Between Foucault and Derrida

Between Foucault and Derrida

Edited by Yubraj Aryal, Vernon W. Cisney,
Nicolae Morar and Christopher Penfield

EDINBURGH
University Press

Edinburgh University Press is one of the leading university presses in the UK. We publish academic books and journals in our selected subject areas across the humanities and social sciences, combining cutting-edge scholarship with high editorial and production values to produce academic works of lasting importance. For more information visit our website: edinburghuniversitypress.com

Edinburgh University Press Ltd
The Tun – Holyrood Road
12(2f) Jackson's Entry
Edinburgh EH8 8PJ

Typeset in 10/12 Goudy Old Style by
Servis Filmsetting Ltd, Stockport, Cheshire,
and printed and bound in Great Britain by
CPI Group (UK) Ltd, Croydon CR0 4YY

A CIP record for this book is available from the British Library

ISBN 978 0 7486 9769 4 (hardback)
ISBN 978 0 7486 9770 0 (webready PDF)
ISBN 978 0 7486 9771 7 (paperback)
ISBN 978 0 7486 9772 4 (epub)

Published with the support of the Edinburgh University Scholarly Publishing Initiatives Fund.

Contents

Acknowledgements

Yubraj, Vernon, Nicolae and Christopher would like to express their gratitude to the following people, all of whom helped to make this project possible.

First, we would like to thank our contributors for both the excellence of their essays and the steadfastness of their support, qualities which have proven indispensable to the crafting of this volume. We would also like to thank the two anonymous reviewers, whose supportive insights and thoughtful suggestions were instructive in orienting our own editorial work.

We would like to extend our sincere gratitude to all of the presses that gave us the opportunity to republish the original source materials that form the foundation of this project.

In particular, thank you to Routledge for giving us permission to republish both 'Cogito and the History of Madness' by Jacques Derrida, first published in Derrida's *Writing and Difference* (London: Routledge, 1978, pp. 36–76), as well as 'My Body, This Paper, This Fire' by Michel Foucault, initially published as Appendix II in Foucault's *History of Madness* (London: Routledge, 2006, pp. 550–74); to the Presses Universitaires de France (PUF) for allowing us to publish '"But Such People Are Insane": On a Disputed Passage from the First Meditation' by Jean-Marie Beyssade, originally published in French as '"Mais quoi ce sont des fous": Sur un passage controversé de la "Première Méditation"' in *Revue de Métaphysique et de Morale*, No. 3 (juillet–septembre 1973), pp. 273–94, and appearing in Jean-Marie Beyssade, *Descartes au fil de l'ordre* (Epimethée series, Paris: PUF, 2001); and to PUF once more for allowing us to publish 'A Return to Descartes' First Meditation' by Michel Foucault, initially published in French as 'Retour sur la Première Méditation' in Beyssade's *Descartes au fil de l'ordre*.

There are, in addition, two scholars whose support has been invaluable to the realisation of this volume, and to whom we are especially grateful. To Daniel W.

Smith, you have been a mentor to all of us, and your unflagging encouragement, friendship and backing have been essential to this project from the moment it was conceived. Thank you. To Leonard Lawlor, from the beginning, your generous guidance, advocacy and participation have elevated this project and facilitated its happy achievement. Thank you.

Thank you to the editorial staff at Edinburgh University Press. To Carol Macdonald, thank you for the constancy of your support, the buoyancy of your encouragement, and the discernment of your judgement. Thank you also to Ersev Ersoy and the rest of the editorial, design and marketing team whose diligent work helped to bring this volume to completion. The editors would also like to thank the Oregon Humanities Center and the College of Arts and Sciences at the University of Oregon for the Humanities Faculty Publication Subvention. Special thanks to Paul Peppis, Julia Heydon, and Melissa Gustafson for their support and encouragement.

Yubraj would like to thank Brian Massumi, Marjorie Perloff, Robert Young, Paul Patton, Peter Nicholls, Fred Evans, Kelly Oliver, William McBride and Leonard Harris for their love and support. He would also like to thank Binod, Arun, Samjhana, Sarita and Milan for always being his inspiration.

Vernon would like to thank Jody for her love, friendship and unwavering support; Jacob and Hayley for being constant sources of joy and inspiration; and Kerry for his friendship, inspiration and encouragement.

Nicolae would like to thank Anca for her support and cherishing love, and Colin Koopman and Ted Toadvine for their constant support and generous insights into how best to think of the volume.

Christopher would like to thank Eden for her sustaining love, Justin Litaker for his intellectual comradery, and James Miller for having first introduced him to a fascinating and lesser known Foucault.

Michel Foucault and Jacques Derrida: A Chronology

Alan D. Schrift

1926	15 October: Michel Foucault born in Poitiers.	
1930		15 July: Jacques Derrida born in El-Biar, a suburb of Algiers.
1945	Fall: Foucault begins *khâgne* at the Lycée Henri-IV in Paris, where he first meets Jean Hyppolite.	
1946	July: Foucault enters the École Normale Supérieure, Rue d'Ulm (ENS).	
1948	Foucault passes the *licence de philosophie* at the Sorbonne.	
1949	Foucault passes the *licence de psychologie* at the Sorbonne.	Derrida moves to Paris and enters *khâgne* at the Lycée Louis-le-Grand.
1951	August: Foucault passes the *agrégation de philosophie*, finishing third. Philosophers appearing on the *programme* for the written examination include the Stoics, Plotinus, Spinoza, Hume, Comte, and Bergson.	
1951	October: Foucault named *répétiteur* of psychology at the ENS.	
1952	June: Foucault passes his *diplôme de psychopathologie* at the Institute of Psychology of Paris.	Fall: Derrida enters the ENS and begins attending Foucault's lectures on experimental psychology. Derrida, along with some other students, occasionally travels with Foucault to see psychiatric patients at the Saint-Anne Hospital.

1953	June: Foucault passes his *diplôme de psychologie expérimentale* at the Institute of Psychology of Paris.	Derrida travels to the Husserl Archive in Louvain, Belgium to do research for his thesis.
1954		Derrida submits his *Diplôme d'études supérieures*, directed by Jean Hyppolite and Maurice Patronnier de Gandillac, on *The Problem of Genesis in Husserl's Philosophy*.
1956		Derrida passes the *agrégation de philosophie*, finishing fourteenth. Philosophers appearing on the *programme* for the written examination include the Stoics, Plotinus, Descartes, Malebranche, Berkeley, and Bergson.
1956		Fall – Spring 1957: Derrida studies at Harvard as a special auditor.
1960	Fall: Foucault begins teaching philosophy and psychology at the University of Clermont-Ferrand.	Fall: Derrida begins teaching at the Sorbonne as *assistant* (to Suzanne Bachelard, Georges Canguilhem, Paul Ricoeur, and Jean Wahl) in general philosophy and logic. He continues at the Sorbonne until 1964.
1961	20 May: Foucault defends his two theses – *Folie et déraison. Histoire de la folie à l'âge classique* and *Introduction à l'*Anthropologie *de Kant* – for the *Doctorat d'État* at the Sorbonne. The jury, presided over by Henri Gouhier, includes Canguilhem as reporter, Daniel Lagache, Hyppolite, and de Gandillac.	
1961	Foucault publishes *Histoire de la folie à l'âge classique*.	Derrida publishes *Introduction to Husserl's Origin of Geometry*.
1963	January: Foucault joins the editorial board of *Critique*. According to Jean Piel, *Critique*'s Director, Foucault only became active on the board after the publication of *The Order of Things* in 1966. His activity declined after 1973, although his name remained on the editorial board until 1977. (*Dits et écrits* I, 24–25)	
1963	27 January: Foucault sends Derrida an enthusiastic letter thanking him for sending a copy of his *Introduction to Husserl's Origin of Geometry*, about which he says he is "filled with admiration" as he admits to knowing "what a perfect connoisseur of Husserl" Derrida was. (Peeters, 129) It is worth noting that throughout their letters of 1963–64, Foucault and Derrida address each other with the familiar *tu*.	3 February: Derrida writes to Foucault that he re-read *History of Madness* over the Christmas break from teaching in anticipation of the paper he would present at the invitation of Jean Wahl to the Collège Philosophique. He informs Foucault that he will focus on his pages addressing Descartes: "I think I'll try to show – basically – that your reading of Descartes is legitimate and illuminating, but at a deep level that in my view cannot be the level of the text you are using and that,

		I think, I will not read altogether the same way that you do." (Peeters, 131)
1963	25 October: Foucault writes to Derrida encouraging him to publish his essay on *History of Madness*: "As for your text being published, in the final analysis I think it's a good thing (I'm here speaking egotistically): only the blind will find your critique severe." (Peeters, 132)	4 March: Derrida presents his first major paper in Paris, at the Collège Philosophique: "Cogito and the History of Madness." Derrida acknowledges having been Foucault's student and describes his own position as the "admiring and grateful disciple." Foucault is in attendance, and his initial reaction to the talk is positive, thanking Derrida in a letter (11 March 1963) for "the immense and marvelous attention [he] gave to [Foucault's] words." About the relationship between the cogito and madness, Foucault writes that he might have treated this theme "too cavalierly" and adds: "You have magisterially showed the right road to take: and you can understand why I owe you a profound debt of gratitude." The letter concludes: "please believe in my deepest and most faithful friendship." (Peeters, 132)
1963	Foucault publishes *Naissance de la clinique: Une archéologie du regard médical.*	
1964	11 February: About the published essay "Cogito and the History of Madness," Foucault writes to Derrida that he was "convinced that it gets to the heart of things and in such a radical, such an all-embracing way that it simultaneously leaves me in an aporia and opens up to me a whole way of thinking that I hadn't thought of." (Peeters, 132)	January: "Cogito and the History of Madness" is published in *Revue de métaphysique et de morale* 4 (octobre-decembre 1963).
1964		Fall: At the invitation of Hyppolite and Althusser, Derrida returns to teach at the ENS. He is named *répétiteur* of philosophy in 1965, and occupies this post until his promotion to *Maître-assistant* in 1967. He continues at the ENS until 1983.
1965	Foucault's *Madness and Civilization* appears in English translation.	
1966	Foucault publishes *Les mots et les choses: Une archéologie des sciences humaines*.	21 October: Derrida presents "Structure, Sign, and Play in the Discourse of the Human Sciences" at a conference titled "The Language of Criticism and the Sciences of Man," organized by Richard Macksey and Eugenio Donato, at Johns Hopkins University, 18–21 October 1966. It is at this conference that he first meets Paul DeMan.

1967		Derrida submits *De la grammatologie: Essai sur la permanence de concepts platonicien, aristotélicien et scolastique de signe écrit*, directed by Maurice Patronnier de Gandillac, for his *Doctorat du troisième cycle* at the Sorbonne. In addition to de Gandillac, the jury was chaired by Henri Gouhier and Paul Ricoeur was its third member.
1967		Derrida publishes *De la grammatologie*, *La Voix et le phénomène* and *L'Écriture et la différence*.
1967		Derrida's "Cogito and the History of Madness" is published in *Writing and Difference*.
1967		Derrida joins Foucault on the editorial board of *Critique*. He remains on the board until 1973.
1967		November: Gérard Granel publishes in *Critique* "Jacques Derrida et la rapture de l'origine," a review of Derrida's three books published earlier in the year (*Speech and Phenomena, Of Grammatology*, and *Writing and Difference*). The review is very complimentary, but includes an extremely critical paragraph on Foucault. Prior to publication, Foucault had asked Derrida to intervene, but Derrida refused, saying he thought it improper to intervene in an essay devoted to his own work; Derrida suggests that this was a prime factor in his break with Foucault, a break that would last until the events in Prague in 1981. (Derrida, "Gérard Granel," in *Chaque fois unique, la fin du monde*.)
1968		Fall: Derrida teaches first seminar at Johns Hopkins University on "Plato's Pharmacy"; he will teach regularly each fall through 1974.
1969	Foucault publishes *L'Archéologie du savoir*.	1 October: Derrida presents the first part of "Force of Law: The 'Mystical Foundation of Authority'" as keynote address at the colloquium on "Deconstruction and the Possibility of Justice," held at the Benjamin Cardozo Law School.
1970	Foucault elected to the Chair of the History of Systems of Thought at the Collège de France.	
1970	Foucault's *The Order of Things* appears in English translation.	

1971	January – March: Foucault lectures on "The Will to Know" at the Collège de France (published in French 2011; English translation 2013).	
1971	1 February: Foucault's "Response to Derrida" is published in the Japanese journal *Paideia*, in a special issue devoted to Foucault. ("Michel Foucault Derrida e no kaino" ("Réponse à Derrida")," *Paideia* 11, in *Dits et écrits* II, 281–95.)	
1971	Foucault publishes *L'Ordre du discours*, his inaugural lecture at the Collège de France.	
1972	January–March: Foucault lectures on 'Penal Theories and Institutions' at the Collège de France (published in French 2015).	Derrida publishes *La Dissémination*, *Marges de la philosophie*, and *Positions*.
1972	Foucault's "My Body, this Paper, this Fire," a revision of his "Response to Derrida," is published as an appendix in the re-edition of *History of Madness*. Foucault sends Derrida a copy, with a dedication that asks him to "forgive [me] for this too slow and partial response." This appendix is removed in the 1976 edition of *History of Madness*, but is included, along with a translation of "Réponse à Derrida," in the 2006 English translation.	10–20 July: Colloquium on Nietzsche at Cerisy-la-Salle, where Derrida presents a paper that will later be published as *Éperons, les styles de Nietzsche*.
1972	Foucault's *The Archeaology of Knowledge* appears in English translation.	
1973	January – March: Foucault lectures on "The Punitive Society" at the Collège de France (published in French 2013; English translation 2015).	
1973	Foucault's *The Birth of the Clinic: An Archeology of Medical Perception* appears in English translation.	Derrida's *Speech and Phenomena* appears in English translation.
1974	January – March: Foucault lectures on "Psychiatric Power" at the Collège de France (published in French 2003; English translation 2008).	Derrida publishes *Glas*.
1975	January – March: Foucault lectures on "Abnormal" at the Collège de France (published in French 1999; English translation 2003).	Foundation of GREPH, the Groupe de Recherches sur l'Enseignement Philosophique.
1975	Foucault begins teaching at the University of California at Berkeley.	Fall: Derrida begins teaching in the English Department at Yale; he will continue teaching for a few weeks each fall until 1986.

1975	Foucault publishes *Surveiller et punir: Naissance de la prison*.	
1976	January – March: Foucault lectures on "Society Must Be Defended" at the Collège de France (published in French 1997; English translation 2003).	
1976	Foucault publishes *Histoire de la sexualité. 1. La Volonté de savoir*.	Derrida's *Of Grammatology* appears in English translation.
1977	Foucault's *Discipline and Punish: The Birth of the Prison* appears in English translation.	
1978	January – March: Foucault lectures on "Security, Territory, Population" at the Collège de France (published in French 2004; English translation 2007).	Derrida publishes *La Vérité en peinture*.
1978		Derrida's *Writing and Difference* appears in English translation.
1979	January – March: Foucault lectures on "The Birth of Biopolitics" at the Collège de France (published in French 2004; English translation 2008).	16–17 June: Derrida plays a major role in the organization of the Etats Généraux de la Philosophie at the Sorbonne. Other notable members of the organizing committee include François Châtelet (Paris VIII), Gilles Deleuze (Paris VIII), Jean-Touissaint Desanti (Paris I), Elizabeth de Fontenay (Paris I), Vladimir Jankélévitch (Paris I), Philippe Lacoue-Labarthe (Strasbourg), Jean-Luc Nancy (Strasbourg), Paul Ricœur (Paris X), and Hélène Védrine (Paris I).
1979		Derrida's *Spurs: Nietzsche's Styles* appears in English translation.
1980	Foucault's *The History of Sexuality, Vol. One* appears in English translation.	Derrida publishes *La Carte postale de Socrate à Freud et au-delà*.
1980	January – March: Foucault lectures on "On the Government of the Living" at the Collège de France (published in French 2012; English translation 2014).	2 June: Derrida receives his *Doctorat d'État* from the Sorbonne for ten works already published: *Edmund Husserl's Origin of Geometry: An Introduction, Writing and Difference, Speech and Phenomena, Of Grammatology, Dissemination, Margins of Philosophy, The Archeology of the Frivolous, Fors, Scribble*, and *The Truth in Painting*. The jury, presided over by Maurice Patronnier de Gandillac, included Pierre Aubenque, Jean-Toussaint Desanti (who served as the thesis Director), Henri Joly, Gilbert Lascault, and Emmanuel Levinas.

1981	January – March: Foucault lectures on "Subjectivity and Truth" at the Collège de France (published in French 2014; English translation forthcoming 2017).	30 December: When leaving Prague following his participation in an unofficial seminar on philosophy organized by the dissident Charter 77 human rights group, Derrida is arrested for allegedly smuggling drugs. Following the active intervention of François Mitterand and the French government, he is released 1 January, and returns to Paris the following morning. Foucault was among the most active intellectuals working on Derrida's behalf, as he spoke on several radio stations denouncing the arrest and demanding Derrida's release. Several days after he returned to France, Derrida phoned Foucault to thank him and the two again resumed friendly contact. (Eribon, 121–22; Peeters, 340)
1981		Derrida's *Positions* appears in English translation.
1982	January – March: Foucault lectures on " *The Hermeneutics of the Subject* " at the Collège de France (published in French 2001; English translation 2004)	Foundation of the Collège International de Philosophie by François Châtelet, Jacques Derrida, Jean-Pierre Faye, and Dominique Lecourt.
1982		Derrida's *Dissemination* and *Margins of Philosophy* appear in English translation.
1982		Derrida named A.D. White Professor at Large at Cornell University.
1983	January – March: Foucault lectures on "The Government of Self and Others" at the Collège de France (published in French 2008; English translation 2010)	Derrida leaves the ENS after his election as *Directeur d'études* in "Philosophical Institutions" at the École des Hautes Études in Sciences Sociales.
1984	January – March: Foucault lectures on "The Courage of Truth: The Government of Self and Others II" at the Collège de France (published in French 2009; English translation 2012)	
1984	Foucault publishes *Histoire de la sexualité. 2. L'Usage des plaisirs* and *Histoire de la sexualité. 3. Le Souci de soi.*	
1984	9 June: Foucault is transported from the Saint-Michel Clinic to the Hospital *Salpêtrière*.	
1984	25 June: Foucault dies at the Hospital *Salpêtrière in Paris*.	

1984 29 June: Gilles Deleuze reads the eulogy at a small ceremony in the courtyard near the mortuary at the Hospital Salpêtrière. Derrida is among the several hundred in attendance.

1985 Foucault's *The History of Sexuality. Vol. Two. The Use of Pleasure* appears in English translation.

1986 Foucault's *The History of Sexuality. Vol. Three. Care of the Self* appears in English translation.

Derrida's *Glas* appears in English translation.

1986 Spring: Following the departure of his friend J. Hillis Miller from Yale to the University of California at Irvine, Derrida begins teaching the spring quarter at UC-Irvine in the Department of Critical Theory, sharing this post with Jean-François Lyotard (fall quarter) and Wolfgang Iser (winter quarter).

1987 Derrida publishes *De l'esprit: Heidegger et la question* and *Psyché: Inventions de l'autre*. His *The Truth in Painting* and *The Post Card: From Socrates to Freud and Beyond* appear in English translation.

1989 Derrida's *Edmund Husserl's "Origin of Geometry": An Introduction* and *Of Spirit: Heidegger and the Question* appear in English translation.

1989 Derrida and Jacques Bouveresse serve as co-presidents of the Commission de réflexion pour l'épistémologie et la philosophie established by the French Ministry of National Education.

1990 Derrida pledges to donate his literary estate to the Critical Theory Archive at the University of California at Irvine.

1991 23 November: Derrida presents "'To Do Justice to Freud': The History of Madness in the Age of Psychoanalysis" at a conference of the International Society for the History of Psychiatry and Psychoanalysis marking the thirtieth anniversary of Foucault's *History of Madness*.

1991 Derrida publishes *Donner le temps. 1. La Fausse monnaie*.

1992 Derrida's *Given Time: I. Counterfeit Money* appears in English translation.

1993		Derrida publishes *Spectres de Marx: L'État de la dette, le travail deuil et la nouvelle Internationale*.
1994	Publication of Foucault's *Dits et écrits*.	Derrida publishes *Politiques de l'amitié*. His *Specters of Marx: The State of the Debt, the Work of Mourning, and the New International* appears in English translation.
1997	Foucault's archive is moved from the Bibliothèque du Saulchoir in Paris, where they had been preserved since 1986, to IMEC (Institut Mémoires de l'édition contemporaine).	Derrida publishes *Adieu à Emmanuel Lévinas*. His *Politics of Friendship*
1999		Derrida's *Adieu to Emmanuel Levinas* appears in English translation.
2000		Derrida publishes *Le Toucher, Jean-Luc Nancy*.
2001		Derrida's *The Work of Mourning* appears in English translation.
2003		Derrida publishes *Voyous*.
2004		25 July: In response to a contested judgment by the University of California at Irvine against a long-time friend – Professor Dragan Kunundzić – Derrida informs the university of his wish to suspend his relationship with the university and his intention to suspend any further donations to his archive there. At present, the archive at Irvine contains Derrida's student work and manuscripts for his courses, seminars, books, essays, and lectures from 1959–1995. Beginning in 2002, Derrida's manuscripts from 1995–2004 were deposited in Le Fonds Derrida at IMEC, where Foucault's archive is also located.
2004		9 October: Derrida dies at the Hospital Curie, around the corner from the ENS.
2005		Derrida's *On Touching: Jean-Luc Nancy* and *Rogues: Two Essays on Reason* appear in English translation.
2006	Foucault's *History of Madness* in its entirety appears in English translation, along with his earlier responses to Derrida.	Derrida publishes *L'Animal que donc je suis*.
2006		Establishment of an editorial team to begin editing and publishing Derrida's seminars
2007		Derrida's *Psyche: Inventions of the Other, Vol. 1* appears in English translation.

2008		Derrida's *Psyche: Inventions of the Other, Vol. 2* and *The Animal That Therefore I Am* appear in English translation.
2008		Publication by Derrida's long-time publisher Éditions Galilée of the first of his seminars: *Séminaire: La Bête et le souverain, Volumes I (2001–2002)*. It is estimated that about 40 volumes of Derrida's seminars will be published in the coming years.
2009		The first volume of *The Seminars of Jacques Derrida, The Beast and the Sovereign, Volume I* appears in English translation.
2010		Publication of Derrida's *Séminaire: La Bête et le souverain. Volume II (2002–2003)*.
2011		*The Seminars of Jacques Derrida. The Beast and the Sovereign, Volume II* appears in English translation.
2012	Publication of *Mal faire, dire vrai: Fonction de l'aveu en justice. Cours de Louvain, 1981*.	Publication of Derrida's *Séminaire: La Peine de mort. Volume 1 (1999–2000)*.
2013		Publication of Derrida's *Heidegger: la question de l'Être et l'Histoire. Cours de l'ENS-Ulm: 1964–1965*.
2014	Publication of Foucault's *Wrong-Doing, Truth-Telling: The Function of Avowal in Justice* appears in English translation.	*The Seminars of Jacques Derrida. The Death Penalty, Volume I* appears in English translation.
2015		Publication of Derrida's *Séminaire: La Peine de mort. Volume II (2000–2001)*.
2016		*The Seminars of Jacques Derrida. Heidegger: The Question of Being and History* appears in English translation.[1]

NOTES

1 In compiling this chronology, the following sources have been consulted: Jacques Derrida, *Chaque fois unique, la fin du monde*, edited by Pascale-Anne Brault and Michael Naas (Paris: Galilée, 2003); Didier Eribon, *Michel Foucault*, trans. Betsy Wing (Cambridge: Harvard University Press, 1992); Michel Foucault, *Dits et écrits* (Paris: Gallimard, 1994); David Macey, *The Lives of Michel Foucault* (New York: Vintage, 1995); Marie-Louise Mallet and Ginette Michaud, *Derrida* (Paris: L'Herne, 2004); Benoît Peeters, *Derrida*, trans. Andrew Brown (Cambridge: Polity, 2012). Information regarding the *agrégation de philosophie* is from the *Bulletin Officiel de l'éducation nationale* and the *Revue Universitaire*.

In the chronology of events in the lives of Michel Foucault and Jacques Derrida, I have had occasion to use some French academic terminology that might not be familiar to all readers. Here let me provide brief explanations of this terminology. For further information about this academic terminology, see 'Appendix 1: Understanding French Academic Culture' in my *Twentieth-Century French Philosophy: Key Themes and Thinkers* (Oxford: Blackwell Publishing, 2006).

Agrégation de philosophie: A competitive examination under the auspices of the Ministry of National Education that credentials students for teaching philosophy in secondary schools (*lycées*) and universities.

Assistant: Roughly the academic rank equivalent to an Assistant Professor (US) or Lecturer (UK).

Collège de France: Founded in 1530, the Collège is not part of the regular university system and it offers no diplomas. Instead, the faculty of the Collège, upon election by current faculty members, offer public lectures and seminars. Election to a Chair at the Collège is recognition that one has risen to the very top of one's field of expertise.

Collège Philosophique: Founded in 1946 by Sorbonne philosopher Jean Wahl, the Collège operated outside the formal university system to provide a forum and audience for controversial and non-institutionally sanctioned thinkers to present their work.

Diplôme d'études supérieures: Degree awarded following the submission of a thesis and marking the completion of one's formal university education. Eliminated in 1963 and replaced by the *Maîtrise* (Masters).

Diplôme de psychologie expérimentale: Degree in experimental psychology.

Diplôme de psychopathologie: Degree in psychopathology.

Directeur d'études: Director of studies, the top rank for teaching faculty at the École des Hautes Études in Sciences Sociales.

Doctorat d'État: Formerly known as the *Doctorat ès Lettres*, the *Doctorat d=État* was awarded following the submission of two theses (*thèse principale* and *thèse complémentaire*) to the Faculty of Letters at the Sorbonne. In the latter half of the century, it became increasingly common for the *Doctorat d=État* to be awarded in recognition and defense of the publication of a significant body of work rather than the presentation and defense of a single principal thesis.

Doctorat du troisième cycle: Created in 1954 (for the sciences) and 1958 (for humanities and social sciences) as a less demanding doctoral degree than the *Doctorat d=État*, this *Doctorat* also helped meet the increasing need for more university teachers. In 1984, the *Doctorat de troisième cycle* became the only doctoral degree granted.

École des Hautes Études in Sciences Sociales (EHESS): Established in 1975 (from the former Sixth Section of the École Pratique des Hautes Études) as an institution authorized to grant doctoral degrees, the EHESS is a center for history and social science that also has always welcomed interdisciplinary research.

École Normale Supérieure (ENS): Founded in 1794, the ENS has been traditionally the school that recruits the most promising *lycée* graduates in the liberal arts with the expectation that its graduates will enter the intellectual elite following completion of their course of study. In particular, it has been at the center of philosophical education for much of its existence. The ENS itself awards no university diplomas; therefore its students (*normaliens*) must also enroll at a university in order to obtain their graduate and postgraduate university degrees.

Etats Généraux de la Philosophie: The 'Estates General of Philosophy' was a meeting that took place June 16–17, 1979 at the Sorbonne of some twelve hundred teachers, scholars, and others interested in the fate of philosophy instruction in French secondary schools. The motivation behind the gathering was in large part to formulate a collective response to the proposal by then Minister of Education René Haby to significantly reduce the teaching of philosophy in French *lycées*.

IMEC (Institut Mémoires de l'édition contemporaine): Presently housed in the Ardenne Abbey in Caen, IMEC collects and preserves the archives of a number of twentieth-century French philosophers and writers as well as the archives of several major publishing houses and journals.

Khâgne: For students who intend to pursue a teaching career, it is common to spend an additional year or two at a *lycée* following the *baccalauréat* (high school diploma) where they study in preparation for the rigorous entrance exams into one of the *Grandes Écoles*, for philosophy students typically the École Normale Supérieure. The first of these years for humanities and social science students is known as the *hypokhâgne* (officially, this course is called the '*Lettres Supérieures*') and the second the *khâgne* (officially, the '*Première Supérieure*').

Licence de philosophie: Prior to the educational reforms of 1973, this was approximately the equivalent of a US master=s degree in philosophy.

Licence de psychologie: Prior to the educational reforms of 1973, this was approximately the equivalent of a US master=s degree in psychology.

Lycée Henri-IV: Founded in 1873, one of the two most prestigious Parisian *lycées* where philosophy students enrolled for their *khâgne* in preparation for the examination for entrance into the École Normale Supérieure.

Lycée Louis-le-Grand: Founded in 1563, one of the two most prestigious Parisian *lycées* where philosophy students enrolled for their *khâgne* in preparation for the examination for entrance into the École Normale Supérieure.

Maître-assistant: Roughly the academic rank equivalent to an Associate Professor (US) or Senior Lecturer or Reader (UK).

Programme: The required reading list of texts that appear on the annual *agrégation* examination.

Répétiteur: Title of an instructor whose primary responsibility is to prepare students for the *agrégation*. In ENS slang, the *répétiteur* is referred to as the '*caiman*'.

Sorbonne: Founded in 1257 by Robert de Sorbon (1201–74), the Sorbonne was originally the name of a single college within the larger University of Paris. As early as the fifteenth century, the name 'Sorbonne' came to be identified with the entire University of Paris. This identification continued until the reorganization of the University of Paris in 1971 into thirteen campuses.

CHAPTER 1

Introduction: Between Foucault and Derrida

Christopher Penfield

The 'between' that separates and joins Michel Foucault and Jacques Derrida would seem to designate an uncertain relational space, a cleft that appears to be at once slight and unbridgeable. On the one hand, both thinkers develop original philosophies of difference that challenge the dominant discourse or logocentrism of western reason. In this capacity as radical critics of the philosophical tradition, Derrida and Foucault together headline the generation of French philosophers from the 1960s and 1970s that Hélène Cixous termed 'the incorruptibles',[1] a prolific group that is often retrospectively assimilated under the headings of poststructuralism, postmodernism, or French theory. Whatever their differences, Foucault and Derrida – who were friends before they were rivals, Derrida having first been a student of Foucault's – would at first glance appear to be philosophical allies.

On the other hand, Derrida and Foucault's contentious interchange indicates the incommensurability of their respective projects concerning that most basic of philosophical questions: what is thinking? Each thinker, disputing the other's conception of the nature and agential force of thought, systematically calls into question the foundation and viability of the other's philosophy of difference. From this perspective, the debate between Foucault and Derrida can be framed quite generally as an irresolvable disaccord over the very relation between thought and difference: for Foucault, difference would be situated *outside* thought, an aleatory encounter for thought that is indeed the occasion for thinking, opening the possibility of thinking-otherwise; by contrast, for Derrida, difference would be situated *within* thought itself as its original impetus and principle of animation.

From this basic difference follows a singularly rich, if polemically charged, philosophical debate spanning at least two decades. The initial occasion is provided by Foucault's first major book, *History of Madness*; two years later, Derrida presented his critique of this work, 'Cogito and the History of Madness', an essay that would be instrumental for his articulation of deconstruction; nine years after that, Foucault, who had remained publicly silent about Derrida's criticism, published two replies, both indicative of his own intellectual and political development. In what follows, we will explore in detail these three stages of the debate, demonstrating not only their conceptual intricacy and interrelation, but also their philosophical significance: that is, both the foundational stakes of the debate itself and the essential role it plays in catalysing the respective trajectories of Derrida and Foucault.

FOUCAULT'S *HISTORY OF MADNESS* (1961)

In the original preface to his work on madness, Foucault situates his project 'beneath the sun of the great Nietzschean quest'[2] in *Birth of Tragedy*, according to which the history of reason begins with Socrates misunderstanding, forgetting, and excluding the disquieting truth of tragic experience. For Nietzsche as for early Foucault, tragic works of art express an abyssal vision revealing 'the nothing of existence' (HM, 31), that is, the absolute groundlessness of reality, including the contingency of reason. For example, Nietzsche, in imagery that recalls Plato's allegory of the cave, describes the tragedy of Sophocles thusly:

> When we turn away blinded after a strenuous attempt to look directly at the sun, we have dark, coloured patches before our eyes, as if their purpose were to heal them; conversely, those appearances of the Sophoclean hero in images of light . . . are the necessary result of gazing into the inner, terrible depths of nature – radiant patches, as it were, to heal a gaze seared by gruesome night.[3]

The nocturnal brilliance of tragic expression effectively inverts the Platonic regime of light, which posits the sun as the analog in the world of sense to the form of the good. Rather than resembling and confirming a universal moral order, the 'sun of the great Nietzschean quest' – the searing incandescence of 'gruesome night' revealing nature's 'terrible depths' as chaos or void – threatens instead to undo any bond posited between metaphysics and morality.[4]

Whence the danger posed by tragic experience: the belief in the moral structure of reality founds the edifice of western reason (to say nothing of monotheistic religion), persisting into the modern period by underpinning the Enlightenment view of history as the teleologically guided trajectory of rational progress. According to Nietzsche, such a belief can only get off the ground, can only first posit itself as ground, after having expelled, defused, or forgotten tragedy. (It would thus be no accident that in Plato's *Republic*, before Socrates discourses upon the allegories of the divided line and the cave, he must first insist upon banishing the tragic poets from the *kallipolis*.) Therefore, one aspect of Nietzsche's 'quest' will be to recover or re-articulate tragic experience in its distinctively modern form, which he later conceives as the death of God, the still latent event of radical finitude constitutive of modernity in the west. And when, in *The Gay Science*, Nietzsche first gives voice to this abyssal vision – 'this earth [unchained] from its sun', 'plunging continually', 'straying as through an infinite nothing', with 'night continually closing in' – it is announced by the character of the 'madman'.[5] Tragic truth thus re-emerges through a certain figure of madness, contesting the foundation of a moral-metaphysical worldview (in this case, God) and unmasking the contingent nature of reason; for

> [n]ot truth and certainty are the opposite of the world of the madman, but the universality and the universal binding force of a faith; in sum, the non-arbitrary character of judgments. . . . Continually, precisely the most select spirits bristle at this universal binding force – the explorers of *truth* above all. . . . *We others are the exception and the danger* – and we need eternally to be defended.[6]

With this Nietzschean backdrop in place, we should be better positioned to understand the project announced in the original preface to *History of Madness*. Taking up Nietzsche's 'defence', Foucault's thesis, in brief, is that the exclusion of tragic forms of limit-experience (of which a certain experience of madness would be one[7]) founds and makes possible the historical formation of western reason and culture:

> We could write a history of *limits* – of those obscure gestures, necessarily forgotten as soon as they are accomplished, through which a culture rejects something which for it will be the Exterior. . . . [T]his is the originary thickness in which a culture takes shape. To interrogate a culture about its limit-experiences is to question it at the confines of history about a tear that is something like the birth of its history. . . . At the center of these limit-experiences of the Western world is the explosion, of course, of the tragic itself – Nietzsche having shown that the tragic structure from which the history of the Western world is made is nothing other than the refusal, the forgetting, and the silent collapse of tragedy. (HM, xxix–xxx)

The world of reason takes form by expelling the tragic encounter with the 'nothing of existence' and then disavowing this original gesture of expulsion. Foucault stresses that what is 'constitutive' is the very act of division itself by which a culture, exteriorising what it rejects, 'gives itself the face of its positivity' (HM, xxx): 'The caesura that establishes the distance between reason and non-reason is the origin [*originaire*] . . .' (HM, xxviii). That is, an arbitrary and unjustifiable violence underlies the ostensibly necessary foundation that reason professes for itself, belying the rationalist conception of history as the linear march of human progress.

Indeed, one of the principal targets of *History of Madness*, as of Foucault's later archaeological and genealogical works, is the roughly Hegelian model of historical development as teleological continuity – a view which had been made prominent in France by Jean Hyppolite, who served as a thesis advisor for both Foucault and Derrida. It is therefore by contrast to this 'horizontal' vector of reason that Foucault counterposes a vertical vector, which 'would confront the dialectics of history with the immobile structures of the tragic' (HM, xxx), contesting the dominant historical forms and practices of western culture from the site of its exclusion:

> Where might this interrogation lead, following not reason in its *horizontal* becoming, but seeking to retrace in time this *constant verticality*, which, the

> length of Western culture, confronts it with what it is not, measuring it with its own extravagance [*démesure*]? Towards what region might it take us, which is neither the history of knowledge nor history plain and simple, which is commanded neither by the teleology of the truth nor the rational concatenation of causes, which only have value or meaning beyond the division? A region, no doubt, where it would be a question more of the limits than of the identity of a culture. (HM, xxix, translation slightly modified, my emphasis)

Foucault's project is therefore a tragic counter-history of the western world. In opposition to the horizontal discourse of psychiatry that 'grows up in the calm that returns after the division is made' (HM, xxviii), narrating reason's progressive mastery of non-reason, Foucault orients his work from the perspective of the excessive and 'constant verticality' that is excluded as an exterior limit of the social formation, 'confront[ing] the dialectics of history' by attesting to the unacknowledged and illegitimate first condition of reason.

History of Madness is thus a 'history of limits' in at least two senses: (1) because madness in its tragic form is itself an experience of the limit, 'the still undivided experience of division itself' (HM, xiv); and (2) because this very division, situated at the 'degree zero of the history of madness' (HM, xxvii), is *constitutive* not only for madness but for western culture, a 'tear' at the 'confines of history' that ushers in 'the birth of its history'. The limit-experience of madness, in other words, bears witness to the originary or genetic violence that institutes the order of the social world and must be covered over as a condition for that order's retroactive self-legitimation. Foucault's work will thus function both as 'the archeology of that silence' (HM, xxviii), aiming to recover tragic experience and make visible the arbitrary force of its refusal, as well as a critical counter-history of reason, locating in this 'silent collapse of tragedy' a singular and contingent (rather than universal and necessary) condition of possibility for the western social formation. A history of limits, then, conducted at the limits of history.

The tragic structure of constitutive division between non-reason and reason would thus be 'the degree zero of the history of madness' and the history of reason alike. In turn, on the side of non-reason, Foucault counterposes two very different kinds of madness that correspond to the horizontal and vertical vectors, respectively: *mental illness*, which becomes the object of a rational science formulated through medical and juridical discourses and historically supported by institutional practices of confinement; and *unreason*, which is a tragic limit-experience expressed in literary and artistic works that contest the authority of rationalist thought and its horizontal history. The cleft between these divergent modes of madness, which Foucault treats in his opening chapter ('*Stultifera Navis*'), first emerges during the early Renaissance in the disparity between the moralising humanist discourse on folly (paradigmatically, Desiderius Erasmus's *The Praise of Folly*) and the apocalyptic phantasmagoria of tragic painting (exemplified by the works of Hieronymus Bosch).[8]

Along the horizontal vector, which ultimately issues into the positivism of clinical psychiatry, madness becomes appropriated by the language of reason to designate the broad field of abnormal human attributes and activities: to use Foucault's language, madness takes the form *within man* of an errant and defective self-relation for which he is ultimately to blame. An experience of madness thus emerges that is bound up in normalising relations of moral guilt, social division, and political exclusion, all of which constitutes the continuity of 'the passage from the medieval and humanist experience of madness to the experience that is our own, which confines madness in mental illness' (HM, xxxiii).[9] Two singular events along this trajectory will bookend the history of madness in the classical period: 'in 1657, the founding of the Hôpital Général, and the Great Confinement of the poor', marking the major internment of the mad alongside other marginalised figures unable or unwilling to labour (criminals, vagabonds, mendicants, etc.); and 'in 1794, the liberation of the mad in chains at Bicêtre' (HM, xxxiii), ushering in the 'birth of the asylum' and advent of modern psychiatry.

Along the vertical vector, by contrast, the tragic-cosmic experience of madness during the Renaissance discloses 'the vertiginous unreason of the world' (HM, 13) through the painterly delirium of chaotically concatenated bestial images. Unmoored from the rigorous theological organisation of Gothic symbology, these images herald a double revelation: (1) that madness, as 'that which goes against nature, or the seething mass of a senseless presence immanent in the earth' (HM, 18), expresses an abyssal or subterranean truth beyond the order of God; and (2) that this terrible truth is none other than the secret of man's own nature in its infernal and contingent animality,[10] 'the experience of an *animal unreason* that formed the absolute limit of the incarnation of reason, and the scandal of the human condition' (HM, 158, my emphasis).[11] We can thus already see that the tragic expression of unreason in apocalyptic painting cryptically announces the double death of God and man, which will find its fuller articulation centuries later in the works of Nietzsche, Antonin Artaud and Georges Bataille – that is, the discovery that the 'death of God restores us not to a limited and positivistic world but to a world exposed by the experience of its limits, made and unmade by that excess which transgresses it'.[12] Indeed, this disclosure of radical finitude through the limit-experience of unreason is the key for threading together 'the great broken line that stretches from the Ship of Fools to the last words of Nietzsche and perhaps Artaud's cries of rage' (HM, 344).

In sum, Foucault's history of madness charts the ever-widening difference between mental illness and unreason: between, on the one hand, the horizontal conception of madness as pathology, as medico-moral abnormality that institutionalised forms of knowledge (psychiatry, psychology, pharmacology, psychoanalysis) will be able to progressively control and treat; and, on the other hand, the vertical conception of madness as tragic experience, as dangerous insight into the groundlessness of reason that western culture must expel or defuse.[13]

> The linearity that led rationalist thought to consider madness as a form of mental illness *must be reinterpreted in a vertical dimension*. Only then does it become apparent that each of its incarnations is a more complete, but more perilous masking of tragic experience – an experience that it nonetheless

> failed to obliterate. When constraints were at their most oppressive, an explosion was necessary, and that is what we have seen since Nietzsche. (HM, 28, my emphasis)

When reinterpreted vertically – that is, from the perspective of tragic limit-experiences and the constitutive force of their exclusion – the history of the discursive and institutional forms by which reason apprehends madness as mental illness, from the Great Confinement to the birth of the asylum, can be grasped as so many attempts to refuse and forget the tragic truth of groundlessness at the heart of existence. And if tragic experience fails to be 'obliterated' by the 'linearity' of rationalist thought, this is owed to the works of unreason that provide it with a form of expression through literature, painting and philosophy.

Along the vertical axis of Foucault's counter-history, then, there emerges a discontinuous lineage of artists and poets whose expressive power opens 'the possibility . . . of rediscovering tragic experience beyond the promises of dialectics', forming a privileged site at the exterior limit of the social order 'from which all contestation becomes possible, as well as the contestation of all things [*la contestation totale*]' (HM, 532, 535).[14] The subversive effect of these works of unreason is to call into question the justification of reason and its sciences of man (especially psychiatry), arraigning the modern world before the baseless founding violence by which it expels the tragic from itself. Hence the reversal with which the book concludes:

> Ruse and new triumph of madness: the world that thought to measure and justify madness through psychology must justify itself before madness, since in its struggles [*effort*] and agonies [*débats*] it measures itself by the excess [*démesure*] of works like those of Nietzsche, of Van Gogh, of Artaud. And nothing in itself, especially not what it can know of madness, assures the world that it is justified by such works of madness.[15]

Foucault's earliest formulation of resistance – what might be termed *a politics of tragic expression* – first emerges here through this concept of an experience of unreason, made manifest in modern literary and artistic works, that disrupts the horizontal history of reason, problematising the latter's forms of thought and institutional structures and practices. However, as though this power of expression were impossible to sustain, all the voices of unreason, from Goya and Sade to Van Gogh and Artaud, collapse into madness, deprived of the support necessary to prolong their limit-vision; the height of their lucidity anticipates their breakdown into catatonia or suicide. It is *this* silence, the tragic silence of suicided poets, whose archaeology Foucault sets out to write, for the dividing practices of western culture that exclude the tragic are the very same that render the experience of unreason unsupportable.[16] And if, for Foucault, 'total contestation' against the dominant organisation of western culture and society is made possible by the expression of unreason, then to inquire into what prevents this expression from being sustained will be to pose a problem of power that is essential to modernity. Naming Hölderlin, Nerval, Nietzsche, Van Gogh, Roussel and Artaud, Foucault writes:

> And each of those existences, each of the words that made up those existences repeats with the insistence of time the same question, which probably concerns the essence of the modern world: why is it not possible to remain in the difference that is unreason? Why is it that unreason always has to separate from itself, fascinated in the delirium of the sensible and trapped in the retreat that is madness? How was it at this point deprived of language? What is this power that petrifies all those who dare look upon its face, condemning to *madness* all those who have tried the test [*l'épreuve*] of *Unreason*? (HM, 352, translation slightly modified)

This set of questions cuts to the heart of Foucault's work and would perhaps explain its original title of *Folie et déraison* ['Madness and Unreason']. The movement from tragic experience and expression (unreason) to suicidal breakdown (madness) is not the necessary consequence of a mental disorder, but the result of an arbitrary if fundamental violence that founds the modern world and makes it impossible to maintain oneself 'in the difference that is unreason'. Foucault's effective project is thus twofold: (1) to critically diagnose the historically contingent conditions of impossibility for sustaining the experience of unreason, conditions which are political in so far as they derive from a structure of division itself constitutive of the social formation; and (2) to recover, to compose itself as, a tragic form of expression, thereby (a) restoring access to a limit-experience systematically excluded from the modern world and (b) confronting reason with its own groundlessness or lack of self-justification. In short, the transformative aim of *History of Madness* is to provide the conditions of tragic expression capable of sustaining unreason in its difference and contesting western culture in its arbitrary constraint.

Everything thus turns on this problem of expression; and indeed, Foucault will pursue a closely related literary politics for much of the 1960s, where what is at stake in modern literature (e.g., Bataille's concept of transgression or Maurice Blanchot's thought of the outside) is a kind of subversive writing able to articulate a limit-experience of language that would undermine the philosophical subject and inaugurate a new form of thought. However, in order to perceive the crux of Foucault's project, including the status and performative effect of his own discourse, one must first attend to the difference between madness qua mental illness and tragic unreason. Failing to do so might make it appear that the only alternative to reason would be the sterile silence of madness as breakdown, as 'the absence of an oeuvre': either intelligible speech or catatonic collapse. Such would be to neglect Foucault's politics of tragic expression – which is to say, from the vertical perspective of *History of Madness*, to once more forget the truth of unreason.

DERRIDA'S 'COGITO AND THE HISTORY OF MADNESS' (1963)

Although Foucault's first major book enjoyed relative academic success, garnering the praise of such prominent French intellectuals as Blanchot, Roland Barthes, Gaston Bachelard and Fernand Braudel, it did not initially achieve the deeper transformative impact or reach the wider reading public to which Foucault aspired.[17] Perhaps this is why he first responded enthusiastically two years later when one of his former students, perceiving the novelty and depth of *History of Madness*'s thoroughgoing critique of reason, presented a significant talk at the Collège Philosophique in Paris that both emphasised the radicality of Foucault's project and submitted the latter to systematic criticism.[18] The student, of course, was Jacques Derrida, and the paper, 'Cogito and the History of Madness', provided something of a launch pad for Derrida's own novel critical engagement with *Logos* or western reason, which would become known as 'deconstruction'.

It is worth lingering over how Derrida begins his lecture, for which Foucault was present at Derrida's invitation. Derrida commences with the problem of commencing and the bad conscience of the student, who, entering a critical dialogue with his teacher, struggles within and against himself to break with his teacher and speak in his own voice:

> And when, as is the case here, the dialogue is in danger of being taken – incorrectly – as a challenge [*contestation*], the disciple knows that he alone finds himself already challenged by the master's voice within him that *precedes* his own. He feels himself indefinitely challenged, or rejected or accused; as a disciple, he is challenged by the master who speaks within him and before him, to reproach him for making this challenge and to reject it in advance, having elaborated it before him; and having *interiorised the master*, he is also challenged by the disciple that he himself is. This interminable unhappiness of the disciple perhaps stems from the fact that he does not yet know – or is still concealing from himself – that *the master, like real life, may always be absent*. The disciple must break the glass, or better the mirror, the reflection, his infinite speculation on the master. And start to speak.[19]

Derrida insists that his engagement with Foucault not be taken 'as a challenge', using the French word *contestation* – which, as we have seen, is the term Foucault reserves in *History of Madness* for the transgressive achievement of tragic works of unreason in relation to reason (the 'ruse and new triumph of madness' providing, as Foucault puts it, the point 'from which all contestation becomes possible, as well as the contestation of all things'). This model of resistance is based upon the disruptive emergence of that which has been excluded, expelled, and produced as 'the Exterior'. By contrast, Derrida's model of transformation will involve a movement that acts from within, inhabiting and destabilising, rather than threatening from without. As he later puts it, the 'movements of deconstruction do not destroy structures from the outside. They are not possible and effective, nor can they take accurate aim, except by inhabiting those structures', operating 'necessarily from the inside, borrowing all the strategic and economic resources of subversion from the old structure'.[20] Setting the terms of the debate, we might say that whereas Foucault privileges the outer limit of western culture, Derrida instead privileges the inner limit of reason, that 'zero point' (WD, 68 [p. 51]) of the Cogito where thought is most proximate to madness. Thus, while it may be true that Derrida's challenge to

Foucault is not a form of 'contestation', this is not because it refrains from seeking to undercut and, in its own way, supplant Foucault's project, but rather because it deploys a different strategy of subversion.

At issue here is an essential philosophical difference over how to conceive and evaluate the relation between inner and outer – a difference, no doubt, that goes to the heart of the dispute and will later be formulated politically as a strategic disaccord regarding the transformative efficacy of thought. Indeed, Derrida has already implicitly begun this debate in the passage above. Positioning Foucault as the 'master' and himself as the 'disciple', he then subtly performs deconstruction's distinctive method of 'reversal and displacement',[21] a double manoeuvre by which the hierarchically related terms of a binary opposition are inverted, but in such a way as to transform the binary relation itself, allowing a new concept to emerge. As we will see, for example, Derrida's general argument takes this form in deconstructing the privilege accorded by Foucault to madness's exteriority over reason's interiority, inverting their order of priority (showing how reason contains within itself the difference attributed to madness) in a manner that dislocates their very opposition (showing how the inner limit of reason is actually closest and most hospitable to madness), thereby elucidating a more profound concept of reason. In the specific case above of Derrida's commencement, the master position (occupied, for Derrida, by Foucault), located outside and anterior to the disciple, becomes both 'interiorised' (reversal) and absented (displacement), disclosed in the end as having been 'always absent'. Derrida, having thus undone the master-disciple dyad, can finally emerge and 'start to speak', has indeed already begun speaking.

The critique of *History of Madness* proceeds on two levels, taking aim, respectively, at Foucault's original preface and at his interpretation of Descartes. At the first level, Derrida claims to lay bare the fundamental 'infeasibility [*impossibilité*]' of Foucault's project: namely, its attempt 'to write a history of madness *itself*' (WD, 39 [p. 31]),[22] whether as an 'archeology of silence' or in terms of a constitutive division between reason and madness. For Derrida, this attempt, in so far as Foucault's history is itself necessarily a work of reason, is consigned to failure in advance. *Either* madness would have to be the subject of the work, which is impossible, since to speak the language of madness would require that one actually be mad, and, following Foucault's own formula, where there is madness there is no work; *or* madness would have to be the object of the work, in which case it would already have been ineluctably appropriated by reason, and Foucault would thus be recommitting the very gesture of violence that he condemns. Madness, then, as disqualified subject or already-captured object: either way, it is impossible to render a history of madness in which the truth of madness itself would speak.

On Derrida's reading, the founding impossibility of *History of Madness* follows from what is both 'the most audacious and seductive aspect' and 'the maddest aspect' of the work, namely, Foucault's effort to avoid 'the trap or objectivist naiveté that would consist in writing a history of untamed madness utilizing the concepts that were the historical instruments of the capture of madness' (WD, 40 [p. 32]). In other words, Derrida diagnoses the inner untenability of Foucault's project as rooted precisely in the problem of its expression, of finding a language suited to give voice to what is in principle either silent or unintelligible.[23] Confronted with this problem, Foucault would vacillate between two equally problematic projects, resulting in a major methodological dilemma: (1) either an impossible language that necessarily betrays the madness it would seek to praise; or (2) a historical perspective that both (a) implies just the kind of metaphysics that Nietzsche had proclaimed dead, and (b) diminishes its own historical claims about the classical period.

On the one hand, Foucault sometimes refuses the language of reason altogether in the name of an archaeology of silence; but this project, Derrida argues, is doubly impossible, for silence itself has no history (since history is composed of things said), and archaeology itself is a form of reason that could not but repeat the appropriation of madness. On the other hand, Foucault sometimes presents his project as an analysis of the constitutive division between reason and non-reason ('the degree zero of the history of madness') that gave birth to western culture. However, this task, too, faces a double problem. First, by treating the beginning of history as itself a historical event of division, Foucault would seem to imply a prelapsarian unity preceding this history (since an act of division suggests that the two parts which result originally formed a unity), which is to say, a metaphysics of presence characteristic of the very logocentric tradition that *History of Madness* would contest: the 'attempt to write the history of the decision, division, difference runs the risk of construing the division as an event or a structure subsequent to the unity of an original presence, thereby confirming metaphysics in its fundamental operation' (WD, 48 [p. 37]). Second, by positing the decision of constitutive division as that which inaugurates the historicity of history, Foucault, in addition to the apparent contradiction of writing 'the history of the origin of history' (WD, 51 [p. 39]),[24] would seem to undermine his claim for the singular historical importance of the Great Confinement in the classic period; for, since what preceded the seventeenth century cannot be considered pre-historic, the Great Confinement would be merely one example of a larger structure (rather than being itself the original partition), the more archaic historical grounds of which remain unexplored.

In sum, whether taken as an archaeology of silence or a history of limits, the essential impossibility of *History of Madness* is that one can neither write a work outside of reason, nor appeal to an original exclusion without 'exhum[ing] the virgin and unitary ground upon which the decisive act linking and separating madness and reason obscurely took root' (WD, 46 [p. 36]). In both cases, Derrida, beginning to mount reason's apologia, constructs his argument by summoning Hegel, casting the shadow of Hyppolite over the debate. First, marking his strategic difference from Foucault with respect to a philosophy of transformation, Derrida denies the possibility that reason could be contested from without:

> The unsurpassable, unique, and imperial grandeur of the order of reason, that which makes it not just another actual order or structure (a determined historical structure, one structure among other possible ones), is that one cannot speak out against it except by being for it. . . . The revolution against reason . . . can be made only within it, in accordance with a Hegelian law [*dimension*] to which I myself was very sensitive in Foucault's book, despite the absence

> of any precise reference to Hegel. Since the revolution against reason, from the moment it is articulated, can operate only within reason, it always has the limited scope of what is called, precisely in the language of a department of *internal* affairs, a disturbance. (WD, 42 [pp. 33–4])

At stake here is the question of thought itself: is there a way to think outside the domain of reason that would not simply articulate another form of reasoning, or does meaningful thought per se necessarily participate in the 'order of reason', that is, a transhistorical institution that would remain irreducible to any of its particular historical instantiations? Affirming the latter as 'an essential and principled truth' (WD, 65 [p. 49]),[25] Derrida calls into question the coherence of Foucault's concept of a counter-history of reason, that is, of a historical critique that would free itself from 'following reason in its horizontal becoming' (Foucault). Foucault's strategy of *contestation totale* would thus remain unintelligible because it violates Hegel's principle that 'the revolution against reason' can only ever be an 'internal' agitation. Of course, it remains an open question whether what Derrida identifies here as the 'Hegelian dimension' of *History of Madness* – the totalising view (with respect to what can be thought, written or said) of the unsurpassable unicity of reason in its 'imperial grandeur' – captures Foucault's own perspective or remains itself (and functions within Foucault's work as) the self-conception of a certain, historically determinate form of reason (namely, that of the modern period beginning in the late eighteenth century).[26]

If Derrida's first summons of Hegel effectively denies the ability of an archaeology (or any other form of thought) to escape the interiority of reason, his second Hegelian invocation confronts Foucault's history of limits by denying the exteriority of that which is originally divided by reason:

> The Decision, through a single act, links and separates reason and madness, and it must be understood at once both as the original act of an order, a fiat, a decree, and as a schism, a caesura, a separation, a dissection. I would prefer *dissension*, to underline that in question is a self-dividing action, a cleavage and torment interior to meaning *in general*, interior to logos in general, a division within the very act of *sentire*. As always, the dissension is internal. The exterior (is) the interior, is the fission that produces and divides it along the lines of the Hegelian *Entzweiung*. (WD, 46 [p. 36])

The source of divergence between Foucault and Derrida's respective philosophies of difference can be grasped here in the implicit opposition between the tragic (Nietzschean) and dialectical (Hegelian) conceptions of constitutive division. Refusing the model of exclusion, that is, of an expulsion that produces an outside, Derrida holds that an 'original act' of severance, if it is not to imply a metaphysics of presence, can only be an auto-differentiation: 'a self-dividing action' 'interior to logos in general', to 'a logos that preceded the split of reason and madness, a logos which within itself permitted dialogue between what were later called reason and madness' (WD, 45 [p. 36]). In other words, if the constitutive division between reason and madness is a decision, a meaningful (and meaning-bestowing) act, then the decision-making agency that institutes that division, logos, (1) must have already contained within itself what come to be called 'reason' and 'madness' and (2) must always exceed the particular historical forms of reason that result from that decision. Thus, like any process of fission that generates through self-division, 'the dissension is internal', an auto-production of difference intrinsic to logos that motors the dialectical course of reason.

In short, Derrida has thus deconstructed the inner-outer relation at the heart of *History of Madness*. 'The exterior (is) the interior': not only are the terms in the binary relation inverted and revalued (reversal), but the oppositional form of the relation itself is undone (displacement), allowing a more profound concept of interiority to emerge. The project that follows from this conceptual substitution of *dissension* for *exclusion*, charting 'a different and more ambitious design', is therefore 'one that should lead to a praise of reason . . . but this time of a reason more profound than that which opposes and determines itself in a historically determined conflict. Hegel again, always . . .' (WD, 51 [p. 40]). Rather than try to recover what is rejected as Exterior by a superficial and historically determinant form of reason, Derrida will aim to articulate the innermost ground of a deeper logos. Indeed, such a project will proceed to deconstruct the very relation between reason and madness, enacting both their reversal (what appears to be exterior, madness, is 'welcomed into the most essential interiority of thought' by a reason that 'acknowledges madness as its liberty and its very possibility', WD, 64, 68 [pp. 49, 52]) and the displacement of their opposition (the 'zero point' of reason is in essence that point most proximate to 'the possibility of a *total madness*', WD, 63 [p. 48]).

In the service of just this project, Derrida, at the second level of his critique, turns to Foucault's treatment of Descartes, offering his own interpretation of the Cartesian Cogito (the 'I think') that completes his deconstructive reading of *History of Madness* by doubling as both a praise and a radicalisation of reason. In dispute is a three-page passage on the First Meditation that appears at the beginning of Foucault's second chapter, 'The Great Confinement'. Here, Foucault suggests that the exclusion of madness proper to the classical period, realised at a socio-institutional level through widespread practices of internment, becomes realised at the epistemico-discursive level through the surreptitiously grounding decision taken by the meditating subject to dogmatically refuse the possibility of being mad as a sceptical reason for doubt. That is, before reason can lay claim to its own necessary and indubitable foundation – which the subject will accomplish in the Second Meditation through the insight *Cogito, sum* ('I think, I am') – and in order to establish the subject's right to reason, madness as mere possibility must be rejected out of hand.

Derrida argues that Foucault's reading is both unfaithful to Descartes and symptomatic of the basic impossibility of *History of Madness*. It is *unfaithful* because Foucault does not sufficiently attend to the Cartesian 'order of reasons', according to which the madness hypothesis is first surpassed by an equivalent but more universally accessible reason for doubt (the dreaming hypothesis) and then covered by the evil genius hypothesis (which is the madness hypothesis hyperbolised). That is, in the economy of doubt that organises the First Meditation, the doubt resulting from the madness hypothesis (were it to be entertained) would be partial (since it does not call into question the existence of the world as such, nor that of the subject's body) and restricted to the domain of sensory ideas (since, for Descartes, madness is merely 'a disorder of the body', WD, 64 [p. 48]). By contrast, the doubt engendered by the evil genius hypothesis – the possibility that a demon has deceived the meditating subject into falsely believing not only in the existence of the extended world (including the subject's body), but also in necessary intellectual truths, such as those of mathematics and logic – is apparently total, including all received ideas of both sensible and intelligible origin. For Derrida, this amounts to the universalisation of the madness hypothesis:

> Total derangement is the possibility of a madness . . . that will bring subversion to pure thought and to its purely intelligible objects, to the field of its clear and distinct ideas, to the realm of the mathematical truths which escape natural doubt. This time madness, insanity, will spare nothing, neither bodily nor purely intellectual perceptions. . . . Thus, ideas of neither sensory nor intellectual origin will be sheltered from this new phase of doubt, and everything that was previously set aside as insanity is now welcomed into the most essential interiority of thought. (WD, 63–4 [pp. 48–9])

Rather than dogmatically foreclose madness's possibility, the Cartesian subject would thus be exposed absolutely before that most insidious form of madness which subverts the innermost activity of thought. Making itself hospitable to what it had 'previously set aside', reason endures the ordeal of the hyperbolic madness that rushes in to possess it; and when, having traversed the long night of radical doubt, the subject arrives at the thought of the Cogito, the 'certainty thus attained need not be sheltered from an emprisoned madness, for it is attained and ascertained within madness itself. It is valid *even if I am mad* – a supreme self-confidence that seems to require neither the exclusion nor the circumventing of madness' (WD, 67 [p. 51]). Indeed, '[t]hought no longer fears madness' because the bedrock of indubitability remains so, whether or not one is mad: the founding truth 'attained and ascertained within madness itself' ensures that '[m]adness is therefore, in every sense of the word, only one case of thought (*within* thought)' (WD, 67–8 [p. 51]).

A moment of reversal thus takes place in the 'critical [*aigüe*] experience' (WD, 67 [p. 51]) of the Cogito: the reason that was possessed by (and dispossessed before) the possibility of 'total derangement' now takes possession of madness, not through exclusion and confinement but by incorporation. On Derrida's reading of Descartes, thought must first be inhabited by madness before arriving at the zero point of reason; and this inner ground of logos itself supports, houses madness as its intimate possibility: 'nothing is less reassuring than the Cogito at its proper and inaugural moment' (WD, 69 [p. 52]). Reason and madness can therefore no longer be understood as interior and exterior in relation to one another, for the very form of their opposition has been displaced.

In turn, for Derrida, the fact that Foucault sees in Descartes only a forced and unattested exclusion is not only unfaithful to the text of the *Meditations*, but *symptomatic* of the essential infeasibility of *History of Madness*; for this work conceives of difference on the model of exteriorisation and therefore can only see the refusal of madness by reason, there where thought confronts the 'mad audacity' (WD, 67 [p. 51]) proper to philosophy itself. In other words, for Derrida, what Foucault in his preface calls 'the obscure common root' (HM, xxxiii) of reason and madness is not a (tragic) limit-experience expelled by philosophy as the latter's first condition. Rather, before any historical act of founding division would have been instituted, this common root is embedded in the very ground of philosophy, in the 'hyperbolical audacity of the Cartesian Cogito', the 'impenetrable point of certainty' that makes possible any 'project of thinking' (WD, 67–8 [pp. 51–2]).

There would be no thought outside of this philosophy, no 'thought of the outside' that would not also be thought from a more profound inside. For not only does the zero point of reason make thought itself possible, but the difference introduced by the 'outside' is always already housed as an innermost possibility of logos, contained in the inaugural experience of the Cogito; and this experience, in turn – 'which, at its furthest reaches, is perhaps no less adventurous, perilous, nocturnal, and pathetic than the experience of madness' (WD, 39 [p. 31]) – remains irreducible to any of the forms of determinate historical reason that follow and thus 'cannot be objectified as an event in a determined history' (WD, 70 [p. 53]). The deeper concept of reason that Derrida's deconstructive reading would praise is thus at once the most vulnerable and the most 'supremely self-confident', taking hold by passing through total derangement and measuring itself by its test with hyperbolic madness. In a word, *pace* Foucault, it is reason rather than madness (reversal) – or rather, philosophy in its 'mad audacity' (displacement) – that opens onto the most radical possibilities of thought.

FOUCAULT'S TWO REPLIES (1972)

> Not truth and certainty are the opposite of the world of the madman, but the universality and the universal binding force of a faith . . .
>
> (Nietzsche, *The Gay Science*, §76: 'The greatest danger')

> What is at stake in the debate is indicated clearly: is it possible that there might be something anterior or exterior to philosophical discourse? Could it have its condition in an exclusion, a refusal, a risk eluded, and, why not, in a fear? A suspicion that Derrida rejects with passion. *Pudenda origo* (shameful origin!), said Nietzsche of religious people and their religion.
>
> (Foucault, 'My Body, This Paper, This Fire')

Nearly a decade would pass before Foucault responded to Derrida in print, a decade that included the insurrectionary political events of the late 1960s, including the student revolts of March 1968 in Tunisia (in which Foucault actively participated, and which would be for him a formative political experience[27]) and May 1968 in France (towards which Derrida, while taking part, remained ambivalent[28]). When the famously polemical response did come, it would sever personal ties between the two for nearly another decade. There are assuredly biographical reasons for the deterioration of relations between Derrida and Foucault, and these may well have contributed to the latter's decision to reply as he did.[29] However, we will focus our analysis on the philosophical reasons for why Foucault was compelled to respond, and to respond in such an uncharacteristically violent way; for these, grounded in the conceptual and political developments of his thought during this time, take us further in mining the difference between Foucault and Derrida.

Foucault, in fact, penned two replies, both of which appeared in 1972: 'Reply to Derrida', written for a special issue of the Japanese literary review, *Paideia*; and 'My Body, This Paper, This Fire', which Foucault appended to the second edition of *History of Madness*. The more famous second essay, appearing in the present volume, is the longer and exegetically richer of the two, and it focuses almost entirely on the second level of Derrida's critique, namely, the disputed reading of Descartes. This, no doubt, accounts for the perhaps puzzling fact that despite much of the force of Derrida's argument being directed at Foucault's original preface, most of the attention regarding the Foucault-Derrida debate has centred on their competing interpretations of the *Meditations*. Moreover, Foucault in fact suppressed his original preface from the second edition and removed the original title, *Folie et Déraison* ['Madness and Unreason'], leaving instead what had been the subtitle, *Histoire de la folie à l'âge classique* ['History of Madness in the Classical Period']. It is thus indeed possible to be left with the impression that Foucault largely concedes Derrida's first line of criticism regarding philosophical and methodological foundations – an impression that we will have cause to question below.

One thing is clear in any case: the methodology guiding Foucault's own work changed considerably between 1961 and 1972, moving from a tragic archaeology of silence to a still-incipient genealogy of power-knowledge by way of the more thoroughly articulated concept of archaeology as an analysis of discursive events and practices. At issue over the course of this trajectory is the question of the transformative efficacy of thought. While Foucault, throughout most of the previous decade, pursued an answer to this question through his politics of literary transgression, by 1970, he had abandoned this project altogether. In an interview given in Japan that year, during the same trip that he proposed writing a reply to Derrida for *Paideia*,[30] Foucault suggests that modern literature has been divested of its erstwhile subversive force, losing its position of exteriority in relation to the capitalist social formation and becoming appropriated as a commodity. Perhaps alluding to the celebrated category of *writing* that Derrida had made famous in *Of Grammatology* and *Writing and Difference*, Foucault asks:

> Does the subversive function of writing still remain? Hasn't the time already past when the sole act of writing . . . sufficed for expressing a form of contestation against modern society? Hasn't the time now come to move on to truly revolutionary actions? Now that the bourgeoisie and capitalist society have totally dispossessed writing of these actions, doesn't the fact of writing serve only to re-enforce the repressive system of the bourgeoisie? Mustn't we cease writing?[31]

For Foucault, then, what will replace literary exteriority conceptually as the locus or source of thought's powers of contestation is the 'dangerous [*redoubtable*] materiality' of discourse, which is to say, the 'material reality' of discourse as both practice and event situated in the historical field of force relations.[32] In so far as it is constituted by and as so many events, discourse arises as the 'effect of, and in, material dispersion'; it is thus material not in the sense of being 'corporeal', but by virtue of the 'level' at which it 'takes effect, becomes effect'.[33] In other words, the *materiality* of discourse refers to its *efficacy*, understood in two ways: (1) discourses, as events, are effectuated historically, that is, are themselves contingent effects; and (2) discourses, as practices, in turn produce effects in the historical domain of their emergence (not least of which upon the very subjects of discourse). Indeed, the fact that materiality is 'dangerous' owes precisely to its double efficacy as contingent and effective force: for, although 'in every society the production of discourse is at once controlled, selected, organised and redistributed according to a certain number of procedures, whose role is to avert its powers and its dangers', the very constitution of discourse as 'aleatory event' and practice escapes the ability of society to master it in advance.[34]

In short, Foucault's new concept of discourse enables him to reconceive the material agency of thought. There is a more involved story to tell here about how this concept informed both his emergent analytic of power and his novel experiments in political activism, notably, the efforts of the Prison Information Group (GIP) in the early 1970s to construct conditions of discursive agency for prisoners and thereby to contest the prison regime itself as a site of power-knowledge. For our present purposes, however, it may suffice to show how the opposition Foucault posits between his notion of discursivity and Derridean 'textuality' provides the basis for both his counter-interpretation of Descartes and broader critique of Derrida. As Foucault himself notes, in order to articulate his difference with Derrida concerning how to understand the exclusion of madness performed in the First Meditation, '[i]t was necessary that my attention be drawn towards "discursive events", the modalities of inclusion of the subject in discourse . . .'.[35]

In emphasising the discursive rather than merely textual dimension of Descartes' work, Foucault's strategy is to show how the refusal of the madness hypothesis can best be grasped by reading the *Meditations* as an *exercise* of thought rather than simply a demonstration of truth, which is to say, by attending to its ascetic aspects as a meditation in addition to the 'order of reasons' given by the meditating subject:

> Any discourse, whatever its nature, is made up of a group of enunciations which are produced in their space and in their time, as so many discursive events. If they form a pure demonstration, these enunciations can be read as a series of events, linked to each other according to a certain number of formal rules . . . A 'meditation', by contrast . . . implies . . . a subject who is mobile and capable of being modified by the very effect of the discursive events that take place . . . The *Meditations* require such a double reading: a group of propositions, forming a *system*, which each reader must run through if he wishes to experience their truth; and a group of modifications forming an *exercise*, which each reader must

> carry out, and by which each reader must be affected, if he wishes in his turn to be the subject enunciating this truth on his own account.[36]

From the perspective of this 'double reading', the relations between the sceptical hypotheses of madness, dreaming and the evil genius appear quite different than would be suggested by Derrida's fidelity to the order of reasons. To begin with, the reason the dreaming hypothesis surpasses the madness hypothesis is not that dreams are more universal than madness, but that they are more familiar and accessible to memory: the subject can remember having the experience of mistaking what was merely a dream for reality, whereas the example of madmen remains wholly exterior and alien to the one who meditates. The dreaming hypothesis thus 'takes' in a way that imagining oneself mad cannot, resulting in an essential practical advantage – namely, the continuation of the meditation. For the meditating subject can be disturbed by the doubt that what seems to be reality is in fact a dream, without thereby losing the ability to maintain control over the mechanics of thought and method of doubting. In other words, the validity of the meditation is preserved, for even as a dreamer, *dormiens*, the subject retains the full licence to meditate (HM, 553–5 [pp. 64–5]).

By contrast, Foucault argues, the subject as madman, *demens*, would be disqualified from the right to reason, invalidated as a meditating subject; and this can be seen in the very Latin terminology Descartes employs in the First Meditation. As a reason for doubting the present situation of the body and its near surroundings, the meditator considers whether she or he might be like a madman, *insanus*, who believes himself to be a king when he is poor or to be made of earthenware, etc. But before this hypothesis can be tested, the comparison fails, for the meditator exclaims: 'But such people are insane (*sed amentes sunt isti*), and I would be [thought] equally mad (*demens*) if I took anything from them as a model for myself' (HM, 558 [p. 68]). Now, the word *insanus* is chiefly a medical term distinguishing one who, suffering from a physical condition ('the brain swollen with vapors'), mistakes herself or himself for something other than she or he is. On the other hand, 'when Descartes wishes not to characterise madness, but to affirm that I should not take my example from the mad', he instead employs the terms *demens* and *amens*, which are principally juridical and 'designate a whole category of people who are incapable of certain religious, civil and judicial acts', which is to say, who are dispossessed of their discursive agency as legal subjects: 'the *dementes* do not have all their rights in matters of speaking, promising, committing themselves, signing, bringing legal actions, etc. *Insanus* is a term of characterisation; *amens* and *demens* are disqualifying terms' (HM, 559 [p. 69]).

Unlike the prospect of dreaming, then, the madness hypothesis threatens the disqualification of the meditator as subject of enunciation. Lacking the same resources of memory that allow the dreaming hypothesis entrance into the meditation, the prospect of being mad is never fully elevated to the level of hypothesis; for the meditative imagination cannot entertain the possibility of madness, even *as an exercise*, without thereby having succumbed to insanity: 'It is not by imitating madmen that I will be persuaded that I am mad (just as, a moment ago, the thought of dreaming convinced me that perhaps I am asleep); it is the very project of imitating them that is' (HM, 557 [p. 67]).

It is thus at the discursive level of the meditation, as an ascetic practice or technique, that the forcible exclusion of madness is required before the subject can be assured the necessary standing to continue the meditation and found the rational project.

Indeed, once the position of the subject is itself secured in the meditation, before yet arriving at the grounding insight of the Cogito, the meditator is equipped to entertain the hyperbolic doubt of the evil genius; and as extreme as that hypothesis may be with respect to the domain it calls into question, that is, at the level of the order of reasons, it never compromises the rational mastery of the discoursing subject at the level of meditative exercise. Foucault thus concludes that in order for Derrida to posit the evil genius as the radicalisation of the madness hypothesis,

> it is necessary to remove from Descartes' texts themselves everything which shows that the episode of the evil genius is a voluntary exercise, controlled, mastered and carried out from beginning to end by a meditating subject who never allows himself to be surprised . . . It could even be said that [the evil genius] is [madness's] contrary: in madness *I believe* that an illusory robe covers my nudity and my poverty, whereas the hypothesis of the evil genius *allows me not to believe* that this body and these hands exist. As for the scope of the trap, the evil genius, it is true, differs not from madness; but regarding the positioning of the subject in relation to the trap, the evil genius and madness are rigorously opposed. The evil genius takes over the power of *madness*, but only after the exercise of the meditation has excluded the risk of being *mad*. (HM, 571–2 [p. 78])

For Foucault, then, Derrida's interpretation of Descartes levels the 'discursive differences' essential to the movement of the *Meditations*, reducing the 'series of events (acts, effects, qualifications)', which modify 'the subject through the very exercise of the discourse', to 'the signifying organisation of the text' (HM, 562 [p. 71]).[37] In turn, this '"textualisation" of discursive practices' (HM, 573 [p. 79]), which offers a reading that is not only naïve and protective but deforming, effectively enacts a higher order exclusion by philosophy: 'in the end, it is excluded that philosophical discourse should exclude madness' (HM, 570 [p. 77]).

Rather than radicalise reason, Derrida's reading is thus merely 'recalling an old tradition', the very one *History of Madness* had set out to contest; and if he fails to grasp the singularity of the passage on madness in the First Meditation, this is not by chance or by inattention. Instead, it 'is part of a system, a system of which Derrida is today the most decisive representative, in its waning light: a reduction of discursive practices to textual traces; the elision of events that are produced there, leaving only marks for a reading . . .' (HM, 573 [p. 79]). Therefore, although 'Cogito and the History of Madness' begins by deconstructing the master-pupil dyad and concludes by praising a reason irreducible to historical determination, Derrida, Foucault suggests, fails on both counts: for deconstruction itself is nothing but a historically well-determined little pedagogy . . . A pedagogy which teaches the student that there is nothing outside the text . . . [and] that inversely gives to the voice of the masters that unlimited sovereignty that allows it indefinitely to re-say the text' (HM, 573 [p. 79]).

What, more precisely, is this system which Derrida would represent – and which, in 1972, just after the university as institution had become the object of political struggle, would be singing its swansong? The answer to this question remains obscure unless we consider Foucault's first, relatively neglected response, 'Reply to Derrida';[38] for that essay shows not only that Foucault does marshal an answer to Derrida's first set of charges regarding the coherence of a history of limits, but that he does so in the strongest of terms, clarifying the philosophical and political stakes of the debate.

At issue are both the historical contingency of reason and the possibility of thinking outside it, which is to say, for Foucault, thinking-otherwise. Foucault argues that if Derrida cannot conceive of a form of thought that would open onto the outside – if he is 'so preoccupied with remaining in the interiority of philosophy' that he cannot 'recognize this external event, this *limit event*, this primary division' (HM, 589, my emphasis) by which the positivity of reason is predicated on the exclusion of madness – then this is because Derrida's own thought is determined by three 'postulates' that serve as the traditional armature for the institution of philosophy in France. First, every form of knowledge or rational discourse 'entertains a fundamental relation with philosophy' (HM, 575–6), which confers on the former its epistemic justification as rational or as knowledge (*philosophy as law of discourse*). Second, any mistake made in regard to philosophy is not an error in argument so much as 'a blend of Christian sin and Freudian slip' (HM, 576), a moral fault inadvertently revealing a wayward inner logic that only philosophy can disclose and correct (*philosophy as totalisation of meaning* and *moralisation of truth*). Third, philosophy, as 'the repetition of an origin that is more than originary, and which infinitely exceeds, in its retreat, anything that it could say in any of its historical discourses' (HM, 577), is sealed off from any event, any encounter with singular forces outside it that it would not have been able to master in advance (*philosophy as impermeable to the event*).[39]

In other words, Foucault's reply to the first level of Derrida's critique is to disclose the dominant conditions of discourse that make his argument possible – and then to call these conditions themselves into question. Indeed, for Foucault, the three postulates summarise everything in the intellectual domain from which he had tried 'for so long' to free himself (HM, 577). In opposition to them, he advances three counter-theses, following from the archaeological method that he had developed in the intervening years since Derrida's essay. First, philosophy is not foundational for knowledge; on the contrary, the formation of philosophy as a kind of knowledge is itself subject to historico-epistemic conditions that are exterior to it. Second, 'the systematicity which links together forms of discourse, concepts, institutions and practices is not of the order of a forgotten radical thought that has been covered over and hidden from itself, nor is it a Freudian unconscious' (HM, 578), but rather, the unconscious of knowledge is constituted by a specific set of rules governing the emergence of statements and discursive practices. Third, far from being impermeable to events, thought itself can be understood *as* an event, and the history of thought can be analysed in terms of 'the "events" that can come about in the order of knowledge, and which cannot be reduced either to the general law of some kind of "progress," or the repetition of an origin' (HM, 578); it is in this sense that Foucault refers to *History of Madness* as 'the analysis of an event' (HM, 577).

If, for Foucault, what is thus at stake philosophically in this debate is the evental status of thought (which is also to say, thought's material agency as discourse), conversely, the political stakes concern the thought of the event. In an interview given just three months prior to the publication of 'Reply to Derrida', Foucault identifies the categories of *power* and *the event* as central to the kind of counter-knowledge that he would aim to produce or facilitate:

> Under the categories of what has alternately been called 'truth', 'man', 'culture', 'writing', etc., it is always a matter of warding off the shock of that which happens [*ce qui se produit*]: the event. . . . In the broadest sense, *the event and power are what are excluded from knowledge*, such as it is organised in our society. This is to be expected, since class power (which determines this knowledge) must appear inaccessible to the event; and the event, in its dangerous aspect, must be dominated and dissolved in the continuity of a class power that remains unnamed. On the other hand, the proletariat develops a form of knowledge where it is a question of the struggle for power, of what must be done to give rise to the event, respond to its urgency, or avoid it, etc.; this is a knowledge that is absolutely inassimilable to the first kind, since it is *centered around power and the event.*[40]

The appearance of impermeability to the event is required for the organisation of a dominant form of power-knowledge that must present itself as necessary or universal so as to cover over its own contingency (hence mutability, fragility); in turn, this concealment functions to safeguard the invisibility of power, to mask its exercise and its effects. Seen in this light, when Foucault opposes his own mode of analysis to deconstruction by asserting that Derrida 'does not know the category of the singular event' (HM, 577), at issue is less a methodological question than the implied political charge that Derrida's thought is determined by, and unwittingly reinforces, 'class power'.

Thus, far from tacitly conceding Derrida's essential claim that 'the exterior (is) the interior', and thereby abandoning the thesis of constitutive exclusion along with his original preface, Foucault instead situates Derrida's critique itself, and his philosophical project more generally, within the regime of power-knowledge that functions by excluding the double thought of the singular event ('this external event, this limit event, this primary division') and power. Such, finally, is the historically determinate 'system' the 'final glory' of which Derrida would represent – the very same system that regulates the production of discourse in society so as to defuse or contain the dangerous materiality of discursive events and practices. We can therefore see the full extent of Foucault's charge that deconstruction is but a historically determined pedagogy: by positioning Derrida as 'the most profound and the most radical' (HM, 577) contemporary example of philosophy qua dominant discourse, Foucault seeks to flip deconstruction on its head, effectively charging it with being a monolithic, logocentric, totalising form of discourse that forecloses any relation to an outside and thus to difference as such, which is to say, to the singular event as production of the new and force of transformation.

On the one hand, then, the debate between Foucault and Derrida can thus be understood as a fundamental clash between two philosophers of difference over (1) what it means to think difference and (2) what difference can be introduced by means of thought. Derrida would deny the transgressive efficacy of Foucault's appeal to a radical outside (the exterior limit as site of contestation), while Foucault would deny the subversive reversal and displacement of Derrida's appeal to a radical inside (the zero degree of reason as original and irreducible ground of thought).

On the other hand, this clash is not a direct confrontation so much as a relation of mutual incompossibility, for both Derrida and Foucault critically evaluate the other's work by means of criteria proper to their own. *History of Madness* can already be understood in terms of what Foucault will later call *discourse* because it aims to generate transformative effects in the historical field of force relations (with respect to social and cultural forms and practices) by providing the conditions of material expression for tragic unreason ('ruse and new triumph of madness'). Derrida, denying the intelligibility of this counter-history of reason, *treats Foucault's discourse as a text* – 'a logic, that is, an organized language, a project, an order, a sentence, a syntax, a work' (WD, 41 [p. 32]) – which, precisely as a piece of philosophical logos, is either self-defeating or forced to implicitly appeal to a metaphysics of presence, therefore requiring deconstruction. In turn, in his two replies, Foucault also shifts levels of analysis, *treating Derrida's text as discourse*, which is to say, evaluating Derrida's critique as a historically determined discursive practice performing a conservative institutional function within the field of power-knowledge. From this perspective, Derrida, failing to conceive the double thought of the event and power, and despite claiming to destabilise and radicalise the foundations of the logocentric tradition, effectively insulates reason from forms of counter-thought that might threaten it from outside.

Upon closer examination, then, what initially appears to be the space of a sharply delineated if temporally discontinuous polemic instead emerges as the non-place of competing but incommensurable projects. Like Foucault's description of the relation between the man of reason and the madman, the debate between Derrida and Foucault would thus read as the broken communication of two voices that 'fall away, like things henceforth foreign to each other, deaf to any exchange, as though dead to each other' (HM, xxvii, translation slightly modified). In turn, the work of the present volume will aim to re-establish the space of an 'in-between', of a proximity bespeaking the possibility of new connections between these voices, articulating 'the dialogue of their rupture, which proves, in a fleeting fashion, that they are still on speaking terms' (HM, xxviii).

NOTES

1. In addition to Cixous, this generation would also include Gilles Deleuze, Luce Irigaray, Jean-François Lyotard and Emmanuel Levinas, all of whom, in their own ways, articulate philosophies of difference that fundamentally critique the philosophical tradition.
2. Michel Foucault, *History of Madness*, ed. Jean Khalfa, trans. Jonathan Murphy and Jean Khalfa (London: Routledge, 2006), p. xxx. Hereafter cited in the text as HM.

3. Friedrich Nietzsche, *The Birth of Tragedy*, trans. Ronald Speirs (Cambridge: Cambridge University Press, 1999), §9, p. 46. In his final book, Nietzsche, characterising himself as 'the first *tragic philosopher*', will refer to this section from *Birth of Tragedy* as describing and anticipating 'the *style* of *Zarathustra*' (Friedrich Nietzsche, *Ecce Homo*, in *On the Genealogy of Morals and Ecce Homo*, trans. Walter Kaufmann (New York: Vintage Books, 1989), 'Why I Write Such Good Books: "The Birth of Tragedy"', §§3–4, pp. 273–5).
4. Antonin Artaud, whom Foucault places alongside Nietzsche throughout *History of Madness* as a poet of tragic unreason in the late modern period, refers to this tragic insight or abyssal vision as the 'superior lucidity' of the 'authentically insane'; see 'Van Gogh, the Man Suicided by Society', in Antonin Artaud, *Selected Writings*, ed. Susan Sontag (Berkeley: University of California Press, 1992). Cf., in the same volume, 'To Have Done with the Judgment of God', and especially 'The Rite of the Black Sun'.
5. 'Have you not heard of that madman who lit a lantern in the bright morning hours, ran to the market place, and cried incessantly: "I seek God! I seek God! . . . Whither is God?" he cried; "I will tell you. *We have killed him* – you and I. . . . What were we doing when we unchained this earth from its sun? Whither is it moving now? Whither are we moving? Away from all suns? Are we not plunging continually? . . . Are we not straying as through an infinite nothing? Do we not feel the breath of empty space? . . . Is not night continually closing in on us? Do we not need to light lanterns in the morning? . . . God is dead. God remains dead. And we have killed him"' (Friedrich Nietzsche, *The Gay Science*, trans. Walter Kaufmann (New York: Vintage Books, 1974), §125: 'The madman', p. 181).
6. Nietzsche, *Gay Science*, §76: 'The greatest danger', pp. 130–1.
7. Foucault, anticipating a series of further studies that were never to materialise, names as other tragic limit-experiences that of the Orient, the oneiric, and sexual transgression (HM, xxx).
8. See Foucault's historical overview of the division and opposed trajectories of these two regimes: 'Despite these crossovers, the division is nonetheless made, and from now on the gap between these two radically different visions of madness will not cease to widen. The paths taken by the figure of the cosmic vision and the incisive movement that is moral reflection, between the tragic and the critical elements, now constantly diverge, creating a gap in the fabric of the experience of madness that will never be repaired. . . . In short, the critical consciousness of madness was increasingly brought out into the light, while its more tragic components retreated ever further into the shadows, soon to almost vanish entirely. Only much later can a trace of the tragic element be again discerned, and a few pages in Sade and the work of Goya bear witness to the fact that this disappearance was merely an eclipse; the dark, tragic experience lived on in dreams and in the dark night of thoughts, and what happened in the sixteenth century was not a radical destruction but a mere occultation. . . . Behind the critical consciousness of madness in all its philosophical, scientific, moral and medicinal guises lurks a second, tragic consciousness of madness, which has never really gone away. It is that tragic consciousness that is visible in the last words of Nietzsche and the last visions of Van Gogh. . . . And it is that same consciousness that finds expression in the work of Antonin Artaud' (HM, 26–8).
9. Cf.: 'The dark cosmic forces at work in madness that are so apparent in the work of Bosch are absent in Erasmus. Madness no longer lies in wait for man at every crossroads; rather, it slips into him, or is in fact a subtle relationship that man has with himself. . . . In that respect, madness now opens out onto an entirely moral universe. Evil was no longer a punishment or the end of time, but merely a fault or flaw . . . – in short, every possible irregularity invented by man himself [*tout ce que l'homme a pu inventer lui-même d'irrégularités dans sa conduite*]' (HM, 23–4).
10. 'By a strange paradox, that which was born of the most singular delirium was already hidden, like a secret inaccessible truth, buried in the bowels of the earth. When the arbitrary nature

of madness was exhibited, man encountered the sombre necessity of the world: the animal that haunted his nightmares and visions born of ascetic deprivation was man's own nature, revealed in the unpitying truth of hell' (HM, 20–1).

11. Cf.: 'The animality that raged in madness dispossessed man of his humanity, not so that he might fall prey to other powers, but rather to fix him at the degree zero of his own nature' (HM, 148).
12. Michel Foucault, 'A Preface to Transgression', in *Aesthetics, Method, and Epistemology: Essential Works of Foucault, Volume 2*, ed. James Faubion (New York: The New Press, 1998), p. 72. See Foucault's remarks on Nietzsche at the end of *Introduction to Kant's Anthropology*, Foucault's secondary doctoral thesis, which was written contemporaneously with *History of Madness*: 'The Nietzschian enterprise can be understood as at last bringing that proliferation of the questioning of man to an end. For is not the death of God in effect manifested in a doubly murderous gesture which, by putting an end to the absolute, is at the same time the cause of the death of man himself? For man, in his finitude, is not distinguishable from the infinite of which he is both the negation and the harbinger; it is in the death of man that the death of God is realized. Is it not possible to conceive of a critique of finitude which would be as liberating with regard to man as it would be with regard to the infinite . . . ?' (Michel Foucault, *Introduction to Kant's Anthropology*, trans. Roberto Nigro and Kate Briggs (Los Angeles: Semiotext(e), 2008), p. 124). Cf. Artaud's pithy formulation in 'To Have Done with the Judgment of God': 'although nobody believes in god any more everybody believes more and more in man. / So it is man whom we must now make up our minds to emasculate' (Artaud, *Selected Writings*, p. 570).
13. Cf.: 'In this disparity between the consciousness of madness and the consciousness of unreason, we find, in the late eighteenth century, the starting point of what was to be a decisive moment, where the experience of unreason, such as is evident in Hölderlin, Nerval and Nietzsche, always leads back to [*remonter toujours plus haut vers*] the roots of time – unreason thereby becoming the untimely within the world *par excellence* – while the knowledge of madness sought on the contrary to situate it ever more precisely within the direction of nature and history in their development. It is from this period onwards that the time of unreason and the time of madness were to be affected by *two opposing vectors*: unreason becoming an unconditional return, and an absolute plunge; madness developing along the chronology of a history' (HM, 363–4, my emphasis).
14. This lineage includes Bosch, Francisco Goya, Marquis de Sade, Friedrich Hölderlin, Gérard de Nerval, Nietzsche, Vincent Van Gogh, Raymond Roussel and Artaud.
15. Michel Foucault, *Madness and Civilization*, trans. Richard Howard (New York: Pantheon, 1965), p. 289; cf. HM, 538. I have cited Richard Howard's older translation of this passage because, among other advantages, it retains Foucault's language of 'justification', which is a more faithful rendering. The original French reads: 'Ruse et nouveau triomphe de la folie: ce monde qui croit la mesurer, la justifier par la psychologie, c'est devant elle qu'il doit se justifier, puisque dans son effort et ses débats, il se mesure à la démesure d'œuvres comme celle de Nietzsche, de Van Gogh, d'Artaud. Et rien en lui, surtout pas ce qu'il peut connaître de la folie, ne l'assure que ces œuvres le justifient' (Michel Foucault, *Histoire de la folie à l'âge classique* (Paris : Éditions Gallimard, 1972), p. 663).
16. Foucault here follows Artaud, whose thesis in his essay on Van Gogh is that the 'authentically insane' – those artists, such as Hölderlin, Nerval, Nietzsche and Van Gogh, who possess a form of 'superior lucidity' that psychiatry institutionalises and treats as mental illness – become suicided by society because the dangerous subversive force that their works express would undermine the foundation of social institutions. See Artaud, 'Van Gogh, the Man Suicided by Society': 'And what is an authentic madman? / It is a man who preferred to become mad, in the socially accepted sense of the word, rather than forfeit a certain superior idea of human honor. / So society has strangled in its asylums all those it wanted to get rid of

or protect itself from, because they refused to become its accomplices in certain great nastiness. / For a madman is also a man whom society did not want to hear and whom it wanted to prevent from uttering certain intolerable truths' (*Selected Writings*, p. 485). See also: 'This is why a tainted society has invented psychiatry to defend itself against the investigations of certain superior intellects [*lucidités supérieures*] whose faculties of divination would be troublesome. / . . . For it is not a certain conformity of manners that the painting of van Gogh attacks, but rather the conformity of institutions themselves' (ibid., pp. 483–4).

17. See James Miller, *The Passion of Michel Foucault* (Cambridge MA: Harvard University Press, 1993), p. 118.
18. See Benoît Peeters, *Derrida: A Biography* (Cambridge: Polity, 2013), p. 132.
19. Jacques Derrida, 'Cogito and the History of Madness', in *Writing and Difference*, trans. Alan Bass (London and New York: Routledge, 2001), p. 37 [pp. 29–30], my emphasis. Hereafter cited in the text as WD, with corresponding in-volume pagination noted in brackets.
20. Jacques Derrida, *Of Grammatology*, trans. Gayatri Chakravorty Spivak (Baltimore: Johns Hopkins University Press, 1997), p. 24.
21. Spivak, 'Translator's Preface', in Derrida, *Of Grammatology*, p. lxxvi.
22. Derrida elaborates: 'In writing a history of madness, Foucault has attempted – and this is the greatest merit, but also the very infeasibility of his book – to write a history of madness *itself*. *Itself*. Of madness itself. That is, by letting madness speak for itself. Foucault wanted madness to be the *subject* of his book in every sense of the word: its theme and its first-person narrator, its author, madness speaking about itself. Foucault wanted to write a history of madness *itself*, that is madness speaking on the basis of its own experience and under its own authority, and not a history of madness described from within the language of reason, the language of psychiatry *on* madness – the agonistic and rhetorical dimensions of the preposition *on* overlapping here – on madness already crushed beneath psychiatry, dominated, beaten to the ground, interned, that is to say, madness made into an object and exiled as the other of a language and a historical meaning which have been confused with logos itself' (WD, 39 [p. 31]).
23. Note, however, that Derrida does not attend to *History of Madness* as a tragic work, limiting the expressive possibilities of non-reason to the silence or oeuvre-lessness of madness (without distinguishing mental illness and tragic unreason). That is, for both Derrida and Foucault, the problem of expression cuts to the heart of Foucault's project, but each poses the problem in different terms, or better, in terms of a different set of possibilities. Here as elsewhere on both sides of this debate, one senses both a true disaccord and the drift of misunderstanding.
24. 'Finally, a last question: if this great division is the possibility of history itself, the historicity of history, what does it mean, here, "to write the history of this division"? To write the history of historicity? To write the history of the origin of history? . . . If there is a historicity proper to reason in general, the history of reason cannot be the history of its origin (which, for a start, demands the historicity of reason in general), but must be that of one of its determined figures' (WD, 51 [p. 39]). It is in this light, no doubt, that Derrida will later claim that grammatology is superior to archaeology in providing the history of the origin of history, in so far as writing constitutes that first condition for historicity: 'historicity itself is tied to the possibility of writing; to the possibility of writing in general, beyond those particular forms of writing in the name of which we have long spoken of peoples without writing and without history. Before being the object of a history – of an historical science – writing opens the field of history – of historical becoming. . . . The history of writing should turn back towards the origin of historicity. . . . A history of the possibility of history which would no longer be an archaeology . . .' (Derrida, *Of Grammatology*, pp. 27–8).
25. Derrida continues: 'if discourse and philosophical communication (that is, language itself) are to have an intelligible meaning, that is to say, if they are to conform to their essence and vocation as discourse, they must simultaneously in fact and in principle escape madness.

They must carry normality within themselves. And this is . . . an essential and universal necessity from which no discourse can escape, for it belongs to the meaning of meaning' (WD, 65 [p. 49]).

26. See Amy Allen's contribution to the present volume, 'The History of Historicity: The Critique of Reason in Foucault (and Derrida)', for a Foucauldian defence of the latter position. It would follow from this view that Foucault's appeal to expressive unreason as 'total contestation' refers specifically to contesting the epistemic formation of the modern period – what Gilles Deleuze, in his book on Foucault, calls the 'Man-form' (Deleuze, *Foucault*, trans. Seán Hand (Minneapolis: University of Minnesota Press, 1988), p. 126) – rather than 'Reason' as Derrida understands it, that is, meaning or intelligible thought as such. Of course, Derrida could still deny the coherence of this project by maintaining the Hegelian position that the deeper ground of reason (which would contain madness and difference within itself) must first be grasped and held at a remove before – indeed as the basis for – undertaking to subvert any historically determinate form of reason. Indeed, such a position describes how Derrida's deconstruction of Foucault's opposition between reason and madness, which becomes a 'praise of reason', is not only consistent with but helps makes possible the deconstructive critique of logocentrism.
27. See, for example, Foucault's interview with Duccio Trombadori, 'Interview with Michel Foucault', in *Power: Essential Works of Foucault, Volume 3*, ed. James Faubion (New York: The New Press, 2001), pp. 279ff.
28. In particular, Derrida was leery of what he perceived as the 'spontaneism' of the '*soixante-huitards*'; see Peeters, *Derrida: A Biography*, p. 197.
29. For example, in their respective biographies of Foucault and Derrida, both James Miller and Benoît Peeters suggest that an important role was played by Derrida's increasing fame, which had grown considerably with the publication of both *Of Grammatology* and *Writing and Difference* in 1967. See Miller, *The Passion of Michel Foucault*, p. 120; and Peeters, *Derrida: A Biography*, p. 238. Derrida himself blamed the initial cooling of relations with Foucault on their quarrel in 1967 over the publication of a review of *Writing and Difference* by Derrida's friend, Gérard Granel, in *Critique* (whose editorial board included both Derrida and Foucault), which review was extremely hostile towards Foucault; see Peeters, *Derrida: A Biography*, pp. 182–3, and, in the present volume, Alan Schrift, 'Michel Foucault and Jacques Derrida: A Chronology'.
30. See 'Chronologie', in Michel Foucault, *Dits et écrits I, 1954–1975*, ed. Daniel Defert and François Ewald with Jacques Lagrange (Paris: Quarto Gallimard, 2001), p. 49.
31. Foucault, 'Folie, littérature, société', in ibid., p. 983, my translation.
32. Foucault, 'The Discourse on Language', in *The Archaeology of Knowledge*, trans. A. M. Sheridan Smith (New York: Pantheon, 1972), p. 216, translation slightly modified.
33. Ibid., p. 231. The fuller passage reads: 'If discourses are to be treated first as ensembles of discursive events, what status are we to accord this notion of event, so rarely taken into consideration by philosophers? Of course, an event is neither substance, nor accident, nor quality nor process; events are not corporeal. And yet, an event is certainly not immaterial; it takes effect, becomes effect, always on the level of materiality. Events have their place; they consist in relation to, coexistence with, dispersion of, the cross-checking accumulation and the selection of material elements; it occurs as an effect of, and in, material dispersion. Let us say that the philosophy of event should advance in the direction, at first sight paradoxical, of an incorporeal materialism' (ibid.). This lecture, 'The Discourse on Language' (*L'ordre du discours*), was given in December of 1970; the previous month, Foucault had articulated the concept of 'incorporeal materiality' in terms of Gilles Deleuze's thought of intensity, which Foucault calls 'a metaphysics of the incorporeal event'; see Foucault, 'Theatrum Philosophicum', in *Aesthetics, Method, and Epistemology*, pp. 346–52.
34. Foucault, 'Discourse on Language', p. 216.

35. Foucault, 'A Return to Descartes' First Meditation' (Chapter 5 in the present volume).
36. Foucault, 'My Body, This Paper, This Fire,' in *History of Madness*, pp. 562–3 [pp. 71–2]. Hereafter cited in the text as HM, with corresponding in-volume pagination noted in brackets.
37. In a dialogue with Deleuze from the same year as his replies to Derrida, Foucault, anticipating his genealogical analytic of power, praises Deleuze for precisely breaking with this tendency to subordinate events and practices to a governing meaning: 'If the reading of your books (from *Nietzsche* to what I anticipate in *Capitalism and Schizophrenia*) has been essential for me, it is because they seem to go very far in exploring this problem: under the ancient theme of meaning, of the signifier and the signified, etc., you have developed the question of power, of the inequality of powers and their struggles' (Michel Foucault, 'Intellectuals and Power', in *Language, Counter-memory, Practice*, ed. D. F. Bouchard (New York: Cornell University Press, 1977), pp. 213–4).
38. 'Reply to Derrida' was first translated into English in 2006 as an appendix to *History of Madness*, which may account in part for why, at least in the Anglophonic world, this essay has remained so uncommented upon. Still, it is perhaps indicative of a more general attitude – to wit, that the first essay is merely a rough draft of the second – that in his introduction, Jean Khalfa, the editor and co-translator of *History of Madness*, says nothing about the content of 'Reply to Derrida' other than describing it as 'an earlier and different version of Foucault's answer to Derrida' (Khalfa, 'Introduction', HM, xxiii).
39. Anticipating this line of argument against Derrida in an essay four years prior (1968), Foucault characterises this last postulate as the 'historico-transcendental recourse: to try to find, beyond every manifestation and every historical birth, an originary foundation, the opening of an endless horizon, a project that would remain at a distance in relation to every event' (Foucault, 'Réponse à une question', *Dits et écrits I*, p. 703, my translation). In turn, he defines his own archaeological project as the attempt 'to free the discursive field from the historico-transcendental structure that the philosophy of the nineteenth century has imposed upon it' (ibid., p. 712, my translation). This would also be, of course, Foucault's attempt to free himself from Hegel, whom Derrida incidentally had summoned to testify against the methodological foundations of *History of Madness*.
40. Foucault, 'Revolutionary Action: "Until Now"', in *Language, Counter-memory, Practice*, pp. 220–1, translation modified, my emphasis; cf. Foucault, 'Par-delà le bien et le mal', *Dits et écrits I*, p. 1094.

PART I

The History of Madness Debate

CHAPTER 2

Cogito and the History of Madness

Jacques Derrida
Translated by Alan Bass

> The Instant of Decision is Madness. (Kierkegaard)

> In any event this book was terribly daring. A transparent sheet separates it from madness. (Joyce, speaking of *Ulysses*)

These reflections have as their point of departure, as the title of this lecture[1] clearly indicates, Michel Foucault's book *Folie et déraison: Histoire de la folie à l'âge classique*.[2]

This book, admirable in so many respects, powerful in its breadth and style, is even more intimidating for me in that, having formerly had the good fortune to study under Michel Foucault, I retain the consciousness of an admiring and grateful disciple. Now, the disciple's consciousness, when he starts, I would not say to dispute, but to engage in dialogue with the master or, better, to articulate the interminable and silent dialogue which made him into a disciple – this disciple's consciousness is an unhappy consciousness. Starting to enter into dialogue in the world, that is, starting to answer back, he always feels 'caught in the act', like the 'infant' who, by definition and as his name indicates, cannot speak and above all must not answer back. And when, as is the case here, the dialogue is in danger of being taken – incorrectly – as a challenge, the disciple knows that he alone finds himself already challenged by the master's voice within him that precedes his own. He feels himself indefinitely challenged, or rejected or accused; as a disciple, he is challenged by the master who speaks within him and before him, to reproach him for making this challenge and to reject it in advance, having elaborated it before him; and having interiorised the master, he is also challenged by the disciple that he himself is. This interminable unhappiness of the disciple perhaps stems from the fact that he does not yet know – or is still concealing from himself – that the master, like real life, may always be absent. The disciple must break the glass, or better the mirror, the reflection, his infinite speculation on the master. And start to speak.

As the route that these considerations will follow is neither direct nor unilinear – far from it – I will sacrifice any further preamble and go straight to the most general questions that will serve as the focal points of these reflections. General questions that will have to be determined and specified along the way, many of which, most, will remain open.

My point of departure might appear slight and artificial. In this 673-page book, Michel Foucault devotes three pages – and, moreover, in a kind of prologue to his second chapter – to a certain passage from the first of Descartes' *Meditations*. In this passage madness, folly, dementia, insanity seem, I emphasise *seem*, dismissed, excluded and ostracised from the circle of philosophical dignity, denied entry to the philosopher's city, denied the right to philosophical consideration, ordered away from the bench as soon as summoned to it by Descartes – this last tribunal of a Cogito that, by its essence, *could not possibly* be mad.

In alleging – correctly or incorrectly, as will be determined – that the sense of Foucault's entire project can be pinpointed in these few allusive and somewhat enigmatic pages, and that the reading of Descartes and the Cartesian Cogito proposed to us engages in its problematic the totality of this *History of Madness* as regards both its intention and its feasibility, I shall therefore be asking myself, in two series of questions, the following:

1. First, and in some ways this is a prejudicial question: is the *interpretation* of Descartes' intention that is proposed to us justifiable? What I here call interpretation is a certain passage, a certain semantic relationship proposed by Foucault between, *on the one hand*, what Descartes said – or what he is believed to have said or meant – and *on the other hand*, let us say, with intentional vagueness for the moment, a certain 'historical structure', as it is called, a certain meaningful historical totality, a total historical project through which we think what Descartes said – or what he is believed to have said or meant – can *particularly* be demonstrated. In asking if the interpretation is justifiable, I am therefore asking about two things, putting two preliminary questions into one: (a) Have we fully understood the *sign* itself, in itself? In other words, has what Descartes said and meant been clearly perceived? This comprehension of the sign in and of itself, in its immediate materiality as a sign, if I may so call it, is not only the first moment but also the indispensable condition of all hermeneutics and of any claim to transition from the sign to the signified. When one attempts, in a general way, to pass from an obvious to a latent language, one must first be rigorously sure of the obvious meaning.[3] The analyst, for example, must first speak the same language as the patient. (b) Second implication of the first question: once understood as a sign, does Descartes' stated intention have with the total historical structure to which it is to be related the relationship assigned to it? *Does it have the historical meaning assigned to it?* 'Does it have the historical meaning assigned to it?' That is, again, two questions in one: Does it have *the* historical meaning assigned to it? does it have *this* meaning, a *given* meaning Foucault assigns to it? Or, second, does it have the *historical* meaning assigned to it? Is this meaning exhausted by its historicity? In other words, is it

fully, in each and every one of its aspects, historical, in the classical sense of the word?

2. Second series of questions (and here we shall go somewhat beyond the case of Descartes, beyond the case of the Cartesian Cogito, which will be examined no longer in and of itself but as the index of a more general problematic): in the light of the rereading of the Cartesian Cogito that we shall be led to propose (or rather to recall, for, let it be said at the outset, this will in some ways be the most classical, banal reading, even if not the easiest one), will it not be possible to interrogate *certain* philosophical and methodological presuppositions of this history of madness? *Certain ones* only, for Foucault's enterprise is too rich, branches out in too many directions to be preceded by a method or even by a *philosophy*, in the traditional sense of the word. And if it is true, as Foucault says, as he admits by citing Pascal, that one cannot speak of madness except in relation to that 'other form of madness' that allows men 'not to be mad', that is, except in relation to reason,[4] it will perhaps be possible not to add anything whatsoever to what Foucault has said, but perhaps only to *repeat* once more, on the site of this *division* between reason and madness of which Foucault speaks so well, the meaning, a meaning of the Cogito or (plural) Cogitos (for the Cogito of the Cartesian variety is neither the first nor the last form of Cogito); and also to determine that what is in question here is an experience which, at its furthest reaches, is perhaps no less adventurous, perilous, nocturnal and pathetic than the experience of madness, and is, I believe, much less adverse to and accusatory of madness, that is, accusative and objectifying of it, than Foucault seems to think.

As a first stage, we will attempt a commentary, and will accompany or follow as faithfully as possible Foucault's intentions in reinscribing an interpretation of the Cartesian Cogito within the total framework of the *History of Madness*. What should then become apparent in the course of this first stage is the meaning of the Cartesian Cogito as read by Foucault. To this end, it is necessary to recall the general plan of the book and to open several marginal questions, destined to remain open and marginal.

In writing a history of madness, Foucault has attempted – and this is the greatest merit, but also the very infeasibility of his book – to write a history of madness *itself*. *Itself*. Of madness itself. That is, by letting madness speak for itself. Foucault wanted madness to be the *subject* of his book in every sense of the word: its theme and its first-person narrator, its author, madness speaking about itself. Foucault wanted to write a history of madness *itself*, that is madness speaking on the basis of its own experience and under its own authority, and not a history of madness described from within the language of reason, the language of psychiatry *on* madness – the agonistic and rhetorical dimensions of the preposition *on* overlapping here – on madness already crushed beneath psychiatry, dominated, beaten to the ground, interned, that is to say, madness made into an object and exiled as the other of a language and a historical meaning which have been confused with logos itself. 'A history not of psychiatry', Foucault says, 'but of madness itself, in its most vibrant state, before being captured by knowledge.'

It is a question, therefore, of escaping the trap or objectivist naiveté that would consist in writing a history of untamed madness, of madness as it carries itself and breathes before being caught and paralysed in the nets of classical reason, from within the very language of classical reason itself, utilising the concepts that were the historical instruments of the capture of madness – the restrained and restraining language of reason. Foucault's determination to avoid this trap is constant. It is the most audacious and seductive aspect of his venture, producing its admirable tension. But it is also, with all seriousness, the *maddest* aspect of his project. And it is remarkable that this obstinate determination to avoid the trap – that is, the trap set by classical reason to catch madness and which can now catch Foucault as he attempts to write a history of madness itself without repeating the aggression of rationalism – this determination to bypass reason is expressed in two ways difficult to reconcile at first glance. Which is to say that it is expressed uneasily.

Sometimes Foucault globally rejects the language of reason, which itself is the language of order (that is to say, simultaneously the language of the system of objectivity, of the universal rationality of which psychiatry wishes to be the expression, and the language of the body politic – the right to citizenship in the philosopher's city overlapping here with the right to citizenship anywhere, the philosophical realm functioning, within the unity of a certain structure, as the metaphor or the metaphysics of the political realm). At these moments he writes sentences of this type (he has just evoked the broken dialogue between reason and madness at the end of the eighteenth century, a break that was finalised by the annexation of the totality of language – and of the right to language – by psychiatric reason as the delegate of societal and governmental reason; madness has been stifled): 'The language of psychiatry, which is a monologue of reason *on* madness, could be established only on the basis of such a silence. I have not tried to write the history of that language but, rather, the archaeology of that silence.'[5] And throughout the book runs the theme linking madness to silence, to 'words without language' or 'without the voice of a subject', 'obstinate murmur of a language that speaks by itself, without speaker or interlocutor, piled up upon itself, strangulated, collapsing before reaching the stage of formulation, quietly returning to the silence from which it never departed. The calcinated root of meaning.' The history of madness itself is therefore the archaeology of a silence.

But, first of all, is there a history of silence? Further, is not an archaeology, even of silence, a logic, that is, an organised language, a project, an order, a sentence, a syntax, a work?[6] Would not the archaeology of silence be the most efficacious and subtle restoration, the *repetition*, in the most irreducibly ambiguous meaning of the word, of the act perpetrated against madness – and be so at the very moment when this act is denounced? Without taking into account that all the signs which allegedly serve as indices of the origin of this silence and of this stifled speech, and as indices of everything that has made madness an interrupted and forbidden, that is, arrested, discourse – all these signs and documents are borrowed, without exception, from the juridical province of interdiction.

Hence, one can inquire – as Foucault does also, at moments other than those when he contrives to speak of silence (although in too lateral and implicit a fashion from my point of view) – about the source and the status of the language of this archaeology, of this language which is to be understood by a reason that is not classical reason. What is the historical responsibility of this logic of archaeology? Where should it be situated? Does it suffice to stack the tools of psychiatry neatly, inside a tightly shut workshop, in order to return to innocence and to end all complicity with the rational or political order which keeps madness captive? The psychiatrist is but the delegate of this order, one delegate among others. Perhaps it does not suffice to imprison or to exile the delegate, or to stifle him; and perhaps it does not suffice to deny oneself the conceptual material of psychiatry in order to exculpate one's own language. All our European languages, the language of everything that has participated, from near or far, in the adventure of Western reason – all this is the immense delegation of the project defined by Foucault under the rubric of the capture or objectification of madness. *Nothing* within this language, and *no one* among those who speak it, can escape the historical guilt – if there is one, and if it is historical in a classical sense – which Foucault apparently wishes to put on trial. But such a trial may be impossible, for by the simple fact of their articulation the proceedings and the verdict unceasingly reiterate the crime. If the *Order* of which we are speaking is so powerful, if its power is unique of its kind, this is so precisely by virtue of the universal, structural, universal and infinite complicity in which it compromises all those who understand it in its own language, even when this language provides them with the form of their own denunciation. Order is then denounced within order.

Total disengagement from the *totality* of the historical language responsible for the exile of madness, liberation from this language in order to write the archaeology of silence, would be possible in only two ways.

Either do not mention a certain silence (a *certain* silence which, again, can be determined only within a *language* and an *order* that will preserve this silence from contamination by any given muteness), *or* follow the madman down the road of his exile. The misfortune of the mad, the interminable misfortune of their silence, is that their best spokesmen are those who betray them best; which is to say that when one attempts to convey their silence *itself*, one has already passed over to the side of the enemy, the side of order, even if one fights against order from within it, putting its origin into question. There is no Trojan horse unconquerable by Reason (in general). The unsurpassable, unique and imperial grandeur of the order of reason, that which makes it not just another actual order or structure (a determined historical structure, one structure among other possible ones), is that one cannot speak out against it except by being for it, that one can protest it only from within it; and within its domain, Reason leaves us only the recourse to strategems and strategies. The revolution against reason, in the historical form of classical reason (but the latter is only a determined example of Reason in general. And because of this oneness of Reason the expression 'history of reason' is difficult to conceptualise, as is also, consequently, a 'history of madness'), the revolution against reason can be made only within it, in accordance with a Hegelian law to which I myself was very sensitive in Foucault's book, despite the absence of any precise reference to Hegel. Since the revolution against reason, from the moment it is articulated, can operate only *within* reason, it always has the limited scope of what is called, precisely in the language of a department of *internal* affairs, a disturbance. A history, that is, an archaeology against reason doubtless cannot be written, for, despite all appearances to the contrary, the concept of history has always been a rational one. It is the meaning of 'history' or *archia* that should have been questioned first, perhaps. A writing that exceeds, by questioning them, the values 'origin', 'reason' and 'history' could not be contained within the metaphysical closure of an archaeology.

As Foucault is the first to be conscious – and acutely so – of this daring, of the necessity of speaking and of drawing his language from the wellspring of a reason more profound than the reason which issued forth during the classical age, and as he experiences a necessity of speaking which must escape the objectivist project of classical reason – a necessity of speaking even at the price of a war declared by the language of reason against itself, a war in which language would recapture itself, destroy itself, or unceasingly revive the act of its own destruction – the allegation of an archaeology of silence, a purist, intransigent, nonviolent, nondialectical allegation, is often counterbalanced, equilibrated, I should even say contradicted by a discourse in Foucault's book that is not only the admission of a difficulty, but the formulation of *another* project, a project that is not an expediency, but a different and more ambitious one, a project more effectively ambitious than the first one.

The admission of the difficulty can be found in sentences such as these, among others, which I simply cite, in order not to deprive you of their dense beauty:

> The perception that seeks to grasp them [in question are the miseries and murmurings of madness] in their wild state, necessarily belongs to a world that has already captured them. The liberty of madness can be understood only from high in the fortress that holds madness prisoner. And there madness possesses only the morose sum of its prison experiences, its mute experience of persecution, and we – we possess only its description as a man wanted.

And, later, Foucault speaks of a madness 'whose wild state can never be restored in and of itself' and of an 'inaccessible primitive purity'.

Because this difficulty, or this impossibility, must reverberate within the language used to describe this history of madness, Foucault, in effect, acknowledges the necessity of maintaining his discourse within what he calls a 'relativity without recourse', that is, without support from an absolute reason or logos. The simultaneous necessity and impossibility of what Foucault elsewhere calls 'a language without support', that is to say, a language declining, in principle if not in fact, to articulate itself along the lines of the syntax of reason. In principle if not in fact, but here the fact cannot easily be put between parentheses. The fact of language is probably the only fact ultimately to resist all parenthisation. 'There, in the simple problem of articulation,' Foucault says later, 'was hidden and expressed the major difficulty of the enterprise'.

One could perhaps say that the resolution of this difficulty is *practised* rather than *formulated*. By necessity. I mean that the silence of madness is not *said*, cannot be said in the logos of this book, but is indirectly, metaphorically, made present by its *pathos* – taking this word in its best sense. A new and radical praise of folly whose intentions cannot be admitted because the *praise* [*éloge*] of silence always takes place within *logos*,[7] the language of objectification. 'To speak well of madness' would be to annex it once more, especially when, as is the case here, 'speaking well of' is also the wisdom and happiness of eloquent speech.

Now, to state the difficulty, to state the difficulty of stating, is not yet to surmount it – quite the contrary. First, it is not to say in which language, through the agency of what speech, the difficulty is stated. Who perceives, who enunciates the difficulty? These efforts can be made neither in the wild and inaccessible silence of madness, nor simply in the language of the jailer, that is, in the language of classical reason, but only in the language of someone *for whom* is meaningful and *before whom* appears the dialogue or war or misunderstanding or confrontation or double monologue that opposes reason and madness during the classical age. And thereby we can envision the historic liberation of a logos in which the two monologues, or the broken dialogue, or especially the breaking point of the dialogue between a *determined* reason and a *determined* madness, could be produced and can today be understood and enunciated. (Supposing that they can be; but here we are assuming Foucault's hypothesis.)

Therefore, if Foucault's book, despite all the acknowledged impossibilities and difficulties, was capable of being written, we have the right to ask what, in the last resort, supports this language without recourse or support: who enunciates the possibility of nonrecourse? Who wrote and who is to understand, in what language and from what historical situation of logos, who wrote and who is to understand this history of madness? For it is not by chance that such a project could take shape today. Without forgetting, *quite to the contrary*, the audacity of Foucault's act in the *History of Madness*, we must assume that a certain liberation of madness has gotten underway, that psychiatry has opened itself up, however minimally, and that the concept of madness as unreason, if it ever had a unity, has been dislocated. And that a project such as Foucault's can find its historical origin and passageway in the opening produced by this dislocation.

If Foucault, more than anyone else, is attentive and sensitive to these kinds of questions, it nevertheless appears that he does not acknowledge their quality of being prerequisite methodological or philosophical considerations. And it is true that once the question and the privileged difficulty are understood, to devote a preliminary work to them would have entailed the sterilisation or paralysis of all further inquiry. Inquiry can prove through its very act that the movement of a discourse on madness is possible. But is not the foundation of this possibility still too classical?

Foucault's book is not one of those that abandons itself to the prospective lightheartedness of inquiry. That is why, behind the admission of the difficulty concerning the archaeology of silence, a *different* project must be discerned, one which perhaps contradicts the projected archaeology of silence.

Because the silence whose archaeology is to be undertaken is not an original muteness or nondiscourse, but a subsequent silence, a discourse arrested by *command*, the issue is therefore to reach the origin of the protectionism imposed by a reason that insists upon being sheltered, and that also insists upon providing itself with protective barriers against madness, thereby making itself into a barrier against madness; and to reach this origin from within a logos of free trade, that is, from within a logos that preceded the split of reason and madness, a logos which within itself permitted dialogue between what were later called reason and madness (unreason), permitted their free circulation and exchange, just as the medieval city permitted the free circulation of the mad within itself. The issue is therefore to reach the point at which the dialogue was broken off, dividing itself into two soliloquies – what Foucault calls, using a very strong word, the *Decision*. The Decision, through a single act, links and separates reason and madness, and it must be understood at once both as the original act of an order, a fiat, a decree, and as a schism, a caesura, a separation, a dissection. I would prefer *dissension*, to underline that in question is a self-dividing action, a cleavage and torment interior to meaning *in general*, interior to logos in general, a division within the very act of *sentire*. As always, the dissension is internal. The exterior (is) the interior, is the fission that produces and divides it along the lines of the Hegelian *Entzweiung*.

It thus seems that the project of convoking the first dissension of logos against itself is quite another project than the archaeology of silence, and raises different questions. This time it would be necessary to exhume the virgin and unitary ground upon which the decisive act linking and separating madness and reason obscurely took root. The reason and madness of the classical age had a common root. But this common root, which is a logos, this unitary foundation is much more ancient than the medieval period, brilliantly but briefly evoked by Foucault in his very fine opening chapter. There must be a founding unity that already carries within it the 'free trade' of the Middle Ages, and this unity is already the unity of a logos, that is, of a reason; an already historical reason certainly, but a reason much less determined than it will be in its so-called classical form, having not yet received the determinations of the 'classical age'. It is within the element of this archaic reason that the dissection, the dissension, will present itself as a modification or, if you will, as an overturning, that is, a revolution but an internal revolution, a revolution affecting the self, occurring within the self. For this logos which is in the beginning, is not only the common ground of all dissension, but also – and no less importantly – the very atmosphere in which Foucault's language moves, the atmosphere in which a history of madness during the classical age not only appears *in fact* but is also *by all rights* stipulated and specified in terms of its limits. In order to account simultaneously for the origin (or the possibility) of the decision and for the origin (or the possibility) of its narration, it might have been necessary to start by reflecting this original logos in which the violence of the classical era played itself out. This history of logos before the Middle Ages and before the classical age is not, if this need be said at all, a nocturnal and mute prehistory. Whatever the momentary break, if there is one, of the Middle Ages with the Greek tradition, this break and this alteration are late and secondary developments as concerns the fundamental permanence of the logico-philosophical heritage.

That the embedding of the decision in its true historical grounds has been left in the shadows by Foucault is bothersome, and for at least two reasons:

1. It is bothersome because at the outset Foucault makes a somewhat enigmatic allusion to the Greek logos, saying that, unlike classical reason, it 'had no contrary'.

To cite Foucault: 'The Greeks had a relation to something that they called *hybris*. This relation was not merely one of condemnation; the existence of Thrasymacus or of Callicles suffices to prove it, even if their language has reached us already enveloped in the reassuring dialectic of Socrates. But the Greek Logos had no contrary.'[8]

[One would have to assume, then, that the Greek logos had no contrary, which is to say, briefly, that the Greeks were in the greatest proximity to the elementary, primordial and undivided Logos with respect to which contradiction in general, all wars or polemics, could only be ulterior developments. This hypothesis forces us to admit, as Foucault above all does *not*, that the history and lineage of the 'reassuring dialectic of Socrates' in their *totality* had already fallen outside and been exiled from this Greek logos that had no contrary. For if the Socratic dialectic is reassuring, in the sense understood by Foucault, it is so only in that it has already expulsed, excluded, objectified or (curiously amounting to the same thing) assimilated and mastered as one of its moments, 'enveloped' the contrary of reason; and also only in that it has tranquilised and reassured itself into a pre-Cartesian certainty, a *sophrosyne*, a wisdom, a reasonable good sense and prudence.

Consequently, it must be *either* (a) that the Socratic moment and its entire posterity immediately partake in the Greek logos that has no contrary; and that consequently, the Socratic dialectic could not be reassuring (we may soon have occasion to show that it is no more reassuring than the Cartesian cogito). In this case, in this hypothesis, the fascination with the pre-Socratics to which we have been provoked by Nietzsche, then by Heidegger and several others, would carry with it a share of mystification whose historico-philosophical motivations remain to be examined. *Or* (b) that the Socratic moment and the victory over the Calliclesian *hybris* already are the marks of a deportation and an exile of logos from itself, the wounds left in it by a decision, a difference; and then the structure of exclusion which Foucault wishes to describe in his book could not have been born with classical reason. It would have to have been consummated and reassured and smoothed over throughout all the centuries of philosophy. It would be essential to the entirety of the history of philosophy and of reason. In this regard, the classical age could have neither specificity nor privilege. And all the signs assembled by Foucault under the chapter heading *Stultifera navis* would play themselves out only on the surface of a chronic dissension. The free circulation of the mad, besides the fact that it is not as simply free as all that, would only be a socioeconomic epiphenomenon on the surface of a reason divided against itself since the dawn of its Greek origin. What seems to me sure in any case, regardless of the hypothesis one chooses concerning what is doubtless only a false problem and a false alternative, is that Foucault cannot *simultaneously* save the affirmation of a reassuring dialectic of Socrates and his postulation of a specificity of the classical age whose reason would reassure itself by excluding its contrary, that is, by *constituting* its contrary as an object in order to be protected from it and be rid of it. In order to lock it up.

The attempt to write the history of the decision, division, difference runs the risk of construing the division as an event or a structure subsequent to the unity of an original presence, thereby confirming metaphysics in its fundamental operation.

Truthfully, for one or the other of these hypotheses to be true and for there to be a real choice between them, it must be assumed in *general* that reason can have a contrary, that there can be an other of reason, that reason itself can construct or discover, and that the opposition of reason to its other is *symmetrical*. This is the heart of the matter. Permit me to hold off on this question.

However one interprets the situation of classical reason, notably as regards the Greek logos (and whether or not this latter experienced dissension) *in all cases* a doctrine of *tradition*, of the tradition of logos (is there any other?) seems to be the prerequisite implied by Foucault's enterprise. No matter what the relationship of the Greeks to *hybris*, a relationship that was certainly not simple . . . (Here, I wish to open a parenthesis and a question: in the name of what invariable meaning of 'madness' does Foucault associate, whatever the meaning of this association, Madness and *Hybris*? A problem of translation, a philosophical problem of translation is posed – and it is serious – even if *Hybris* is not *Madness* for Foucault. The determination of their difference supposes a hazardous linguistic transition. The frequent imprudence of translators in this respect should make us very wary. I am thinking in particular, and in passing, of what is translated by madness and fury in the *Philebus* (45e).[9] Further, if madness has an invariable meaning, what is the relation of this meaning to the a posteriori *events* which govern Foucault's analysis? For, despite everything, even if his method is not empiricist, Foucault proceeds by inquiry and inquest. What he is writing is a history, and the recourse to events, in the last resort, is indispensable and determining, at least in principle. Now, is not the concept of madness – never submitted to a thematic scrutiny by Foucault – today a false and disintegrated concept, outside current and popular language which always lags longer than it should behind its subversion by science and philosophy? Foucault, in rejecting the psychiatric or philosophical material that has always emprisoned the mad, winds up employing – inevitably – a popular and equivocal notion of madness, taken from an unverifiable source. This would not be serious if Foucault used the word only in quotation marks, as if it were the language of others, of those who, during the period under study, used it as a historical instrument. But everything transpires as if Foucault *knew* what 'madness' means. Everything transpires as if, in a continuous and underlying way, an assured and rigorous precomprehension of the concept of madness, or at least of its nominal definition, were possible and acquired. In fact, however, it could be demonstrated that as Foucault intends it, if not as intended by the historical current he is studying, the concept of madness overlaps everything that can be put under the rubric of *negativity*. One can imagine the kind of problems posed by such a usage of the notion of madness. The same kind of questions could be posed concerning the notion of truth that runs throughout the book . . . I close this long parenthesis.) Thus, whatever the relation of the Greeks to *hybris*, and of Socrates to the original logos, it is in any event certain that classical reason, and medieval reason before it, bore a relation to Greek reason, and that it is within the milieu of this more or less immediately perceived heritage, which itself is more or less crossed with other traditional lines, that the adventure or misadventure of classical reason developed. If dissension dates from Socrates, then the situation of the madman in the Socratic and post-Socratic worlds – assuming that there is, then, something that can be called mad – perhaps deserves to be examined first. Without this examination, and as Foucault does not proceed in a simply aprioristic fashion, his historical description poses the banal but inevitable problems of periodisation and of geographical, political, ethnological limitation, etc. If, on the contrary, the unopposed and unexcluding unity of logos were maintained until the classical 'crisis', then this latter is, if I may say so, secondary and derivative. It does not engage the entirety of reason. And in this case, even if stated in passing, Socratic discourse would be nothing less than reassuring. It can be proposed that the classical crisis developed from and within the elementary tradition of a logos that has no opposite but carries within itself and says all determined contradictions. This doctrine of the tradition of meaning and of reason would be even further necessitated by the fact that it alone can give meaning and rationality in *general* to Foucault's discourse and to any discourse on the war between reason and unreason. For these discourses intend above all to be understood.]

2. I stated above that leaving the history of the preclassical logos in the shadows is bothersome for two reasons. The second reason, which I will adduce briefly before going on to Descartes, has to do with the profound link established by Foucault between the division, the dissension and the possibility of history itself. '*The necessity of madness*, throughout the history of the West, is linked to the deciding gesture which detaches from the background noise, and from its continuous monotony, a meaningful language that is transmitted and consummated in time; briefly, it is linked to the *possibility of history*.'

Consequently, if the decision through which reason constitutes itself by excluding and objectifying the free subjectivity of madness is indeed the origin of history, if it is historicity itself, the condition of meaning and of language, the condition of the tradition of meaning, the condition of the work in general, if the structure of exclusion is the fundamental structure of historicity, then the 'classical' moment of this exclusion described by Foucault has neither absolute privilege nor archetypal exemplarity. It is an example as sample and not as model. In any event, in order to evoke the singularity of the classical moment, which is profound, perhaps it would be necessary to underline, not the aspects in which it is a structure of exclusion, but those aspects in which, and especially for what end, its own structure of exclusion is historically distinguished from the others, from all others. And to pose the problem of its exemplarity: are we concerned with an example among others or with a 'good example', an example that is revelatory by privilege? Formidable and infinitely difficult problems that haunt Foucault's book, more present in his intentions than his words.

Finally, *a last question*: if this great division is the possibility of history itself, the historicity of history, what does it mean, here, 'to write the history of this division'? To write the history of historicity? To write the history of the origin of history? The *hysteron proteron* would not here be a simple 'logical fallacy', a fallacy within logic, within an established rationality. And its denunciation is not an act of ratiocination. If there is a historicity proper to reason in general, the history of reason cannot be the history of its origin (which, for a start, demands the historicity of reason in general), but must be that of one of its determined figures.

This second project, which would devote all its efforts to discovering the common root of meaning and nonmeaning and to unearthing the original logos in which *a* language and *a* silence are divided from one another is not at all an expediency as concerns everything that could come under the heading 'archaeology of silence', the archaeology which simultaneously claims to say madness itself and renounces this claim. The expression 'to say madness itself' is self-contradictory. To say madness without expelling it into objectivity is to let it say itself. But madness is what by essence cannot be said: it is the 'absence of the work', as Foucault profoundly says.

Thus, not an expediency, but a different and more ambitious design, one that should lead to a praise of reason (there is no praise [*éloge*], by essence, except of reason),[10] but this time of a reason more profound than that which opposes and determines itself in a historically determined conflict. Hegel again, always . . . Not an expediency, but a more ambitious ambition, even if Foucault writes this: '*Lacking* this inaccessible primitive purity [of madness itself], a structural study must go back towards the decision that simultaneously links and separates reason and madness; it must aim to uncover the perpetual exchange, the obscure common root, the original confrontation that gives meaning to the unity, as well as to the opposition, of sense and non-sense' [my italics].

Before describing the moment when the reason of the classical age will reduce madness to silence by what he calls a 'strange act of force', Foucault shows how the exclusion and internment of madness found a sort of structural niche prepared for it by the history of another exclusion: the exclusion of leprosy. Unfortunately, we cannot be detained by the brilliant passages of the chapter entitled *Stultifera navis*. They would also pose numerous questions.

We thus come to the 'act of force', to the great internment which, with the creation of the houses of internment for the mad and others in the middle of the seventeenth century, marks the advent and first stage of a classical process described by Foucault throughout his book. Without establishing, moreover, whether an event such as the creation of a house of internment is a sign among others, whether it is a fundamental symptom or a cause. This kind of question could appear exterior to a method that presents itself precisely as structuralist, that is, a method for which everything within the structural totality is interdependent and circular in such a way that the classical problems of causality themselves would appear to stem from a misunderstanding. Perhaps. But I wonder whether, when one is concerned with history (and Foucault wants to write a history), a strict structuralism is possible, and, especially, whether, if only for the sake of order and within the order of its own descriptions, such a study can avoid all etiological questions, all questions bearing, shall we say, on the centre of gravity of the structure. The legitimate renunciation of a certain style of causality perhaps does not give one the right to renounce all etiological demands.

The passage devoted to Descartes opens the crucial chapter on 'the great internment'. It thus opens the book itself, and its location at the beginning of the chapter is fairly unexpected. More than anywhere else, the question I have just asked seems to me unavoidable here. We are not told whether or not this passage of the First Meditation, interpreted by Foucault as a *philosophical* internment of madness, is destined, as a prelude to the historical and sociopolitical drama, to set the tone for the *entire* drama to be played. Is this 'act of force', described in the dimension of theoretical knowledge and metaphysics, a symptom, a cause, a language? What must be assumed or elucidated so that the meaning of this question or dissociation can be neutralised? And if this act of force has a structural affinity with the totality of the drama, what is the status of this affinity? Finally, whatever the place reserved for philosophy in this total historical structure may be, why the sole choice of the Cartesian example? What is the exemplarity of Descartes, while so many other philosophers of the same era were interested or – no less significantly – not interested in madness in various ways?

Foucault does not respond directly to any of these more than methodological questions, summarily, but inevitably, invoked. A single sentence, in his preface, settles the question. To cite Foucault: 'To write the history of madness thus will mean the execution of a structural study of an historical ensemble – notions, institutions, juridical and police measures, scientific concepts – which holds captive a madness whose wild state can never in itself be restored.' How are these elements organised in the 'historical ensemble'? What is a 'notion'? Do philosophical notions have a privilege? How are they related to scientific concepts? A quantity of questions that besiege this enterprise.

I do not know to what extent Foucault would agree that the prerequisite for a response to such questions is first of all the internal and autonomous analysis of the philosophical content of philosophical discourse. Only when the totality of this content will have become manifest in its meaning for me (but this is impossible) will I rigorously be able to situate it in its total historical form. It is only then that its reinsertion will not do it violence, that there will be a legitimate reinsertion of *this* philosophical meaning *itself*. As to Descartes in particular, no historical question about him – about the latent historical meaning of his discourse, about its place in a total structure – can be answered before a rigorous and exhaustive internal analysis of his manifest intentions, of the manifest meaning of his philosophical discourse, has been made.

We will now turn to this manifest meaning, this properly philosophical intention that is not legible in the immediacy of a first encounter. But first by reading over Foucault's shoulder.

There had to be folly so that wisdom might overcome it. (Herder)

Descartes, then, is alleged to have executed the act of force in the first of the *Meditations*, and it would very summarily consist in a summary expulsion of the possibility of madness from thought itself.

I shall first cite the decisive passage from Descartes, the one cited by Foucault. Then we shall follow Foucault's reading of the text. Finally, we shall establish a dialogue between Descartes and Foucault.

Descartes writes the following (at the moment when he undertakes to rid himself of all the opinions in which he had hitherto believed, and to start all over again from the foundations: *a primis fundamentis*. To do so, it will suffice to ruin the ancient foundations without being obliged to submit all his opinions to doubt one by one, for the ruin of the foundations brings down the entire edifice. One of these fragile foundations of knowledge, the most naturally apparent, is sensation. The senses deceive me sometimes; they can thus deceive me all the time, and I will therefore submit to doubt all knowledge whose origin is in sensation): 'All that up to the present time I have accepted as most true and certain I have learned either from the senses or through the senses; but it is sometimes proved to me that these senses are deceptive, and it is wiser not to trust entirely to any thing by which we have once been deceived.'

Descartes starts a new paragraph.

'But . . .' (*sed forte* . . . I insist upon the *forte* which the Duc de Luynes left untranslated, an omission that Descartes did not deem necessary to correct when he went over the translation. It is better, as Baillet says, to compare 'the French with the Latin' when reading the *Meditations*. It is only in the second French edition by Clerselier that the *sed forte* is given its full weight and is translated by 'but yet perhaps . . .'. The importance of this point will soon be demonstrated.) Pursuing my citation: 'But it may be that although the senses sometimes deceive us concerning things which are *hardly perceptible*, or *very far away*, there are yet many others to be met with as to which we cannot reasonably have any doubt . . .' [my italics]. There would be, *there would perhaps be* data of sensory origin which cannot reasonably be doubted.

> And how could I deny that these hands and this body are mine, were it not perhaps that I compare myself to certain persons, devoid of sense, whose cerebella are so troubled and clouded by the violent vapours of black bile, that they constantly assure us that they think they are kings when they are really quite poor, or that they are clothed in purple when they are really without covering, or who imagine that they have an earthenware head or are nothing but pumpkins or are made of glass . . .

And now the most significant sentence in Foucault's eyes: 'But they are mad, *sed amentes sunt isti*, and I should not be any the less insane (*demens*) were I to follow examples so extravagant.'[11]

I interrupt my citation not at the end of this paragraph, but on the first words of the following paragraph, which reinscribe the lines I have just read in a rhetorical and pedagogical movement with highly compressed articulations. These first words are *Praeclare sane* . . . Also translated as *toutefois* [but at the same time – trans.]. And this is the beginning of a paragraph in which Descartes imagines that he can always dream, and that the world might be no more real than his dreams. And he generalises by hyperbole the hypothesis of sleep and dream ('Now let us assume that we are asleep . . .'); this hypothesis and this hyperbole will serve in the elaboration of doubt founded on natural reasons (for there is also a hyperbolical moment of this doubt), beyond whose reach will be only the truths of nonsensory origin, mathematical truths notably, which are true 'whether I am awake or asleep' and which will capitulate only to the artificial and metaphysical assault of the evil genius.

How does Foucault read this text?

According to Foucault, Descartes, encountering madness alongside (the expression *alongside* is Foucault's) dreams and all forms of sensory error, refuses to accord them all the same treatment, so to speak. 'In the economy of doubt', says Foucault, 'there is a fundamental imbalance between madness, on the one hand, and error, on the other . . .' (I note in passing that elsewhere Foucault often denounces the classical reduction of madness to error.) He pursues: 'Descartes does not avoid the peril of madness in the same way he circumvents the eventuality of dream and error.'

Foucault establishes a parallelism between the following two procedures:

1. The one by which Descartes wishes to demonstrate that the senses can deceive us only regarding 'things which are hardly perceptible, or very far away. These would be the limits of the error of sensory origin. And in the passage I just read, Descartes did say: 'But it may be that although the senses sometimes deceive us concerning things which are hardly perceptible, or very far away, there are yet many others to be met with as to which we cannot reasonably have any doubt . . .'. Unless one is mad, a hypothesis seemingly excluded in principle by Descartes in the same passage.

2. The procedure by which Descartes shows that imagination and dreams cannot themselves create the simple and universal elements which enter into their creations, as, for example, 'corporeal nature in general, and its extension, the figure of extended things, their quantity or magnitude and number',[12] that is, everything which precisely is not of sensory origin, thereby constituting the objects of mathematics and geometry, which themselves are invulnerable to natural doubt. It is thus tempting to believe, along with Foucault, that Descartes wishes to find in the analysis (taking this word in its strict sense) of dreams and sensation a nucleus, an element of proximity and simplicity irreducible to doubt. It is *in* dreams and *in* sensory perception that I surmount or, as Foucault says, that I 'circumvent' doubt and reconquer a basis of certainty.

Foucault writes thus:

> Descartes does not avoid the *peril* of madness in the same way he circumvents the *eventuality* of dreams or of error. . . . Neither image-peopled sleep, nor the clear consciousness that the senses can be deceived is able to take doubt to the extreme point of its universality; let us admit that our eyes deceive us, 'let us assume that we are asleep' – truth will not entirely slip out into the night. For madness, it is otherwise.

Later: 'In the economy of doubt, there is an imbalance between madness, on the one hand, and dream and error, on the other. Their situation in relation to the truth and to him who seeks it is different; dreams or illusions are surmounted within the structure of truth; but madness is inadmissible for the doubting subject.'

It indeed appears, then, that Descartes does not delve into the experience of madness as he delves into the experience of dreams, that is, to the point of reaching an irreducible nucleus which nonetheless would be interior to madness itself. Descartes is not interested in madness, he does not welcome it as a hypothesis, he does not consider it. He excludes it by decree. I would be insane if I thought that I had a body made of glass. But this is excluded, since I am thinking. Anticipating the moment of the Cogito, which will have to await the completion of numerous stages, highly rigorous in their succession, Foucault writes: 'impossibility of being mad that is essential not to the object of thought, but to the thinking subject.' Madness is expelled, rejected, denounced in its very impossibility from the very interiority of thought itself.

Foucault is the first, to my knowledge, to have isolated delirium and madness from sensation and dreams in this First Meditation. The first to have isolated them in their philosophical sense and their methodological function. Such is the originality of his reading. But if the classical interpreters did not deem this dissociation auspicious, is it because of their inattentiveness? Before answering this question, or rather before continuing to ask it, let us recall along with Foucault that this decree of inadmissibility which is a forerunner of the political decree of the great internment, or corresponds to it, translates it, or accompanies it, or in any case is in solidarity with it – this decree would have been impossible for a Montaigne, who was, as we know, haunted by the possibility of being mad, or of becoming completely mad in the very action of thought itself. The Cartesian decree therefore marks, says Foucault, 'the advent of a *ratio*'. But as the advent of a *ratio* is not 'exhausted' by 'the progress of rationalism', Foucault leaves Descartes there, to go on to the historical (politico-social) structure of which the Cartesian act is only a sign. For 'more than one sign', Foucault says, 'betrays the classical event'.

We have attempted to read Foucault. Let us now naïvely attempt to reread Descartes and, before repeating the question of the relationship between the 'sign' and the 'structure', let us attempt to see, as I had earlier mentioned, what the *sense of the sign itself* may be. (Since the sign here already has the autonomy of a philosophical discourse, is already a relationship of signifier to signified.)

In rereading Descartes, I notice two things:

1. That in the passage to which we have referred and which corresponds to the phase of *doubt* founded on *natural* reasons, Descartes *does not* circumvent the eventuality of sensory error or of dreams, and does not 'surmount' them 'within the structure of truth'; and all this for the simple reason that he apparently does not ever, nor in any way, surmount them or circumvent them, and does not ever set aside the possibility of total error for *all* knowledge gained from the senses or from imaginary constructions. It must be understood that the hypothesis of dreams is the radicalisation or, if you will, the hyperbolical exaggeration of the hypothesis according to which the senses could *sometimes* deceive me. In dreams, the *totality* of sensory images is illusory. It follows that a certainty invulnerable to dreams would be *a fortiori* invulnerable to *perceptual* illusions of the sensory kind. It therefore suffices to examine the case of dreams in order to deal with, on the level which is ours for the moment, the case of natural doubt, of sensory error in general. Now, which are the certainties and truths that escape perception, and therefore also escape sensory error or imaginative and oneiric composition? They are certainties and truths of a nonsensory and nonimaginative origin. They are *simple* and *intelligible* things.

In effect, if I am asleep, everything I perceive while dreaming may be, as Descartes says, 'false and illusory', particularly the existence of my hands and my body and the actions of opening my eyes, moving my head, etc. In other words, what was previously excluded, according to Foucault, as insanity, is admissible within dreams. And we will see why in a moment. But, says Descartes, let us suppose that all my oneirical representations are illusory. Even in this case, there must be some representations of things as naturally certain as the body, hands, etc., however illusory this representation may be, and however false its relation to that which it represents. Now, within these representations, these images, these ideas in the Cartesian sense, everything may be fictitious and false, as in the representations of those painters whose imaginations, as Descartes expressly says, are 'extravagant' enough to invent something so new that its like has never been seen before. But in the case of painting, at least, there is a final element which cannot be analysed as illusion, an element that painters cannot counterfeit: colour. This is only an *analogy*, for Descartes does not posit the necessary existence of colour in general: colour is an object of the senses among others. But, *just* as there always remains in a painting, however inventive and imaginative it may be, an irreducibly simple and real element – colour – *similarly*, there is in dreams an element of noncounterfeit simplicity presupposed by all fantastical compositions and irreducible to all analysis. But this time – and this is why the example of the painter and of colour was only an analogy – this element is neither sensory nor imaginative: it is intelligible.

Foucault does not concern himself with this point. Let me cite the passage from Descartes that concerns us here:

> For, as a matter of fact, painters, even when they study with the greatest skill to represent sirens and satyrs by forms the most strange and extraordinary, cannot give them natures which are entirely new, but merely make a certain medley of the members of different animals; or if their imagination is extravagant enough to invent something so novel that nothing similar has ever before been seen, and that then their work represents a thing purely fictitious and absolutely false, it is certain all the same that the colours of which this is composed are necessarily real. And for the same reason, although these general things, to wit, a body, eyes, a head, hands, and such like, may be imaginary, we are bound at the same time to confess that there are at least some other objects yet more simple and more universal, which are real and true; and of these just in the same way as with certain real colours, all these images of things which dwell in our thoughts, whether true and real or false and fantastic, are formed.
>
> To such a class of things pertains corporeal nature in general, and its extension, the figure of extended things, their quantity or magnitude and number, as also the place in which they are, the time which measures their duration, and so on.
>
> That is possibly why our reasoning is not unjust when we conclude from this that Physics, Astronomy, Medicine and all other sciences which have as their end the consideration of composite things, are very dubious and uncertain; but that Arithmetic, Geometry and other sciences of that kind which only treat of things that are very simple and very general, without taking great

> trouble to ascertain whether they are actually existent or not, contain some measure of certainty and an element of the indubitable. For whether I am awake or asleep, two and three together always form five, and the square can never have more than four sides, and it does not seem possible that truths so clear and apparent can be suspected of any falsity.[13]

And I remark that the following paragraph also starts with a 'nevertheless' (*verumtamen*) which will soon be brought to our attention.

Thus the certainty of this simplicity of *intelligible* generalisation – which is soon after submitted to metaphysical, artificial and hyperbolical doubt through the fiction of the evil genius – is in no way obtained by a continuous reduction which finally lays bare the resistance of a nucleus of sensory or imaginative certainty. There is discontinuity and a transition to another order of reasoning. The nucleus is purely intelligible, and the still natural and provisional certainty which has been attained supposes a radical break with the senses. At this moment of the analysis, no imaginative or sensory signification, as such, has been saved, *no* invulnerability of the senses to doubt has been experienced. *All* significations or 'ideas' of sensory origin are *excluded* from the realm of truth, *for the same reason as madness* is excluded from it. And there is nothing astonishing about this: madness is only a particular case, and, moreover, not the most serious one, of the sensory illusion which interests Descartes at this point. It can thus be stated that:

2. The hypothesis of insanity – at this moment of the Cartesian order – seems neither to receive any privileged treatment nor to be submitted to any particular exclusion. Let us reread, in effect, the passage cited by Foucault in which insanity appears. Let us resituate it. Descartes has just remarked that since the senses sometimes deceive us, 'it is wiser not to trust entirely to any thing by which we have once been deceived'.[14] He then starts a new paragraph with the *sed forte* which I brought to your attention a few moments ago. Now, the entire paragraph which follows does not express Descartes' final, definitive conclusions, but rather the astonishment and objections of the nonphilosopher, of the novice in philosophy who is frightened by this doubt and protests, saying: I am willing to let you doubt certain sensory perceptions concerning 'things which are hardly perceptible, or very far away', but the others! that you are in this place, sitting by the fire, speaking thus, this paper in your hands and other seeming certainties! Descartes then assumes the astonishment of this reader or naïve interlocutor, pretends to take him into account when he writes: 'And how could I deny that these hands and this body are mine, were it not perhaps that I compare myself to certain persons, devoid of sense, whose . . . and I should not be any the less insane were I to follow examples so extravagant.'

The pedagogical and rhetorical sense of the *sed forte* which governs this paragraph is clear. It is the 'but perhaps' of the feigned objection. Descartes has just said that all knowledge of sensory origin could deceive him. He pretends to put to himself the astonished objection of an imaginary nonphilosopher who is frightened by such audacity and says: no, not all sensory knowledge, for then you would be mad and it would be unreasonable to follow the example of madmen, to put forth the ideas of madmen. Descartes *echoes* this objection: since I am here, writing, and you understand me, I am not mad, nor are you, and we are all sane. The example of madness is therefore not indicative of the fragility of the sensory idea. So be it. Descartes acquiesces to this natural point of view, or rather he feigns to rest in this natural comfort in order better, more radically and more definitively, to unsettle himself from it and to discomfort his interlocutor. So be it, he says, you think that I would be mad to doubt that I am sitting near the fire, etc., that I would be insane to follow the example of madmen. I will therefore propose a hypothesis which will seem much more natural to you, will not disorient you, because it concerns a more common, and more universal experience than that of madness: the experience of sleep and dreams. Descartes then elaborates the hypothesis that will ruin *all* the *sensory* foundations of knowledge and will lay bare only the *intellectual* foundations of certainty. This hypothesis above all will not run from the possibility of an insanity – an epistemological one – much more serious than madness.

The reference to dreams is therefore not put off to one side – quite the contrary – in relation to a madness potentially respected or even excluded by Descartes. It constitutes, in the methodical order which here is ours, the hyperbolical exasperation of the hypothesis of madness. This latter affected only certain areas of sensory perception, and in a contingent and partial way. Moreover, Descartes is concerned here not with determining the concept of madness but with utilising the popular notion of insanity for juridical and methodological ends, in order to ask questions of principle regarding only the *truth* of ideas.[15] What must be grasped here is that *from this point of view* the sleeper, or the dreamer, is madder than the madman. Or, at least, the dreamer, in so far as concerns the problem of knowledge which interests Descartes here, is further from true perception than the madman. It is in the case of sleep, and not in that of insanity, that the *absolute totality* of ideas of sensory origin becomes suspect, is stripped of 'objective value' as M. Guéroult puts it. The hypothesis of insanity is therefore not a good example, a revelatory example, a good instrument of doubt – and for at least two reasons. (a) It does not cover the *totality* of the field of sensory perception. The madman is not always wrong about everything; he is not wrong often enough, is never mad enough. (b) It is not a useful or happy example pedagogically, because it meets the resistance of the nonphilosopher who does not have the audacity to follow the philosopher when the latter agrees that he might indeed be mad at the very moment when he speaks.

Let us turn to Foucault once more. Confronted with the situation of the Cartesian text whose principles I have just indicated, Foucault could – and this time I am only extending the logic of his book without basing what I say on any particular text – Foucault could recall *two truths* that on a second reading would justify his interpretations, which would then only apparently differ from the interpretation I have just proposed.

1. It appears, on this second reading, that, for Descartes, madness is thought of only as a single case – and not the most serious one – among all cases of sensory error. (Foucault would then assume the perspective of the factual determination of the concept of madness by Descartes, and not his juridical usage of it.) Madness is only a sensory and corporeal fault, a bit more serious than the fault which threatens all waking but normal men, and much less serious, within the epistemological order,

than the fault to which we succumb in dreams. Foucault would then doubtless ask whether this reduction of madness to an example, to a case of sensory error, does not constitute an exclusion, an internment of madness, and whether it is not above all a sheltering of the Cogito and everything relative to the intellect and reason from madness. If madness is only a perversion of the senses – or of the imagination – it is corporeal, in alliance with the body. The real distinction of substances expels madness to the outer shadows of the Cogito. Madness, to use an expression proposed elsewhere by Foucault, is confined to the interior of the exterior and to the exterior of the interior. It is the other of the Cogito. I cannot be mad when I think and when I have clear and distinct ideas.

2. Or, while assuming our hypothesis, Foucault could also recall the following: Descartes, by inscribing his reference to madness within the problematic of knowledge, by making madness not only a thing of the body but an *error* of the body, by concerning himself with madness only as the modification of ideas, or the faculties of representation or judgment, intends to neutralise the originality of madness. He would even, in the long run, be condemned to construe it, like all errors, not only as an epistemological deficiency but also as a moral failure linked to a precipitation of the will; for will alone can consecrate the intellectual finitude of perception as error. It is only one step from here to making madness a sin, a step that was soon after cheerfully taken, as Foucault convincingly demonstrates in other chapters.

Foucault would be perfectly correct in recalling these two truths to us if we were to remain at the naïve, natural and premetaphysical stage of Descartes' itinerary, the stage marked by natural doubt as it intervenes in the passage that Foucault cites. However, it seems that these two truths become vulnerable in turn, as soon as we come to the properly philosophical, metaphysical and critical phase of doubt.[16]

Let us first notice how, in the rhetoric of the First Meditation, the first *toutefois* [at the same time] which announced the 'natural' hyperbole of dreams (just after Descartes says, 'But they are mad, and I should not be any the less insane', etc.) is succeeded by a second *toutefois* [nevertheless] at the beginning of the next paragraph.[17] To 'at the same time', marking the *hyperbolical moment within natural doubt*, will correspond a 'nevertheless', marking the *absolutely hyperbolical moment* which gets us out of natural doubt and leads to the hypothesis of the evil genius. Descartes has just admitted that arithmetic, geometry and simple notions escape the first doubt, and he writes, 'Nevertheless I have long had fixed in my mind the belief that an all-powerful God existed by whom I have been created such as I am.'[18] This is the onset of the well-known movement leading to the fiction of the evil genius.

Now, the recourse to the fiction of the evil genius will evoke, conjure up, the possibility of a *total madness*, a total derangement over which I could have no control because it is inflicted upon me – hypothetically – leaving me no responsibility for it. Total derangement is the possibility of a madness that is no longer a disorder of the body, of the object, the body-object outside the boundaries of the *res cogitans*, outside the boundaries of the policed city, secure in its existence as thinking subjectivity, but is a madness that will bring subversion to pure thought and to its purely intelligible objects, to the field of its clear and distinct ideas, to the realm of the mathematical truths which escape natural doubt.

This time madness, insanity, will spare nothing, neither bodily nor purely intellectual perceptions. And Descartes successively judges admissible:

(a) That which he pretended not to admit while conversing with the nonphilosopher. To cite Descartes (he has just evoked 'some evil genius not less powerful than deceitful'): 'I shall consider that the heavens, the earth, colours, figures, sound, and all other external things are nought but the illusions and dreams of which this genius has availed himself in order to lay traps for my credulity; I shall consider myself as having no hands, no eyes, no flesh, no blood, nor any senses, yet falsely believing myself to possess all these things.'[19] These ideas will be taken up again in the Second Meditation. We are thus quite far from the dismissal of insanity made above.

(b) That which escapes natural doubt: 'But how do I know that Hell (i.e., the deceiving God, before the recourse to the evil genius) has not brought it to pass that . . . I am not deceived every time that I add two and three, or count the sides of a square . . .?'[20]

Thus, ideas of neither sensory nor intellectual origin will be sheltered from this new phase of doubt, and everything that was previously set aside as insanity is now welcomed into the most essential interiority of thought.

In question is a philosophical and juridical operation (but the first phase of doubt was already such) which no longer names madness and reveals all principled possibilities. *In principle* nothing is opposed to the subversion named insanity, although *in fact* and from a natural point of view, for Descartes, for his reader, and for us, no natural anxiety is possible regarding this actual subversion. (Truthfully speaking, to go to the heart of the matter, one would have to confront directly, in and of itself, the question of what is *de facto* and what *de jure* in the relations of the Cogito and madness.) Beneath this natural comfort, beneath this apparently prephilosophical confidence is hidden the recognition of an essential and principled truth: to wit, if discourse and philosophical communication (that is, language itself) are to have an intelligible meaning, that is to say, if they are to conform to their essence and vocation as discourse, they must simultaneously in fact and in principle escape madness. They must carry normality within themselves. And this is not a specifically Cartesian weakness (although Descartes never confronts the question of his own language),[21] is not a defect or mystification linked to a determined historical structure, but rather is an essential and universal necessity from which no discourse can escape, for it belongs to the meaning of meaning. It is an essential necessity from which no discourse can escape, even the discourse which denounces a mystification or an act of force. And, paradoxically, what I am saying here is strictly Foucauldian. For we can now appreciate the profundity of the following affirmation of Foucault's that curiously also saves Descartes from the accusations made against him: 'Madness is the absence of a work.' This is a fundamental motif of Foucault's book. Now, the work starts with the most elementary discourse, with the first articulation of a meaning, with the first syntactical usage of an 'as such',[22] for to make a sentence is to manifest a possible meaning. By its essence, the sentence is normal. It carries normality within it, that is, *sense*, in every sense of the word – Descartes' in particular. It carries normality and sense within it, and does so whatever the state, whatever the health or madness of him who propounds it, or whom it passes through, on whom, in whom it is articulated. In its most impoverished syntax, logos is reason and, indeed, a historical reason. And if madness in general, beyond any factitious and determined historical structure, is the absence of a work, then madness is indeed, essentially and generally, silence, stifled speech, within a caesura and a wound that *open up* life as *historicity in general*. Not a determined silence, imposed at one given moment rather than at any other, but a silence essentially linked to an act of force and a prohibition which open history and speech. *In general*. Within the dimension of historicity in general, which is to be confused neither with some ahistorical eternity, nor with an empirically determined moment of the history of facts, silence plays the irreducible role of that which bears and haunts language, outside and *against* which alone language can emerge – 'against' here simultaneously designating the content from which form takes off by force, and the adversary against whom I assure and reassure myself by force. Although the silence of madness is the absence of a work, this silence is not simply the work's epigraph, nor is it, as concerns language and meaning, outside the work. Like nonmeaning, silence is the work's limit and profound resource. Of course, in essentialising madness this way one runs the risk of disintegrating the factual findings of psychiatric efforts. This is a permanent danger, but it should not discourage the demanding and patient psychiatrist.

So that, to come back to Descartes, any philosopher or speaking subject (and the philosopher is but the speaking subject par excellence) who must evoke madness from the *interior* of thought (and not only from within the body or some other extrinsic agency), can do so only in the realm of the *possible* and in the language of fiction or the fiction of language. Thereby, through his own language, he reassures himself against any actual madness – which may sometimes appear quite talkative, another problem – and can keep his distance, the distance indispensable for continuing to speak and to live. But this is not a weakness or a search for security proper to a given historical language (for example, the search for certainty in the Cartesian style), but is rather inherent in the essence and very project of all language in general; and even in the language of those who are apparently the maddest; and even and above all in the language of those who, by their praise of madness, by their complicity with it, measure their own strength against the greatest possible proximity to madness. Language being the break with madness, it adheres more thoroughly to its essence and vocation, makes a cleaner break with madness, if it pits itself against madness more freely and gets closer and closer to it: to the point of being separated from it only by the 'transparent sheet' of which Joyce speaks, that is, by itself – for this diaphaneity is nothing other than the language, meaning, possibility and elementary discretion of a nothing that neutralises everything. In this sense, I would be tempted to consider Foucault's book a powerful gesture of protection and internment. A Cartesian gesture for the twentieth century. A reappropriation of negativity. To all appearances, it is reason that he interns, but, like Descartes, he chooses the reason of yesterday as his target and not the possibility of meaning in general.

2. As for the second truth Foucault could have countered with, it too seems valid only during the natural phase of doubt. Descartes not only ceases to reject madness

during the phase of radical doubt, he not only installs its possible menace at the very heart of the intelligible, he also in principle refuses to let any determined knowledge escape from madness. A menace to all knowledge, insanity – the hypothesis of insanity – is not an internal modification of knowledge. At no point will knowledge alone be able to dominate madness, to master it in order to objectify it – at least for as long as doubt remains unresolved.

For the end of doubt poses a problem to which we shall return in a moment.

The act of the Cogito and the certainty of existing indeed escape madness the first time; but aside from the fact that for the first time, it is no longer a question of objective, representative knowledge, it can no longer literally be said that the Cogito would escape madness because it keeps itself beyond the grasp of madness, or because, as Foucault says, '*I* who think, I cannot be mad'; the Cogito escapes madness only because at its own moment, under its own authority, it is valid *even if I am mad*, even if my thoughts are completely mad. There is a value and a meaning of the Cogito, as of existence, which escape the alternative of a determined madness or a determined reason. Confronted with the critical experience of the Cogito, insanity, as stated in the *Discourse on Method*, is irremediably on a plane with scepticism. Thought no longer fears madness: '. . . remarking that this truth "*I think, therefore I am*" was so certain and so assured that all the most extravagant suppositions brought forward by the sceptics were incapable of shaking it'.[23] The certainty thus attained need not be sheltered from an emprisoned madness, for it is attained and ascertained within madness itself. It is valid *even if I am mad* – a supreme self-confidence that seems to require neither the exclusion nor the circumventing of madness. Descartes never interns madness, neither at the stage of natural doubt nor at the stage of metaphysical doubt. *He only claims to exclude it during the first phase of the first stage, during the nonhyperbolical moment of natural doubt.*

The hyperbolical audacity of the Cartesian Cogito, its mad audacity, which we perhaps no longer perceive as such because, unlike Descartes' contemporary, we are too well assured of ourselves and too well accustomed to the framework of the Cogito, rather than to the critical experience of it – its mad audacity would consist in the return to an original point which no longer belongs to either a *determined* reason or a *determined* unreason, no longer belongs to them as opposition or alternative. Whether I am mad or not, *Cogito, sum*. Madness is therefore, in every sense of the word, only one *case* of thought (*within* thought). It is therefore a question of drawing back towards a point at which all determined contradictions, in the form of given, factual historical structures, can appear, and appear as relative to this zero point at which determined meaning and nonmeaning come together in their common origin. From the point of view which here is ours, one could perhaps say the following about this zero point, determined by Descartes as Cogito.

Invulnerable to all determined opposition between reason and unreason, it is the point starting from which the history of the determined forms of this opposition, this opened or broken-off dialogue, can appear as such and be stated. It is the impenetrable point of certainty in which the possibility of Foucault's narration, as well as of the narration of the totality, or rather of *all* the determined forms of the exchanges between reason and madness are embedded. It is the point[24] at which the project of thinking this totality by escaping it is embedded. By escaping it: that is to say, by exceeding the totality, which – within existence – is possible only in the direction of infinity or nothingness; for even if the totality of what I think is imbued with falsehood or madness, even if the totality of the world does not exist, even if nonmeaning has invaded the totality of the world, up to and including the very contents of my thought, I still think, I am *while* I think. Even if I do not *in fact* grasp the totality, if I neither understand nor embrace it, I still formulate the project of doing so, and this project is meaningful in such a way that it can be defined only in relation to a precomprehension of the infinite and undetermined totality. This is why, by virtue of this margin of the possible, the principled and the meaningful, which exceeds all that is real, factual and existent, this project is mad, and acknowledges madness as its liberty and its very possibility. This is why it is not human, in the sense of anthropological factuality, but is rather metaphysical and demonic: it first awakens to itself in its war with the demon, the evil genius of nonmeaning, by pitting itself against the strength of the evil genius, and by resisting him through reduction of the natural man within itself. In this sense, nothing is less reassuring than the Cogito at its proper and inaugural moment. The project of exceeding the totality of the world, as the totality of what I can think in general, is no more reassuring than the dialectic of Socrates when it, too, overflows the totality of beings, planting us in the light of a hidden sun which is *epekeina tes ousias*. And Glaucon was not mistaken when he cried out: 'Lord! what demonic hyperbole? *daimonias hyperboles*', which is perhaps banally translated as 'marvelous transcendence'.[25] This demonic hyperbole goes further than the passion of *hybris*, at least if this latter is seen only as the pathological modification of the being called man. Such a *hybris* keeps itself within the world. Assuming that it is deranged and excessive, it implies the fundamental derangement and excessiveness of the hyperbole which opens and founds the world as such by exceeding it. *Hybris* is excessive and exceeds only *within* the space opened by the demonic hyperbole.

The extent to which doubt and the Cartesian Cogito are *punctuated* by this project of a singular and unprecedented excess – an excess in the direction of the nondetermined, Nothingness or Infinity, an excess which overflows the totality of that which can be thought, the totality of beings and determined meanings, the totality of factual history – is also the extent to which any effort to reduce this project, to enclose it within a determined historical structure, however comprehensive, risks missing the essential, risks dulling the *point* itself. Such an effort risks doing violence to this project in turn (for there is also a violence applicable to rationalists and to sense, to good sense; and this, perhaps, is what Foucault's book definitely demonstrates, for the victims of whom he speaks are always the bearers of sense, the *true* bearers of the *true* and *good* sense hidden and oppressed by the *determined* 'good sense' of the 'division' – the 'good sense' that never divides itself enough and is always determined too quickly) – risks doing it violence in turn, and a violence of a totalitarian and historicist style which eludes meaning and the origin of meaning.[26] I use 'totalitarian' in the structuralist sense of the word, but I am not sure that the two meanings do not beckon each other historically. Structuralist totalitarianism here would be responsible for an internment of the Cogito similar to the violences of the classical age. I am not saying that Foucault's book is totalitarian, for at least at its outset it poses the question of the origin of historicity in *general*, thereby freeing itself of historicism; I am saying, however, that by virtue of the construction of his project he sometimes runs the risk of being totalitarian. Let me clarify: when I refer to the forced entry into the world of that which is not there and is supposed by the world, or when I state that the *compelle intrare* (epigraph of the chapter on 'the great internment') becomes *violence itself* when it turns towards the hyperbole in order to make hyperbole re-enter the world, or when I say that this reduction to intraworldliness is the origin and very meaning of what is called violence, making possible all straitjackets, I am not invoking an *other world*, an alibi or an evasive transcendence. That would be yet another possibility of violence, a possibility that is, moreover, often the accomplice of the first one.

I think, therefore, that (in Descartes) everything can be reduced to a determined historical totality except the hyperbolical project. Now, this project belongs to the narration narrating itself and not to the narration narrated by Foucault. It cannot be recounted, cannot be objectified as an event in a determined history.

I am sure that within the movement which is called the *Cartesian Cogito* this hyperbolical extremity is not the only element that should be, like pure madness in general, silent. As soon as Descartes has reached this extremity, he seeks to reassure himself, to certify the Cogito through God, to identify the act of the Cogito with a reasonable reason. And he does so as soon as he *proffers* and *reflects* the Cogito. That is to say, he must temporalise the Cogito, which itself is valid only during the instant of intuition, the instant of thought being attentive to itself, at the point, the sharpest point, of the instant. And here one should be attentive to this link between the Cogito and the movement of temporalisation. For if the Cogito is valid even for the maddest madman, one must, in fact, not be mad if one is to reflect it and retain it, if one is to communicate it and its meaning. And here, with the reference to God *and* to a certain memory,[27] would begin the hurried repatriation of all mad and hyperbolical wanderings which now take shelter and are given reassurance within the order of reasons, in order once more to take possession of the truths they had left behind. Within Descartes' text, at least, the internment takes place at this point. It is here that hyperbolical and mad wanderings once more become itinerary and method, 'assured' and 'resolute' progression through our existing world, which is given to us by God as terra firma. For, finally, it is God alone who, by permitting me to extirpate myself from a Cogito that at its proper moment can always remain a silent madness, also insures my representations and my cognitive determinations, that is, my discourse against madness. It is without doubt that, for Descartes, God alone[28] protects me against the madness to which the Cogito, left to its own authority, could only open itself up in the most hospitable way. And Foucault's reading seems to me powerful and illuminating not at the stage of the text which he cites, which is anterior and secondary to the Cogito, but from the moment which immediately succeeds the instantaneous experience of the Cogito at its most intense, when reason and madness have not yet been separated, when to take the part of the Cogito is neither to take the part of reason as reasonable order, nor the part of disorder and madness, but is rather to grasp, once more, the source which permits reason *and* madness to be determined and stated. Foucault's interpretation seems to me illuminating from the moment when the Cogito must reflect and proffer itself in an organised philosophical discourse. That is, *almost always*. For if the Cogito is valid even for the madman, to be mad – if, once more, his expression has a singular philosophical meaning, which I do not believe: it simply says the other of each determined form of the logos – is not to be able to reflect and to say the Cogito, that is, not to be able to make the Cogito appear as such for an other; an other who may be myself. From the moment when Descartes pronounces the Cogito, he inscribes it in a system of deductions and protections that betray its wellspring and constrain the wandering that is proper to it so that error may be circumvented. At bottom, leaving in silence the problem of speech posed by the Cogito, Descartes seems to imply that thinking *and* saying what is clear and distinct are the same thing. One can say *what* one thinks and *that* one thinks without betraying one or the other. Analogously – analogously only – Saint Anselm saw in the *insipiens*, the insane man, someone who could not think because he could not think what he said. Madness was for him, too, a silence, the voluble silence of a thought that did not think its own words. This also is a point which must be developed further. In any event, the Cogito is a work as soon as it is assured of what it says. But before it is a work, it is madness. If the madman could rebuff the evil genius, he could not tell himself so. He therefore cannot say so. And in any event, Foucault is right in the extent to which the project of constraining any wandering already animated a doubt which was always proposed as methodical. This identification of the Cogito with reasonable – normal – reason need not even await – in fact, if not in principle – the proofs of the existence of a veracious God as the supreme protective barrier against madness. This identification intervenes from the moment when Descartes *determines natural light* (which in its undetermined source should be valid even for the mad), from the moment when he pulls himself out of madness by determining natural light through a series of principles and axioms (axiom of causality according to which there must be at least as much reality in the cause as in the effect; then, after this axiom permits the proof of the existence of God, the axioms that 'the light of nature teaches us that fraud and deception necessarily proceed from some defect').[29] These dogmatically determined axioms escape doubt, are never even submitted to its scrutiny, are established only reciprocally, on the basis of the existence and truthfulness of God. Due to this fact, they fall within the province of the history of knowledge and the determined structures of philosophy. This is why the act of the Cogito, at the hyperbolical moment when it pits itself against madness, or rather lets itself be pitted against madness, must be repeated and distinguished from the language or the deductive system in which Descartes must inscribe it as soon as he proposes it for apprehension and communication, that is, as soon as he reflects the Cogito for the other, which means for oneself. It is through this relationship to the other as an other self that meaning reassures itself against madness and nonmeaning. And philosophy is perhaps the reassurance given against the anguish of being mad at the point of greatest proximity to madness. This silent and specific moment could be called *pathetic*. As for the functioning of the hyperbole in the structure of Descartes' discourse and in the order of reasons, our reading is therefore, despite all appearances to the contrary, profoundly aligned with Foucault's. It is indeed Descartes – and everything for which this name serves as an index – it is indeed the system of certainty that first of all functions in order to inspect, master and limit hyperbole, and does so both by determining it in the ether of a natural light whose axioms are from the outset exempt from hyperbolical doubt, and by making of hyperbolical doubt a point of transition firmly maintained within the chain of reasons. But it is our belief that this movement can be described within its own time and place only if one has previously disengaged the extremity of hyperbole, which Foucault seemingly has not done. In the fugitive and, by its essence, ungraspable moment when it still escapes the linear order of reasons, the order of reason in general and the determinations of natural light, does not the Cartesian Cogito lend itself to repetition, up to a certain point, by the Husserlian Cogito and by the critique of Descartes implied in it?

This would be an example only, for some day the dogmatic and historically determined grounds – ours – will be discovered, which the critique of Cartesian deductivism, the impetus and madness of the Husserlian reduction of the totality of the world, first had to rest on, and then had to fall onto in order to be stated. One could do for Husserl what Foucault has done for Descartes: demonstrate how the neutralisation of the factual world is a neutralisation (in the sense in which to neutralise is also to master, to reduce, to leave free in a straitjacket) of nonmeaning, the most subtle form of an act of force. And in truth, Husserl increasingly associated the theme of normality with the theme of the transcendental reduction. The embedding of transcendental phenomenology in the metaphysics of presence, the entire Husserlian thematic of the living present is the profound *reassurance* of the certainty of *meaning*.

By separating, within the Cogito, *on the one hand*, hyperbole (which I maintain cannot be enclosed in a factual and determined historical structure, for it is the project of exceeding every finite and determined totality), and, *on the other hand*, that in Descartes' philosophy (or in the philosophy supporting the Augustinian Cogito or the Husserlian Cogito as well) which belongs to a factual historical structure, I am not proposing the separation of the wheat from the tares in every philosophy in the name of some *philosophia perennis*. Indeed, it is exactly the contrary that I am proposing. In question is a way of accounting for the very historicity of philosophy. I believe that historicity in general would be impossible without a history of philosophy, and I believe that the latter would be impossible if we possessed only hyperbole, on the one hand, or, on the other, only determined historical structures, finite *Weltanschauungen*. The historicity proper to philosophy is located and constituted in the transition, the dialogue between hyperbole and the finite structure, between that which exceeds the totality and the closed totality, in the difference between history and historicity; that is, in the place where, or rather at the moment when, the Cogito and all that it symbolises here (madness, derangement, hyperbole, etc.) pronounce and reassure themselves then to fall, necessarily forgetting themselves until their reactivation, their reawakening in another statement of the excess which also later will become another decline and another crisis. From its very first breath, speech, confined to this temporal rhythm of crisis and reawakening, is able to open the space for discourse only by emprisoning madness.

This rhythm, moreover, is not an alternation that additionally would be temporal. It is rather the movement of temporalisation itself as concerns that which unites it to the movement of logos. But this violent liberation of speech is possible and can be pursued only in the extent to which it keeps itself resolutely and consciously at the greatest possible proximity to the abuse that is the usage of speech – just close enough to say violence, to dialogue with itself as irreducible violence, and just far enough to *live* and live as speech. Due to this, crisis or oblivion perhaps is not an accident, but rather the destiny of speaking philosophy – the philosophy which lives only by emprisoning madness, but which would die as thought, and by a still worse violence, if a new speech did not at every instant liberate previous madness while enclosing within itself, in its present existence, the madman of the day. It is only by virtue of this oppression of madness that finite-thought, that is to say, history, can reign. Extending this truth to historicity in general, without keeping to a determined historical moment, one could say that the reign of finite thought can be established only on the basis of the more or less disguised internment, humiliation, fettering and mockery of the madman within us, of the madman who can only be the fool of a logos which is father, master and king. But that is another discourse and another story. I will conclude by citing Foucault once more. Long after the passage on Descartes, some three hundred pages later, introducing *Rameau's Nephew* Foucault writes, with a sigh of remorse: 'In doubt's confrontation with its major dangers, Descartes realised that he could not be mad – though he was to acknowledge for a long time to come that all the powers of unreason kept vigil around his thought.'[30] What we have attempted to do here this evening is to situate ourselves within the interval of this remorse, Foucault's remorse, Descartes' remorse according to Foucault; and within the space of stating that, 'though he was to acknowledge for a long time to come', we have attempted not to extinguish the *other* light, a black and hardly natural light, the vigil of the 'powers of unreason' around the Cogito. We have attempted to *requite* ourselves towards the gesture which Descartes uses to requite himself as concerns the menacing powers of madness which are the adverse origin of philosophy.

Among all Foucault's claims to my gratitude, there is thus also that of having made me better anticipate, more so by his monumental book than by the naïve reading of the *Meditations*, to what degree the philosophical act can no longer be in memory of Cartesianism, if to be Cartesian, as Descartes himself doubtless understood it, is to attempt to be Cartesian. That is to say, as I have at least tried to demonstrate, to-attempt-to-say-the-demonic-hyperbole from whose heights thought is announced to itself, *frightens* itself, and *reassures* itself against being annihilated or wrecked in madness or in death. *At its height* hyperbole, the absolute opening, the uneconomic expenditure, is always re-embraced by an *economy* and is overcome by economy. The relationship between reason, madness and death is an economy, a structure of deferral whose irreducible originality must be respected. This attempt to-say-the-demonic-hyperbole is not an attempt among others; it is not an attempt which would occasionally and eventually be completed by the saying of it, or by its object, the direct object of a wilful subjectivity. This attempt to say, which is not, moreover, the antagonist of silence, but rather the condition for it, is the original profundity of will in general. Nothing, further, would be more incapable of regrasping this will than voluntarism, for, as finitude and as history, this attempt is also a first passion. It keeps within itself the trace of a violence. It is more written than said, it is *economised*. The economy of this writing is a regulated relationship between that which exceeds and the exceeded totality: the *différance* of the absolute excess.

To define philosophy as the attempt-to-say-the-hyperbole is to confess – and philosophy is perhaps this gigantic confession – that by virtue of the historical enunciation through which philosophy tranquilises itself and excludes madness, philosophy also betrays itself (or betrays itself as thought), enters into a crisis and a forgetting of itself that are an essential and necessary period of its movement. I philosophise only in *terror*, but in the *confessed* terror of going mad. The confession is simultaneously, at its present moment, oblivion and unveiling, protection and exposure: economy.

But this crisis in which reason is madder than madness – for reason is nonmeaning and oblivion – and in which madness is more rational than reason, for it is closer to the wellspring of sense, however silent or murmuring – this crisis has always begun and is interminable. It suffices to say that, if it is classic, it is not so in the sense of the *classical age* but in the sense of eternal and essential classicism, and is also historical in an unexpected sense.

And nowhere else and never before has the concept of *crisis* been able to enrich and reassemble all its potentialities, all the energy of its meaning, as much, perhaps, as in Michel Foucault's book. Here, the crisis is on the one hand, in Husserl's sense, the danger menacing reason and meaning under the rubric of objectivism, of the forgetting of origins, of the blanketing of origins by the rationalist and transcendental unveiling itself. Danger as the movement of reason menaced by its own security, etc.

But the crisis is also decision, the caesura of which Foucault speaks, in the sense of *krinein*, the choice and division between the two ways separated by Parmenides in his poem, the way of logos and the nonway, the labyrinth, the *palintrope* in which logos is lost; the way of meaning and the way of nonmeaning; of Being and of non-Being. A division on whose basis, after which, logos, in the necessary violence of its irruption, is separated from itself as madness, is exiled from itself, forgetting its origin and its own possibility. Is not what is called finitude possibility as crisis? A certain identity between the consciousness of crisis and the forgetting of it? Of the thinking of negativity and the reduction of negativity?

Crisis of reason, finally, access to reason and attack of reason. For what Michel Foucault teaches us to think is that there are crises of reason in strange complicity with what the world calls crises of madness.

NOTES

1. With the exception of several notes and a short passage (in brackets), this paper is the reproduction of a lecture given 4 March 1963 at the Collège Philosophique. In proposing that this text be published in the *Revue de métaphysique et de morale*, M. Jean Wahl agreed that it should retain its first form, that of the spoken word, with all its requirements and, especially, its particular weaknesses: if in general, according to the remark in the *Phaedrus*,

the written word is deprived of 'the assistance of its father', if it is a fragile 'idol' fallen from 'living and animated discourse' unable to 'help itself', then is it not more exposed and disarmed than ever when, miming the improvisation of the voice, it must give up even the resources and lies of style?

2. Michel Foucault, *Folie et déraison: Histoire de la folie à l'âge classique* (Paris: Plon, 1961); trans. Richard Howard, *Madness and Civilization: A History of Insanity in the Age of Reason* (New York: Pantheon, 1965). [Howard has translated the abridged version of Foucault's book. Whenever possible I have used Howard's translations of passages cited by Derrida. All nonfootnoted translations of Foucault are my own.]
3. In *The Interpretation of Dreams* (trans. and ed. James Strachey in *The Standard Edition of the Complete Psychological Works of Sigmund Freud*, vol. 4 (London: Hogarth Press, 1955), p. 99 n.1), speaking of the link between dreams and verbal expression, Freud recalls Ferenczi's remark that every language has its own dream language. The latent content of a dream (and of any behaviour or consciousness in general) communicates with the manifest content only through the unity of a language – a language that the analyst must thus speak as well as possible. (On this subject cf. Daniel Lagache, 'Sur le polyglottisme dans l'analyse', in *La psychanalyse*, vol. 1 (Paris: 1956), pp. 167–78.) *As well as possible:* progress in the knowledge and practice of a language being by nature infinitely open (*first* by virtue of the original and essential equivocality of the signifier, at least in the language of 'everyday life', its indeterminateness and playing-space being precisely that which liberates the difference between hidden and stated meaning; *then*, by virtue of the original and essential communication between different languages throughout history; *finally*, by virtue of the play, the relation to itself, or 'sedimentation', of every language), are not the insecurities and insufficiencies of analysis axiomatic or irreducible? And does not the historian of philosophy, whatever his method or project, abandon himself to the same dangers? Especially if one takes into account a certain embedding of philosophical language in nonphilosophical language.
4. That all history can only be, in the last analysis, the history of meaning, that is, of Reason in general, is what Foucault could not fail to experience – we shall come to this in a moment. What he could not fail to experience is that the general meaning of a difficulty he attributes to the 'classical experience' is valid well beyond the 'classical age'. Cf., for example: 'And when it was a question, in seeking it in its most withdrawn essence, of peeling it away to its last structure, we would discover, in order to formulate it, only the *very language of reason* employed in the impeccable logic of delirium; precisely that which made it accessible counterfeited it as madness.' The very language of reason . . . but what is a language that would not be one of reason *in general*? And if there is no history, except of rationality and meaning in general, this means that philosophical language, as soon as it speaks, reappropriates negativity – or forgets it, which is the same thing – even when it allegedly affirms or recognises negativity. More surely then, perhaps. The history of truth is therefore the history of this *economy* of the negative. It is necessary, and it is perhaps time to come back to the ahistorical in a sense radically opposed to that of classical philosophy: not to misconstrue negativity, but this time to affirm it – silently. It is negativity and not positive truth that is the nonhistorical capital of history. In question then would be a negativity so negative that it could not even be called such any longer. Negativity has always been determined by dialectics – that is to say, by metaphysics – as *work* in the service of the constitution of meaning. To affirm negativity in silence is to gain access to a nonclassical type of dissociation between thought and language. And perhaps to a dissociation of thought and philosophy as discourse, if we are conscious of the fact that this schism cannot be enunciated, thereby erasing itself, except within philosophy.
5. Foucault, *Folie et déraison*, pp. x–xi. [I have modified Howard's translation of this sentence to include the 'on' whose double sense was played upon above.]

6. TN. I have consistently translated *oeuvre* as 'work' throughout this essay to avoid confusions that could be caused by translating it as 'work of art', as Howard does. To translate Foucault's definition of madness, commented upon by Derrida, as 'the absence of the work of art' (*l'absence d'oeuvre*) does not convey Foucault's sense of the absence of a work governed by institutionalised rationalism.
7. TN. Derrida is making use of the fact that the word *éloge* (praise) is derived from the same word as 'logos'.
8. Foucault, *Folie et déraison*, p. xi.
9. Cf. also, for example, *Symposium* 217e/218b; *Phaedrus* 244b–c/245a/249/265a ff.; *Theatetus* 257e; *Sophist* 228d/229a; *Timaeus* 86b; *Republic* 382c; *Laws* X 888a.
10. TN. Cf. note 7 above.
11. TN. *The Philosophical Works of Descartes*, trans. Elizabeth S. Haldane and G. R. T. Ross (Cambridge: Cambridge University Press, 1970), p. 146.
12. TN. Ibid., p. 146.
13. TN. Ibid., pp. 146–7.
14. TN. Ibid., p. 145.
15. *Madness, theme or index:* what is significant is that Descartes, at bottom, never speaks of madness itself in this text. Madness is not his theme. He treats it as the index of a question of principle, that is, of epistemological value. It will be said, perhaps, that this is the sign of a profound exclusion. But this silence on madness itself simultaneously signifies the opposite of an exclusion, since *it is not a question of madness* in this text, if only to exclude it. It is not in the *Meditations* that Descartes speaks of madness itself.
16. To underline this vulnerability and touch on the greatest difficulty, we would have to specify that the expressions 'sensory or corporeal fault' or 'corporeal error' could have no meaning for Descartes. There is no corporeal error, particularly in illness: jaundice or melancholy are only the *occasions* of an error that itself is born only with the consent or affirmation of the will in judgment, when 'one who is ill with jaundice judges everything to be yellow because his eye is tinged with yellow. So finally, too, when the imagination is diseased, as in cases of melancholia, and a man thinks that his own disorderly fancies represent real things' (*Rule XII*. Descartes emphasises this point: the most abnormal sensory or imaginative experience, considered in and of itself, at its own level and at its proper moment, never deceives us; or never deceives understanding, 'if it restrict its attention accurately to the object presented to it, just as it is given to it either firsthand or by means of an image; and if it moreover refrain from judging that the imagination faithfully reports the objects of the senses, or that the senses take on the true forms of things, or in fine that external things always are as they appear to be' (ibid., p. 44).)
17. TN. The paragraph organisation of Haldane and Ross does not correspond to the paragraph organisation of the edition of Descartes cited by Derrida.
18. TN. Ibid., p. 147.
19. TN. Ibid., p. 148.
20. Ibid. It is a question here of the order of reasons, as it is followed in the *Meditations*. It is well known that in the *Discourse* (part 4) doubt very promptly attacks the 'simplest geometrical questions' in which men sometimes 'commit paralogisms'.
21. Like Leibniz, Descartes has confidence in 'scientific' or 'philosophical' language, which is not necessarily the language taught in the Schools (*Rule III*) and which must also be carefully distinguished from the 'terms of ordinary language' which alone can 'deceive us' (*Meditations* II).
22. That is to say, as soon as, more or less implicitly, *Being* is *called upon* (even before its determination as essence and existence) – which can only mean, *to be called upon by Being*. Being would not be what it is if speech *simply* preceded or invoked it. Language's final protective barrier against madness is the meaning of Being.

23. TN. Ibid., p. 101.
24. It is a question less of a *point* than of a temporal originality in general.
25. TN. The reference is to Plato's *Republic* 509b–c.
26. It risks erasing the excess by which every philosophy (of meaning) is related, in some region of its discourse, to the nonfoundation of unmeaning.
27. In the next to last paragraph of the Sixth Meditation, the theme of normality communicates with the theme of memory, at the moment when the latter, moreover, is confirmed by absolute Reason as 'divine veracity', etc. Generally speaking, does not God's confirmation of the remembrance of obvious truths signify that only the positive infinity of divine reason can absolutely reconcile temporality and truth? In the infinite alone, beyond all determinations, negations, 'exclusions' and 'internments', is produced the reconciliation of time and thought (truth) which Hegel claimed was the task of nineteenth-century philosophy, while the reconciliation of thought and space was to have been the aim of the so-called 'Cartesian' rationalisms. That this divine infinity is the proper location, condition, name, or horizon of these two reconciliations is what has never been contested by any *metaphysician*, neither by Hegel, nor by the majority of those, such as Husserl, who have attempted to think and to name the essential temporality or historicity of truth and meaning. For Descartes, the crisis of which we are speaking would finally have its intrinsic (that is, *intellectual*) origin in time itself, as the absence of a necessary link between its parts, as the contingency and discontinuity of the transition from instant to instant; which supposes that here we follow all the interpretations opposed to Laporte's on the question of the role of the instant in Descartes' philosophy. In the last retort, only continuous creation, uniting conservation and creation, which 'differ only as concerns our way of thinking', reconciles temporality and truth. It is God who excludes madness and crisis, that is to say, embraces them in the presence that encompasses all traces and differences. Which amounts to saying that crisis, anomaly, negativity, etc. are irreducible within the experience of finitude, or of a finite moment, a *determination* of absolute reason, or of reason in general. To attempt to deny this, and allegedly to affirm positivity (the positivity of truth, meaning, norms, etc.) outside the horizon of this infinite reason (reason in general, beyond all its specific determinations), is to attempt to erase negativity, and is to forget finitude at the very moment when one allegedly denounces as mystification the theologism of the great classical rationalisms.
28. But God is the other name of the absolute of reason *itself*, of reason and meaning in general. And what could exclude, reduce, or – amounting to the same thing – *absolutely embrace* madness, if not reason in general, absolute and undetermined reason, whose other name is God, for the classical rationalists? One cannot accuse those, individuals or societies, who use God as a recourse against madness of seeking to *shelter themselves*, to be sure of having protections against madness – the safe boundaries of asylums – except by construing this shelter as a *finite* one, within the world, by making God a third party or finite power, that is, except by deceiving oneself; by deceiving oneself not concerning the content and effective finality of this gesture in history, but concerning the philosophical specificity of the idea and name of God. If philosophy has taken place – which can always be contested – it is only in the extent to which it has formulated the aim of thinking beyond the finite shelter. By describing the historical constitution of these finite protective barriers against madness within the movement of individuals, societies and all finite totalities in general – a legitimate, immense and necessary task – one can finally describe everything except the philosophical project itself. And except the project of this description itself. One cannot allege that the philosophical project of the 'infinitivist' rationalisms served as an instrument or as an alibi for a finite historico-politico-social violence (which is doubtless the case) without *first* having to acknowledge and respect the intentional meaning of this project itself. Now, within its own intentional meaning, this project presents itself as the conceptualisation of the infinite, that is, of that which cannot be exhausted by any finite totality, by any

function or by any instrumental, technical, or political determination. It will be said that this presentation of the philosophical project by itself as such is its greatest lie, its violence and its mystification – or, further, its bad faith. And, certainly, the structure which links this intention to exceed the world to the totality of history must be described rigorously, and its economy must be determined. But like all ruses, these economic ones are possible only for finite words and finite intentions, substituting one finitude for another. One cannot lie when one says *nothing* (that is finite or determined), or when one says God, Being, or Nothingness, or when one does not modify the finite by the declared meaning of one's words, or when one says the infinite, that is, when one lets the infinite (God, Being, or Nothingness, for part of the meaning of the infinite is its inability to be an ontic determination among others) be said and conceived. The theme of divine veracity and the difference between God and the evil genius are thus illuminated by a light which is only apparently indirect.

In short, Descartes knew that, without God, finite thought never had the *right* to exclude madness, etc. Which amounts to saying that madness is never excluded, except *in fact*, violently, in history; or rather that this exclusion, this *difference* between the fact and the principle is historicity, the possibility of history itself. Does Foucault say otherwise? '*The necessity of* madness . . . is linked to the *possibility of history*' (author's italics).

29. Haldane and Ross, *The Philosophical Works of Descartes*, p. 171.

30. Foucault, *Folie et déraison*, p. 199.

CHAPTER 3

My Body, This Paper, This Fire

Michel Foucault
Translated by Jonathan Murphy and Jean Khalfa

On pages 44 to 47 of the *History of Madness*, I said that dreams and madness did not at all have the same status nor the same role in the development of Cartesian doubt: dreaming allows me to doubt the place where I am, the paper that I see, and the hand that I stretch out; but madness is in no sense an instrument or a stage of doubt; because '*I*, who think, cannot be mad.'[1] Exclusion, therefore, for madness, whereas the sceptical tradition, by contrast, had made it one of the reasons for doubting.

To sum up the objection that Derrida makes to this thesis,[2] it is probably best to quote the passage where he gives, in the most vigorous manner, his reading of Descartes:

> Descartes has just said that all knowledge of sensory origin could deceive him. He pretends to put to himself the astonished objection of an imaginary non-philosopher who is frightened by such audacity and says: no, not all sensory knowledge, for then you would be mad and it would be unreasonable to follow the example of madmen, to put forth the ideas of madmen. Descartes *echoes* this objection: since I am here, writing, and you understand me, I am not mad, nor are you, and we are all sane. The example of madness is therefore not indicative of the fragility of the sensory idea. So be it. Descartes acquiesces to this natural point of view, or rather he feigns to rest in this natural comfort in order better, more radically and more definitively, to unsettle himself from it and to discomfort his interlocutor. So be it, he says, you think that I would be mad to doubt that I am sitting near the fire, etc., that I would be insane to follow the example of madmen. I will therefore propose a hypothesis which will seem much more natural to you, will not disorient you, because it concerns a more common, and more universal experience than that of madness: the experience of sleep and dreams. Descartes then elaborates the hypothesis

> that will ruin *all* the *sensory* foundations of knowledge and will lay bare only the *intellectual* foundations of certainty. This hypothesis above all will not run from the possibility of an insanity – an epistemological one – much more serious than madness.
>
> The reference to dreams is therefore not put off to one side – quite the contrary – in relation to a madness potentially respected or even excluded by Descartes. It constitutes, in the methodical order which here is ours, the hyperbolical exasperation of the hypothesis of madness. This latter affected only certain areas of sensory perception, and in a contingent and partial way. Moreover, Descartes is concerned here not with determining the concept of madness but with utilising the popular notion of insanity for juridical and methodological ends, in order to ask questions of principle regarding only the *truth* of ideas.[3] What must be grasped here is that *from this point of view* the sleeper, or the dreamer, is madder than the madman. Or, at least, the dreamer, in so far as concerns the problem of knowledge which interests Descartes here, is further from true perception than the madman. It is in the case of sleep, and not in that of insanity, that the *absolute totality* of ideas of sensory origin becomes suspect, is stripped of 'objective value' as M. Guéroult puts it. The hypothesis of insanity is therefore not a good example, a revelatory example, a good instrument of doubt – and for at least two reasons. (a) It does not cover the *totality* of the field of sensory perception. The madman is not always wrong about everything; he is not wrong often enough, is never mad enough. (b) It is not a useful or happy example pedagogically, because it meets the resistance of the nonphilosopher who does not have the audacity to follow the philosopher when the latter agrees that he might indeed be mad at the very moment when he speaks.

Derrida's argumentation is remarkable. For its depth, and even more so for its frankness. What is at stake in the debate is indicated clearly: is it possible that there might be something anterior or exterior to philosophical discourse? Could it have its condition in an exclusion, a refusal, a risk eluded, and, why not, in a fear? A suspicion that Derrida rejects with passion. *Pudenda origo* (shameful origin!), said Nietzsche of religious people and their religion.

Let us confront the analyses of Derrida and the texts of Descartes.

THE PRIVILEGES OF DREAM OVER MADNESS

Derrida: 'Dreaming is an experience more common, and also more universal than that of madness.' 'The madman is not always wrong about everything.' 'Madness only affects in a contingent and partial manner certain regions of sensible perception.'

Now Descartes does not at all say that dreaming is 'more common and also more universal than madness', and neither does he say that madmen are only mad from time to time and regarding particular points. Let us listen instead to his reference to people who 'constantly claim to be kings'.[4] Is the madness of these people who take themselves for kings, or who believe that they have a body of glass, more intermittent than dreaming?

And yet it is a fact: Descartes, along the path of doubt, privileges dreaming over madness. Let us put to one side for a moment the problem of knowing whether madness is excluded, merely neglected, or taken up again later in a wider and more radical experiment.

Immediately after he has mentioned, in order to abandon it, the example of madness, Descartes evokes the case of dreams: 'In any case, I must consider here that I am a man, consequently that I am in the habit of dreaming, and of seeing the same things in my dreams, and sometimes seeing things more improbable than the waking visions of these insane people.'[5]

A double advantage therefore of the dream. On the one hand, it is capable of creating eccentricities that equal, or sometimes surpass madness; on the other, it has the property of producing itself in an habitual manner. The first advantage is of a logical and demonstrative order: everything of which madness (the example of which I have just set aside) could make me doubt, dreams too could make uncertain for me; as a power of uncertainty, dreaming has nothing to fear from madness, and none of the demonstrative force of madness is lost by dreaming when I have to convince myself of everything that I must revoke in doubt. The other advantage of the dream is of a different order: it is frequent, it often happens; I have recent memories of it, and it is not difficult to draw on the extremely vivid memories that it leaves. A practical advantage, in short, when what is at stake is no longer demonstrating, but carrying out an exercise and calling up a memory, a thought, a state, in the very movement of meditation.

The extravagance of the dream guarantees its *demonstrative* character as *example*: its frequency assures its *accessible* character as *exercise*. And it is certainly this accessible character that worries Descartes here, certainly more so than its demonstrative character, which is signalled once and for all, as though he were assuring himself that the hypothesis of madness could be abandoned without regrets. The theme that dreams happen quite often, by contrast, returns several times. We can find: 'I am a man, and consequently, I am in the habit of dreaming', 'how often at night have I not dreamt', 'what happens during sleep', 'considering the matter carefully, I remember often being deceived while sleeping'.[6]

My fear is that Derrida may have confused these two aspects of dreaming. Everything happens as though he had covered them with a word that forcibly joins them together: 'universal'. As 'universal', dreaming would happen to everyone and regarding everything. The dream: a dubiousness of all things for all men. But this is forcing words, and going well beyond what the Cartesian text says: or rather, stopping well short of its singularities, effacing the quite distinct character of the eccentricity of dreaming and its frequency, erasing the specific role of these two characteristics in the Cartesian discourse (demonstration and exercise) and omitting the greater importance accorded to custom over extravagance.

But why is it so important that dreaming should be familiar and accessible?

MY EXPERIENCE OF DREAMING

Derrida: 'The reference to dreaming constitutes, in the methodical order that is our own here, the hyperbolic exasperation of the hypothesis of madness.'

Before rereading the paragraph about dreaming[7] let us keep in our ears the sentence that has just been spoken: 'But so what? Such people are insane, and I would be no less eccentric if I modelled myself on their example.'[8]

And then the discourse goes on as follows: a resolution in the meditating subject to take into consideration the fact that he is a man, that he often sleeps and dreams; the appearance of a memory (or rather of a multitude of memories), of dreams which coincide exactly, trait for trait, with today's perception (being seated here in this place, fully dressed, beside the fire); the feeling that somehow there is a difference between the perception and the memory, a difference that is not simply noted, but effected by the subject in the very movement of his meditation (I look at this paper, I shake my head, I stretch out my hand, so that the difference between wakefulness and sleeping appears quite vividly); but then come new memories, on a second level (the vividness of this impression has often been a part of my dreams); with these memories, the vivid feeling that I am awake begins to disappear; it is replaced by the clear vision that there is no certain indication that might separate sleeping and wakefulness: a conclusion that provokes an astonishment in the meditating subject such that the indifference between sleep and wakefulness provokes the quasi-certainty that one is sleeping.

And so we can see it: the resolution to think about dreams does not merely have the consequence of turning sleep and wakefulness into a theme for reflection. This theme, in the movement that proposes it and causes it to vary, *takes effect* in the meditating subject in the form of memories, vivid impressions, voluntary movements, differences experienced, memories again, clear vision, astonishment, and an indifferentiation which is close to the feeling of sleeping. To think of dreaming is not at all to think of something exterior, of which I would know the effects and the causes; it is not simply to evoke a whole strange phantasmagoria, or the movements of the brain that might provoke it; thinking of dreaming is such, when one applies oneself to it, that its effect is to scramble for the meditating subject, and at the very heart of his meditation, the perceived limits of sleeping and wakefulness. The dream *troubles the subject* who thinks about it. Turning one's mind to dreams is not an indifferent task: it is perhaps at first a theme that one proposes to oneself, but it quickly reveals itself to be a risk to which one exposes oneself. The risk for the subject that he might be modified, the risk that he may no longer be at all certain of being awake, the risk of *stupor*, says the Latin text.

And it is here that the example of the dream reveals another of its privileges. However much it modifies the meditating subject on this matter, it does not prevent him, at the very heart of this stupor, from continuing to meditate, and to meditate in a valid fashion, and to see clearly a certain number of things or principles despite the indistinction, however profound it might be, between sleeping and wakefulness. Even if I am not sure of being awake, I remain certain of what my meditation allows me to see; and that is what is demonstrated by the passage that follows, beginning precisely with a sort of hyperbolic resolution: 'Suppose then that we are dreaming', or as the Latin text says even more forcibly, *Age somniemus*. The thought of dreaming had led me to uncertainty; the latter, by the astonishment that it provokes, to the quasi-certainty of sleep; that quasi-certainty is now turned by my resolutions into a systematic feint. This is the artful putting to sleep of the meditating subject: *Age somniemus*, and from that point on, the meditation, once again, may be pursued.

We can now see all the possibilities that are given by the character, certainly not 'universal', but modestly customary, of dreaming.

1. It is a possible experience, immediately accessible, of which the model is proposed by a thousand memories.

2. This possible experience is not simply a theme for meditation; it is really and presently produced in meditation, according to the following series: thinking about dreaming; remembering dreaming; seeking to make the distinction between dreaming and waking; no longer knowing if one is dreaming or not, and voluntarily acting as though one were dreaming.

3. Through this meditative exercise, the thought of the dream has an effect on the subject himself: it modifies him by filling him with *stupor*.

4. But by modifying him, by turning him into a subject uncertain of his waking state, it does not disqualify him as a meditating subject: even transformed into a 'subject supposed to be dreaming', the meditating subject can pursue, in a sure fashion, the path of his doubt.

But we must go further back, and compare this experience of dreaming with the example of madness that immediately precedes it.

THE 'GOOD' EXAMPLE AND THE 'BAD' ONE

Derrida: 'What must be retained here is that from this point of view, the sleeper or the dreamer is more mad than the madman.'

For Derrida, madness is not excluded by Descartes; it is simply neglected. Neglected for a better, more radical example. The example of the dream prolongs, completes and generalises what the example of madness indicated in such unsuitable fashion. To go from madness to the dream is to go from a 'bad' to a 'good' instrument of doubt.

But I believe that the opposition between dreaming and madness is of a quite different type. We must compare step by step the two paragraphs of Descartes, and follow in detail the system of their opposition.

1. The *nature* of the meditative exercise. It appears clearly in the *vocabulary* employed. In the paragraph on madness, there is the vocabulary of comparison. If I want to deny that 'these hands and this whole body are mine' I must 'liken myself to madmen' (*comparare*); but I would be quite eccentric 'if I took anything from them as a model' (*si quod ab iis exemplum ad me transferrem*). The madman is an exterior term to which I compare myself.

In the paragraph on dreams there is the vocabulary of memory. 'I am in the habit of dreaming', 'How often have I not', 'Considering the matter carefully, I remember'.[9] The dreamer is what I recall having been myself; from the depths of my memory rises up the dreamer that I myself have been, and that I will be again.

2. The *themes* of the meditative exercise. They appear in the examples that the meditating subject proposes to himself.

For madness: to take oneself for a king when one is poor; to believe oneself dressed in gold when one is naked; to imagine that one has a body of glass, or that one is a water pitcher. Madness is when all is other, it deforms and transports, it evokes a different scene.

For the dream: to be seated (as I am now); to feel the heat of the fire (as I feel it today); to stretch out my hand (as I decide to do, right now). Dreams do not transport the scene; they reproduce demonstratives that point towards the scene where I am (this hand? Perhaps a picture of another hand. This fire? Perhaps a different fire, in a dream). The oneiric imagination matches the current perception exactly.

3. The *central test*[10] of the exercise. It is to be found in the search for difference: will I be able to incorporate the themes proposed into my meditation? Can I seriously ask myself if I have a body of glass, and if I am not quite naked in my bed? If so, I will be obliged to doubt even my own body. But it will be spared if, on the other hand, my meditation remains quite distinct from madness and from dreaming.

From dreaming? I try the test: I remember having dreamt that I was nodding my head. I will therefore nod it again here, right now. Is there a difference? Yes. A certain clarity, a certain distinctiveness. But, and this is the second part of the test, can that clarity and distinctiveness be found in dreams? Yes, I have a clear memory of that. Therefore what I thought to be the criterion of difference (clarity and distinctiveness) belongs indifferently to dreaming and wakefulness. It cannot therefore make the difference.

From madness? The test is immediately done. Or rather, when one looks closely, one sees that it does not take place, in the manner that it is carried out for the dream. There is in fact no question of me trying to take myself for a madman who takes himself for a king; and neither is there any question of me wondering if I am a king (or a captain from Touraine) who thinks himself to be a philosopher who has locked himself away to meditate. The difference from madness does not have to be tested: it is noted. No sooner are the themes of eccentricity evoked than the distinction bursts out like a cry: *sed amentes sunt isti.*

4. The *effect* of the exercise. It appears in the two sentences, or rather in the sentence-decisions that finish each of the two passages.

The paragraph about madness: 'But so what? Such people are insane' (third person plural, they, the others, *isti*); 'I would be no less eccentric if I modelled myself on their example';[11] it would be (note the conditional) madness even to try the test, to want to imitate all these delights, and to play the madman with the mad, like the mad. It is not by imitating madmen that I will be persuaded that I am mad (just as, a moment ago, the thought of dreaming convinced me that perhaps I am asleep); it is the very project of imitating them that is eccentric. The eccentricity relates to the very idea of putting it to the test, and for that reason it is absent, replaced by a mere acknowledgement of difference.

The paragraph about dreaming: the phrase, '*such people* are insane' is answered exactly by '*I* begin to feel dazed' (*obstupestere:* to the cry of difference corresponds the stupor of indistinction); and the phrase 'I would be no less eccentric if . . .' corresponds to 'my astonishment (*stupor*) is such that it is almost enough to persuade me that I am sleeping'. The test that has been tried out has 'worked' so well that I am now (note the present indicative) in the uncertainty of my own wakefulness. And it is in that uncertainty that I decide to continue my meditation.

It would be mad to want to play the madman (and I give up); but to think of dreaming is to already have the impression that one sleeps (and that is what I am going to meditate on).

It is extremely difficult to remain deaf to the echo between these two paragraphs. And difficult not to be struck by the system of complex oppositions that underlies them. Difficult not to recognise there two exercises that are at once parallel and different: the exercise of the *demens* and that of the *dormiens*. Difficult not to understand the words and the phrases that confront each other on either side of this 'In any case'[12] of which Derrida has so profoundly underlined the importance, but of which he is wrong, I feel, not to analyse the function in the play of discourse. Difficult, truly, to say simply that madness is an insufficient and pedagogically clumsy example among the reasons for doubting, because the dreamer is in any case madder than the madman.

The whole discursive analysis demonstrates it: the acknowledgement of non-madness (and the rejection of the test) is not in continuity with the sleep test (and the acknowledgement that one might be sleeping).

But why this rejection of the test of the *demens*? Can we conclude from the fact that it has not happened that it is excluded? After all, Descartes speaks so little, and so quickly, of madness.

THE DISQUALIFICATION OF THE SUBJECT

Derrida: 'What is significant is that Descartes, at bottom, never actually speaks of madness itself in this text . . . this text does not speak of madness, it is not in question, not even to be excluded.'

Several times Derrida wisely remarks that in order to understand Descartes' text properly, we must refer to the original Latin version. He recalls – and he is quite right – the words used by Descartes in the famous phrase: 'But such people are insane (*sed amentes sunt isti*), and I would be [thought] equally mad (*demens*) if I took anything from them as a model for myself.' Unfortunately, his analysis does not go beyond this simple recollection of the words.

Let us return to the passage itself: 'How could it be denied that these hands or this whole body are mine? Unless perhaps I were to liken myself to madmen' (the term employed here is *insani*). But what are these *insani* who take themselves for kings or earthenware? They are *amentes*; and I would be no less *demens* if I applied their example to myself. Why these three terms, or rather why employ first of all the term *insanus*, and then the couple *amens-demens*? When it is a question of characterising them by the improbability of their imaginings, the mad are called *insani:* a word that belongs as much to everyday vocabulary as it does to medical terminology. To be *insanus* is to take oneself for what one is not, it is to believe in chimeras, to be the victim of delusions; these are at least the signs. The cause is a brain swollen with vapours. But when Descartes wishes not to characterise madness, but to affirm that I should not take my example from the mad, he employs the terms *demens* and *amens*, terms that are legal before being medical, and which designate a whole category of people who are incapable of certain religious, civil and legal acts; the *dementes* do not have all their rights in matters of speaking, promising, committing themselves, signing, bringing legal actions, etc. *Insanus* is a term of characterisation; *amens* and *demens* are disqualifying terms. The first refers to signs; the other two to capability.

The two sentences, in order to doubt my body, I must 'liken myself to madmen', and 'but such people are insane', are not proof of an impatient and irritated tautology. In no sense is it a matter of saying 'one should be or act like madmen', but 'they are mad, and I am not'. To summarise the text as Derrida does, 'Since I am here, I'm not mad, neither are you, and we are among sane people here', is singularly to flatten it. The development of the text is quite different: to doubt one's body is to be like those of deranged mind, the sick, the *insane*. Can I follow their example, and on my own account at least feign madness, and become in my own eyes uncertain whether I am mad or not? I neither can nor should. For those *insani* are *amentes*; and I would be no less *demens* than them, and juridically disqualified if I followed their example.

Derrida obscurely sensed the juridical connotation of the word. He returns to it several times, insistent and hesitating. Descartes, he says, 'treats [madness] as the index of a question of principle, that is, of epistemological value'.[13] Or again, 'Moreover, Descartes is concerned here not with determining the concept of madness but with utilising the popular notion of insanity for juridical and methodological ends, in order to ask questions of principle regarding only the *truth* of ideas.' Derrida is correct to underline that at this point it is indeed a question of law. And he is right again to say that Descartes did not want to 'determine the concept of madness' (who ever claimed that anyway?). But he is wrong not to have seen that Descartes' text plays on the gap between two types of determination of madness (the medical ones and the juridical ones). And more than anything he is wrong to conclude hastily that the question of law that is posed here concerns 'the truth of ideas', while, as the words clearly state, it concerns the qualification of the subject.

The problem can then be posed thus. Can I doubt my own body, can I doubt my own actuality? The example of the mad, the *insani*, invites me to do so. But comparing myself to them, doing as they do, implies that I too will become like them, demented, incapable and disqualified from my meditative enterprise: I would be no less *demens* if I followed their example. But if, on the other hand, I take the example of dreams, if I pretend that I am dreaming, then, however *dormiens* I am, I will still be able to meditate, reason, and see clearly. *Demens*, I would be unable to continue: I have to stop with the very hypothesis, and envisage something else, and see if another example might allow me to doubt my own body. *Dormiens*, I can continue my meditation: I am still qualified to think; and so I make my resolution: *Age somniemus*, which introduces a new moment of the meditation.

It would take quite a distant reading to conclude that 'it is not a question of madness in this text'.

Perhaps, you might say. Let us admit, despite Derrida, that we should pay such detailed attention to the text, and to all its little differences. For all that, have you demonstrated that madness is well and truly excluded from the path of doubt? Will Descartes not refer to it again with reference to imagination? Is it not to that that he refers when talking of the eccentricity of painters, and all those fantastical chimeras that they invent?

THE ECCENTRICITY OF PAINTERS

Derrida: 'What Descartes seemed to exclude as eccentricity above is here admitted as a possibility . . . but in these representations, these images, these ideas in the Cartesian sense, everything can be false and fictitious, like the representations of these painters whose imagination, Descartes explicitly says, "manages to think up something so new that nothing remotely like it has been seen before."'

Granted, madness is dealt with several times elsewhere in the Cartesian *oeuvre*. And its disqualifying role for the meditating subject in no way prevents meditation from bearing upon it, for it is not for the content of such eccentricities that madness is removed from the game: it is removed for the subject who would at once 'play the madman' and meditate, when it is a question of knowing whether the subject can assume madness for himself, imitate it, feign it, and risk no longer really knowing if he is reasonable or not. As I think I have said quite clearly, madness is excluded by the subject who doubts, in order that he may qualify himself as a doubting subject. But it is in no sense rejected as an object of reflection and knowledge. Is it not typical that the madness of which Descartes speaks in the paragraph studied above should be defined in medical terms, the result of 'brains . . . damaged by the persistent vapours of melancholia'?

But Derrida could insist and underline that madness is still to be found in the movement of the doubt, mixed with the imagination of the painters. It is clearly present in the French text, as indicated by the word '*extravagant*' (eccentric), used to describe the imagination of painters: 'if perhaps their imagination is sufficiently eccentric to invent something so new that we have never seen anything like it before . . . at least the colours they use must be true to life'. Derrida has understood perfectly what was singular in the expression 'if their imagination is sufficiently eccentric'. He understands it so well that he underlines it in his quotation probably as the point on which his demonstration is to hang. I subscribe entirely to the necessity of sufficiently isolating these few words.

But for a different reason: quite simply because *they are not to be found* in the original text. They are an addition by the French translator. The Latin text simply says '*si forte aliquid ex cogitent ad eon ovum ut nihil*', 'if perhaps they manage to think up something so new'. It is curious that Derrida, to demonstrate the validity of his thesis, has spontaneously chosen, retained and underlined that which can *only* be found in the French translation of the *Meditations*; curious too that he insists, and claimed, that the word 'eccentric' was used 'on purpose' [*expressément*] by Descartes.

It does not therefore seem that the example of the dream is simply for Descartes a generalisation or a radicalisation of the case of madness. It is not as a feeble, less good, insufficient, insufficiently 'revealing', 'ineffective' example that madness is to be distinguished from dreaming. And it is not at all for its lesser value that it is to be left aside after being evoked. The example of madness faces that of dreams; they are confronted and placed in opposition to each other according to a system of differences that are clearly articulated in the Cartesian discourse.

But Derrida's analysis neglects, I fear, many of these differences. Literal differences between words (*comparare/reminiscerere*; *exemplum transferre*/to persuade; conditional/indicative). Thematic differences of images (to be beside the fire; to stretch out one's hand and open one's eyes/to take oneself for a king, to be covered with gold, to have a body made of glass); textual differences in the arrangement and the opposition of the paragraphs (the first plays on the distinction between *insanus* and *demens*, and on the *juridical implication* of *demens* by *insanus*; the second plays on the distinction 'remembering one has slept/convincing oneself that one is asleep', and on the *real passage* from the one to the other in a mind that applies itself to such a memory). But differences above all on the level of what is happening in the meditation, on the level of *events* that succeed one another; *acts* carried out by the meditating subject (comparison/remembering); *effects* produced inside the meditating subject (sudden and immediate perception of a difference/astonishment-stupor-experience of an indistinction); qualification of the meditating subject (invalidity if he is *demens*; validity even if he is *dormiens*).

We can see it quite clearly: this last group of differences commands all the others; it refers less to the signifying organisation of the text than to the series of events (acts, effects, qualifications) that the discursive practice of the meditation brings in its wake; it concerns the modification of the subject through the very exercise of the discourse. And I have the impression that if a reader, even a reader as remarkably assiduous as Derrida, has missed so many literary, thematic or textual differences, it is because he has misunderstood those that are their principle, i.e. the 'discursive differences'.

*

We must keep in mind the title itself of 'Meditations'. Any discourse, whatever its nature, is made up of a group of enunciations which are produced in their space and in their time, as so many discursive events. If they form a pure demonstration, these enunciations can be read as a series of events, linked to each other according to a certain number of formal rules; the subject of the discourse is in no sense implied in the demonstration; it remains, in relation to it, fixed, invariant and as though neutralised. A 'meditation', by contrast, produces, as so many discursive events, new enunciations that bring in their wake a series of modifications in the enunciating subject: through what is said in the meditation, the subject passes from darkness to light, from impurity to purity, from the constraint of passions to detachment, from uncertainty and disordered movements to the serenity of wisdom, etc. In the meditation, the subject is ceaselessly altered by his own movement; his discourse elicits movements inside which he is caught up; it exposes him to risks, subjects him to tests [*épreuves*] or temptations, produces in him states, and confers a status or a qualification upon him which he in no sense possessed at the initial moment. A meditation implies, in short, a subject who is mobile and capable of being modified by the very effect of the discursive events that take place. We can see from this what a demonstrative meditation would be: a set of discursive events that form at the same time groups of enunciations linked to each other by formal rules of deduction, and series of modifications in the enunciating subject, modifications that continually follow on from each other; and more precisely, in a demonstrative meditation, enunciations which are formally linked modify the subject as they develop, and liberate him from his convictions or induce systematic doubts, provoke illuminations or resolutions, free him from his attachments or his immediate certainties, induce new states, but inversely the decisions, fluctuations, displacements, primary or acquired qualifications of the subject make possible sets of new enunciations, which are regularly deduced from the others.

The *Meditations* require such a double reading: a group of propositions, forming a *system*, which each reader must run through if he wishes to experience their truth; and a group of modifications forming an *exercise*, which each reader must carry out, and by which each reader must be affected, if he wishes in his turn to be the subject enunciating this truth on his own account. And while it is true that there are certain passages in the *Meditations* which can be deciphered, in an exhaustive manner, as a systematic concatenation of propositions – moments of pure deduction – there are also sorts of 'chiasms' where the two forms of discourse intersect, and where the exercise modifying the subject orders the succession of propositions, or commands the junction of distinct demonstrative groups. It would appear that the passage on madness and dreaming is of that order.

Let us take it up again in its entirety, and as an intersection of the demonstrative and the ascetic threads.

1. The passage that immediately precedes it has the appearance of a practical syllogism:

> *I must be wary of anything that has deceived me once*
> *But my senses, which have given me all that I hold most true and most certain, have deceived me, and more than once*
> *Therefore I must no longer trust them.*

We can see it quite clearly: this section is a deductive fragment whose implications are quite general – *everything* that we have held to be most *true* is suddenly in doubt, together with the senses that brought it. *A fortiori*, there is therefore nothing that remains which does not become at least as doubtful. Is there any need to generalise any further? Derrida's hypothesis, that the (ineffective) example of madness and the (effective) example of dreaming are called upon to operate this generalisation, and to lead on the syllogism of doubt, cannot therefore be retained. By what, then, are they summoned?

2. They are summoned less by an objection or a restriction than by a resistance; there are sensible things about which 'doubt is quite impossible' [in French, 'dont on ne peut pas *raisonnablement* douter', 'which we cannot reasonably doubt']. It is the word '*plane*' that Descartes' French translator renders by '*raisonnablement*'. What

then is this 'impossibility', when we have just established a totally compelling syllogism? What is the obstacle that prevents us from doubting 'entirely', 'wholly', 'completely', (reasonably?), when we have just presented a rationally unassailable reasoning? It is the impossibility for the subject of really carrying out, in the exercise that modifies his self, a doubt so general. It is the impossibility of constituting oneself as a universally doubting subject. What presents a problem, following a syllogism of such general import, is the conversion of a counsel of prudence into effective doubt, the transformation of a subject 'knowing that he must doubt all things' into a subject who is 'applying to all things his resolution to doubt'. We can see very well why the translator rendered '*plane*' by '*raisonnablement*'; in attempting to carry out this rationally necessary doubt, I expose myself to losing the qualification of '*raisonnable*' that I brought into play from the very beginning of the meditations (and in at least three forms: having a mind that is sufficiently mature, having a mind that is free of cares and passions, and being sure of a peaceful retreat). In order to take the resolution to doubt everything, should I disqualify myself as reasonable? If I wish to maintain my qualification as reasonable, should I give up attempting to effect this doubt, or at least to effect it in its generality?

The importance of the words 'to be able to doubt completely' comes from the fact that they mark a point of overlap of the two discursive forms – that of the system and that of the exercise: on the level of the ascetic discursivity, we cannot yet reasonably doubt. It is thus the latter that will command the following development, and what finds itself engaged there is not the panoply of doubtful things, but the status of the doubting subject, the qualificatory elaboration which permits him at once to be 'omnidoubting' and reasonable.

But what then is the obstacle, the point of resistance in the exercise of the doubt?

3. Is it my body, and the immediate perception that I have of it? Or more exactly, the domain that can be defined as that of the 'vivid and near' (as opposed to all those things that are 'faint and distant' which I can unproblematically *put* in doubt): I am here, wearing a dressing gown, seated near the fire, in short the whole system of actuality that characterises this particular moment of my meditation. It is of capital importance that Descartes here does not evoke the certainty that one can have in general of one's own body, but clearly all that which, in this precise *instant* of the meditation, resists *in fact* the effectuation of the doubt by the subject who is *actually* meditating. We see clearly that it is not at all certain things which in themselves (their nature, their universality, their intelligibility) might resist doubt; but, rather, that which characterises the actuality of the meditating subject (the place of his meditation, the action that he is carrying out, the sensations that strike him). If he really doubted this system of actuality, would he still be reasonable? Would he not precisely renounce all those guarantees of a reasonable meditation he gave himself by choosing, as was said above, the moment of his enterprise (quite advanced in years, but not excessively so; the moment has come which must not be passed up), its conditions (to be seated quietly, without any care that might form a distraction), its place (a peaceful retreat)? If I am to start doubting the place where I am, the attention I am paying to this paper, and the heat of the fire that marks my present instant, how will I be able to remain convinced of the reasonable character of my

undertaking? Would I not, by doubting this actuality, by the same token, make reasonable meditation impossible, and deny any value in my resolution to finally discover the truth?

Two examples are called up, both of which make it necessary to put into doubt the system of the actuality of the subject.

4. First example: madness. The mad, in effect, entirely delude themselves about what constitutes their actuality: they believe they are dressed when they are naked, they believe themselves to be kings when they are poor. But can I use this example for myself? Is it by such means that I will be able to transform into an effective resolution the proposition that I must doubt everything that comes to us in dreams? Impossible: *isti sunt dementes*, which is to say that they are juridically disqualified as reasonable subjects, and to qualify myself as them, in the same fashion as them ('if I took anything from them'), would disqualify me in turn and I could no longer be a reasonable subject for meditation ('I would be [thought] equally mad'). If one uses the example of madness to pass from systems to ascesis, from proposition to resolution, one can effectively constitute oneself as a subject ready to put everything in doubt, but one cannot remain qualified as a subject reasonably leading his meditation through doubt towards a possible truth. The resistance of actuality to the exercise of doubt is reduced by an example that is too strong: with it the possibility of meditating in a valid fashion disappears; the two qualifications 'doubting subject' and 'meditating subject' are not in this case simultaneously possible.

That madness be posited as disqualifying in any search for the truth, that it should not be 'reasonable' to call it to oneself to carry out the necessary doubting, that one cannot feign it even for an instant, and that the impossibility appears immediately in the very assignation of the term '*demens*'; this is indeed the decisive point where Descartes departs from all those for whom madness may be in some way or other a bearer or revealer of truth.

5. Second test [*épreuve*]: dreams. Madness has thus been excluded, not at all as an insufficient example but as an excessive and impossible test. Dreaming is then invoked: not that it renders the actuality of the subject less doubtful than madness (one believes that one is seated at one's table while one is naked in bed); but it presents a number of differences in relation to madness – it is part of the virtualities of the subject (I am a man), of his frequently actualised virtualities (it is my custom to sleep and to dream), his memories (I remember very well having dreamt), and his memories that can be called up most vividly (to the point that I can validly compare my actual impression and my memory of a dream). On the basis of these properties of dreaming, it is possible for the meditating subject to carry out the exercise of doubting his own actuality. The first moment (which defines the test): I remember having dreamt what I currently perceive as my actuality. Second moment (which seems for an instant to invalidate the test): the movement that I make in the very instant of my meditation to know if I am sleeping, seems to have the clarity and distinctiveness of waking. The third moment (which validates the test): I remember not only the images of my dream, but their clarity, which is equal to that of my actual impressions. The fourth moment (which concludes the test): at the same time I *see manifestly* that there is no certain mark to allow a distinction between

dreaming and reality; *and* I no longer know, in this precise moment, *so astonished* am I, if I am in the process of dreaming or not. These two sides of the successful test (an uncertain stupor and a manifest vision) constitute very well the subject as *effectively doubting* his own actuality, and as *validly continuing a meditation* which disregards all that which is not manifest truth. The two qualifications (doubting everything that comes from the senses, and validly meditating) are carried out in reality. The syllogism had required their simultaneous enactment: the consciousness of actuality of the meditating subject was an obstacle to the accomplishment of that requirement. The attempt to follow the example of the mad had confirmed that incompatibility; on the other hand the effort to actualise the vividness of dreaming showed that that incompatibility was not insurmountable. And the meditating subject finds himself a doubting subject at the issue of two tests that are opposed to each other: the one that composed the subject as reasonable (as opposed to the disqualified madman), and the other that constituted the subject as doubting (in the indistinction of dreaming and wakefulness).

Once this qualification of the subject is at last acquired (*Age somniemus*), the systematic discursivity will then be able once more to intersect with the discourse of the exercise and take the upper hand, to begin to call intelligible truths into question, until a new ascetic moment constitutes the subject as threatened by falling into the universal error by the 'great deceiver'. But even in that moment of the meditation, the qualification of 'non-mad' (like the qualification of 'possible dreamer') will remain valid.

*

It seems to me that Derrida felt, vividly and in depth, that this passage on madness had a unique place in the development in the *Meditations*. And he transcribes this feeling in his text, at the very moment he is trying to master it.

1. To explain the discussion of madness here, and at this particular point of the *Meditations*, Derrida invents an alternation of voices which would displace, push to the exterior and banish from the text itself the difficult exclamation: 'Mais quoi, ce sont des fous'.

Derrida found himself faced with a difficult problem here. If it is the case, as he supposes, that the whole movement of the First Meditation operates a generalisation of doubt, why should it stop, even if only for a moment, at madness or even at dreaming? Why take pains to demonstrate that vivid and immediate sensations are no less doubtful than the faintest and most distant ones, when it has been established, *in a general manner*, that one should not trust what comes from the senses? Why this detour via a particular point of my body, this paper, this fire, why a detour through the singular deceptions of madness and dream?

Derrida gave this inflection the status of a rupture. He imagined a foreign intervention, the scruple or reticence of a simpleton worried by the movement that surrounds him, and who fights a reargued action at the last minute. No sooner has Descartes said that the senses cannot be trusted, than a voice protests, that of a peasant who is a stranger to any philosophical urbanity; in his simple manner, he would like to breach or at least to limit the thinker's resolve: 'I am willing to let you doubt certain sensory perceptions concerning 'things which are hardly perceptible, or very far away', but . . . that you are in this place, sitting by the fire, speaking thus, this paper in your hands and other seeming certainties ',[14] one would have to be mad to doubt them, or more exactly, only madmen can commit errors regarding things that are so certain. And mad is one thing that I most certainly am not. At that point Descartes takes over again, and says to this rustic, to this stubborn person: yes, I am happy to admit that you are not mad, as you are resolved not to be so; but you should remember that you dream every night, and that your nightly dreams are no less mad than this madness that you are refusing. And the naïve reticence of the objector who cannot doubt the existence of his own body because he does not want to be mad would be conquered by the example of the dream, which is so much 'more natural', 'more common', 'more universal'.

Derrida's hypothesis is seductive. It solves his problem most neatly, showing that the philosopher goes straight to the questioning of the 'totality of beings'[15] and that the philosophical form and mark of his method is to be found precisely here: if it is the case that he stops for a moment at a 'Being' as singular as madness, it can only be because some naïve person has tugged his sleeve and posed the question; of his own accord, he would never have lingered on these stories of naked kings and water jugs. In this way, the rejection of madness, the abrupt exclamation 'mais quoi, ce sont des fous', are themselves rejected by Derrida and three times confined *outside* the philosophical discourse: because it is another subject who is speaking (no longer the philosopher of the *Meditations*, but this gruff-voiced objector); because it speaks from a place which is that of nonphilosophical naïvety; and because the philosopher then begins to speak again, and by quoting the 'stronger' and 'more convincing' example of the dream, disarms the objection and imposes something much worse than madness on the person who refuses it.

But we can now see the price that Derrida must pay for his clever hypothesis. The omission of a certain number of *literal* elements (which appear as soon as one makes the effort to compare the Latin text and the French translation); the elision of *textual* differences (the whole play of semantic and grammatical oppositions between the paragraph on dreaming and the paragraph on madness); finally, and above all, the effacing of the essential *discursive* determination (the double weave of the exercise and the demonstration). Curiously, Derrida, by imagining this other objecting and naïve voice behind Descartes' writing, has swept away all the differences in the text; or rather, by effacing all these differences, by bringing together so closely the test of madness and the test of dreaming, making the one a pale and failed draft of the other, and by reabsorbing the insufficiency of the first in the universality of the second, Derrida was pursuing the Cartesian exclusion. The meditating subject, for Descartes, was to exclude madness by qualifying himself as not mad. But that exclusion in its turn is perhaps too dangerous for Derrida: no longer because of the disqualification with which it risks tarring the philosophising subject, but by the qualification with which it would mark the philosophical discourse; it would thus determine it as 'other' than the mad discourse, it would establish between them a relation of exteriority, and it would force philosophical discourse into the 'other side', into the pure presumption of not being mad. A division, an exteriority and a determination that the discourse of the philosopher must be spared if it is to be the 'project of exceeding every finite and determined totality'. It is therefore necessary to exclude, because it is determining, this Cartesian exclusion. And to do this, Derrida, as we can see, is obliged to carry out three operations: to affirm, against the whole visible economy of the text, that the power of doubt proper to madness is included, *a fortiori*, in the dream; to imagine (to admit that it is, despite everything, a question of madness) that it is an other who excludes madness, on his own account and according to the diagonal of an objection; and finally to remove any philosophical status from this exclusion by denouncing its naïve rusticity. To turn the Cartesian exclusion into inclusion; to exclude the one who excludes by giving his discourse the status of an objection; to exclude the exclusion by rejecting it into pre-philosophical naïvety: Derrida needed all of that to master the Cartesian text, and to reduce to nothing the question of madness. We can see the results: the elision of the differences in the text and the compensatory invention of a difference of voices lead the Cartesian exclusion to a second level; in the end, it is excluded that philosophical discourse should exclude madness.

2. But perhaps madness does not allow itself to be reduced in this fashion. If we suppose that Descartes 'did not speak' of madness, there in his text where it is a question of *insani* and *dementes*, if we suppose that he made way for a moment for a rustic to raise such a clumsy question, could we not say that he proceeded, although in an insidious and silent manner, towards the exclusion of madness?

Could we not say that, in fact and constantly, he avoided the question of madness?

To this objection Derrida replies in advance: the risk of madness is indeed well and truly confronted by Descartes, not as you claim in a prior and almost marginal manner, regarding some business with water jugs and naked kings, but at the very heart of his philosophical enterprise; there precisely where his discourse, wrenching itself away from natural considerations about errors of the senses or swellings of the brain, takes, in the hyperbolic doubt and the hypothesis of the evil genius, its most radical dimension. It is precisely there that madness is put to the test and confronted; with the evil genius, I suppose I am deceived even more radically than those who believe they have a body made of glass; I go as far as to persuade myself that perhaps 2 and 3 do not make 5; then, with the Cogito, I reach that extreme point, that excess in relation to all determination, which allows me to say that mad or not, deceived or not, I am. The evil genius would be the point where philosophy single-handedly, and in the excess which is its own, risked madness; and the Cogito, the moment when madness disappeared (not at all because it was excluded, but because its determination in the face of reason would cease to be relevant). In no way, according to Derrida, should one attach too much importance to the farce of the peasant who interrupts at the beginning of the text, with his village idiots; despite their caps and bells, they would never manage to raise the issue of madness. On the other hand, all the threats of Unreason would play beneath the incarnations, which are so much more worrying and dark, of the evil genius. Equally, the taking up again by dreams of the worst eccentricities of the madmen would be, at the beginning of the text, an easy victory; on the other hand, after the great maddening that is the evil genius, what is required is nothing less than the point of the Cogito (and its excess on the 'totality of beings') for the determinations of madness and reason to appear as not radical. The great solemn theatre of the universal deceiver and the 'I think' would repeat, but this time in philosophical radicality, the still-natural fable of the madman [*dement*] and the sleeper.

For such an interpretation, Derrida needed first of all to deny that madness was in question in the place where it was named (and in specific terms, carefully differentiated), then he needed to demonstrate that it is in question in the place in which it is not named. Derrida operates this demonstration by two series of semantic derivations. Let's recall them:

Evil genius: 'total madness', 'a total maddening', 'disorder of the body' and 'subversion of pure thought', 'eccentricity', 'a maddening I am unable to master'.

Cogito: 'mad audacity', 'mad project', 'project that recognises madness as its liberty', 'disorder and excess of hyperbole', 'unheard of and unique excess', 'excess towards Nothingness and Infinity', 'hyperbolic extreme which should be, like all pure madness in general, silent'.

All these derivations are necessary surrounding Descartes' text for the evil genius and the Cogito to become, as Derrida wishes, the true scene of the confrontation with madness. But even more is required: it is necessary to remove from Descartes' texts themselves everything which shows that the episode of the evil genius is a voluntary exercise, controlled, mastered and carried out from beginning to end by a meditating subject who never allows himself to be surprised. If it is true that the hypothesis of the evil genius pushes the suspicion of error well beyond the errors of the senses, of which certain madmen provide the example, the person who makes this fiction (and by the very fact that he voluntarily performs it as an exercise) escapes the risk of 'assenting to any falsehoods', as is the case and the misfortune of the mad. He is deceived, but he is not imposed upon. Everything is perhaps illusion, but with no credulity. The evil genius, no doubt, deceives more effectively than a swollen brain; he can conjure up the illusory backdrop of madness, but he is something quite different from madness. It could even be said that he is its contrary: in madness *I believe* that an illusory robe covers my nudity and my poverty, whereas the hypothesis of the evil genius allows *me not to believe* that this body and these hands exist. As for the scope of the trap, the evil genius, it is true, differs not from madness; but regarding the positioning of the subject in relation to the trap, the evil genius and madness are rigorously opposed. The evil genius takes over the power of *madness*, but only after the exercise of the meditation has excluded the risk of *being mad*.

Let us return to Descartes' text. 'I shall think that the sky, the earth, colours, shapes, sounds and all external things are merely the delusions of dreams' (whereas the madman believes that his illusions and dreams really are the sky, the air and external things). 'I shall consider myself as not having hands or eyes . . . but as falsely believing that I have all these things' (whereas the madman wrongly believes that his body is made of glass, but *does not* consider himself to be believing it wrongly). 'I shall at least do what is in my power, that is, resolutely guard against assenting to any falsehoods' (whereas the madman assents to them all).

We can now see quite clearly: when faced with the cunning deceiver, the meditating subject behaves not at all like a madman ruled by universal error, but like an adversary who is no less cunning and always on the lookout, constantly reasonable, remaining in the position of a master in relation to his fiction: 'I shall resolutely guard against assenting to any falsehoods, so that the deceiver, however cunning or powerful he might be, will be unable to impose upon me in the slightest degree.' How far we are from the themes so prettily varied by Derrida: 'Total madness, a total maddening *I would be unable to master*, since it was *inflicted* upon me by hypothesis and *I am not responsible for it*.' How could it be imagined that the meditating subject was no longer responsible for what he himself terms 'this arduous undertaking'?

*

It might well be asked how an author as meticulous as Derrida, and one so attentive to texts, managed not only to allow so many omissions, but also to operate so many displacements, interventions and substitutions. But perhaps we should do that while remembering that Derrida is recalling an old tradition in his reading. He is well aware of this, of course; and this faithfulness seems, quite rightly, to comfort him. He is reluctant, in any case, to think that classical commentators missed, through inattentiveness, the importance and singularity of the passage on madness and dreaming.

I am in agreement on one fact at least: that it was not at all on account of their inattentiveness that classical scholars omitted, before Derrida and like him, this passage from Descartes. It is part of a system, a system of which Derrida is today the most decisive representative, in its waning light: a reduction of discursive practices to textual traces; the elision of events that are produced there, leaving only marks for a reading; the invention of voices behind the text, so as not to have to examine the modes of implication of the subject in discourses; the assignation of the originary as said and not-said in the text in order to avoid situating discursive practices in the field of transformation where they are carried out.

I would not say that it is a metaphysics, metaphysics *itself*, or its closure, that is hiding behind this 'textualisation' of discursive practices. I would go much further: I would say that it is a historically well-determined little pedagogy, which manifests itself here in a very visible manner. A pedagogy which teaches the student that there is nothing outside the text, but that in it, in its interstices, in its blanks and silences, the reserve of the origin reigns; that it is never necessary to look beyond it, but that here, not in the words of course, but in the words as crossings-out, in their *lattice*, what is said is 'the meaning of being'. A pedagogy that inversely gives to the voice of the masters that unlimited sovereignty that allows it indefinitely to re-say the text.

Father Bourdin[16] supposed that, according to Descartes, it was not at all possible to doubt things that were certain, even if one was asleep or mad. In relation to a well-founded certainty, the fact of dreaming or being delirious was not at all relevant. But Descartes replied to this interpretation in a quite explicit manner. 'I have no recollection of having said any such thing, nor even dreamt it while sleeping.' Quite so: nothing that is perceived clearly and distinctly can be untrue (and on that level, the problem of knowing whether or not the person conceiving is dreaming or delirious does not need to be asked). But, Descartes immediately adds, who then can distinguish 'that which is clearly conceived, and that which merely seems and appears to be so'? Who then, as a thinking and meditating subject, can know if he knows clearly or not? Who then is capable of not deluding himself about his own certainty, and not letting himself be impressed? If not precisely those who are not mad? Those who are 'wise'? And Descartes retorts, targeting Father Bourdin, 'But as it is clearly only people who are wise who can distinguish between that which is clearly conceived, and that which merely seems and appears to be so, I am not surprised that the good man takes the one for the other.'

NOTES

1. TN. In this text Foucault mostly refers to the *Méditations métaphysiques*, the French translation (by the Duc de Luynes) of *Renati Descartes Mediationes de prima philosophia in qua Dei existentia et animæ immortalitas demonstrator* (Paris, 1641) read and approved by Descartes. This translation is sometimes significantly different from the Latin text. Quotes here are therefore translated from the French, with the standard English translation from the original Latin text (*The Philosophical Writings of Descartes*, vol. 2, trans. John Cottingham, Robert Stoothoff and Dugald Murdoch (Cambridge: Cambridge University Press, 1984)) given in the footnotes.
2. Jacques Derrida, '*Cogito* et *Histoire de la Folie*', in *L'Écriture et la difference* (Paris: Seuil, 1967), pp. 61–97, translated as 'Cogito and the History of Madness', in *Writing and Difference*, trans. Alan Bass (Chicago: University of Chicago Press, 1980), pp. 31–63.
3. [Derrida's note] *Madness, theme or index:* what is significant is that Descartes, at bottom, never speaks of madness itself in this text. Madness is not his theme. He treats it as the index of a question of principle, that is, of epistemological value. It will be said, perhaps, that this is the sign of a profound exclusion. But this silence on madness itself simultaneously signifies the opposite of an exclusion, since *it is not a question of madness* in this text, if only to exclude it. It is not in the *Meditations* that Descartes speaks of madness itself.
4. '[F]irmly maintain they are kings'. Descartes, 'First Meditation', in *The Philosophical Writings of Descartes*, vol. 2, p. 13 (AT, IX, 14).
5. 'A brilliant piece of reasoning! As if I were not a man who sleeps at night, and regularly has all the same experiences while asleep as madmen do when awake – indeed sometimes even more improbable ones.'
6. 'A man who sleeps at night, and regularly has all the same experiences', 'how often, asleep at night, am I convinced of just such familiar events', 'this would not happen . . . to someone asleep', 'As if I did not remember other occasions when I have been tricked by similar thoughts while asleep.'
7. I employ the term paragraph out of convenience, amusement and faithfulness to Derrida. Derrida says, in a picturesque and rather amusing manner, 'Descartes va à ligne' – Descartes starts a new paragraph. Whereas we know very well that this is not the case.
8. TN. 'But such people are insane, and I would be thought equally mad if I took anything from them as a model for myself.' Descartes' text in French begins with an interjection: 'Mais quoi? Ce sont de fous, et je ne serais pas moins extravagant si je me réglais sur les exemples.' At issue is the colloquial interjection, 'Mais quoi', rendered here as 'But so what?', but absent from the Latin original.
9. 'A man who regularly has the same experiences', 'how often am I convinced', 'as if I did not remember'.

10. TN. In French, *épreuve*, importantly, has two meanings: not just a tool for verification, but also a difficult experience undergone by the subject.
11. 'I would be thought equally mad if I took anything from their example.'
12. 'A brilliant piece of reasoning!' In French, *Toutefois*.
13. TN. Foucault takes Derrida's text literally here, assuming that 'question de droit' has only a juridical meaning (hence its translation here as 'point of law'), whereas Derrida uses the phrase in the Kantian sense of a question of principle (as opposed to an empirical one).
14. I am quoting Derrida. As we know, in Descartes' text, these things, which it is so difficult to doubt, are not characterised by their 'nature', but by their proximity and their vividness. By their relation to the meditating subject.
15. TN. In French, *Etantité* – the Heideggerian characteristic of being a specific being.
16. TN. Pierre Bourdin, a Jesuit priest whose objections to Descartes were included in the second (1642) edition (in Latin) of the *Meditationes*.

CHAPTER 4

'But Such People Are Insane': On a Disputed Passage from the First Meditation

Jean-Marie Beyssade
Translated by Christopher Penfield

In the first edition of his *History of Madness*,[1] Michel Foucault offered an original interpretation of the comparison established between sensible knowledge and the visions of the madman in the First Meditation.[2] He reconstructed there a speculative echo of what was, historically, 'the great confinement' of the mad, the philosophical text manifesting in an exemplary way the attitude of the classical age towards madness: reduced to silence 'by a strange *coup de force*', madness would cease to concern the man of reason, no longer having anything to teach him.

However interesting the light thus shed on a mental attitude may be, this reading drew the admonition of Jacques Derrida in *Writing and Difference*:[3] 'When one attempts, in a general way, to pass from an obvious to a latent language, one must first be rigorously sure of the obvious meaning' (WD, 38). What is, in this case, the *obvious* meaning of the *Meditations*? Derrida's monition is, in fact, a call to order, a call to the *order of reasons* (WD, 64 n.20): it consists in establishing that the episode of madness, dismissed without explanation after having been summoned to testify against natural opinions, does not signify a fundamental and decisive exclusion since, according to the order, Descartes will later assume the risk of an even greater madness. Now, if Foucault had once agreed to orient his reading by the order of reasons in so far as he had undertaken to reconstitute, with as much acuity as brevity, a new organisation of the Cartesian reasons for doubt, his long response to Derrida in the second edition of his book[4] dissociates the 'double web of exercise and demonstration' within the meditation in order to render its 'essential *discursive* determination' (AME, 412). Suffice it to say, this is the interest, for a historian of Cartesian philosophy little accustomed today to such feasts, of a discussion that was not at first strictly historical, between two philosophers who from the beginning did not take themselves to be enclosed within the history of philosophy.

In order to assess the significance of the reading proposed by Foucault, we will have to revisit some commonly accepted principles in the history of philosophy about Descartes. For, taken as a set of theses, Foucault's reading would seem to call for the kind of correctives that, in Derrida's critique, restrict the former's significance to the point of cancelling it entirely. However, perhaps Foucault's reading should not be transformed into a set of theses: it would then enable the disturbance of a certain dogmatism of order, helping in particular to bring out a specificity of the First Meditation and, more generally, to establish that the order of reasons is not a universal instrument for analysing Descartes' texts.

1.

Let us first present the classic event as seen by Foucault, followed by the reading he proposes of the First Meditation.

'Between Montaigne and Descartes an event has taken place': 'Madness has been banished' (HM, 47), 'is no longer a peril lurking in the domain where the thinking subject holds rights over truth' (HM, 46). This event causes a double mutation: in the relations of madness with reason and the rational project to reach the truth; and in the relations of madness with dreams and error, which also serve as obstacles for this rational project.

In the sixteenth century, typified here by the name of Montaigne, madness had not been banished: the experience is 'familiar to the Renaissance – unreasonable Reason, or reasoned Unreason' (HM, 47); 'madness traces what was still in the sixteenth century one of the most commonly taken paths of doubt'; in short, 'man was . . . never sure that he was not mad' (HM, 46). By contrast, in the seventeenth century, 'the danger has been excluded'. A dividing line is now drawn: madness closes in on itself, and even as a thought experiment it is excluded from the rational project of truth, for 'it would be an eccentricity to suppose oneself eccentric' (HM, 46, translation slightly modified). Reason 'rules a domain where the only possible enemies are errors and illusions' (HM, 46), expelling madness outside the self. Having become estranged from 'a subject seeking the truth' (HM, 47), madness can no longer pose 'a threat to the link between subjectivity and truth' (HM, 46); it no longer has a place along the path of doubt.

At the same time, the relations of madness with error and dreams were modified. In the sixteenth century, madness was situated '[a]mongst all other forms of illusion' (HM, 46), and no difference in kind separated it from them. In the seventeenth century, 'there is a fundamental disequilibrium between on the one hand madness, and dreams and error on the other' (HM, 45). But here we come to the text on the First Meditation, where the strange coup of the classical period would reduce to silence the madness whose voices the Renaissance had freed.

For ease of discussion, we will consider as one thesis the text that Foucault devoted to Descartes in 1961 (HM, 44–7) and that he republished without altering, taking the appendix from 1972 as it is given, namely, as an effort to 'confront' Derrida's 'remarkable' critique (AME, 395) and to resolve 'Derrida's objection to this thesis' (AME, 393). And we will reduce this thesis of Foucault's, this reading of Descartes, to several propositions, which we take the liberty of separating and numbering.

1. 'On the methodical path of his doubt, Descartes came across madness alongside dreams and all the other forms of error' (HM, 44, translation slightly modified).
2. 'Might the possibility of his own madness rob him of his own body, in the manner in which the outside world occasionally disappears through an error of the senses, or in which consciousness sleeps while we dream?' (HM, 44).
3. 'In the economy of doubt, there is a fundamental disequilibrium between on the one hand madness, and dreams and errors on the other' (HM, 45).
4. 'However deceptive they might be, the senses can only alter "things that are barely perceptible, or at a great distance", and however strong the illusion, there is still a residue of truth assuring him that he is "sitting by the fire, wearing a dressing gown"' (HM, 44–5).[5]
5. Since the dream can 'never create "simpler or more universal things" that make fantastical images possible' (HM, 45), the force of its illusions also leaves behind a residue of truth, these simple natures that are 'so slight that they lend dreams their verisimilitude, and . . . are the inevitable marks of a truth that dreams themselves can never undo' (HM, 45).
6. Accordingly, 'neither sleep peopled with images nor the clear consciousness that the senses are deceived can lead doubt to its most universal point': in one case as in the other, 'the truth will never slip away entirely into darkness' (HM, 45).
7. 'Madness is an altogether different affair': 'It is not the permanence of truth that ensures that thought is not madness, in the way that it freed it from an error of perception or a dream' (HM, 45). Taken by itself, this latter formula could be understood in a weak sense: madness perhaps lets subsist some residue of truth, but Descartes takes no interest in it and chooses a different way to avoid the peril of madness. Situated alongside the former formula, it must be understood in a strong sense: madness, such as Descartes and the classical period represent it, allows no residue of truth to subsist, so that the meditating subject need only suppose himself mad in order to disqualify himself in his own eyes and dissolve his project of truth; in short, 'as a way of thinking, madness implies itself, and thus excludes itself from his project' (HM, 46). It is the strong sense that we will discuss here.
8. Because the impossibility of being mad is 'inherent in the thinking subject rather than the object of his thoughts', 'madness is simply excluded by the doubting subject' (HM, 45). Thus, even before what is called the Cogito, a first decision is made; madness is excluded by the doubting subject 'in the same manner that it will soon be excluded that he is not thinking or that he does not exist' (HM, 45). This exclusion is necessarily tied to the act of thinking: 'While *man* can still go mad, *thought*, as the sovereign exercise carried out by a subject seeking the truth, can no longer be devoid of reason' (HM, 47). But this first decision concerns the body, since in rejecting madness the meditating subject decides that he holds, with his belief in having a body, a 'grasp on the truth [that] is stronger than that of the man who believes his body to be made of glass' (HM, 45).

These propositions constitute a set the coherence of which is manifest and the originality, seductive. But we would now like to test its truth or, more precisely, its fidelity to the metaphysical thought of Descartes.

II.

Taken as so many *theses*, which would fall under the history of philosophy, the propositions identified all seem inaccurate or excessive, or in some cases even inadmissible in so far as they formally contradict Descartes' texts. Yet we do not always manage to agree with Derrida against Foucault, or rather with Derrida's reasons, his *counter-theses*. The quality of the debate, leading us each time towards a kind of margin of incertitude, might well succeed in shaking some of the beliefs of the historian of Cartesian philosophy.

1. It is not enough to say that, on the path of doubt, Descartes encounters madness *alongside* the dream and all the other forms of error. '[T]he expression *alongside* is Foucault's', as Derrida notes (WD, 55); Foucault is doubtless fond of the expression, which again appears in his appendix: 'It is in order to reply to this question that two examples are called on, one alongside the other, both of which force one to call into doubt the subject's system of actuality' (AME, 408, translation slightly modified). But Descartes encounters madness over the course of doubting, in the progress of doubting, at a certain moment of this progress: the expression *alongside* misses the importance of this chronological order.

'Whatever I have up till now accepted as most true I have acquired either from the senses or through the senses' (CSM II, 18, l. 15–16). Does this mean that madness, summoned thusly (and dismissed quickly) concerning 'certain areas of sensory perception' (WD, 61), is thereby declared insignificant as regards the forms of knowledge proper to the pure understanding? For example, does madness pose no threat to geometric certainty? Derrida would gladly think so, knowing already that mathematical truths are 'of nonsensory origin' (WD, 55), that the simple things uncompromised by the dream hypothesis are 'intelligible' (WD, 58, 59, 60), and that the foundations laid bare by this hypothesis are 'intellectual' (WD, 61). And he is perfectly right, since the Fifth Meditation asserts the nonsensory origin of geometric figures (CSM II, 64–5); since the *Principles of Philosophy* exposes the doubt by dissociating the truth of 'things that can be perceived by the senses' (CSM I, 4) and 'mathematical demonstrations' (CSM I, 5); and since the 'Conversation with Burman' interprets in this sense the disjunction of our text, *from the senses or through the senses, vel a sensibus vel per sensus* (CSM III, 146). Or rather, he is only wrong for having been right too early, for the reader of the First Meditation does not yet know anything of all that, remaining ignorant that sensibility is only '[o]ne of these fragile foundations of knowledge' (the expression *one of* is Derrida's, WD, 54). The word *understanding* had not yet been pronounced and will not be at any point in this Meditation.

At a time when the senses are taken to be *the* foundation of our forms of knowledge, madness is not encountered alongside something else; rather, it is summoned, before or after other witnesses falling under the general heading of *reasons for doubt*, for a confrontation, here named comparison, *comparem* (CSM II, 18, l. 26). In order to cast doubt on opinions, reasons for doubting are summoned to testify in turn, and the procedure follows this strange rule – to which we will henceforth refer as the rule of hyperbole, since it renders Cartesian doubt hyperbolic, that is, excessive – that any questionable opinion be deemed false since it has not been proven to be indubitable. Certainly, madness appears alongside dreams and all the forms of error in the classical list of reasons for doubt. Descartes and his interlocutors, Hobbes ('Third Set of Objections', CSM II, 171) or Father Bourdin ('Seventh Set of Objections', CSM II, 469, l. 17–21), were perfectly aware of it; the historian of philosophy would add only that a deceiving God and evil genius are less common and less ruminated upon by the sceptics and academics. But, on the path of Cartesian doubt, what is properly Cartesian is the order of summons. Madness is summoned *after* sensory error (CSM II, 18, l. 16ff) and *before* dreams (CSM II, 19, l. 8ff), at a moment when the one who inquires has not yet hit upon the originality of things that are simple and general, or the originality of the mathematical sciences that study them.

We must therefore determine the significance of the chronological order, without either effacing it as Foucault does by an *alongside* . . . , or converting it as Derrida does into a hierarchy among kinds of knowledge: it authorises both of these readings without either one quite managing to forbid the other.

2. Should we oppose, with Foucault, among the things cast into doubt, my body (of which I would be dispossessed by the possibility of madness), the external world (which would slip away into error), and consciousness (which would slumber in the dream)? This tripartite distinction risks doing violence to the first Cartesian division, between 'objects which are very small or in the distance' (CSM II, 18, l. 19–20) and 'particulars' (*particularia ista*, CSM II, 19, l. 23), which are also very common (*usuata ista*, CSM II, 19, l. 11) or, as it will later be put, quotidian (*quae mihi quotidie a sensibus exhibentur*, CSM II, 89, l. 18). This division is the only one known to the First Meditation, since the dream hypothesis did not bring to light mathematical things, utterly simple and utterly general, and the boundary between error and madness passes through the sense data of the body proper (for there are errors at the level of internal senses, and the amputee is not mad despite being mistaken about his own body, CSM II, 77, l. 1–7) as well as through the representations of the external world (since, in the residue of the *particularia*, near objects are not disconnected from the body proper, the paper from the hands that hold it, the clothes from the body that wears them, CSM II, 18, l. 23–4; 19, l. 3 and l. 12).

Behind the misleading tripartite division into qualitatively heterogeneous regions, we must locate a division, fragile perhaps and provisional, between degrees of intensity. The weak (very small) and the distant are opposed to everyday certitudes, the proximity of which (marked in the Cartesian text by the demonstrative, CSM II, 18, l. 22–5; 19, l. 13–16; and again 30, l. 8 for 'this piece of wax') assures the commonality of nature, *et similia* (CSM II, 18, l. 24). This commonality of nature manifests itself in their common resistance to the doubt motivated by sensory error: about these everyday certitudes, perhaps,[6] one cannot doubt, cannot at all (*plane*, CSM II, 18, l. 21) doubt, or at least cannot *reasonably* doubt (as in the French edition, AT IX, 14).

3. In the economy of Cartesian doubt, there is a fundamental equilibrium between dreams and madness, and a disequilibrium between sensory error on the one hand, and dreams and madness on the other. Sensory errors let subsist a residue of truth, my everyday certitudes. We will have to return to the status of this resistance, which

is as much objection or restriction in the order of the demonstration and system, as it is reticence or impossibility in the order of the exercise and ascetic discursivity: it is the same sense of *forte* that we have just noted. The fact remains that in order to cast into doubt my everyday certitudes, I need stronger reasons: madness and dreams are summoned to this end, 'one alongside the other', as Foucault says (AME, 408, translation slightly modified) – this is why we speak of a fundamental equilibrium – but they will also meet with such different success that one can equally speak with Foucault of disequilibrium. Let us resume.

'[H]ow could it be denied that these hands or this whole body are mine?' (CSM II, 18, l. 24–5): here are the everyday certitudes that withstand their confrontation with sensory error and, of this sensory error, are never again a question. 'Unless perhaps[7] I were to liken myself to madmen' (CSM II, 18, l. 26): they are sure they are dressed in gold and purple despite being completely naked; why should I not be completely naked when I believe myself clothed? The comparison would permit me perhaps to give up my everyday certitudes. But the testimony of the madman is rejected and the comparison refused (CSM II, 19, l. 5–7). By the end of this second test, everyday certitudes thus retain their lustre unaltered. I invoke against them, then, a new reason for doubt, the imposture of dreams: though I am not mad, I am human, and I am accustomed to dreaming; 'How often, asleep at night, am I convinced of just such familiar events – that I am here in my dressing-gown, sitting by the fire – when in fact I am lying undressed in bed' (CSM II, 19, l. 11–13). The comparison is more welcome this time – after several vicissitudes to which we will return. It almost succeeds in compelling me to give up my everyday certitudes: 'The result is that I begin to feel dazed, and this very feeling only reinforces the notion that I may be asleep' (CSM II, 19, l. 21–2). The rule of hyperbole effaces the restriction of *may be*: 'Suppose then that I am dreaming' (CSM II, 19, l. 23). Only then arise, in their privileged resistance, the utterly simple and utterly general mathematical objects, of which it had not previously been a question, and which alone are 'real and exist' (*vera esse*, CSM II, 20, l. 11).

Descartes' project thus concerns 'all the images of things . . . that occur in our thought', obeying the rule developed by sceptics and academics[8] to discredit those which are 'true and real' by establishing that they are indiscernible from the 'fictitious and unreal'; and the doubt is provisionally defeated by the simple natures, 'the real colours from which we form all the images of things' (CSM II, 20, l. 12–14). The simple natures demand recourse to a new reason for doubt, which would constitute a second stage in the doubt, dedicated to the deceiver God, or more exactly to the author (still unknown) of my being. In the first stage, which is all that concerns us at the moment, the genus that Descartes calls fictitious and unreal, false, *falsae* (CSM II, 20, l. 13) indifferently gathers together the fictions of dreams and the phantasms of delirium. Foucault's thesis had motivated Derrida's counter-thesis: 'The reference to dreams is therefore not put off to one side – quite the contrary – in relation to a madness potentially respected or even excluded by Descartes' (WD, 61). *Quite the contrary* a bit disquieting, which invites one to think that madness 'does not cover the *totality* of the field of sensory perception' (WD, 62), that the dream is 'a more common, and more universal experience than that of madness'

(WD, 61), and, finally, that madness is 'much less serious' (WD, 62): this would be to forget that Descartes reaches the worlds (of waking, madness, or dreams) only through the particularity of images that he compares, and to bestow upon dreams a privilege they do not have in favour of the language of totality and universality. But Foucault is, on this point, even more illuminating in his response, excellently recognising that 'everything that madness (the example I have just left to one side) could make me doubt can also be rendered uncertain by dreams. In their power to make uncertain, dreams are not outdone by madness' (AME, 395–6). And it is indeed extremely difficult to remain deaf to the echo made by the compared images, notwithstanding some insignificant thematic differences: the same example is systematically reused in the three cases, that of nudity and clothing. To be wearing a robe is an everyday certitude that withstands its confrontation with sensory error; that would be shaken (if I were to accept the comparison) by the example of the madmen who believe themselves clothed in gold and purple despite being completely naked; and that finally comes to ruin in the memory I have of having often believed, while dreaming, that I was clothed when I was completely naked in my bed. We do not claim the competency to interpret the latent meaning of this example, but it will be enough to lay claim to the obvious meaning: dreams and madness are, regarding the thematic of their images, in profound agreement, since they mimic (in the element of the false) the same everyday certitudes and counterfeit equally what Foucault calls 'the actuality of the meditating subject' (AME, 408).

It is thus unnecessary to appeal to texts that would establish, in the Cartesian system of science, the profound kinship of dreams and madness: in the economy of doubt, an appeal to dreams and an appeal to madness have the same function, and, in a sense, their images are equivalent.

4. Against the doubt motivated by sensory errors, certain certitudes perhaps resist. What significance is acknowledged by this *perhaps*, *forte* (CSM II, 18, l. 19)? For Derrida, it would signal in advance that the reticence (of the subject who doubts) and the restriction (in the extension of doubt) are only 'the astonishment and objections of the nonphilosopher, of the novice in philosophy who is frightened by this doubt and protests', by contrast to 'Descartes' final, definitive thought', which 'feigns to rest in this natural comfort in order better, more radically and more definitively, to unsettle himself from it and to discomfort his interlocutor' (WD, 60–1, translation slightly modified). Yet the reserve has a foundation, according to the final thought of Descartes, since the senses rediscover a truth value under the supervision of the superior faculties and in the majority of cases; in lifting the hyperbolic doubts, the Sixth Meditation will re-establish a division within sensible forms of knowledge: 'I should not have any further fears about the falsity of what my senses tell me every day, *quotidie*' (CSM II, 89, l. 17–18). More importantly, however, we must ask whether or not the intellectual exercise of the meditation authorises us to distinguish a plurality of voices in the Cartesian text. What warrants us to attribute the resistance of everyday certitudes to some unknown 'peasant foreign to all philosophical urbanity', and to oppose this 'scarcely refined voice' to the thought of the philosopher? Providing the First Meditation with an invaluable doublet, an unfinished and undated dialogue by Descartes, *The Search for Truth*, allows a response

to be given to Foucault's question (AME, 411–2) by analysing what he calls 'the modes of implication of the subject in discourses' (AME, 416). For, in this dialogue, Polyander, who 'has never studied at all', is doubtless a novice in philosophy, but he is also 'among the most outstanding and inquiring [minds] of our time' (CSM II, 498–9). Now, it is he who addresses to Eudoxus, Descartes' representative, the very objection whose status is presently under discussion, namely, that sensory error does not suffice to discredit 'everything which ordinarily appears to my senses' (CSM II, 510). But Eudoxus, faced with this objection, which is addressed to him externally, is obliging enough to adopt it: 'So if I wish to make you fear that the senses are deceptive on occasions when you are unaware of the deception, it is not enough for me to tell you that the senses deceive you on certain occasions when you perceive the deception. I shall have to go further' (CSM II, 511). *Go further* means to search for other, stronger reasons for doubt; and the Cartesian *has to* (that is, is willing, consents to) take this detour demanded by the non-Cartesian. Let us return to the meditation, which ignores the distinction proper to the dialogue between the one who knows already and the one who is learning, and gather together the plurality of voices that the dialogue exteriorises. Many passages would remain unintelligible if this implicit plurality of voices were neglected, and, in particular, if it were forgotten that within everyone, while in the process of becoming Cartesian, a Polyander subsists and resists: hence the analysis of the piece of wax in the Second Meditation. At the moment of the path we are considering, it is impossible to enclose the plurality of voices in the straightjacket of a hierarchy: no 'final, definitive' thought would give the philosopher licence to judge the resistances that he encounters, so as to attribute them to a naïve objector and, for example, 'feign' to rest there.

The resistance of everyday certitudes is doubtless encountered by the philosopher and, in this sense, is exterior to his project. But he accepts it, provisionally; the *perhaps* signals this consent, this will that is more than a feigning, this willingness that already distances itself from a complete and spontaneous adherence. At this moment of the path, philosophy is reduced to this mode of implication in discourse, to this provisional consenting to dogmatic discourse.

5. The dream, which overcomes everyday certitudes, fails to undermine simple natures, which will later reveal themselves to be of nonsensory origin. In order to know whether or not the dream, as a reason for doubt, is set apart from the madness hypothesis, we must examine this residue of truth and the manner in which it is drawn out.

Foucault had formerly suggested that the true-seeming implies the true, and that the verisimilitude of dreams implies the persistence, even in the dream, of a certain truth and its inevitable marks, simple natures. However, from this point of view, the very text of the First Meditation precludes the claim that madness is more perilous than the dream: 'As if I were not a man who sleeps at night, and regularly has all the same experiences while asleep as madmen do when awake – indeed sometimes even more improbable ones' (CSM II, 19, l. 8–11). And Foucault himself admits in his reply that 'none of the demonstrative force of madness is lost by dreams when I need to convince myself of all that I must call into doubt' (AME, 396). In fact, nowhere does Descartes seek in the experience of the dreamer a specific characteristic of verisimilitude that would attest to a presence of truth, or to the truth. He finds, in the experience of the subject who doubts, certain truths that subsist even when one supposes oneself asleep, because these simple natures are the constitutive elements of all the images of things, fictitious and unreal as well as true and real.

Once again, a group of truths resists, and the philosopher accepts this resistance he encounters, for it motivates a pause and a refusal to doubt: 'It seems impossible that such transparent truths should incur any suspicion of being false' (CSM II, 20, l. 30–1). Once again, a *might* nuances the mode of implication of the philosophical subject in this profession of mathematical faith, and in the division made between what is dashed by the dream hypothesis and what *seems* indubitable: 'So a reasonable conclusion from this might be, *forsan*, that physics, astronomy, medicine, and all other disciplines which depend on the study of composite things, are doubtful; while arithmetic, geometry and other subjects of this kind . . . contain something certain and indubitable' (CSM II, 20, l. 20–7). Once again, the division, which will only be validated later and retrospectively, is accepted provisionally, motivating the passage to a new reason for doubt.

6. Whether it be motivated by dreams or sensory error, doubt leaves behind a residue of truth: sensible particulars in the one case, mathematical essences in the other. But these two kinds of evidence are not equivalent. In Descartes' metaphysics, doubt is a measuring instrument; a truth is clearer to the extent that it resists stronger reasons for doubting; and the graduated scale of doubts serves notably 'to show the firmness of the truths which I propound later on, in the light of the fact that they cannot be shaken by these metaphysical doubts' (*Third Set of Objections with the Author's Replies*, CSM II, 172). Doubt motivated by sensory error is weaker than doubt motivated by dreams, since the former fails before everyday certitudes; mathematical truths are clearer still, since they alone resist the strongest doubt. Thus, in the domain of sensible things, or rather, to avoid prematurely employing the category of the sensible, in the domain of composite things, dreams carry doubt to the extreme point of its universality, there where sensory error only motivates a limited doubt.

Foucault has very opportunely emphasised the structural analogy between two manners of doubting that generate two groups of truths, resistant and residual; yet it must not be forgotten that to the sequence of steps corresponds an inequality of degrees, and that the two residua of truth have clarity of differing intensity.

7. 'It is not the permanence of truth that ensures that thought is not madness' (HM, 45): in the First Meditation, assuredly. Must we conclude from this that no truth subsists for the madman, or for myself who doubts, if I suppose myself mad? That mathematical truths, even what is called the Cogito, collapse as soon as one supposes oneself mad? This thesis would imply, in Cartesian philosophy, that the madman is as really distinct from the soul, in the metaphysical sense of the formula, as the body itself. Madness would truly be, 'to use an expression proposed elsewhere by Foucault, confined to the interior of the exterior and to the exterior of the interior' (WD, 62). Derrida evades this disquieting consequence by postulating 'that a certainty invulnerable to dreams would be *a fortiori* invulnerable to perceptual illusions of the sensory kind' (WD, 58), and that mathematics and, even more so, what

is called the Cogito, which resist the dream hypothesis, resist *a fortiori* the madness hypothesis. Yet the entire difficulty is to be found in this *a fortiori*. When tests are effectively passed, one can say for example that mathematical truths, which in fact resist the dream hypothesis, resist *a fortiori* the doubt motivated by the experience of my errors. But can one equally say that the madness hypothesis, which fails to take away my sensory everyday certitudes, is *a fortiori* powerless before the truths of the understanding, such as mathematical truths or, what's more, metaphysical truths? In fact, in the First Meditation, the test was not passed, since madness was brusquely dismissed before the originality of mathematics had been remarked upon. Now, it is a common artifice in the judicial arts to trip up a bothersome witness before they can testify to whatever is essential. Foucault makes us suspicious, as regards Descartes and all *a fortiori* reasoning; we would like to know what madness's testimony would have been, if it had been less brusquely dismissed.

'For even though I might be dreaming, if there is anything which is evident to my intellect, *intellectu*, then it is wholly true' (CSM II, 71, l. 1–2). The exercise of the *dormiens*, to speak like Foucault, that is, the assumption that I am sleeping, does not affect the value of mathematics but, on the contrary, highlights its strength. This by no means suggests that mathematicians, in fact, are dreaming, or that dreamers, in fact, are capable of doing mathematics: 'I do not know what kind of analysis has enabled my supremely subtle critic to deduce this from my writings, for I do not remember ever having had such a thought, even in a dream' (*Seventh Set of Objections with the Author's Replies*, CSM II, 461, l. 17–21). Rather, the value of mathematical demonstration is not affected even if I assume I am sleeping. And when I assume I am mad? The exercise of the *demens*, if one consents to practise it, ends with exactly the same result: 'Admittedly he might have inferred from what I wrote that everything that anyone clearly and distinctly perceives is true, although the person in question may from time to time doubt whether he is dreaming or awake, and may even, if you like, be dreaming or mad, *quamvis sit delirus*' (CSM II, 461, l. 21–6). This by no means suggests that metaphysicians, in fact, are delirious, nor that the mad, in fact, are capable of doing mathematics or metaphysics; but only that the value of rational certainty is not at all affected even if I assume I am mad. For one must not, like Father Bourdin, starting from a catalogue of certitudes, proceed from 'things that are completely certain' to factual situations, and then ask oneself whether or not these certitudes, recognised as such by Descartes, are present to the minds of children, or to dreamers, or to the mad; rather, one must begin with the thought experiment, with the assumption that I am sleeping or that I am delirious, to see what kind of certainty emerges by withstanding the test of these assumptions.

The exercise of the *demens* therefore leaves behind the same residue of truth as the exercise of the *dormiens*. Or rather, it would do so if it were undertaken.

8. Yet it is not undertaken; the testimony of the madman, in the First Meditation, was abruptly refused. Important or secondary, the fact is indisputable. It serves as the point of departure for Foucault's reading, prevents us from reasoning *a fortiori*, and, since at the time it happens we have no 'definitive, final' science with which to judge it, compels us to pose the question: why is the voice of the madman, the

speech of the madman (since the Cartesian madman is not silent, cf. CSM II, 19, l. 2), neither understood nor even listened to?

'But such people are insane, and I would be thought equally mad if I took anything from them as a model for myself': the logical weakness and the cutting tone perfectly evoke bias and prejudice, the deep-rooted and discrete underside of clear, classical reason. Once again we will appeal to Eudoxus and *The Search for Truth* to elucidate for us the Cartesian meaning of this strange exclamation. 'To be sure, a good man would be indignant if you told him that his beliefs cannot have any more rational basis than theirs' (that is, those melancholics) 'since he relies, like them, on what the senses and imagination represent to him. But you cannot take it amiss if I ask whether you are not, like all men, liable to fall sleep' (CSM II, 511). The metaphysician is not intolerant here concerning the madman, whom he would banish, but tolerant, obliging, concerning the honest man who already banished him. An honest man like Polyander, who is also man before (Cartesian) metaphysics, or just man. When this honest man refuses an unreasonable doubt that would argue from the premise of sensory error against the everyday, nearby universe, Eudoxus has to (is willing to) provide him with more pressing reasons for doubt; now that he could *take offence* from a disagreeable assumption, or *find it bad* to assimilate him to the mad, he has to (is willing to) again circumvent this reticence, and to provide a less disagreeable reason for doubting. While Derrida rightly notes that it is not at all a question in our text of madness itself, even if only to exclude it, a response must still be given to the objection that he poses to himself straight away: is not this very fact the sign of a profound exclusion (WD, 392 n.15)? In the same way that leniency towards the racism of others comprises a great deal of racism, so the leniency that Eudoxus shows the honest Polyander is not perfectly innocent. Just like the society of *honest* men among themselves, the society of the metaphysician with the honest men is formed here by excluding the *bad* company of the mad.

In the First Meditation, Descartes does not encounter madness, which he would exclude; he encounters the prejudice against madness. Who thus exclaims: 'but such people are insane'? It is an older voice than his, and the history of philosophy can help to identify it. It spoke already in the *Academics* of Cicero, common reading for Montaigne and Descartes and a traditional reference in the Jesuit teachings: it is the voice of Lucullus the dogmatic, which had already excluded the madman, and better yet, had already disqualified the (philosophical) idea of the comparison with the madman. For Lucullus the dogmatic, this desire to make the comparison is itself already more than a little mad: '*quod velle efficere non mediocris insaniae est*' (II, XVII, 54). We recognise the formula, the point that imparts the slight rhetorical flourish to our text. Cicero, in the *Academics*, encountered this dogmatic prejudice against madness, and this dogmatic refusal of any comparison between *honest* perception and phantasm: he encountered them and combated them. Descartes encounters them in turn in the First Meditation, and, in the passage that concerns us, he does not judge them. To say that such is precisely his wrongdoing would be to make use of a respectable ethical category, but even more so an irrelevant one, as the fight against prejudices, for Descartes, is a matter of effort rather than decree. We must thus seek out, at this point of the meditation, the exact attitude of the metaphysician regarding a debarment, or an exclusion, that he encounters without being its author.

'But such people are insane (*amentes*), and I would be equally mad (*demens*) if I took anything from them as a model for myself.'[9] In reading the translation, one might believe that Descartes adopts without restriction the dogmatic exclusion. However, our preceding remarks have prepared us for the nuance introduced by the original Latin: 'I would seem, would be thought [*viderer*] equally mad if I took anything from them as a model for myself.' To compare oneself with the madman *would be* madness: this is the dogmatic language of Lucullus, and, for once, Foucault has been duped by the French translator, the Duc de Luynes, in attributing it to Descartes. To compare oneself with the madman *would seem to be* madness: that is the precise language of the metaphysician, who has not yet come to a definitive or final conclusion, only a suspicion, which nuances his agreement. Now the *amens-demens* couple comes to light. Foucault, a historian of penitentiary and medical systems, found in *insanus*, employed at the moment of summons, a characteristic term belonging equally to common vocabulary and medical terminology; and in *amens* and *demens*, used to dismiss madness, disqualifying terms of juridical value (AME, 401–2). But the historian of philosophy, and of Cartesian philosophy in particular, cannot remain insensitive to what separates *amens* from *demens*. The madman, you say, says the dogmatic voice, has no *mens*, is *a-mens*; if I pretended to follow his example, I would give the impression, *viderer*, of divesting myself of my mind, of depriving myself of it, of being *de-mens*. We recognise the traditional distinction between negation and privation, which the Fourth Meditation will recall (CSM II, 55, l. 1–3). In a world where madness has already been banished, where the madman was considered as having no mind, the comparison, proposed by the philosopher, expresses a scandalous perversion, a voluntary mutilation. Descartes, obliging the honest man who is scandalised, renounces the comparison and seeks a less offensive equivalent to this reason for doubt. Provisional obligingness, as is indicated by the *viderer*.

This obligingness dissimulates no *requisit*. Foucault thinks that Descartes, by rejecting here the possibility of being mad, posits his first assertion, before what is called the Cogito. This would be to introduce, in the order of reasons, with this first unavowed link, an element of the arbitrary. 'But madness is banished in the name of the man who doubts, and who is no more capable of opening himself to unreason than he is of not thinking or not being' (HM, 46); and 'the qualification as "nonmad" (like the qualification as "potential dreamer") will remain valid' (AME, 410). If we compare the modality given to this first assertion and its content – which would be a positive response to the question, 'When I think I have a body, can I be certain that my grasp on the truth is stronger than that of the man who believes his body to be made of glass?' (HM, 45) – we will reject such an interpretation without hesitation. The first Cartesian truth is certainly not the real existence of the body. This existence, which is not demonstrated until the Sixth Meditation, is cast into doubt by all the arguments following the rejection of madness in the First Meditation. Such is the result of the next exercise, the exercise of *dormiens*, as well as the fiction of the evil genius, which, it is worth remembering, strikes the sensible and especially the body proper, not mathematics, and which takes up and reinforces the dream hypothesis (*ludificationes somniorum*, CSM II, 22, l. 28) more than the hypothesis of a deceiving God. To be listened to by honest men, Descartes needs to not seem mad; to be assured of his first truth, he has no need to posit that he has a true body, to posit that he is not mad.

It still remains to understand the difference in fortune, in the assault against everyday certitudes, between the testimony of the madman, which is refused, and the testimony of the dreamer, which 'almost' wins assent. In the two cases, the philosopher seeks to discredit perception by a comparative detour, approximating it to an imaginative appearance that would be indiscernibly similar and indisputably deceiving. Now, the honest man resists the philosopher's approximation of perception to dreams *or* to madness, proclaiming a difference: 'But such people are insane', of course; but also: 'Yet at the moment my eyes are certainly wide awake when I look at this piece of paper. . . . All this would not happen with such distinctness to someone asleep' (CSM II, 19, l. 13–17). The two testimonies seem to fail equally before the immediate consciousness of a difference; Eudoxus would only have renounced *offending* Polyander in order to disturb him (which he seeks to do) to the point of leading him to break off the pact of the dialogue (which would be the ruin of the philosophical enterprise): 'For myself, however, I fear that I should simply go wool-gathering if I tried to consider such abstract matters, for I am a man who has never engaged in study or accustomed himself to turning his mind so far away from things that are perceivable by the senses' (*The Search for Truth*, CSM II, 512). Since the metaphysician seeks (and, in the dialogue, already knows) a truth that withstands these tests, his true problem is to surmount the reticence and refusals of the honest man, who speaks in him as outside of him. How is it possible to shatter the prejudice that I am not sleeping, after I have ceded to the analogous prejudice that I am not mad?

Only here does *memory* intervene, the importance of which Foucault very judiciously reconstructs (AME, 397). *Custom* still consigned to exteriority the two terms under comparison. But a voice arises in everyone that accords with the philosopher's appeal, the voice of the dreamer whom one has been, the memory of having already been duped. 'As if I did not remember other occasions when I have been tricked by exactly similar thoughts while asleep, *a similibus etiam cogitationibus*' (CSM II, 19, l. 17–19). Not only do I remember having dreamt, or having discovered in dreams, as Foucault puts it, this 'clarity and distinction' (AME, 410); I also remember having believed, while dreaming, that I was not dreaming, telling myself, while dreaming, that this time it was not a dream. Whether memory's deception or faithful remembrance, it makes little difference: the honest man had been entirely exterior to madness, and his refusal served as a barrier; by means of memory, he ceases to be exterior to the dream, as though his refusal is suspended as soon as he remembers having previously made a similar but illegitimate refusal. I cannot find it bad to be *compared* to a dreamer, since I myself compare and identify myself with one by *remembering* that I have dreamt yet believed I was not dreaming. 'As I think about this more carefully, I see plainly that there are never any sure signs by means of which being awake can be distinguished from being asleep. The result is that

I begin to feel dazed' (CSM II, 19, l. 20–1). The memory here lifts the barrier of prejudice; the (indignant) refusal of the honest (offended) man gives way to *dazedness* (of someone who finds in his own pocket the object that he is wrongly accused of having stolen): 'and this very feeling, *stupor*, only reinforces the notion that I may be asleep' (CSM II, 19, l. 21–2). This panic, which will later be warded off, which will appear not only hyperbolic but a bit ridiculous (CSM II, 89, l. 19), leads to the verge of a confession. The honest man no longer refuses to join with the philosopher, and, in this company of dreamers, no one will any longer think to exclude the madman, for the qualification of non-mad has ceased to be required. '[A]s a way of thinking, madness implies itself, and thus excludes itself from his project', Foucault asserted (HM, 46). The *thus* raises a problem. The dream also implies itself, for to model oneself after a dreamer leads to the supposition that one is dreaming, just as modelling oneself after a madman would lead to the appearance of being mad. The value of the metaphysical project stems precisely from what it includes, rather than what it excludes, of these marginal experiences. Such is at least the conviction of Descartes, which Foucault passionately rejects.

Madmen and dreamers have their place on the Cartesian vessel heading towards the New World of the Second Meditation. But the example of the madman, by contrast to the example of the dreamer, does not succeed in bringing the honest man aboard this vessel. For, in the precise weighing of reasons – in the balance of reasons for believing and reasons for doubting, where opposing prejudices should reach equilibrium (*velut aequatis utrimque praejudiciorum ponderibus*, CSM II, 22, l. 15–16) – in order to counterbalance the immediate awareness of not being mad, most men do not find in themselves the memory of having been mad, whereas all men remember having dreamt. For a recovered madman, the memory of his delirium would suffice to neutralise the prejudice of the difference. Can one really infer, from Descartes considering this category of readers to be a minority, a classical '*coup de force*', a decisive mutation in the history of the culture? When Foucault proposes that 'while *man* can still go mad, *thought* . . . can no longer be devoid of reason' (HM, 47), the historian of Cartesian philosophy would underscore the necessity of a *distinguo*. If thought, 'as the sovereign exercise carried out by a subject seeking the truth' (HM, 47), is the act of the pure *res cogitons*, leaving aside the *cogitationes* that issue from the union between soul and body, then no doubt thought cannot be mad, and delirium is outside of thought; but then nor can thought be dreaming, and dreams are not thoughts: the one accustomed to sleeping at night is not (in this restrictive sense) the mind or the soul, the *mens*, but man, *homo* (CSM II, 19, l. 8). If, however, thought is understood in the broad sense of the Cartesian *cogitatio*, which *also*, *quoque* (CSM II, 28, l. 22), *etiam* (CSM II, 34, l. 20) encompasses the imagination and sensation, then the visions of the madman are just as much thoughts as are the images of dreams. The faculty of thought, *cogitandi vis*, is not more suppressed in one case than in the other: to a classical comment by the great Arnauld, classical in Foucault's sense and classical in Arnauld's, regarding 'the fact that "the power of thought is . . . extinguished in madmen (*amentibus*)"', Descartes simply responds 'I should say not "extinguished" (*extincta*) but "disturbed" (*perturbata*)' (*Fourth Set of Replies*, CSM II, 228, l. 20–2). It may be that the madman, like the dreamer or the child, is in fact incapable of using the pure understanding and, for example, reflecting on his thought in order to assure himself that he exists, the first truth of metaphysics implying a necessary link that can in no case be reduced to a juxtaposition *Cogito, sum*. Yet, as a thought experiment, the assumption that I am mad does not affect the truths of the understanding any more than the assumption that I am sleeping: even if, in believing myself to have a body made of flesh, I am as mad as the madman who believes himself to have a body made of glass or mistakes himself for earthenware, I think (in the broad sense of the verb), thus I am, and even if my body is nothing but an unreal image, it must remain a constant that I exist, as *mens*, so long as I have this thought.

Far from altering the traditional economy of reasons for doubt, Descartes recognises that he ruminated over 'precooked material' (*Second Set of Replies*, CSM II, 130, l. 21–2), and he even grants that he had the frankness to not 'sell them as novelties' (*Third Set of Objections with the Author's Replies*, CSM II, 171). Considered as a systematic set of theses, Foucault's interpretation thus does not seem adequate to the obvious meaning of the Cartesian discourse.

III.

It bothers us somewhat to obstinately discuss a point of detail in a work whose scope and originality compel admiration. But we believe that Cartesian studies, which are habituated to minutia in the interpretation of the *Meditations on First Philosophy*, have greatly benefited from this debate between Foucault and Derrida, for it raises several questions that do not seem unimportant.

We might first take notice that once again, in contemporary French philosophy, a certain relation between the imaginary and the perceived, which must be termed Cartesian, is called into question and refused. Without being conflated with them, Foucault's reading echoes other readings and other refusals, more elliptical in Sartre (*The Imaginary*, IV, 4) and more explicit in Merleau-Ponty (*The Phenomenology of Perception*, II, III-D). Cartesian philosophy installs the distance, immediately experienced by 'the honest man' between the truth of perception and the impostors of imagination, through the calming language of difference in degree. Metaphysical reflection can first attend to the unity of the genus, in order to reject, in the First Meditation, the assurance of the madman by means of the imposture of dreams and the immediacy of the everyday universe; it can then attend to the diversity of species, in order to separate, in the Sixth Meditation, the truth of sensory experience from the illusion of dreams. However, the French philosophers of yesterday and today refuse to accept that the choice, the *Decision*, to take up Foucault's original term, be dulled down to a simple difference of degree: to the approximations of the First Meditation, they oppose the irreducibility in nature between the thesis of perception and the thesis of the imaginary; to the eliminations of the Sixth Meditation, and, for madness, of the First perhaps already, they oppose the identity of the question to which wakefulness, dreams and madness provide incommensurable and concurrent responses. What Sartre denounces as 'a sophism' in the Cartesian text is to have abandoned the direct inspection of perception in order to attack it obliquely by way of a comparison: the direct inspection would manifest immediately, admitting of no doubt, that perceiving is not dreaming, and that the assumption that I am sleeping, as a thought experiment, would be just as absurd as the denial of my existence. In other words, Sartre criticises Descartes for not having stopped at the moment of exclusion ('Yet at the moment my eyes are certainly wide awake when I look at this piece of paper; I shake my head and it is not asleep; as I stretch out and feel my hand I do so deliberately, and I know what I am doing. All this would not happen with such distinctness to someone asleep'), and for having sought to lift this exclusion through the appeal to memory. In short, he criticises as a *sophism* Descartes' failure to commit on the occasion of dreams what Foucault calls, on the occasion of madness, a *coup de force*. The two objections are in a sense opposites, since Sartre widens the difference at the risk of giving off the brusque appearance of bias for refusing to dream. However, they contribute to bringing out a heterogeneity that disallows the compromise of perception as much as it does the mastery or confinement of dreams or madness. We would also gladly bring together these two readings with the texts that Merleau-Ponty dedicates to hallucination: there, despite 'empiricism' and despite 'intellectualism' (Alain serving as Descartes' double), the exclusion would be *reciprocal*. 'At the level of judgment, [the patients] distinguish hallucination from perception.'[10] This time, an ultra-Cartesianism in a sense justifies the debarment that the First Meditation would institute, according to Foucault, against madness: for Descartes, only the honest man is conscious of his difference, while the madman assures that he is king or has a body made of glass as if it were a matter of perceived truth; for Merleau-Ponty, however, the separation is made through mutual understanding, the madman saying 'but those such as I are insane', the honest man saying 'but such people are insane', and both together saying 'we are not to take anything from the other as a model, respectively, for ourselves'. By this new turn, ultra-Cartesianism again sacrifices the (Cartesian) thesis of difference in degree, leading to a radical choice between irreducible values, to a Decision that reason always presupposes and therefore cannot justify.

Yet we would like to conclude not with considerations on the imaginary and the perceived, but on what Foucault brings to the history of Cartesian philosophy. He isolated the moment when madness is dismissed: if it is true that nothing, in principle, precedes the time of doubt; and *if the order demands that one refuse all retroaction*; then the qualification of 'non-mad' must indeed have been laid down once and for all. In order to avoid this ruinous consequence, one need only oppose, with Derrida, the naïve objection (of the honest man who refuses to consider himself as mad) and the definitive thought of the metaphysician (who accepts this test): though perfectly legitimate in a dialogue and, more generally, in a work of exposition where the one who sets out to reveal the truth knows it already, the dissociation is impossible in the order of the meditation, where one cannot judge from the outside what happens in the moment of discovery. In order to give an acceptable status to the refusal of madness, we must thus search out the extent to which what follows can react back upon what precedes; that is, we must return to what Descartes called the *order of reasons*, to the dogma that led Martial Guéroult to some admirable analyses, but also to some rash consequences that most commentators have just as much difficulty accepting as they do the conclusions of Foucault. Descartes himself had the occasion to explain to Father Bourdin, who converted the propositions of the First Meditation into assertions or theses, that the moment of doubt is irreducible to the rules that govern the order of science in general. 'When you promised me "powerful and well thought-out reasons"' (for doubting), 'I expected ones which were certain and free from all doubt – reasons of the kind which are demanded by . . . that rule of yours', remarked the good Father, who then wondered: 'why do you assert with such confidence that we sometimes dream? Why not follow your first law and reason as follows: "It is not wholly certain that the senses have sometimes deceived us, or that we have sometimes dreamed, or that people have sometimes gone mad; hence I will assert and insist that the senses never deceive us, we never dream and no one goes mad"' (*Seventh Set of Objections with Replies*, CSM II, 469–70). Descartes replied to him that reasons for doubting are not posited as true but as plausible (which is also to say, questionable and uncertain), that the rule of indubitability cannot 'be related to what I said in the First Meditation', in short, that '[t]here is nothing at all that I asserted "with confidence" in the First Meditation', which 'is full of doubt throughout' and where one 'might just as well have found there the statements "We never dream" and "We sometimes dream"' (CSM II, 473–4). The subject who doubts thus posits nothing definitively, not even the rejection of being mad: he is seeking to get a hold, over his reader or over his own prejudices, in order to access a first truth, in order to be able finally to posit the indubitable first proposition that will be *I am, I exist*. If it is illegitimate to determine the events of the First Meditation starting from (Cartesian) theses that are not yet established, it is stipulated that through them direction be given to the project of truth, and that a relation of dependency be maintained between *opinions*, of which I make use provisionally, or better by provision, and the *true and certain science*, still undetermined, towards which I orient myself. This other rule, so obvious in the moment of doubt, when, 'in order to discover what is certain, [I] make use of what is doubtful' (*Seventh Set of Objections and Replies*, CSM II, 479 and 480, l. 26), is found in fact throughout Descartes' metaphysics. Since it is a question of proceeding all the way until God, the final and necessary principle of all true science; since in metaphysics (and this is its difference with mathematics) first principles are also the last discoveries and the most difficult to conceive clearly and distinctly; the *order of reasons* – which 'consists simply in this', that '[t]he items which are put forward first must be known entirely without the aid of what comes later; and the remaining items must be arranged in such a way that their demonstration depends solely on what has gone before' – is subordinated to an inverse rule, where what precedes depends, in its meaning and in its intention, on what comes next. Descartes followed the order, in his *Meditations*, only as far as he could, '*quam accuratissime*' (*Second Set of Replies*, CSM II, 155). For, in the progressive enterprise of liberation, if it is clearly illegitimate to determine in advance the significance of a discursive event based on a truth that is not yet known, one must nevertheless suspend the definitive position of a first proposition until the discovery of the unconditional foundation that alone gives to all propositions of the true and certain science their stability. In an admirable paragraph, of which we would not deny a single word, Foucault described how the 'meditation implies a mobile subject modifiable through the effect of the discursive events that take place' (AME, 406). Descartes calls this reciprocal support *cohaerentia*, and he does not hesitate to tell Gassendi: 'you have not paid sufficient attention to the way in which what I wrote all fits together, *cohaerentiam*. I think this interconnection is such that, for any given point, *ad cujusque rei probationem*, all the preceding remarks and most of those that follow contribute to the proof of what is asserted, *maxima pars eorum quae sequuntur*' (*Fifth Set of Replies*, CSM II, 379, l. 16–19). This coherence is stronger than the order of reasons, the latter constituting only a partial and subordinate formula of the former. It explains how madness, first summoned to testify against sensible knowledge, can be dismissed at the request of the honest man without this obligingness confining the meditating subject by an immutable qualification: on the contrary, it enables other discursive events, particularly the assumption that I am sleeping, which in turn modify the meditating subject, unblock certain resistances, and carry doubt to the extreme point of its universality. The qualification of non-mad will doubtless be rediscovered and placed in the element of true science, but this new event will occur later, coming in the Sixth Meditation. The episode of madness, in this sense, is an excellent example: it compels us to think together the two rules whose convergence makes Descartes' metaphysics, the rule of order and the rule of coherence.

NOTES

1. Michel Foucault, *History of Madness*, ed. Jean Khalfa, trans. Jonathan Murphy and Jean Khalfa (London and New York: Routledge, 2006), Chapter II, pp. 44–7; first published in French as *Folie et déraison: Histoire de la folie à l'âge classique* (Paris: Librarie Plon, 1961). Hereafter cited in the text as HM.
2. René Descartes, 'Meditations on First Philosophy', *The Philosophical Writings of Descartes*, vol. 2, trans. John Cottingham, Robert Stoothoff and Dugald Murdoch (Cambridge: Cambridge University Press, 1984), pp. 18–19. Hereafter cited in the text as CSM.
3. Jacques Derrida, 'Cogito and the History of Madness', in *Writing and Difference*, trans. Alan Bass (London and New York: Routledge, 2001), pp. 36–76. Hereafter cited in the text as WD.
4. The second edition of *Histoire de la folie à l'âge classique* was published in 1972 by Gallimard and includes, as an appendix, Foucault's long response to Derrida, translated into English by Geoff Bennington as 'My Body, This Paper, This Fire', and appearing in Michel Foucault, *Aesthetics, Method, and Epistemology: Essential Works of Foucault, Volume 2*, ed. James Faubion (New York: The New Press, 1998), pp. 393–418. Hereafter cited in the text as AME.
5. Foucault's citations do not completely conform to the French translation by the Duc de Luynes. Though the differences here are apparently insignificant, they may already announce a distrust in regard to this translation, which Foucault will make explicit in his response to Derrida.
6. *Sed forte*, AT, VII, 18, l. 19. Foucault makes no mention of this *forte* ['perhaps']. As for Derrida, who demonstrated its importance (WD, 54 and 60), he criticises the Duc de Luynes for not having translated it. This is too severe a criticism, for in effect, the *forte* was translated together with the first proposition to which it refers: 'il s'en rencontre *peut-être* [*perhaps*] beaucoup d'autres' (AT, IX, 14). [TN. This phrase corresponds to the following one from the English translation, which does not seem to mark the uncertainty as strongly: 'there are many other beliefs about which doubt is quite impossible' (CSM II, 18, l. 21).] The French

translation by Clerselier, which came later and was not authorised by Descartes, doubles the *peut-être* [perhaps] in what is a slightly heavy-handed redundancy.

7. We again encounter the adverb *forte*, the importance of which Derrida had emphasised so judiciously a few lines up. Here, in order for the doubt to be possible (*forte*, CSM II, 18, l. 26), I must make the comparison. It becomes impossible when I refuse the comparison (*sed*, CSM II, 19, l. 5). With this refusal, everything returns to order, and everyday certitudes retain their lustre, unaltered. Such is duly marked by the *praeclare sane* (CSM II, 19, l. 8), with a touch of irony in the *sane*. The reason for this irony will begin to be explained by the *tanquam*, which introduces dreams as a new reason for doubting, and which corresponds to the *toutefois* [TN. 'however', 'nevertheless': in the English translation, 'As if'] in the French translation.
8. We could refer, notably, to the second book of Cicero's *Prior Academics*, entitled *Lucullus or Academica Priora – Liber Secundus*, XIV, 44 and XXXIV, 111.
9. TN. Because the context of this discussion requires the direct comparison of the Latin and its French (rather than English) translation, in this instance, I have modified the English translation of Descartes (by Cottingham, Stoothoff and Murdoch) to more closely mirror the French. As quoted by Beyssade, the French translation reads: 'Mais quoi ce sont des fous, et je ne serais pas moins extravagant si je me réglais sur leurs exemples.' By contrast, the unmodified English translation retains the qualification that drops out of the French: 'But such people are insane, and I would be *thought* equally mad if I took anything from them as a model for myself' (emphasis added).
10. Maurice Merleau-Ponty, *Phenomenology of Perception*, trans. Colin Smith (London and New York: Routledge, 2002), pp. 390–1.

CHAPTER 5

A Return to Descartes' First Meditation

Michel Foucault
Translated by Christopher Penfield

Dear friend,

Thank you for your letter and parcel. You can imagine how greatly your text interested me. Its rigour is remarkable in every regard, and if there are a certain number of small details over which I might quibble, it seems to me – and this is, for me, what is essential – that we are in agreement on the principle of an analysis that would disclose the 'series' of the meditative exercise, too often neglected in favour of the 'order of reasons'; it is at this level of the discursive events of the text that the relation to madness is posed as a problem. You demonstrate this very well using your own method, and the text on the 'cohaerentia' that you cite at the end of your article is most convincing.

Truly, this return to Descartes is most amusing, and I did not think at the beginning that it would give rise to so much discussion. Since you had the kindness to send me your manuscript, will you allow me to continue the debate?

One thing first: you generously ask me if there is anything that bothers me. In all honesty, it is true that there is one thing, and one only. Between the first edition of my book and my reply to Derrida, ten years went by. Meanwhile, my perspective changed quite a bit. In 1960, I had the feeling that this 'exclusion' of madness was poorly integrated into the order of reasons; I thus saw there a furtive, violent gesture, a sudden rupture amid a continuous movement. I was correct, I believe, to sense that it could not be reduced to Cartesian systematicity, such as is typically described; but the status that I accorded it was no doubt not a good one. It was necessary that my attention be drawn towards 'discursive events', the modalities of inclusion of the subject in discourse, in order to grasp the coherence of a movement that is specific, but that is adjusted to the order of reasons; the procedures which then take place, the game of qualifications and disqualifications, do not disturb the order of reasons.

You can see, then, what is problematic to me about your text: it is that you treat as a whole, as though they were continuous, the several lines that I had written in 1960 and the analyses that I have recently conducted using a completely different style, method, and degree of approximation.

You thus critique all that I say about Descartes on the basis of eight propositions that are found in effect in the first edition. However, many of these propositions are clarified, modified, or abandoned in the reply to Derrida. For example:

- '*madness alongside dreams*'; in 1960, I contented myself with indicating this juxtaposition; in my reply, on nearly every page I insist on the series, the succession, the chronological ordering of the two moments, that of madness and that of dreams; I do not believe it would be accurate to say that I 'effaced' the chronological order in the text from 1971.
- *the distinction between body, world and consciousness*: I make no reference to this in my reply; on the contrary, I underscore the decisive importance,[1] for the method of doubt at this point of the meditation, of the difference between the 'weak' or 'distant' and the close, the lively, the actual; I agree with you completely that this is the only division to be found in the First Meditation.
- With respect to the other six theses, I believe that I could point out the same kind of modifications.

You can thus see the point, or rather the two points that bother me:

- you critique two analyses (one of which is developed, modified, displaced in relation to the other) in the name of eight theses that are only present in the first.
- the representation in eight theses does not in any case seem very adequate for describing my reply to Derrida, where all the stress is placed on the method and level of analysis. I have the impression that you 'block off' [*verrouilles*] the second text a bit by the first, and that you sentence them together as one.

Please forgive the frankness with which I speak to you; and be certain that I am deeply appreciative of the work that you have done. It considerably enriches the reading that can now be given of Descartes' text.

Of course, apart from the point that bothers me, I have several theoretical objections to make, but with prudence; you know Descartes so much better than I. It seems to me that the situation can be summarised in the following way: you would agree that the test of madness concerns the qualification of the meditating subject; but you deny that the qualification of non-madness is definitively attained at this level. Your arguments are impressive; however, three of them did not fully gain my assent:

a) *the plurality of voices*. The analogy with the dialogue is extremely interesting. Is it absolutely convincing? The meditation is an exercise during which the subject does not dialogue with others; rather, he himself takes up what may well have been encountered in others' discourse, or even what will retrospectively appear as common prejudice, in order to make of it a test through which he passes. To transform into a test modifying the discoursing subject, what is perhaps only an object of encounter – such is the particularity of the Meditation. There is no plurality of voices.

b) You are perfectly right to underscore the difference between *amens* and *demens*. But this distinction is not only pertinent for the historian of philosophy; it holds in the medical domain. *Amens* (which is doubtless negation): the one who does not have his mind; *demens* (which is doubtless privation): the one who is dispossessed of it, who no longer benefits from it, who deviated, etc. I do not think that *demens* can ever designate the state of someone who voluntarily 'dispossessed himself' of his mind. If I modelled myself on the example of those who have no *mens*, I would appear to be deprived of it. (Let us not forget the '*nec minus demens*' of the Latin text.)
c) It seems to me that you give to *viderer* a weak sense (which is of course possible, but not necessary). Might it not mean 'to appear' rather than 'to seem'?

Such are the first questions that I ask myself regarding your article; but with the prudence that I owe to your erudition and mastery. They are, as you see, of an entirely different nature than the difficulty about which I spoke to you just above.

You may of course do with my letter whatever you please. If you wish for us to pursue the discussion, in any form you like, I would be delighted to.

I wish you a propitious year in Rennes, and I beg you to please accept my fondest remembrance.

Letter from Michel Foucault to Jean-Marie Beyssade, November 1972

NOTE

1. TN. See Michel Foucault, *Aesthetics, Method, and Epistemology: Essential Works of Foucault, Volume 2*, ed. James Faubion (New York: The New Press, 1998), p. 408.

CHAPTER 6

Deconstruction, Care of the Self, Spirituality: Putting Foucault and Derrida to the Test

Edward McGushin

I

> It may be that there is something necessarily mad in every question and every problem, as there is in their transcendence in relation to answers, in their insistence through solutions and the manner in which they maintain their own openness. (Gilles Deleuze)[1]

What madness haunts the questions and problems that draw Foucault and Derrida to each other as teacher and student (master and disciple) and as friends, only to drive them apart as rivals? Of course, initially it is the problem of madness in its relation to history, to the birth of modernity and modern subjectivity, and specifically its presence in, or absence from, Descartes' First Meditation. But in and through their disagreement concerning these problems and questions something else emerges: a *spirituality*. That is to say, a passion for, even a devotion to, the question of how to live, a problematisation of the arts of living, a desire to get free from oneself and find new possibilities of thinking and being. To really get at the spirit of this spirituality, however, we have to ask another question: what exactly is an *épreuve*, a test or trial, an ordeal? How does it function, by what means does it come to pass, and what results does it bring about? Why is it that the self is given to this sort of experience, to find itself, its world, its relationships in the form of the test or trial? What sort of being are we such that we put ourselves to the test, give ourselves to it, put it into play, or that on other occasions we flee from it? The *épreuve* is nothing other than the lived experience of the limit where subjectivity and reason come undone and pass into madness. But this same limit is what carves out and defines the spaces for and thus gives birth to subjectivities or selves of all kinds. Whoever has passed through such an *épreuve* is changed as a result. This is what puts Derrida and Foucault to the test in Descartes' text – the trial and ordeal of madness, the *épreuve* that takes place in Descartes' thought, giving rise to a new sense of life, reason, subjectivity, to new practices and forms of thought, those which we recognise as modernity.[2]

2

My aim in returning to the 'Derrida-Foucault polemic', which has already been so thoroughly discussed and debated, is not to take sides, to decide once again or once and for all, who was right and who wrong about Descartes, the history of madness, the nature and function of signification or textuality, or any of the many possible disputes to which it gave or gives rise. For me what is especially striking about their exchange is that, so far as I can tell, it is in his response to Derrida's 'Cogito and the History of Madness' that Foucault first explicitly characterises philosophy – in the specific case of Descartes' *Meditations* – as an *askésis*, as an exercise through which the subjectivity of the meditating subject is modified and displaced by the thoughts it thinks. What I am curious about is this: why is it that Foucault introduces the notion of philosophy as a meditative practice, as *askésis*, in his response to Derrida? This question is all the more gripping given the perspective we have looking back on it now, knowing that this same experience of philosophy was to return in Foucault's thought and become its centre of gravity.

In what follows I want to test a certain hypothesis, or perhaps something less than a hypothesis, a mere hunch: namely, that this sense of philosophy first appears in Foucault's response to Derrida, because this sense of philosophy is already quietly, implicitly, at play in 'Cogito and the History of Madness'. The test: what happens if we re-read 'Cogito and the History of Madness' through the lens, so to speak, of the later Foucault?[3] Such a reading allows the otherwise silent and implicit ascetic dimension of Derrida's text to be heard.

3

We all know the key dates and events. Michel Foucault's *History of Madness* (*Folie et déraison: Histoire de la folie à l'âge classique*) appears in France in 1961. The first chapter of the book, '*Stultifera Navis*', shows that the 'world of the early seventeenth century is strangely hospitable to madness. Madness is there in the hearts of men and at the heart of things'.[4] The aim of the second chapter, 'The Great Confinement', is to describe a major event in the history of madness – the moment when reason suddenly became inhospitable to madness. Reason and madness were divided from each other and madness was set apart from reason, confined and silenced. This chapter opens with a reading of Descartes' First Meditation, a text Foucault takes to be one of many 'signs' that this division has taken place, a division which finds its social expression in the widespread confinement of the mad, along with the poor, idle, immoral and unproductive of society, that takes place across Europe in the middle of the seventeenth century (HM, 47).

The passage that Foucault takes up concerns Descartes' attempt to determine whether or not he can rely on his senses to provide him with an accurate report on his immediate environment. Having noticed that our senses seem to deceive us about the appearance of objects when we perceive them under certain conditions, for example when they are far away or very small, Descartes notes that under other conditions they seem to be indubitable:

> for example, that I am here, sitting by the fire, wearing a winter dressing-gown, holding this piece of paper in my hands, and so on. Again, how could it be denied that these hands or this whole body are mine? Unless perhaps I were to liken myself to madmen . . . But such people are insane, and I would be thought equally mad if I took anything from them as a model for myself. A brilliant piece of reasoning! As if I were not a man who sleeps at night, and regularly has all the same experiences while asleep as madmen do when awake – indeed sometimes even more improbable ones.[5]

Foucault points to this passage as evidence that for Descartes there is no common ground or dialogue between madness and reason. Descartes cannot entertain the possibility that he could be mad in so far as he is engaged in the methodical application of reason. The separation of madness from reason and consequent exclusion and silencing of madness represent something new in the order of thought. If we look back to Montaigne, we see an experience in which the rational thinking subject can never exclude the possibility that he or she is mad, reason itself cannot be separated from madness. According to Montaigne, 'there is nothing in the whole world madder than bringing matters down to the measure of our own capacities and potentialities'.[6] But Descartes' text, then, represents, and provides evidence of, 'a strange, novel form of pathos, a different relationship between mankind and all that can be inhuman in his existence' (HM, 55). Descartes excludes madness from his rational method just as the mad will soon be physically removed from the social world and placed in a world of confinement.

In 1963, Jacques Derrida devoted his first major lecture in Paris to a critical reading of *History of Madness*. In this talk, 'Cogito and the History of Madness' ('Cogito et l'histoire de la folie'), which poses fundamental questions about the coherence and possibility of writing a history of madness as Foucault has attempted, Derrida challenged Foucault's interpretation of Descartes' First Meditation. Derrida writes:

> is the interpretation of Descartes' intention that is proposed to us justifiable? What I here call interpretation is a certain passage, a certain semantic relationship proposed by Foucault between, *on the one hand*, what Descartes said – or what he is believed to have said or meant – and *on the other hand*, let us say, within intentional vagueness for the moment, a certain 'historical structure', as it is called, a certain meaningful historical totality, a total historical project through which we think what Descartes said – what he is believed to have said or meant – can *particularly* be demonstrated.[7]

Foucault, Derrida contends, moves too quickly from the text to its context, from its manifest meaning as an internally ordered system of signs to its purported latent meaning as a symptom or sign of the times. No attempt to historicise the meaning of the text can be justified prior to a rigorous reading of the text in its own terms; that is, Derrida claims, in terms of the manifest intentions of the author, the intentions of the author as manifest in the signifying system of the text itself. The 'comprehension of the sign in and of itself, in its immediate materiality as a sign, if I may so call it, is not only the first moment but also the indispensable condition of all hermeneutics and of any claim to transition from the sign to the signified' (WD, 32).

Prior to any attempt to move from the text, in its immediate materiality as a system of signs, to its historical context and meaning, one would first have to carry out

> the internal and autonomous analysis of the philosophical content of philosophical discourse. Only when the totality of this content will have become manifest in its meaning for me (but this is impossible) will I rigorously be able to situate it in its total historical form. It is only then that its reinsertion will not do it violence, that there will be a legitimate reinsertion of *this* philosophical meaning *itself*. (WD, 44)

The main part of Derrida's paper represents his attempt to 'turn to this manifest meaning [of Descartes' text], this properly philosophical intention that is not legible in the immediacy of a first encounter' (WD, 45). Derrida contends that a rigorous reading of the text on its own terms shows that Descartes *does not exclude madness* from his systematic doubt. Rather, madness makes its presence, or rather, its absence felt in the form of the dream and the figure of the evil genius. Foucault's failure to let the madness of Descartes' text speak represents a continuation and repetition of the silencing of madness that took place in the great confinement of the seventeenth century. And, what is more, this failure to properly let the text speak is, writes Derrida, symptomatic of the impossibility of his entire project in *History of Madness*, which would be, on one level, to allow madness to tell its own story (WD, 32–42).

It is not until 1972 that Foucault finally responds in public to Derrida's critique.[8] His essay, 'My Body, This Paper, This Fire' ('Mon corps, ce papier, ce feu'), is focused less on the larger challenge to *History of Madness* and more on Derrida's reading of Descartes. His response culminates in a brutal dismissal of what he famously (infamously) calls Derrida's 'little pedagogy' of endless textual interpretation (HM, 573). After the publication of this essay, as an appendix to a new edition of *History of Madness*, Foucault and Derrida broke off all relations for the next ten years. In 1981 Derrida was arrested in Prague in what became an international event. Foucault played a key role in publicising the injustice of the arrest and came to the side of Derrida in the media. This provided the occasion for the two to renew their friendship. Of course, not long after, in 1984, Foucault would pass away. Finally, in 1991 Derrida revisits *History of Madness* but refuses, out of respect to his late friend and former teacher, to resume the debate surrounding the text of Descartes.

4

In 'My Body, This Paper, This Fire', Foucault offers both a critique of Derrida and a highly original interpretation of Descartes' First Meditation. Here I want to focus on his reading of Descartes. As we have seen in 'Cogito and the History of Madness', for Derrida interpretation must begin with the manifest intention of the author, and only once we have grasped the meaning of the text in its own terms are we in a position to locate it within a historical situation or context. In his response, Foucault characterises the text first and foremost as a series of 'discursive events'. Consequently, the meaning of the text cannot be grasped without understanding the discursive functions of the various statements of which it is composed. Derrida, he argues, is representative of a systematic failure on the part of modern philosophy to grasp a text as an event or series of events and a systematic reduction of text to traces, which require infinite commentary. The meaning of the text does not lie behind or within the manifest presence of its statements, according to Foucault, rather it appears at its surface, its exteriority, in the effects statements produce as events that take place in a specific field of practices and other statements, effects they produce in the very being or subjectivity of the reading, thinking subject.

Foucault writes that we 'must keep in mind the title itself of "Meditations"' (HM, 562). A meditation is composed of discursive events and practices that have precise functions and effects that must be understood and put into play. In other words, a statement in a meditation is not grasped through commentary and its meaning is not reducible to the signification or representation of ideas, of a sense or notion. Neither can its truth be verified by its adequacy to a referent or state-of-affairs. Rather its meaning is found in the effects it brings about in the meditating subject. To make this clear Foucault contrasts meditation and demonstration. In a 'pure demonstration', in a text composed exclusively or primarily of assertions and arguments, statements are linked by formal rules and must be understood and evaluated according to their logical validity. This means in effect that 'the subject of the discourse is in no sense implied in the demonstration' (HM, 562). In other words, in a text that functions as a demonstration each statement takes place, or happens, as the result of the application of formal rules, and the aim of the demonstration is to arrive at the proper conclusion, which follows necessarily from the sequence. The essence of an argument lies in the *relation of each statement to the others*. The existence and status of the subject who writes or reads the argument is absolutely inessential to the meaning or structure of the text. In a demonstration we are not interested in the *relation of the statements to the subject* who thinks them or the affects they might bring about in or through that subject. But a meditation, on the other hand, 'produces, as so many discursive events, new enunciations that bring in their wake a series of modifications in the enunciating subject' (HM, 563). Foucault introduces here the notion of the 'ascetic' dimension of the text – the meditation as an exercise that the thinking subject must engage in and undergo. In so far as the meditation aims at bringing about modifications in the subject it is a practice of the self – a practice that aims at the transformation of the subject. On the ascetic level of the text, 'the subject is ceaselessly altered by his own movement; his discourse elicits movements inside which he is caught up; it *exposes* him to *risks*, *subjects* him to *tests* (*épreuves*) or temptations, produces in him states, and *confers a status or a qualification upon him* which he in no sense possessed at the initial moment' (HM, 563, my emphasis).

This characterisation of the ascetic dimension of Descartes' *Meditations* anticipates Foucault's final years of research represented in his lectures on spirituality, care of the self, and *parrésia* and it marks the first appearance in his thinking of the notion of philosophy as a spiritual exercise or care of the self. Ten years later in his lectures at the Collège de France, *The Hermeneutics of the Subject*, Foucault defines meditation 'not as the game the subject plays with his thought but as the game thought plays on the subject'. In the case of the First Meditation Foucault writes: 'Descartes is not thinking about everything in the world that could be doubtful. . . . Descartes puts himself in the position of the subject who doubts everything. . . . This, then, is not at all an exercise carried out on thought and its content. It is an exercise by which, through thought, the subject puts himself in a certain situation.'[9] In his lectures from the 1980s, Foucault is no longer analysing the exclusion of madness, of course. Rather he is excavating the moment, and the event in thought, by which philosophy, and more broadly, reason, intelligibility, the relationship of subjectivity to the truth, undergoes a fundamental mutation. He calls this event the 'Cartesian Moment'.[10] What happens in this moment is nothing less than a transformation in the fundamental experience of subjectivity and truth. Prior to modernity, the subject-truth relation was experienced in the form of what Foucault calls 'spirituality'.[11] Spirituality was foundational to the ancient Greek and Hellenistic notion that philosophy was essentially an attempt to theorise and practise 'care of the self' (*epimeleia heautou, souci de soi*). Spirituality, Foucault holds, entails three basic postulates. First, that the subject does not have a natural right or capacity to know the truth. The very being or subjectivity of the subject cuts the subject off from the truth. In order to gain access to the truth, then, the subject must undergo a conversion, a transformation of its subjectivity that will open it up to the truth. The second postulate of spirituality is that this conversion is brought about either through *eros* or *askésis*. In the erotic conversion the subject is torn away from itself in the overwhelming experience of *eros* that elevates and transforms the subject, raising it to a new perspective on itself and the world. In *The Hermeneutics of the Subject*, Foucault does not spend much time discussing erotic spirituality, but he deals extensively with *askésis*, spiritual exercises and spiritual direction. In *askésis* the subject brings about a conversion through working on itself, through the labour of spiritual exercises. This work transforms the subject in its subjectivity giving it access to truth, to true being. Finally, the third postulate of spirituality is that truth is not experienced as a quality of propositions, it is not the correspondence between a proposition and a state-of-affairs. Rather, truth is experienced in existential terms as salvation – that is, as beatitude, tranquillity, peace, joy, fulfilment, self-mastery. These and other terms characterise the accomplishment of truth in a true life.

The Cartesian Moment, then, names the series of events that displace and disqualify spirituality and allow a new subject-truth relation to take its place. In other words, modern philosophy, modern subjectivity and reason, come into being by disqualifying the idea that philosophy is care of the self. This new experience of subjectivity and truth takes the form of knowledge (*connaissance*) understood in strictly cognitive and discursive terms. Knowledge takes the form of systems of propositions that are linked by rules of inference and that correctly represent or correspond to objects or states-of-affairs. The truth or correctness of these propositions is verified in a mental experience of evidence. The thinking subject, in the modern framework, has the natural right and capacity to access evidence – in fact evidence is precisely what any sane person can see and understand. The modern subject of knowledge does not need to undergo a conversion through *askésis* or *eros* in order to gain access to the truth. Truth is not a characteristic of the ethos or subjectivity of the subject, it is a quality of propositions. In fact, in modernity truth is true precisely to the extent that it is 'disinterested' rather than interested, 'objective' rather than 'subjective'. In the *Meditations*, Descartes arrives at this non-ascetic subject, the Cogito – the subject of modern scientific knowledge. And yet, the way Descartes arrives at the Cogito is through the spiritual exercise of meditation, by undergoing the *épreuve* of radical doubt and modifying his subjectivity or ethos. The framework of spirituality is still present and at work in the *Meditations* even though the goal of the *Meditations* is to displace that very framework and to substitute for it the framework of modern, objective knowledge, the basis of modern science and philosophy.

5

In *The Hermeneutics of the Subject* and the lectures that follow, *The Government of Self and Others*, and *The Courage of the Truth*, Foucault excavates the ancient Greek and Hellenistic model of spirituality and the practice of philosophy as care of the self. Philosophy was, then, both the theorisation and the practice of care of oneself and others. In other words, ancient Greek, Hellenistic and Roman philosophers developed elaborate systems, practices, theories and forms of relationships (pedagogical, therapeutic, formal and informal, friendships, erotic, etc.) all revolving around the attempt to take care of oneself and others, to govern or conduct oneself properly, to learn how to live, to learn and practise the arts of living, in order to bring about the necessary modification in one's subjectivity and gain access to truth in the form of a true life. Central to this care of self and others was the practice of *parrésia*, frank, free, dangerous speech. In order to transform oneself one had to be able to speak the truth, to open up and say what needs to be said and heard but what may be unpleasant to say or hear. This work on oneself, care of the self, took place within relationships of spiritual direction that involved speaking frankly and making manifest one's ethos, one's subjectivity, with the goal of conversion and salvation, the goal of living the true life.

This entire conception and endeavour was taken over by Christian monasticism and asceticism. Spiritual exercises and spiritual direction defined the Christian monastic or ascetic life as a 'true life' and 'the true philosophy', the true arts of living. *Parrésia* was taken over and displaced in the arts of spiritual direction and in confessional practices and relationships, but also manifest in Christian mysticism.[12] Telling the truth of the self became a cornerstone of Christian spiritual direction and spiritual exercise. Of course the specific nature, function and aims of care of the self all changed as it was appropriated by Christianity. The ancient Greek and Hellenistic model in general linked the true life to forms of freedom and power, the capacity to live a beautiful, noble life and to exercise political power in the polis, or to govern one's life or household. *Askésis* was not fundamentally about self-denial but about self-formation, etho-poiesis. An individual would elect to become the disciple of a master, a spiritual director, as a temporary condition the result of which would be self-mastery and the freedom to govern oneself and others. In Christian spirituality, on the other hand, self-care was linked up to self-renunciation and to obedience, to submitting one's will permanently to one's spiritual director and to God. This Christianised form of spirituality, care of the self, and government or direction of oneself and others, developed over the centuries into what is know as the pastorate and what Foucault called in *Security, Territory, Population*, 'pastoral power'.[13] Spirituality and care of the self had become the systematic pastoral government of souls and lives, the systematic deployment of relations of government that took the form of permanent obedience to one's spiritual master and director.

In the *Meditations*, what is at stake is precisely the care of the self, the government of oneself and others and the government of life, the discovery and practice of new arts of living and of mastery of self and world, and a new form of subjectivity capable of gaining access to the truth as the key to true life: 'I do not think', Foucault says in *The Hermeneutics of the Subject*, 'we can understand the meticulousness with which [Descartes] defines his intellectual method unless we have clearly in mind his negative target, which is precisely these methods of spiritual exercise that were frequently practiced within Christianity and which derived from the spiritual exercises of Antiquity.'[14] And in *The Government of Self and Others*, a year later, Foucault says:

> if Descartes' Meditations are in fact an enterprise to found a scientific discourse in truth [they are also] an enterprise of *parrésia* in the sense that it is actually the philosopher as such who speaks in saying 'I', and in affirming his *parrésia* in that precisely founded scientific form of evidence, and he does this in order first of all to play a particular role in relation to the structures of power of ecclesiastical, scientific, and political authority in the name of which he will be able to conduct men's conduct.[15]

The rise of modernity is the break with this pastoral power just as much as it is the break with the Renaissance *episteme* linked to it. This does not mean a break away from the problem of the government of oneself and others but rather the break out of this problem – its breaking free from pastoral power and becoming a general, widespread phenomenon, no longer the exclusive domain of the pastorate. Foucault writes, 'If Descartes' philosophy is taken as the foundation of philosophy, we should also see it as the outcome of this great transformation that brought about the reappearance of philosophy in terms of the question: How to conduct oneself?'[16] Descartes' is trying to break free not just from an *episteme* as a purely intellectual matter. Rather, Descartes is trying to solve the age-old philosophical problem of how to take care of oneself, how to govern oneself and others. He did so by formulating and practising a new government of himself, he developed and practised new 'rules for the conduct of his mind' that opened up, what he saw as, 'the possibility of gaining *knowledge which would be very useful in life*, and of discovering a practical philosophy which might replace the speculative philosophy taught in the schools . . . *we could use this knowledge – as artisans use theirs* – for all the purposes for which it is appropriate, and thus make ourselves, as it were, the lords and masters of nature'.[17]

To accomplish all of this Descartes must undergo his own conversion through the ascetic practice of meditation, he must go through the ordeal (*épreuve*) of hyperbolic doubt as a labour of self-transformation and self-care, as an attempt to modify his subjectivity and gain access to truth as certainty and evidence in the form of the Cogito. Yet, the form of subjectivity and truth that he arrives at in the Cogito will become the foundation of an experience of knowledge that no longer requires *askésis*, spirituality, self-care.[18] The rise of evidence, of the subject as a nature that is capable of just looking and seeing, who arrives at the truth by following the formal rules of inference, will mean that individuals no longer need to undergo a spiritual exercise, a conversion of ethos, to see the truth. Truth in modern philosophy and science is given to anyone and is precisely what is not contingent upon who you are, your ethos. Modern scientific truth is objectivity rather than as *askésis*, ethos, subjectivity.

Just as Descartes invites the mad and their madness into his thoughts only to immediately show them to the door, he adopts the practices of *askésis*, spirituality, only to arrive at a relation to himself and to the truth, the Cogito, which will no longer grasp itself in terms of spirituality, *askésis* and ethos, but rather in the form of evidence, cognition, *connaissance*. Modern philosophy, the form or forms of subjectivity it both requires and makes possible, is premised upon the exclusion of spirituality, of care of the self; it is strangely inhospitable to spirituality. To be hospitable to madness – would that not mean to be hospitable to spirituality, to an experience of the subject's access to truth and to itself that takes the form of *eros* or of *askésis*, of an *épreuve*, a trial, to a truth that is itself a sort of ordeal and a way of living? Is it precisely this sort of experience of subjectivity, of the Cogito itself, that is in play in 'Cogito and the History of Madness'? Would it be crazy to think of deconstruction as a spiritual exercise, a care of the self and others, even a form of *parrésia*?

6

> Derrida's argumentation is remarkable for its depth and perhaps even more so for its frankness [*sa franchise*]. (HM, 552)

Derrida's paper is remarkable for its frankness, that is to say, for its '*parrésia*'. In what sense is 'Cogito and the History of Madness' a case of *parrésia*? Derrida begins his essay with a sort of confession – a personal, biographical note – that could all too easily be read as external to the actual philosophical content of his essay. He inscribes into his text its personal meaning and singularity as an event in his life and in his relationship to Michel Foucault. But if we see this passage in light of Foucault's later work we can understand it very differently.

Derrida confesses that, 'having formerly had the good fortune to study under

Michel Foucault, I retain the consciousness of an admiring and grateful disciple' (WD, 31–2). Perhaps it would be impossible for Derrida to fail to acknowledge this fact under the circumstances, knowing that his former teacher was in the audience. But Derrida goes much further. He elucidates in detail the structure and dynamic movement of the form of consciousness or subjectivity, which he claims as his own, that of the disciple: 'Now the disciple's consciousness, when he starts, I would not say to dispute, but to engage in dialogue with the master or, better, to articulate the interminable and silent dialogue which made him into a disciple – this disciple's consciousness is an unhappy consciousness.' What we have here is the beginning of a description of the disciple, the student, as a form of subjectivity, and the master-disciple pair as a relationship of power-knowledge-subjectivity centred on problems of self-care and the proper use of *parrésia*. This form of subjectivity, then, is at one and the same time a relationship of the self to itself – a way of comprehending oneself and a practical stance towards one's own life, comportment and identity – and a relationship of the self to the other, the master. In the act of speaking, of speaking up and talking back, the disciple becomes acutely conscious of himself as a disciple – that is, just at the crucial moment of passage where one must no longer be a disciple in a relationship to a master or teacher. Of course, speaking back is preceded by the 'internal dialogue' of the self with itself. Yet this internal dialogue cannot be characterised as the spontaneous work of the single isolated thinking subject. Rather the 'internal dialogue' puts into play the words spoken by the other, the master, within the institutional setting of the university. It is this institution – with its codes, traditions, forms of power and authority – that constitutes the one as teacher or master and the other as student or disciple.

It is precisely at the threshold across which one passes into a new relationship to oneself and others that discipleship as a mode of subjectification becomes most intensely present – both to oneself and to the other, the master. 'Starting to enter into dialogue in the world, that is, starting to answer back, he [the disciple] always feels "caught in the act", like the "infant" who, by definition and as his name indicates, cannot speak and above all must not answer back.' The internal tension which structures this mode of subjectivity finally comes fully into view, that is the tension between an enforced but necessary 'silence' on the part of the disciple and the very possibility of his speaking, of having something of his own to say. And what is more, the possibility of being recognised as a speaking subject who claims his own words as his own. In other words, it is part of the subjectivity of the disciple to listen, or to speak only in such a way as to reiterate or internalise the lessons of the master. The disciple then is defined by a certain sort of silence – a silence that may not be literal or complete but rather entails not having one's own truths to impart, one's own knowledge to articulate – rather the disciple must acquire knowledge through listening and repeating, through accepting and internalising. In the dynamics of this relationship to oneself and to others, how could the free speech of the disciple come across as anything other than a challenge? But, Derrida makes clear that the internalised dialogue takes the form of a challenge from the beginning – it gives form to a relationship of power-knowledge, not just knowledge:

> And when, as is the case here, the dialogue is in danger of being taken – incorrectly – as a challenge, the disciple knows that he alone [that is to say, already alone with his thoughts] finds himself challenged by the master's voice within him that precedes his own. He feels himself indefinitely challenged, or rejected or accused; as a disciple, he is challenged by the master who speaks within him and before him, to reproach him for making this challenge and to reject it in advance; and having interiorized the master he is also challenged by the disciple that he himself is.

The master's authoritative voice precedes the disciple's own voice, but not because it comes from outside the disciple, or not only so. Rather, because that voice echoes within the disciple himself, as his own relationship to himself.

The crucial moment, the real test, the *épreuve de soi*, through which one passes to become no longer a disciple is the moment when one must speak in one's own voice and say what one thinks. This moment is the one in which the entire structure and all of the dynamic relationships and possibilities it inaugurated, as well as all this which it cancelled out, is shattered, a mere reflection, mere reflexivity: 'This interminable unhappiness of the disciple perhaps stems from the fact that he does not yet know – or is still concealing from himself – that the master, like real life [*la vrai vie*], may always be absent. The disciple must break the glass, or better the mirror, the reflection, his infinite speculation on the master. And start to speak.' Breaking the glass, liberating oneself from the position of disciple, does not culminate in one's reaching true freedom, true life, one does not become master. To be a disciple means that one is learning, living to learn, learning to live. In other words to be a disciple is to be preparing for life, and in a sense then it means that as a disciple one is not yet truly living. It is the master, presumably, who truly lives and who knows, who has the power to govern and care for those who are not yet ready. At least this is the mode of experience that takes the form of master-disciple. The act of speaking back does not then move the disciple to the other side of the relationship, to the position of master. The true liberation would not be a liberation to true life, to the position of power and knowledge. It would be the tenuous and uncertain insight that 'the master, like true life, may always be absent'. In other words, breaking from the position of disciple would be to realise there is no master, no true master, no true mastery of oneself, of life. We enter into a new set of relationships of self to self and self to other, but this new relationship might no longer command us by offering us the promise of true life and true mastery.

The paradoxical, impossible, task of this art or practice of the government of oneself and others is for the disciple to come to the recognition that the master, like *la vrai vie*, does not exist. The master would be the one who knows – the one who knows what? How to live, fully and truly live. The master would be the one in whom true life and true discourse mutually support, express and confirm each other. The one from whom we can learn how to live, finally.[19] But what if there is no true life to be learned, if there is perhaps only living with that paradoxical, Socratic wisdom? – we become wise, we become freed from the government of the master-disciple relationship when we finally learn that there is no final knowledge to be learned on this topic, there can be no master because there can be no wisdom. And yet the one who learns this – has she become a master of herself, has she now learned how to live?

All of this returns in Derrida's final interview when he was asked to comment on the surprising and personal 'Exordium' to *Specters of Marx* in which he reflects on the notion of learning how to live: 'Someone, you or me, comes forward and says: *I would like to learn to live finally*.'[20] Already, in 1963, this question haunts Derrida, even if it has not yet been able to find such clear articulation. In his final interview Derrida asks: 'Can one learn, through discipline or apprenticeship, through experience or experimentation, to *accept* or, better, to *affirm* life?' Here, he admits, he 'never learned-to-live. In fact not at all!' Learning to live would mean, Derrida claims, just like a philosopher, learning how to die. 'But', he says, 'I remain uneducable when it comes to any kind of wisdom about knowing-how-to-die or, if you prefer, knowing-how-to-live.'[21] Of course, death hovered in the background of this interview. Only a couple of months after it was published Derrida would be gone.

Derrida makes it clear that one must learn of the non-being of the master and of the true life, the two seemingly tied together of necessity. In *Specters of Marx*, these themes return:

> For from the lips of the master this watch word would always say something about violence. It vibrates like an arrow in the course of an irreversible and asymmetrical address, the one that goes most often from father to son, master to disciple, or master to slave ('I'm going to teach you to live'). Such an address hesitates, therefore: between address as *experience* (is not learning to live experience itself), address as *education*, and address as *taming* or *training* [dressage].[22]

A life that is fully alive, a life saturated with life, could not possibly pose this question and there would be no need because life would be living to the fullest. Therefore, it is not in life or from life that we learn to live. We cannot learn it in death – even if there is life after death, the lesson would come too late for living here and now, today. It is not in death that we learn to live. 'If it – learning to live – remains to be done, it can happen only between life and death';[23] only for those who are neither fully alive nor who are dead but who are between the two – those survivors, those who live on, carry on, living in the wake of death, who face it on the horizon, out there somewhere closer than one might think.

The speaking subject, Derrida himself, is constituted by a specific form of relationship: disciple-master. In the opening lines of the text Derrida characterises the dynamics, the affectivity, the modes of constraint as well as the lines of flight that compose it. Is this relationship itself constituted through a movement of internalisation – the internalisation of a historically specific institution, a relationship of power-knowledge? Is this relationship of disciple-master rather formed through a process of externalisation or projection of an internal process, a psycho-dynamic process of ego-formation? It cannot be specified and perhaps cannot be properly located as an internalising or externalising phenomenon. Rather the master-disciple relationship is both a relationship of power or governmentality that defines oneself with respect to another and an institution, and *at the same time* a relationship to oneself that represents a series of self-reflexive activities and processes. It can only function as a mechanism of control if it is taken to be externally real. On the other hand, it can only be taken as an externally real mechanism of control if it internally structures the relationship of the self to itself through self-reflexive choices. This is precisely what Foucault is getting at in his analyses of the practices of freedom of the self, and of governmentality – the way in which these practices seen from one angle function as mechanisms of control and constraint, perhaps even to the point of domination and oppression, and on the other hand represent practices of freedom and of the cultivation of one's ethos, of oneself as an ethical subject, and as a knower.

The opening lines of 'Cogito and the History of Madness' outline the etho-poetic or ascetic function of the discursive events to follow. In other words, Derrida asserts that the act of speech to come must be understood as a practice of the self, as ascesis and an *épreuve* which he must carry out and undergo in order to transform his own subjectivity. In yet other words, this lecture is an act of *parrésia*, a risk, a test, and an intensification of the truth, the reverberations of which will be felt in the very being of the speaking and listening subjects. We can see the degree to which this event, these words spoken at this time and place, in this room with this audience, modified both Derrida and Foucault, they transformed the relationship that each would take to himself and to the other, and the way each would constitute himself as a philosopher.

7

As we have already noted, Derrida argues that Descartes does not exclude madness from his systematic doubt. In the following, I will go once more through this text, reading Descartes through Derrida through the later Foucault. What I hope to show is that despite the fact that Derrida does not have recourse to the language or concepts of care of the self, *askésis*, or spirituality, his reading of Descartes does in fact reveal the text to be primarily a series of discursive practices and events that aim at displacing and modifying the subjectivity of the meditating subject.

So let's return once again to Descartes' First Meditation. As we know, what motivates Descartes is his realisation that so often he believed in things that have turned out to be false. The *Meditations* are driven by Descartes' desire to evade this error and uncertainty – he has erred too often and concerning fundamental, foundational matters. Is it possible then to secure himself from error – from wandering blindly in uncertainty, believing in falsehoods? Can I dispel illusions and get a hold on reality with certainty? The method of course is systematically to pursue and radicalise doubt and uncertainty. This should allow him to see what beliefs, if any, can withstand the most extreme conditions of doubt and uncertainty. But for doubt to be systematic it must adhere to the discipline of reason, method. Doubt only that which I have a reason to doubt. And rather than hopelessly submitting every belief to the test, go straight to the foundational beliefs, the sources of my other beliefs.

First among these: the belief that my senses give me an accurate representation of the material world outside of me. Among the reasons to doubt my senses, Descartes raises, momentarily, the possibility that madmen believe they are kings when in fact they are poor; they believe they are gourds or made of glass. Could I be like them, could my senses be deceiving me about my body and its immediate surroundings? Descartes dismisses the possibility: *but such people are insane*, he writes, and I would be just as mad to compare myself to the mad. I could, on the other hand, be dreaming, and that is not crazy.

Derrida claims that the line, 'but such people are insane', indicates a shift of voice. It represents an interruption of Descartes' train of thought and 'the astonishment and objections of the nonphilosopher, of the novice in philosophy who is frightened by this doubt and protests' (WD, 50). In other words, Derrida here characterises the First Meditation as a sort of implicit, internal dialogue in which Descartes, the philosopher, presents his argument to an interlocutor, who at this point interrupts and represents the voice of common sense, of ordinary everyday opinion. Descartes 'assumes the astonishment of this reader or naïve interlocutor, pretends to take him into account' (WD, 50). It is not Descartes who rules out the possibility of madness, it is the ordinary person – the nonphilosopher. Rather Descartes is pretending here. The philosopher, on the other hand, is always ready to follow the argument even when it transgresses common sense and seems to be mad, even when it might be mad.

But why should Descartes slow down the movement of doubt, why interrupt with this voice of the nonphilosopher? Derrida writes: 'Descartes acquiesces to this natural point of view, or rather he feigns to rest in this natural comfort in order better, more radically and more definitively, to unsettle himself from it and to discomfort his interlocutor' (WD, 50). What is important for us here is that Derrida attributes to this sequence a function or meaning that is not reducible to signification or demonstration. Rather, for Derrida this passage is 'meant' first of all to tranquilise the reader (as well as the author), to induce a sense of comfort and security, but only in order subsequently to bring about a heightened or intensified subjective state of 'discomfort', it is meant to 'unsettle' not only the supposed interlocutor (the reader) but also the philosopher himself, the meditating subject, Descartes.

It seems to me that this reading of the passage takes it, implicitly, as nothing other than a meditation, in the sense given that term by Foucault in 'My Body, This Paper, This Fire' and then later in *The Hermeneutics of the Subject*: an exercise in which the very being or subjectivity of the thinking subject is put into play by the thoughts that subject thinks. Meditation in this sense is a test that the subject must undergo or put itself through and which clarifies, displaces and modifies the thinking subject. Thinking as *épreuve*.

We can already see here the outlines of the ascetic, meditative, movement taking place in the text. Rather than operating on the plane of the intellectual comprehension of concepts or the assessment of the validity of inferences, this text would function as an exercise and a test; it aims at the displacement of the thinking subject. This displacement or ascetic modification of the subject would culminate at the moment of the Cogito. *But this point cannot be reached directly*, or purely demonstratively. Rather, for Derrida, it can occur only when Descartes is able to bring madness into play in his methodical pursuit of certainty via the route of doubt: 'the recourse to the fiction of the evil genus will *evoke*, *conjure up*, the possibility of a *total madness*, a total derangement over which I could have no control because it is inflicted upon me – hypothetically – leaving me no responsibility for it' (WD, 52–3, my emphasis). It is only when this possibility is *evoked* or *conjured* that Descartes will be able to attain the moment of the Cogito. Moreover, we have to specify then what is meant by a 'hypothesis' here – the postulate of the evil genus is not a thesis or statement to be tested, verified, validated. Rather, it is a hypothetical madness that occurs in the course of an exercise and is experienced as a test of the thinking subject, a test which puts the very being and validity of the thinker himself in play. The conditional nature of this thought attaches not to its asserted content so much as to its effect on the meditating subject. At this point, everything I think and perceive *could* turn out to be nothing, *could* turn out to be false and meaningless – my thoughts *could* be totally deranged without any possible recourse to a standard of reason to assure me of that. But it is precisely in the vertigo of this madness that the Cogito suddenly appears on the scene.

How does Derrida characterise the event of the Cogito (as a discursive practice and, it seems to me, as an ascetic event)? For Derrida, the meaning of the Cogito is that it 'escapes madness only because at its own moment, under its own authority, it is valid even if *I am mad*, even if my thoughts are completely mad' (WD, 55). It is in the face of madness that Descartes attains, experiences, or undergoes the full meaning and truth of the Cogito. The Cogito does not attain its truth through evading madness and uncertainty, but rather it recognises its validity precisely in facing the essential possibility of its own madness. This possibility of total madness, brought about through the meditative practice itself, is not the same as any determined, historical or empirical case of madness. The total madness confronting Descartes exceeds any distinction between meaning and nonmeaning because it necessarily abolishes any clear logos or logic, any reason that could be given without doubt, to separate the meaningful thought from the empty one. This is what Derrida calls the 'instantaneous experience of the Cogito at its most intense' (WD, 58).

Descartes *realises* the Cogito – in the dual sense of the term as both comprehending and bringing into existence – in that instantaneous experience sparked by the meditative practice or device of the evil genius. This test or trial – undergoing the meditative exercise of demonic hyperbole – intensifies the subjectivity of the meditator to the highest degree. Here at the point of total madness, at the point of total loss and derangement, in a sort of wild freedom, the subjectivity of the meditating subject is most alive and present – it is most present in this moment of total or nearly total absence of sense. It is only subsequent to this realisation, according to Derrida, that Descartes excludes madness and secures reason and meaning:

> From the moment when Descartes pronounces the Cogito, he inscribes it in a system of deductions and protections that betray its wellspring and constrain the wandering that is proper to it so that error may be circumvented. . . . These dogmatic axioms escape doubt, are never even submitted to its scru-

> tiny, are established only reciprocally, on the basis of the existence and truthfulness of God. Due to this fact, they fall within the province of the history of knowledge and the determined structures of philosophy. (WD, 58–9)

Descartes' hyperbolic doubt, his meditative exercise, evokes an experience that is implicated by and within language/meaning (*vouloir-dire*) itself – that original source, which, however, would lie before or beyond all language and meaning. In his quest for a secure starting point, a pure origin, Descartes undergoes the experience of a certainty, the existence of the Cogito, whose very certainty is most intense at the moment of its greatest uncertainty. Realising his own subjectivity in this moment, Descartes calls upon language and reason to *articulate* that existence and in effect silence the madness of his own subjective life taken to its most acute or intense point. A repression that would be inscribed in the heart of every determinate form of reason and its other, every manner of inscribing nonmeaning as the specific localisable other of a specific meaning and reason.[24]

My claim then is that Derrida gives us a Descartes engaged in a concerted exercise, labouring to unsettle himself, break free of himself, only to come alive in the most intense way in the moment of the Cogito. And then, at precisely this moment, to get a hold on this intensity, to contain and control it within a series of concepts and deductions, within a rational and meaningful order that would stabilise it and protect it from its own naked intensity.

In Derrida's reading, Descartes deliberately unsettles himself, discomforts himself, disrupts the general system of meaning that had been operative in, through, and as his own subjective life in order to find a secure basis for knowledge and science, in order to find certainty so that he can avoid error and blind wandering, in order to think differently and be a different kind of subject. But this exercise leads to the greatest uncertainty, the hyperbolic doubt, the demonic-hyperbole in which every thought is potentially deranged, blind wandering and error. It is precisely at this point that Descartes realises in the most intense way the form of subjective life that he will articulate as the Cogito. But it is also at this moment, wanting to get a hold of the certainty of the Cogito in the very face of its total senselessness, that he encloses the madness of empty thought so that it can then be reduced to determinate and specific forms of unreason.

8

According to Derrida, Descartes' *Meditations* would only be one case of a more general phenomenon. For Derrida, philosophy itself is essentially the will-to-say-the-demonic-hyperbole, the desire to put into words the moment where subjectivity (self-ethos) comes to be, that is, where it is not, or not yet, or no longer itself:

> To define philosophy as wanting-to-say-the-hyperbole [translation slightly modified: *vouloir-dire-l'hyperbole*] is to confess [*avouer*] – and philosophy is perhaps this gigantic confession [*aveu*] – that by virtue of the historical saying of it [translation slightly modified: *le dit historique*] through which philosophy

> tranquilises itself and excludes madness, philosophy also betrays itself (or betrays itself as thought), enters into a crisis and a forgetting of itself that are an essential and necessary period of its movement. (WD, 62)

This movement of confession, fall, test or crisis, and re-awaking, isn't it most fully illuminated by the terms Foucault gives us: care of the self, *askésis*, *parrésia*, spirituality?

Between Derrida and Foucault thinking occurs as an *exercise* and *épreuve*, transforming by intensifying the subjective life that unfolds at the border of language and nonlanguage, reason and madness. On the one side of this border lies the 'total madness' of hyperbolic doubt and naked, solitary existence present only with itself in its emptiness. On the other side lies every historically singular determination of the division between sense and non-sense, between the sane and the mad. This exercise and *épreuve* would also be at the heart of responsibility, of recognising the inevitability of the decision, groundless but necessary, at the root of and hence outside of any justification – the moment of *parrésia*. Learning to live, putting into play arts of living, a care of the self, spirituality, even a political spirituality, all bring us back, ceaselessly to this moment, the absence of the work, the *épreuve* of that absence. The practice of care of the self, spirituality, *askésis*, *parrésia*, puts life, reason and subjectivity to the test by ceaselessly suspending their certainties, disturbing them, razing them to the ground in order to give place to new forms and relations. The madness of the question of how to care for the self, how to practise the art of living, would be the truth, and untruth, haunting every answer, dissolving every solution, in a way that is not simply destructive but also creativity itself.[25]

NOTES

1. Gilles Deleuze, *Difference and Repetition*, trans. Paul Patton (New York: Columbia University Press, 1994), p. 107.
2. Len Lawlor has already argued that the *épreuve* is central to the experience of deconstruction: 'The experience that functions as this undeconstructible measure is the test (*l'épreuve*) of the sign. It seems to me that it is impossible to dissociate deconstruction, Derrida's thought itself, from the experience or test of language' (Leonard Lawlor, *Derrida and Husserl: The Basic Problem of Phenomenology* (Bloomington: Indiana University Press, 2003), p. 3). This essay continues to think through this fact and its implications.
3. Others have already shown that Foucault's later work continues his engagement with Derrida. But none have suggested the tight interweaving of texts and readings that I propose in this chapter. See, for example, Arnold Davidson's Introduction to Michel Foucault, *The Hermeneutics of the Subject: Lectures at the Collège de France 1981–1982*, ed. Frédéric Gros, trans. Graham Burchell (New York: Palgrave Macmillan, 2005), p. xxvii; Frédéric Gros's footnote 20 on p. 257; and his essay on the Course Context in Michel Foucault, *The Government of Self and Others: Lectures at the Collège de France 1982–1983*, ed. Frédéric Gros, trans. Graham Burchell (New York: Palgrave Macmillan, 2010), p. 383. For a much more extensive treatment of the way Foucault's later work is indebted and responding to the criticism and overall positions of Derrida, see Paul Allen Miller, *Post-Modern Spiritual Practices: The Construction of the Subject and the Reception of Plato in Lacan, Derrida, and Foucault* (Columbus: Ohio State University Press, 2007).

4. Michel Foucault, *History of Madness*, ed. Jean Khalfa, trans. Jonathan Murphy and Jean Khalfa (London: Routledge, 2006), p. 42. Hereafter cited in the text as HM.
5. René Descartes, *The Philosophical Writings of Descartes*, vol. 2, trans. John Cottingham, Robert Stoothoff and Dugald Murdoch (Cambridge: Cambridge University Press, 1984), p. 13.
6. Quoted by Foucault, HM, 46.
7. Jacques Derrida, 'Cogito and the History of Madness', in *Writing and Difference*, trans. Alan Bass (Chicago: University of Chicago Press, 1978), p. 32. Hereafter cited in the text as WD.
8. Private letters during the period after this lecture give expression to Foucault's admiration of and gratitude for Derrida's essay and encourage him to publish it. These letters may be consulted, with permission, at the IMEC.
9. Foucault, *The Hermeneutics of the Subject*, p. 358.
10. Ibid., p. 14.
11. Ibid., pp. 15–16.
12. Michel Foucault, *The Courage of Truth. The Government of Self and Others II: Lectures at the Collège de France 1983–1984*, ed. Frédéric Gros, trans. Graham Burchell (New York: Palgrave Macmillan, 2011), p. 337. The genealogy of *parrésia* from its first appearance in Euripides' through its appropriation by and then exclusion from Christian spirituality is far more complex than can be shown in this chapter. I offer a far more extensive account of all these threads in Edward McGushin, *Foucault's* Askésis: *An Introduction to the Philosophical Life* (Evanston, IL: Northwestern University Press, 2007).
13. Michel Foucault, *Security, Territory, Population: Lectures at the Collège de France 1977–1978*, ed. Michel Senellart, trans. Graham Burchell (New York: Palgrave Macmillan, 2007), p. 123.
14. Foucault, *The Hermeneutics of the Subject*, p. 294.
15. Foucault, *The Government of Self and Others*, p. 349.
16. Foucault, *Security, Territory, Population*, p. 230.
17. René Descartes, *The Philosophical Writings of Descartes*, vol. 1, trans. John Cottingham, Robert Stoothoff and Dugald Murdoch (Cambridge: Cambridge University Press, 1985), p. 142.
18. Michel Foucault, 'On the Genealogy of Ethics: An Overview of Work in Progress', in *Ethics, Subjectivity, and Truth: Essential Works of Foucault, Volume I*, trans. Robert Hurley et al., ed. Paul Rabinow (New York: The New Press, 1997), pp. 278–80.
19. Jacques Derrida, *Learning How to Live, Finally: The Last Interview*, trans. Pascale-Anne Brault and Michael Nass (Brooklyn, NY: Melville House, 2007).
20. Jacques Derrida, *Specters of Marx: The State of the Debt, the Work of Mourning, and the New International*, trans. Peggy Kamuf (New York: Routledge, 1994), p. xvi.
21. Derrida, *Learning How to Live, Finally*, pp. 24, 25.
22. Derrida, *Specters of Marx*, p. xvi.
23. Ibid., p. xvii.
24. 'This is why the act of the Cogito, at the hyperbolic moment when it pits itself against madness, or rather lets itself be pitted against madness, must be repeated and distinguished from the language or the deductive system in which Descartes must inscribe it as soon as he proposes it for apprehension and communication, that is, as soon as he reflects the Cogito for the other, which means for oneself. It is through this relationship to the other as an other self that meaning reassures itself against madness and nonmeaning. And philosophy is perhaps the reassurance given against the anguish of being mad at the point of greatest proximity to madness' (WD, 59).
25. The research for this chapter was supported by generous grants from Stonehill College. A SURE grant during the summer of 2013 provided me with time and an excellent research assistant, Lauren Mahncke. I am grateful for her critical readings of my work and her assistance in dealing with the mass of secondary literature on this topic. A Stonehill Faculty Development Grant in 2014 allowed me to travel to Caen, France to work in the IMEC

where I consulted Foucault's letters to Derrida. The staff of the IMEC were extraordinarily patient with my requests for assistance in halting French. I would also especially like to thank Foucault's sister, Francine Fruchaud, and his nephew, Henri-Paul Fruchaud, for granting me permission to read these letters.

PART II

The End of Reason

CHAPTER 7

The History of Historicity: The Critique of Reason in Foucault (and Derrida)

Amy Allen[1]

Much of the published debate between Derrida and Foucault over Foucault's *History of Madness*[2] turns on their disagreement about how to read Descartes. Derrida devotes over half of his rightly famous essay, 'Cogito and the History of Madness',[3] to challenging Foucault's reading of Descartes in the opening pages of the chapter on 'The Great Confinement', and the bulk of Foucault's official responses in the essays 'My Body, This Paper, This Fire' and 'Reply to Derrida' defends his reading. And, on one level, it makes a lot of sense that this should be the focus of debate. After all, at stake is not only the question of the legacy of Descartes – a significant enough question for a debate between two of the most important French philosophers of the twentieth century – but also the question of *how to read* him – whether we must, as Derrida insists, strive to preserve the autonomy of Descartes' text, or whether we may, as Foucault suggests, read the text as in some way related to extra-textual social and historical events. These are undoubtedly important philosophical and interpretive issues. And yet it is a bit strange that so much of their debate turns on what can seem to many readers like quibbling over a few sentences in the First Meditation, especially given that, in the opening pages of his essay, Derrida raises some very fundamental methodological challenges to Foucault's project, challenges that go largely, but, as we shall see, not entirely unanswered in Foucault's replies.

In what follows, I aim to reconsider the Derrida/Foucault debate from the point of view of these methodological challenges. My central claim is that this aspect of their debate is best understood as a disagreement over how best to conduct a critique of reason. One of Derrida's main methodological criticisms of Foucault in 'Cogito and the History of Madness' is that Foucault is guilty of a kind of performative contradiction.[4] In so far as Foucault writes in the language of reason, his critique of psychiatric reason must necessarily perform the very exclusion of madness that he aims to indict. 'The revolution against reason', Derrida writes, 'can be made only within it' (WD, 36). Without taking a position on Derrida's substantive claim here, I argue in the first section of this chapter that he has misconstrued Foucault's aim in the *History of Madness*, which is not a revolution against reason at all, but rather a *critique* of it, in the same modified Kantian sense in which Foucault understands the project of critique in his late work. That is to say, *History of Madness* offers an analysis of the historically, socially and culturally specific conditions of possibility for modern reason. Moreover, I want to suggest that their debate over *History of Madness* shows that although Derrida and Foucault share the aim of offering a critique of reason that will expose its entanglements in relations of power, violence and exclusion, they offer two distinct versions of this critical project. This second section of the chapter sketches out Foucault's deeply historical approach to the critique of reason, and suggests some points of contrast with Derrida's more ahistorical and aporetic approach to this issue. Finally, by way of a conclusion, I defend Foucault's version of that project against what I take to be Derrida's most potent objection to it: the charge of metaphysics. I argue that Derrida is right to claim, as he does in 'Cogito and the History of Madness', that the success of Foucault's approach depends on his ability to write a history of historicity, but that this project is not as quixotic as Derrida seems to think.

THE REVOLUTION AGAINST REASON?

Derrida's critique divides into two parts. The first part centres on Foucault's original preface and considers in detail Foucault's methodology in *History of Madness*; the second focuses on the brief discussion of Descartes that opens Foucault's chapter on 'The Great Confinement'. It is an interesting feature of their exchange that the bulk of Foucault's response to Derrida deals with the question of how to read Descartes, and he remains mostly – though not, as we'll see, completely – silent on the methodological questions that Derrida raises. This fact, combined with Foucault's own self-criticisms of *History of Madness* in his 1969 book *The Archaeology of Knowledge*,[5] could be read as evidence that Foucault conceded Derrida's criticisms.[6] However, as we shall see, on the crucial methodological point, which concerns the history of historicity, this is not the case.

Derrida begins with the now infamous, but in my view dubious, claim that 'in writing a history of madness, Foucault has attempted – and this is the greatest merit, but also the very infeasibility of the book – to write a history of madness *itself*. *Itself*' (WD, 33). This is, Derrida claims, 'with all seriousness, the *maddest* aspect of his project' (WD, 34). For, inasmuch as Foucault is writing a *history* of madness, he must necessarily make madness make sense, and in order to do this, he must to capture it in the language of reason. As a result, Foucault cannot help but fall into 'the trap set by classical reason to catch madness', a trap that compels him repeat the very 'aggression of rationalism' that he aims to critique (WD, 34). The claim that Foucault aims to write a history of madness *itself* has contributed to the image of the early Foucault as a youthful romantic who idealises the pure, primitive, wild experience of madness as the locus of freedom. The question of Foucault's romanticism in this text is a complicated one,[7] but the question of whether or not his aim is to write a history of 'madness itself' is more straightforward. To be sure, Derrida's reading is corroborated by the following line from Foucault's preface: 'A history not of psychiatry, but of madness itself, in all its vivacity, before it is captured by knowledge' (HM, xxxii). However, immediately after this sentence, Foucault goes on to acknowledge that writing the history of madness itself 'is, no doubt, a doubly impossible task' and, moreover, that it is impossible for precisely the reasons that Derrida offers: a history of madness could only be told from the point of view of reason, which means both that one could never write a history of 'madness itself' without either going mad oneself or re-performing the rational exclusion of madness (HM, xxxii).[8] As a result of this double impossibility, Foucault concludes this section of the preface by saying that 'to write the history of madness will therefore mean making a structural study of the historical ensemble – notions, institutions, judicial and police measures, scientific concepts – which hold captive a madness whose wild state can never be reconstituted' (HM, xxxiii).

In other words, *History of Madness* is not, as Derrida suggests, a history of 'madness itself' but rather a history of *reason*;[9] or, to be more precise, it is a history of a form of rationality, as that form is articulated in philosophical conceptions and institutional structures, that defines its own limits via the refusal to be mad, and that in so doing constitutes madness as an object of possible experience. Despite his somewhat misleading initial characterisation of Foucault's aim in *History of Madness*, Derrida's methodological critique does hit in the end on a crucial point, though we will have to lay out more of his critique before we will be in a position to see what that point is. Derrida maintains that the impossibility of Foucault's attempt to write the history of madness itself leaves him in a trap that he can only avoid by one of two contradictory moves. Foucault can attempt to avoid re-enacting the aggression of rationalism either by rejecting the language of reason altogether or by delineating the point of the decision, the point where our form of reason separated itself from its mad, unreasonable other.

According to Derrida, the first strategy, the rejection of the language of reason altogether, leads to a dead end inasmuch as it runs into a more general version of the same performative contradiction objection sketched above: even an archaeology is a kind of history, which means that it must be written in the language of reason, hence, an archaeology cannot succeed in rejecting the language of reason and remain an archaeology. As Derrida puts it,

> The unsurpassable, unique, and imperial grandeur of the order of reason, that which makes it not just another actual order or structure (a determined historical structure, one structure among other possible ones), is that one cannot speak out against it except by being for it, that one can protest it only from within it; . . . the revolution against reason can be made only within it. . . . A history, that is, an archaeology against reason doubtless cannot be written, for, despite all appearances to the contrary, the concept of history has always been a rational one. (WD, 36)

I think we need to ask two sorts of questions about Derrida's argument here. First, would Foucault agree with Derrida that it makes sense to talk about Reason understood as an 'unsurpassable, unique, and imperial' order? Or does he believe, as Derrida suggests, dismissively, in a parenthetical aside in the passage quoted above, that reason can be thought of as 'a determined historical structure, one structure among other possible ones'? In a 1983 interview, Foucault claims that *History of Madness* was an attempt to answer the question: 'how does one elaborate a history of rationality?'[10] If such a project is indeed possible (and we don't yet want to assume that it is, we are just trying to get clear on what it is that Foucault is trying to do), then Foucault is not forced to choose between reiterating the 'unsurpassable, unique, and imperial grandeur of the order of reason', on the one hand, and lapsing into a mad irrationalism, on the other. If rationality has a history, then this means that it takes different forms at different times. And Foucault's project of constructing 'a rational critique of rationality' becomes 'a question of isolating the form of rationality presented as dominant, and endowed with the status of the one-and-only reason, in order to show that it is only *one* possible form among others'.[11] But to say that reason has a history is precisely to reject Derrida's talk of Reason per se understood as an unsurpassable, unique and imperial order, in favour of the plural forms of rationality.[12] To be sure, this does not settle the difficult question of whether and if so how such a project is possible, an issue that I'll return to later on. But, to anticipate just a bit, the response will involve articulating the difference between waging a revolution against reason from within it and attempting to construct an immanent critique of rationality from within one of its determinate historical forms.

A second and related set of questions: is Foucault's history of madness in fact written 'against reason'? Is it even intended, as Derrida suggests, as a 'revolution against reason'? Or is it better understood as a *critique* of reason, in the modified and historicised Kantian sense of a reflection on the historically specific limits and conditions of possibility for us as rational subjects, as reasoning beings operating within a specific form of rationality?[13] If we understand his aim in this way, then *History of Madness* becomes a part of Foucault's overall attempt to address the questions that he would later claim have been central to philosophy and critique since the eighteenth century: '*What* is this Reason that we use? What are its historical effects? How can we exist as rational beings, fortunately committed to practicing a rationality that is unfortunately crisscrossed by intrinsic dangers?'[14] On this reading, Foucault's aim is not to reject reason, but rather to think through this 'spiral' formed by the 'indispensability' and the 'intrinsic dangers' of our form of rationality.[15] And, if Foucault is not mounting a revolution against reason, then the performative contradiction charge levelled by Derrida misses its mark.

Derrida's discussion of the second strategy available to Foucault as a result of the double impossibility of his task, however, leads in a more productive direction. As noted above, Derrida characterises this approach as an attempt to delineate the historical moment of the split between reason and madness. Such a methodology is announced in passages such as this one, from Foucault's preface: 'in the absence of that inaccessible primitive purity, the structural study must go back to that decision that both bound and separated reason and madness; it must tend to discover the perpetual exchange, the obscure common root, the originary confrontation that gives meaning to the unity and the opposition of sense and senselessness' (HM, xxxiii). This Derrida takes to mean an exhumation of 'the virgin and unitary ground' that serves as the 'common root' of both madness and reason (WD, 39). Derrida claims that Foucault locates this virgin and unitary ground in the Middle Ages, and he takes issue with that location, for two reasons.

First, Derrida argues that the split between reason and its other is foundational to western philosophy and reason as a whole; hence, the point of division could not be located in the classical age, as he interprets Foucault to be suggesting (WD, 40). However, this criticism assumes once again the kind of grand, unsurpassable order of Reason that Foucault is attempting to call into question by writing a history of rationality. This leads us to Derrida's second point about Foucault's attempt to articulate the originary confrontation between reason and madness, and it is with this point, I want to suggest, that Derrida gets to the heart of Foucault's methodology in *History of Madness*:

> If the decision through which reason constitutes itself by excluding and objectifying the free subjectivity of madness is indeed the origin of history, if it is historicity itself . . . if the structure of exclusion is the fundamental structure of historicity, then the 'classical' moment of this exclusion described by Foucault has neither absolute privilege nor archetypal exemplarity. It is an example as sample and not as model. (WD, 42)

Here Derrida is discussing Foucault's important and somewhat cryptic claim from the preface to *History of Madness* that 'the *necessity of madness* throughout the history of the West is linked to that decisive action that extracts a significant language from the background noise and its continuous monotony, a language which is transmitted and culminates in time; it is, in short, linked to the *possibility of history*' (HM, xxxii). Furthermore, he seems to be assuming that when Foucault talks about the possibility of history, he is making a claim about western history as a whole, about historicity understood as the very possibility of writing history. However, Foucault's claim does not refer to western history as a whole, but instead, as I'll discuss further in the next section, refers to History with a capital 'H', where this is understood as a particular way of organising knowledge that emerged in the nineteenth century with what is sometimes called the second, historicist enlightenment (which Foucault refers to as 'modernity' as distinct from the classical age). In other words, it refers to a particular historical a priori – what we might call the Historical historical a priori, the historical a priori in which the notion of History understood in a broadly speaking Hegelian sense as the progressive realisation of reason in history emerges – which means that the claim that the necessity of madness is linked to the possibility of history in this sense does not commit Foucault to any claims about the 'origin of history' per se or 'historicity itself'. Nor is the classical age offered by Foucault as an archetype or exemplar or model of some broader exclusion of madness itself by Reason with a capital R. Rather, it is offered as a contingently emergent form of rationality that defines its own limits by refusing and confining madness; this, in turn makes possible the modern, nineteenth-century conception of a historically unfolding progressive realisation of reason that, as we will see, confines madness by incorporating it into its dialectic.

This leads us to Derrida's final methodological question for Foucault, which he simply poses, suggesting that it is so paradoxical and quixotic that it isn't even worth attempting to answer: 'if this great division is the possibility of history itself, the historicity of history, what does it mean, here, "to write the history of this division"? To write the history of historicity? To write the history of the origin of history?' (WD, 43). Here Derrida hits the nail on the head, because he is absolutely right that the methodological aim of *History of Madness* is the attempt to write the history of historicity, to write the history of the origin of History, though, as I shall try to argue in the next two sections, this project is not nearly as quixotic and problematic as Derrida seems to think.

THE HISTORY OF HISTORICITY? FOUCAULT'S HISTORICISED CRITIQUE OF REASON

In what sense does *History of Madness* attempt to write the history of historicity? As I have already suggested, this claim is announced in the preface where Foucault links the necessity of madness to the possibility of history, but it isn't explored in detail until the opening of Part Three of the text, in which Foucault deals with the nineteenth-century experience of madness as mental illness. Central to this discussion is Foucault's complicated and shifting distinction between madness and unreason. Whereas for the classical age, madness had been one of the determinate forms of the broader category of unreason – which included all those whom the bourgeois order deemed to be undesirable or abnormal, not only madmen but also libertines, sexual perverts, criminals and the unemployed – in modernity, the classical age's unified experience of unreason broke apart. Unreason remained the untimely monotonous 'background noise' from which the language of reason that 'culminates in time' was 'extracted' (HM, xxxii), whereas madness was recuperated in the dialectical unfolding of reason in history. From the late eighteenth century onwards, Foucault writes, 'the time of unreason and the time of madness were to be affected by two opposing vectors: unreason becoming an unconditional return, and an absolute plunge; madness developing along the chronology of a history' (HM, 363–4).

This uncoupling of madness from unreason meant that madness had entered a new, historical, phase. Whereas unreason remained associated with the tragic outside of history, an outside that could be glimpsed fleetingly through the tragic consciousness of madness, madness was 'intimately connected to history' (HM, 377) and 'took shape inside a historical consciousness' (HM, 378). This was the case not only because madness was understood to be historically conditioned, but also because it was posited as a moment internal to the dialectical unfolding of history, as a contrary of reason that was posited and then sublated. 'Madness', for the nineteenth century, 'was relative to time, and essential to the temporality of man, more fundamentally historical, in short, than it is for us today' (HM, 378). However, even if, as Foucault says, this relationship between the necessity of madness and the possibility of history was short lived and soon forgotten (HM, 378–9), the internal connection between the nineteenth-century conception of History that remains pivotal for our historical a priori and its dialectical recuperation of madness remained intact. Hence, the challenge of writing a history of our form of rationality, a history that aims to reveal the contingency of that form of rationality-understood-as-historical, is that of 'de-dialectising Hegel', by, as Lynne Huffer puts it, 'undo[ing] Hegel from within'.[16]

History of Madness thus attempts to write the history of historicity, in the sense that it writes a history of the emergence of the modern historical a priori, a historical a priori in which the relationship between reason and madness takes a new form, with reason being understood as something that is realised in and through history and madness being understood as a historically conditioned part of that historical dialectic. The modern historical a priori is historical in two senses: first, like all historical a priori, it is a historically specific, contingent and emergent system of thought or way of ordering things; and, second, it is distinctively Historical in the sense that its way of systematising thought or ordering things is to understand them as progressive realisations of a historically unfolding reason. As Foucault puts it in his essay, 'Nietzsche, Genealogy, History': 'The *Entstehung* of history is found in nineteenth-century Europe.'[17] Since Foucault could not possibly be claiming here that the emergence of recorded history is found in nineteenth-century Europe, I take him to be referring instead to the emergence of a certain philosophical conception of history that can be found in nineteenth- century Europe: one that assumes a 'suprahistorical perspective' from the point of view of which all of the myriad 'displacements of the past' can be reconciled; in short, 'a history whose perspective on all that precedes it implies the end of time, a completed development'.[18] This is what I mean by History, but I take it that it is also what Foucault is referring to in the preface to *History of Madness* when he links the necessity of madness to the possibility of history. Madness is the soon to be incorporated other of a dialectically unfolding historically conditioned reason that is central to our modern Historical historical a priori.

Importantly, then, for Foucault, the very attempt to write the history of historicity is directly opposed to the idea that historicity is a universal feature of human reason (à la Hegel) or that it is a timeless existential characteristic of Dasein (à la Heidegger). And I suspect that on this point Derrida is much closer to Heidegger and Hegel than he is to Foucault. For example, in *Rogues*, Derrida offers his own critique of reason, exposing its aporetic entanglements with power, sovereignty and law, and yet refusing to adopt the stance of the irrationalist. He also articulates the temporal dimensions of reason and Enlightenment, linking them closely to the event, democracy to come, and messianicity without messianism. For example, he writes:

> For deconstruction, if something of the sort exists, would remain above all, in my view, an unconditional rationalism that never renounces – and precisely in the name of the Enlightenment to come, in the space to be opened up of a democracy to come – the possibility of suspending in an argued, deliberated, rational fashion, all conditions, hypotheses, conventions, and

> presuppositions, and of criticizing unconditionally all conditionalities, including those that still found the critical idea . . .[19]

In both its attempt to articulate the entanglement of reason with power without collapsing into irrationalism and its uncovering of a temporal or historical dimension of reason, Derrida's critique of reason overlaps substantially with Foucault's. And yet, unlike Foucault, Derrida tends to present the entanglement of power or force and reason as an ineliminable aporia or paradox, understood in ahistorical terms. Hence, he writes:

> As soon as I speak to the other, I submit to the law of giving reason(s), I share a virtually universalizable medium. . . . The paradox, *which is always the same*, is that sovereignty is incompatible with universality even though it is called for by every concept of international, and thus universal or universalizable, and thus democratic law. There is no sovereignty without force, without the force of the strongest, whose reason – the reason of the strongest – is to win out over everything.[20]

Similarly, rather than historicising the notion of historicity, Derrida contrasts the closed teleological accounts of historicity found in thinkers such as Kant and Husserl with a fundamentally open-ended, future-oriented thinking of the to-come or becoming of the event.[21] Thus, for Derrida, the critique of reason is a matter not of revealing the idea of the historicity of reason to be part of a contingent, historically emergent system of thought; rather, the critique of reason consists in rethinking the historicity of reason in terms of an open-ended, ecstatic temporality, but without letting go of the moment of unconditionality built into the idea of reason.

For Foucault, by contrast, historicity itself has a history, which means that human beings *become Historical* at a specific point in time and that, henceforth, historicity constitutes part of their historical a priori. In particular, Foucault suggests that the notion of a rational, teleological, progressive History as a way of understanding and organising human knowledge and experience emerges in the nineteenth century, though it continues to cast a long shadow over the twentieth.[22] All of which suggests that just as Foucault is sceptical of the notion of a Reason in general, he is likewise sceptical of the idea that there is a historicity proper to reason in general. The most that he would say is that there is a historicity proper to our modern form of rationality – a form which, following Hegel, takes reason to be Historical, and history to be rational – and it is precisely the historicity of History that Foucault aims to reveal, as part of his critical effort to uncover the contingency of that form of knowledge, thus opening up the possibility of moving beyond it.

Interestingly enough, this is the one methodological point raised in Derrida's original critique of *History of Madness* to which Foucault actually responds, and his response runs along the lines I just suggested. He writes:

> For Derrida, what happened in the seventeenth century could only ever be a 'sample' (i.e., a repetition of the identical) or a 'model' (i.e. the inexhaustible

> excess of origin). He does not know the category of the singular event; it is therefore pointless for him – and probably impossible – to read that which occupies the essential part, if not the totality of my book: the analysis of an event. (HM, 577)

In other words, just as Derrida assumes that there is one order of Reason, an order that is not just any old historically determined order, but the 'unsurpassable, unique, imperial' order, he also seems to assume that historicity must be thought of as a timeless structure, a basic structural feature of human Reason itself. (Or at least he assumes that Foucault assumes this.) But Foucault is suggesting precisely the opposite: instead of one 'unsurpassable, unique, imperial' order of Reason, Foucault theorises multiple, shifting, contingently emergent forms of rationality, and instead of historicity as a timeless, ahistorical feature of human reason, Foucault understands the complex and shifting relationship between reason, madness and history as so many emergent, singular, contingent events.[23] In other words, Foucault's own historico-philosophical method is itself historically conditioned; it is an attempt to think through the modern historical a priori from within, by historicising the Hegelian understanding of History that constitutes its core.[24] Which explains why Foucault, a thinker so associated with the project of historicising philosophical concepts that he has sparked a heated debate among Foucault scholars over whether he is a historian or a philosopher,[25] could write the following: 'if history possesses a privilege, it would be . . . insofar as it would play the role of an internal ethnology of our culture and our rationality, and consequently would embody the very possibility of any ethnology'.[26] In other words, Foucault, the pre-eminent historian of systems of thought, is interested in history not because rationality is essentially historically conditioned or because we are essentially historically conditioned beings but rather because our modern age is historical, because History is central to our historical a priori. Hence if we want to engage in a critique of our modern historical a priori, we must attempt to think through and beyond this notion of History, and Foucault's historical-philosophical method aims to give us the tools to do just that.

THE PROBLEM OF METAPHYSICS

Thus far, I have been trying to articulate how Foucault understands the project of the critique of reason and how his attempt to write the history of historicity in *History of Madness* is central to that project. But I have not yet attempted to answer Derrida's most potent objection to this project, to explain how it is possible to write the history of historicity. Above I argued that the most productive thread of Derrida's critique of Foucault is the one that construes his task as delineating the point of division between reason and madness, since this is what leads Derrida to the core idea of the history of historicity. But this reading of Foucault's method also leads to Derrida's most famous criticism of Foucault, the charge of metaphysics: 'The attempt to write the history of the decision, division, difference runs the risk of construing the division as an event or a structure subsequent to the unity of an original presence, thereby confirming metaphysics in its fundamental operation' (WD,

p. 40). As Derrida presents it, this charge rests on his assumption of single, grand, imperial order of Reason; hence, he claims that in order for the charge of metaphysics to stick, 'it must be assumed in *general* that reason can have a contrary, that there can be an other of reason, that reason itself can construct or discover, and that the opposition of reason to its other is *symmetrical*' (WD, 41). As I have already argued, Foucault rejects the idea of the grand imperial order of Reason, thus, he would have to reject the idea that there is an other or a contrary to Reason.

And yet Derrida's worry about metaphysics is not totally misplaced. To see why, we need to return to the idea of unreason, as distinct from madness. One of the key methodological presuppositions of *History of Madness* is the refusal to understand history in terms of the idea of progress towards some endpoint or goal. As Foucault announces in the preface: 'We must therefore speak of this primitive debate [between reason and non-reason] without supposing a victory, nor the right to victory; we must speak of these repeated gestures in history, leaving in suspense anything that might take on the appearance of an ending, or of rest in truth' (HM, xxviii). To refrain from supposing the right to victory on the part of reason is to hold in abeyance strong teleological ideas about the goal of historical development as the point at which the real and the rational converge; to refrain from supposing a victory on the part of reason is to refuse somewhat weaker but still arguably Whiggish notions that we are entitled to or even, perhaps, in some sense, required to reconstruct history as a developmental learning process that vindicates our point of view. These refusals are central to Foucault's attempt to de-dialectise Hegel.

But Foucault's attempt to de-dialectise Hegel goes further than this. For the suspension of 'anything that might take on the appearance of an ending, or of rest in truth' seems to require the assumption or perhaps it would be better to say the *positing* of something that can never be fully conceptualised in the language of reason or reconciled in the dialectical unfolding of history. This something goes by the name of unreason, understood as the untimely outside of history that resists recuperation within the Hegelian dialectic.[27] Indeed this is another meaning of the enigmatic passage from the preface discussed above, which links the necessity of madness to the possibility of history. 'The necessity of madness . . . is linked to that decisive action that extracts a significant language from the background noise and its continuous monotony, a language which is transmitted and culminates in time' (HM, xxxii). Here, unreason is figured as the monotonous 'background noise' from which the language of rational thought, a language that 'culminates in time', was extracted. Hence, the recurrent suggestion in *History of Madness* that something about unreason escapes language and linear temporality itself – and this is what the tragic consciousness of madness allows us to glimpse, however fleetingly. In this vein, Foucault announces in the preface that *History of Madness* was to be the first of a series of works, 'beneath the sun of the great Nietzschean quest', that 'would confront the dialectics of history with the immobile structures of the tragic' (HM, xxx).

But this still doesn't quite address the question of how such a project is possible. Where, after all, does the archaeologist who attempts to trace the outlines of our historical a priori stand? Does he stand within his own historical a priori or outside of it, on the shifting ground of unreason? If the former, then does this undermine his critical reflections on his own historical a priori, transforming the history of reason into that of 'one of its determined figures' (WD, 43)? If the latter, then is Foucault guilty of presupposing a point of view outside of reason and history, and thus of implicitly, if indirectly, positing a unity to Reason after all? Foucault seems to have only two options here: either he's stuck within the determined figures of the history of reason, and thus he can't really write the history of the origin of the split between madness and reason that founds that history; or he can write this history, but only by accessing some point of view outside of that history, which could only be a suprahistorical, metaphysical standpoint. (As Derrida puts it: 'Hegel again, always . . .', WD, 43).

But perhaps Foucault would simply refuse this way of posing the question, just as he refused to be *either* a philosopher *or* a historian. In a sense, Foucault is obviously inside of his own historical a priori, the Historical historical a priori, taking it up and attempting to transform or undo it from within. But in another sense he thinks that from *within* that historical a priori, spaces can be opened up that allow for the possibility of a critique *of* that historical a priori. Sometimes, in his early work, he suggests that what makes this possible is that our own historical a priori is in the process of breaking up and transforming into something new. Indeed, Derrida also suggests this possibility, when he notes that in order for *History of Madness* to be possible 'we must assume that a certain liberation of madness has gotten underway, that psychiatry has opened itself up, however minimally, and that the concept of madness as unreason, if it ever had a unity, has been dislocated' and that 'a project such as Foucault's can find its historical origin and passageway in the opening produced by this dislocation' (WD, 38). But later, Foucault puts more emphasis on the role that critique might play in transforming our historical a priori, precisely by revealing it as an historical a priori, as a contingently emergent way of thinking, experiencing and acting. Our historical a priori is neither closed nor unified; it contains 'lines of fragility' or 'kinds of virtual fracture' that allow us to see how 'that-which-is might no longer be that-which-is'.[28] The figure of the outside or of unreason that Foucault traces in *History of Madness* is, I submit, one such line of fragility or fracture. Precisely because it is defined as what resists recuperation within the dialectical realisation of reason, the figure of unreason opens up the possibility of a critical reflection on the limits of our Hegelian, Historical modernity. The critique of our modern Historical historical a priori consists in tracing these lines of fragility and fracture, using them to open up a difference, a discontinuity between ourselves and our historical a priori. This opening up generates a 'space of concrete freedom, that is of possible transformation'.[29]

NOTES

1. An earlier and very different version of this paper was presented to philosophy colloquia at the New School for Social Research, Miami University, the University of Oregon, the Humboldt University Berlin, and at the 2011 SPEP meeting. I am grateful to audiences on those occasions, and especially to Andrew Cutrofello, Béatrice Han-Pile, Lynne Huffer, Colin Koopman, Rahel Jaeggi and Kevin Thompson, for their helpful comments and questions.

2. Michel Foucault, *History of Madness*, ed. Jean Khalfa, trans. Jonathan Murphy and Jean Khalfa (New York: Routledge, 2006). Hereafter cited in the text as HM.
3. Jacques Derrida, 'Cogito and the History of Madness', in *Writing and Difference*, trans. Alan Bass (Chicago: University of Chicago Press, 1978), pp. 31–63. Hereafter cited in the text as WD.
4. Derrida doesn't use this term to describe his criticism, but I think it fits. It is worth noting the curious convergence here between Derrida's and Habermas's critiques of Foucault. For the latter see Jürgen Habermas 'The Critique of Reason as an Unmasking of the Human Sciences: Michel Foucault', in *The Philosophical Discourse of Modernity: Twelve Lectures*, trans. Frederick G. Lawrence (Cambridge: MIT Press, 1987). For an insightful discussion of this convergence, see Colin Koopman, 'Revising Foucault: The History and Critique of Modernity', *Philosophy and Social Criticism*, 36: 5 (2010), pp. 545–65. I discuss this issue in more detail and explore some possible reasons for it in my paper 'Philosophies of Immanence and Transcendence: Reading *The History of Madness* with Derrida and Habermas' (forthcoming in Olivia Custer, Penelope Deutscher and Samir Haddad (eds), *Foucault/Derrida: Fifty Years On* (New York: Columbia University Press)), which is in many ways a companion piece to this essay.
5. Foucault insists that the aim of archaeology is not 'to reconstitute what madness itself might be', and then notes, in a footnote, that 'This is written against an explicit theme of my book *Madness and Civilization*, and one that recurs particularly in the Preface' (Michel Foucault, *The Archaeology of Knowledge*, trans. A. M. Sheridan Smith (New York: Pantheon, 1972), p. 47).
6. For an alternative reading of the exchange, see Colin Gordon, '*Histoire de la folie*: An Unknown Book by Michel Foucault', *History of the Human Sciences*, 3: 1 (1990), pp. 3–26.
7. I discuss this issue in detail in Amy Allen, 'Feminism, Foucault, and the Critique of Reason: Re-reading the *History of Madness*', *Foucault Studies*, 16 (September 2013), pp. 15–31.
8. For similar critiques of Derrida's reading of this passage from Foucault's preface, see Gordon, '*Histoire de la folie*', p. 19, and Deborah Cook, 'Madness and the Cogito: Derrida's Critique of *Folie et déraison*', *Journal of the British Society for Phenomenology*, 21: 2 (May 1990), pp. 164–74.
9. As Colin Gordon puts it: 'it is strictly impossible to find in Foucault's book anything remotely resembling a "history of madness itself"' (Gordon, '*Histoire de la folie*', p. 19). Indeed, one of the more prominent themes of Foucault's book is his critique of the very idea of a 'madness itself' that could be the object of historical knowledge (which is not at all the same as saying that Foucault thinks that madness isn't 'real'). On this point, see HM, 78–80 and 108–22.
10. Michel Foucault, 'Critical Theory/Intellectual History', in *Critique and Power: Recasting the Foucault/Habermas Debate*, ed. Michael Kelly (Cambridge: MIT Press, 1994), p. 114.
11. Ibid., p. 118.
12. On this point, see Michel Foucault, 'Afterword: The Subject and Power', in Hubert Dreyfus and Paul Rabinow, *Michel Foucault: Beyond Structuralism and Hermeneutics*, 2nd edn (Chicago: University of Chicago Press, 1983), p. 210.
13. I discuss Foucault's subversive transformation of the Kantian notion of critique in more detail in Amy Allen, *The Politics of Our Selves: Power, Autonomy, and Gender in Contemporary Critical Theory* (New York: Columbia University Press, 2008), chapter 2.
14. Michel Foucault, 'Space, Knowledge, and Power', in *Power: Essential Works of Michel Foucault, Volume 3*, ed. James Faubion (New York: The New Press, 2000), p. 358.
15. Ibid.
16. Lynne Huffer, *Mad for Foucault: Rethinking the Foundations of Queer Theory* (New York: Columbia University Press, 2010), p. 199. I am deeply indebted to Huffer's brilliant reading of the section on Rameau's Nephew in *History of Madness*, and her general argument that Foucault's text is best understood as an implicit critical dialogue with Hegel. For further

discussion of Huffer and an articulation of some of my disagreements with her, see Allen, 'Feminism, Foucault, and the Critique of Reason'.

17. Michel Foucault, 'Nietzsche, Genealogy, History', in *Aesthetics, Method, Epistemology: Essential Works of Michel Foucault, Volume 2*, ed. James Faubion (New York: The New Press, 1998), p. 384.
18. Ibid., p. 379.
19. Jacques Derrida, *Rogues: Two Essays on Reason*, trans. Pascale-Anne Brault and Michael Naas (Stanford: Stanford University Press, 2005), p. 142.
20. Ibid., p. 101, emphasis added.
21. See ibid., pp. 134–6.
22. This explains Foucault's claim that Sartre is a man of the nineteenth century trying to think the twentieth: because Sartre is still in the grips of a dialectical conception of history. Michel Foucault, 'L'homme, est-il mort?', *Dits et Écrits: 1954–1988*, vol. 1 (Paris: Éditions Gallimard, 1994), pp. 541–2.
23. To be sure, Derrida also invokes the notion of the event as part of this thinking of the temporal or historical aspects of reason, but it is worth noting that his understanding of the event is primarily futural: the event is always to come. Foucault's notion of the event, by contrast, has both forward and backward looking aspects. With respect to the latter, the point is that our historical a priori, our system of thought or mode of rationality, is made up of a series of contingent events, and reveals that history is central to the work of critique. When Foucault criticises Derrida for lacking a conception of the event, I take it that he is referring to this backward looking notion; thus, the central point of contrast is between Foucault's thoroughly historicised critique of reason and Derrida's more ahistorical approach.
24. On this point, see Foucault, 'Nietzsche, Genealogy, History', p. 384.
25. See Gary Gutting, review of Béatrice Han, *Foucault's Critical Project*, *Notre Dame Philosophical Reviews*, at http://ndpr.nd.edu/review.cfm?id=1262, posted 1 May 2003. Han-Pile's reply to Gutting's review is posted online at: http://privatewww.essex.ac.uk/~beatrice/Gutting%20_answer_%202003–05.pdf. Subsequent discussions of this issue can be found in Gary Gutting, 'Foucault, Hegel and Philosophy', in Timothy O'Leary and Christopher Falzon (eds), *Foucault and Philosophy* (London: Wiley-Blackwell, 2010), and Béatrice Han-Pile, 'Is Early Foucault a Historian? History, history and the Analytic of Finitude', *Philosophy and Social Criticism*, 31: 5–6 (2005), pp. 585–608.
26. Foucault, 'On the Ways of Writing History', in *Aesthetics, Method, Epistemology*, p. 293.
27. Recall that Foucault argues that in the nineteenth-century madness is incorporated into the dialectic.
28. Foucault, 'Critical Theory/Intellectual History', pp. 126–7.
29. Ibid., p. 127.

CHAPTER 8

The End of Man: Foucault, Derrida and the Auto-Bio-Graphical

Ellen T. Armour

> As the archaeology of our thought easily shows, man is an invention of recent date. And one perhaps nearing its end.
>
> (Foucault, *The Order of Things*)

> Man, since always, is his proper end, that is, the end of his proper. Being, since always, is its proper end, that is, the end of its proper.
>
> (Derrida, 'The Ends of Man')

To step into the terrain that lies between Michel Foucault and Jacques Derrida is a risky business. For one thing, as the portion of the exchange between them that appears in this volume documents, that terrain was emotionally and intellectually fraught for these two French philosophers. For another, while we conventionally group Foucault and Derrida together as major figures in what we in the world of Anglophone philosophy have dubbed 'continental philosophy', the two figures are rarely engaged together. There are, of course, notable exceptions, including Judith Butler's *Gender Trouble*, which draws on both – in conversation with Lacanian and post-Lacanian psychoanalytic theory – to creative and generative ends. That intersection – where Foucault, Derrida and psychoanalysis meet – is the portion of the terrain traversed in the exchange between them that will be my particular focus here.

I approach this inquiry into what lies between Derrida and Foucault not as an exercise in comparative philosophy, but through the nexus of what I'll call the auto-bio-graphical. I reference here more than the conventionally autobiographical dimensions of the terrain: the hyphens disaggregate the various components of the term in order to call attention to the various ways *graphe* (writing), *bios/thanatos* (life/death) and *autos* (the authorial 'I') come together across this terrain. The auto-bio-graphical in various senses constitutes what the exchange between Foucault and Derrida opens up and opens onto – in each philosopher's *oeuvre* and beyond.

BETWEEN FOUCAULT AND DERRIDA I: TRACING THE AUTO-BIO-GRAPHICAL

I begin with the ways I am implicated in the auto-bio-graphical as a reader and a writer whose work is in-formed by theirs. Those contours of the space between Derrida and Foucault that I have come to occupy include aspects I know and can name and aspects that I cannot. I first encountered Derrida and Foucault as a doctoral student. Derrida first in a course on religious language taught by my *doktormutter*, the eminent feminist theologian Sallie McFague. That experience intrigued me sufficiently to enrol in a second course – on Derrida and Foucault, coincidentally enough – taught by the eminent American continental philosopher Charles Scott. Yet, until recently, though I regularly taught texts by both Derrida and Foucault, my scholarship engaged only with the former, not the latter. My latest book, *Signs and Wonders: Theology After Modernity*, is positioned between Derrida and Foucault.[1] Though the project had its genesis in Derrida, it became a Foucauldian project (for reasons too complicated to set forth here). A set of photographs – of the consecration of the Rt. Rev. Gene Robinson as the first openly gay bishop in the worldwide Anglican communion, of prisoner mistreatment at Abu Ghraib prison in Iraq, of Terri Schiavo, and of the aftermath of Hurricane Katrina – anchors this project. Drawing on Foucault, I consider modernity as *episteme* and *ethos*; that is, as a time and place constituted by ways of knowing, doing and being informed by and imbued with biopower and disciplinary power. The photographs and the events they index render legible a major channel where these two distinctively modern forms of power converge: a 'fourfold' (a term I borrow from Martin Heidegger) of 'man' (a term Foucault reserves for the post-Enlightenment subject) and his 'others' ([explicitly] sexed and raced, animal and divine). I trace bio-disciplinary power's benevolent and malevolent effects *and* emergent fractures and fissures in the structures and systems that contain and channel it – including in the fourfold itself. Foucault provides the book's framework, but texts by Derrida do more than a little of its intellectual labour. A risky move, some would say, to blithely insert one into a framework constructed from the other, especially given their history with one another (and the import of that history for the philosophical landscape). But perhaps emboldened by the fact that I occupy another space between – between theology and philosophy – I plunged bravely ahead. From time to time, as the book moved towards completion, I have been made aware of the impact of this Foucauldian turn on me. We speak often of our fields as disciplines, but rarely attend to the way we are disciplined by them. We take up (with some degree of struggle) and, if successful, take on certain habits of mind under the (gentle, in my case) guidance of adepts in their practice and in the teaching of that practice. This (mostly freely willed) self-subjection opens up certain ways of thinking not just *to* us but *in* us even as it closes off others.

The question of what lies between Derrida and Foucault is personal and philosophical for them, as well; a question of their own formation as students of philosophy (and more) in a certain time and place (post-war France) and of their subsequent stature as bearers (not without resistance) of that formation, of their complicated history with one another. See, for example, the infamous exchange (of sorts) between Derrida and Foucault over Foucault's magisterial second book, *History of Madness*, first published in English in abridged form as *Madness and Civilization*. I say 'exchange (of sorts)' for a number of reasons. For one thing, 'exchange' usually connotes a collegial relationship, but Foucault's interpretation of what Derrida wrote in his initial response to *Madness* led to a ten-year rupture in their relationship. The rupture ended in 1981 – just three years before Foucault's death – when Foucault came to Derrida's assistance following his imprisonment in Czechoslovakia. 'Exchange' also can connote a relationship between equals, but Derrida had been Foucault's student. While Derrida acknowledges and navigates this dimension of their past with considerable care – even a degree of deference – in 'Cogito and the History of Madness', the tone and content of Foucault's response in 'My Body, This Paper, This Fire' is anything but careful, its undisguised anger reflecting a (begrudging?) acknowledgment of a change in status. No longer professor and student, but uneasy peers in the hallowed halls of French academe (its own habitat, to be sure).

Exchange may also presume a temporal and spatial proximity to its give and take. With the exception of Derrida's original lecture, this particular exchange took place in print, not in person, and in essays published at different times and in different places. Indeed, the exchange is constituted more by extended silences than by timely responses. What might be considered the last salvo is an essay Derrida wrote after Foucault's death. 'To Do Justice to Freud' was Derrida's contribution to a symposium on *History of Madness*. An excerpt from it serves as Derrida's elegy of sorts to the late Foucault in *The Work of Mourning*. These questions – of space and time, of life and death, of mastery and its limits – are central to what lies between Derrida and Foucault in these exchanges; a terrain marked by the convergence and divergence of philosophy, history and psychoanalysis.

BETWEEN FOUCAULT AND DERRIDA II: RUPTURES OF/ IN HISTORY

More so, perhaps, than any of Foucault's other works, *History of Madness* arguably reads on the surface like a traditional history. For one thing, Foucault tracks madness across (relatively) recognisable epochal periods – medieval, Renaissance, classical, modern – that unfold (relatively) linearly, one after the other. Readers of Foucault know, of course, that what are here epochs (of a sort) become *epistemes* in the works that follow (notably in *The Order of Things*, to which I return later): ways of knowing and organising knowledge distinguishable only in hindsight. Epistemic change is anything but smooth and linear. *Epistemes* morph into one another.

Though the concept has yet to appear, the mode and the effect of epochal change as Foucault traces it here anticipates, to a degree, epistemic change. To track madness across time is also to track it through space. *History of Madness* traces transitions from a largely itinerant existence for the mad (exemplified in the literary figure – occasionally literalised – of the Ship of Fools) to their (mere) confinement, to the rise of the modern asylum, a place (ostensibly) of healing and restoration. The history of madness may seem to be one of progress, yet another example of modernity's superiority to what came before it. But it's precisely that notion of historicity that Foucault calls into question. For one thing, these spatial shifts are at best ambivalent in their effects. However insecure and uncomfortable itinerancy might have been, the mad were (usually) cared for as signs of divine (dis)order. The modern asylum may no longer confine merely to contain, but embedded in its promise of diagnosis and cure are forms of control that, though more subtle than applying shackles and chains, similarly deprive those subjected to it of (a certain) freedom. But more to the point, to track the history of madness through time and across space is to trace its virtual disappearance (though not without remainder). Madness is banished to the realm of unreason and mental illness – the brainchild (so to speak) of reason – comes to take its place. It falls to the now regnant science of psychology to divide and conquer mental illnesses; to establish a system of classification that distinguishes one from another, to determine their etiologies and appropriate courses of treatment with the goal of restoring its victims to health (or its proximity). Madness's disappearance is, for Foucault, more of a loss to be mourned than a victory to be celebrated.

Much of what concerns Derrida in 'Cogito and the History of Madness' is evident in the title. Though he acknowledges *History of Madness* as a work of great importance, he finds he must trouble the very project of a history of madness. The linchpin for Derrida's critique is a brief excursus on Descartes that opens Foucault's account of the change that occurred between the seventeenth and eighteenth centuries in how madness was treated. Early in the First Meditation, Descartes takes up the question of madness. Illusions – believing we are experiencing something real when we are not – seem to pose a challenge to his quest to establish the foundation of knowledge. Instead, they open up onto what becomes its key. Illusions do alert us to the limits of *sensory* knowledge, Descartes acknowledges, but in doing so, they also call our attention to knowing's foundation in rational thinking manifest here as doubt. The presence of doubt – no matter how small – distinguishes illusion from utter delusion, reason from madness, Descartes claims. One can doubt, for example, whether this hand is really attached to one's body, whether the piece of paper it holds is real or whether the heat one feels is from sitting by a fire, but one cannot *think* that one might be mad and actually *be* mad. To *think* oneself (possibly) mad – to doubt one's sanity – is still to think and to think is to be rational. And, as we know from the line that sums up the Cartesian project, to think is to be (human). This line drawn between thinking and madness sunders unreason from reason, a turning point not only in the history of madness, but in western philosophy and the larger culture in which it is embedded. 'Madness has been banished', Foucault writes. 'While *man* can still go mad, *thought*, as the sovereign exercise carried out by a subject seeking the truth, can no longer be devoid of reason.'[2]

Derrida takes issue with Foucault's interpretation of Descartes on these questions, but that dispute ultimately serves as a point of entry into a larger question, which is what interests me here. What does it mean – for madness and for philosophy – to attempt to give an account of its history? Such a project presumes that madness can be an object of knowledge; a presumption that rests on yet more presumptions – of what it is to know, of who does the knowing. The project presumes, in other words, the very philosophical apparatus (if I may) that Foucault seems, in turning to Descartes, to see as embedded in that history. Certainly, this is what Foucault takes to be the import of Derrida's response. Derrida has set himself up as the spokesperson for philosophy, a discipline that may *have* a history (of ideas, say), but which pursues what lies outside the vicissitudes of history. So, for example, philosophy is the discipline that seeks not just to know (something), but to know *how* we know (we know), in other words. (That Foucault would so align Derrida and philosophy reads ironically, to say the least, here and now – that is, many decades after his appearance on the American landscape where his status as a philosopher was highly contested to say the least. Indeed, that they would distinguish themselves one from the other will surprise those who know them by their American reputations as united by certain alleged methodological commitments; a 'poststructuralist' turn to language, for example. But I digress . . .)

BETWEEN FOUCAULT AND DERRIDA III: PSYCHOANALYSIS AND THE AUTO-BIO-GRAPHICAL

Fast forward, if you will, to the first instalment in their posthumous exchange. From the title ('To Do Justice to Freud', recall) one would hardly know it was an homage to Foucault (indeed, readers aware of Foucault's take on Freud might think it anything but). Nor would one suspect that it might resurrect the spectre of their exchange now decades old. And yet Derrida begins his paper by acknowledging this particular past. He notes that the organisers of the event (Elisabeth Roudinesco and René Major) invited him to revisit the exchange – an invitation that he overtly declines. Instead, he proposes a new point of entry into *History of Madness*. Where his original 'Cogito' paper looked to Descartes, 'To Do Justice' looks to Freud. If 'Cogito' called into question the project of writing a history of madness, 'Justice' inquires after the conditions that enable such a project. Yet, as Derrida acknowledges, this new query bears spectral traces of its predecessor both in form and content. Freud, like Descartes, is relatively marginal to the text of *History of Madness* itself; indeed they are bookends of a sort. Descartes appears briefly early on, Freud (in scattered references) towards the end. In Derrida's hands, these two points of entry result in similar insights. If 'Cogito' exposed the (unacknowledged) philosophical underpinnings of *History of Madness*, 'Justice' inquires after their (unacknowledged) psychoanalytic underpinnings.

Hovering over Derrida's reading of Freud in Foucault is a particular text of Freud's, *Beyond the Pleasure Principle*, which Derrida evokes both explicitly and implicitly throughout 'Justice'. Freud's presence/absence in Foucault's *oeuvre* recalls for Derrida Freud's famous analysis in *Beyond the Pleasure Principle* of his grandson's *fort/da* game. Readers of that text will recall that the game involves a spool on a string that Freud's grandson, Ernst, tosses onto and then pulls out from a curtained bed. As the spool disappears, Ernst says 'o-o-o-o' (to Freud's ear, an approximation of 'Fort', 'away/lost/gone'). When it reappears, Ernst says, 'Da' ('there'). Freud interprets this game as Ernst's attempt to manage his frustration at his mother's comings and goings by restaging them (with the spool as her stand-in). The game commemorates the child's 'great cultural achievement – the instinctual renunciation (that is, the renunciation of instinctual satisfaction) which he had made in allowing his mother to go away without protesting'.[3] Some of Freud's contemporaries used the connection between his daughter Sophie's death, this autobiographical episode, and the timing of *Beyond the Pleasure Principle*'s publication to challenge psychoanalysis's claim to scientific status. The autobiographical is the anecdotal, the singular; the very antithesis, it would seem, of the scientific – constructed on the firm foundation of the objective, the repeatable.

This episode plays a significant role in Derrida's *The Post Card*; a text that, like the exchange between Foucault and Derrida under discussion here, is marked by questions of life and death, time and space, knowledge and its limits, framed in and around Freud and psychoanalysis through the question of the auto-bio-graphical. On Derrida's read, Freud's account of Ernst's game opens onto multiple *fort/da* games played by multiple versions of Freud himself – as founder of psychoanalysis and as a family man (father, grandfather, husband and son). These *fort/da* games involve but are not limited to Freud's own losses, on Derrida's read. Reflected in Freud-the-scientist's account of a grandson's attempt to manage his mother's presence and absence, Derrida finds the father's displacement of the work of mourning his daughter. Reflected in Freud-the-scientist's account of Ernst's jealousy towards his brother is Freud-the-family-man's jealousy of his daughter's husband. This circuit of disavowed grief extends forward into Freud's future and backward into his past, as well – it anticipates the death of his mother and his anticipation of his own death, it recalls the death of Ernst's brother (Freud's favourite grandson) and through that loss the death of Freud's brother, Julius.[4]

Derrida's interest, however, does not lie in Freud's psychobiography *per se* or in what it suggests about psychoanalysis' claim to status as a science. The connection between Freud and little Ernst calls for a rethinking of the relationship between autobiography and psychoanalysis as a rethinking of what I am calling here the auto-bio-graphical that opens up yet more dimensions of what lies between Derrida and Foucault. It is clear, from 'Justice', that Derrida reads Freud's place in Foucault's *oeuvre* as a repetition of this game, though in precisely what sense – or, better, senses – is an open question, in my view. On the surface, of course, is the obvious (if banal) psychoanalytic reading; Derrida, the master analyst, knows – *really* knows – what his putative analysand (Foucault) doesn't (want to) know: that his masterwork isn't really his after all, but is indebted to Freud; a debt that his analyst demands be acknowledged (for Foucault's own good, of course!). 'Would Foucault's project have been possible without psychoanalysis, with which it is contemporary and of which it speaks little and in such an equivocal or ambivalent manner in the book?' Derrida asks. 'Does the project owe psychoanalysis anything? What? Would the debt, if it had been contracted, be essential? Or would it, on the contrary, define the very thing from which the project had to detach itself, in a critical fashion, in order to take shape?'[5]

On this read, Derrida pursues justice for Freud through Foucault's *oeuvre*, following the traces of Freud and psychoanalysis from *History of Madness* through the works that follow it. But following those traces complicates that banal reading of this *fort/da* game. These two figures – 'Freud' and 'psychoanalysis' – converge and diverge internally and in relationship to each other. In part, those convergences and divergences reflect the subsequent effects of the division between madness and unreason that Descartes inaugurated and that *History of Madness* pursued; in part, notably, *they resist it*.

Key to this *fort/da* game is the complex relationship between psychology and psychoanalysis, between psychology and Freud, between psychoanalysis and Freud. At times, on Derrida's read, Foucault aligns Freud (and/or psychoanalysis) with what we might call a Cartesian legacy. In so far as Freud valorises the analyst as master knower, for example, he contributes to reason's triumph. At other times, however, Foucault aligns Freud (and/or psychoanalysis) against this trend. Although Derrida claims he ultimately decouples them, Foucault sometimes speaks of Freud in company with Nietzsche and others whom he credits as custodians of the lingering traces of madness. So, for example, Foucault credits Freudian psychoanalysis with giving madness a language of its own, if you will, thus allowing unreason to speak and be heard (think here not only of the infamous 'Freudian slip', but of the content of any of Freud's case studies) – at least, from time to time and in certain settings.

That Foucault's treatment of Freud and/or psychoanalysis exhibits such ambivalence is not an indication of a failure on Foucault's part, Derrida hastens to say. Said ambivalence, rather, inheres in both Freud and psychoanalysis. More to the point, it inheres in *History of Madness* – both as its ground and as that from which it must detach itself. The attempts that Foucault makes to detach from psychoanalysis – in part, by attaching it firmly to madness's disappearance – render legible the debt that *History of Madness* owes it in the first place, Derrida suggests. Derrida argues that Freud serves as the hinge or pivot around which the book (and much of Foucault's *oeuvre*) turns. And this claim returns us to the specific problematic of the 'Cogito' essay, that of historicity and its limits. Freud, perhaps even more than Descartes, undoes any neatly linear temporal scheme in *History of Madness*. Through Freud – epochally speaking, a decidedly modern figure – the door that purportedly divides the classical from the modern swings open and shut. In so far as madness crosses its threshold from time to time, the division between classical and modern is undone. Yet, by Derrida's own acknowledgment, that door was never firmly or permanently closed on Foucault's read; the question is, rather, who makes way for said openings and closings – or who attends to what passes through them. For Foucault, those figures include not only (occasionally, if only accidentally) Freud, but philosophers and poets – Nietzsche, for one – a philosopher not easily contained in or by the philosophy that Foucault, in 'My Body, This Paper, This Fire', reads Derrida as speaking for.

Once again, we find ourselves on terrain where the lines between philosophy, psychoanalysis and history are called into question – perhaps even redrawn. This redrawing calls to mind not only the Foucault of 'Justice', but the Foucault of 'My Body' and, more to the point, the Derrida of 'Cogito'. Philosophy, like psychoanalysis, resists containment in and by its Cartesian history. The relatively banal round of *fort/da* ostensibly being played here opens up and onto a dizzying array of rounds. Between Foucault and Freud, Freud and Descartes, Derrida and Foucault; between history and psychoanalysis, psychoanalysis and philosophy, philosophy and history;

all set in motion by the as-yet unacknowledged (and thus unmourned) loss of madness. To do justice to Freud, then, is to acknowledge the debt, if you will, owed to madness; a debt that *History of Madness* exposes. To do justice to Freud, then, *is* to do (a certain) justice to Foucault.

To do (Derridean) justice to Foucault, though, is not to restore to him proper authorship understood as auto-bio-graphical mastery over *History of Madness*. Neither Foucault nor Derrida 'believed', if you will, in the author as the masterful 'I' who writes a book into life. As both have argued (on different grounds and in different contexts), such a notion is itself a useful but limited fiction; the product of a specific history, according to Foucault in 'What is an Author?', whose supposed mastery over what a text intends to say, according to Derrida in 'Signature Event Context', is always already undercut by the very distinction between speaking and writing that founds textuality in the first place.[6]

If 'Cogito' launched the public exchange between Derrida and Foucault, 'Justice' would seem to conclude it. Foucault was already dead when Derrida wrote it and so couldn't respond (though Derrida takes the liberty of imagining his response in its last paragraphs). And yet, the exchange arguably lives on; it survives (*survivre*) not only Foucault's death, but Derrida's as well (he died in 2004). By proxy and quite explicitly in the essays that comprise this volume; by proxy and less explicitly in the larger corpus of the many students of both thinkers – in which I include myself. (I also include in this group both those who studied under them in person and those who have studied their work under the tutelage of others.) Indeed, these exchanges exhibit many of the dynamics of the exchanges between Foucault and Derrida I have just surveyed – including their strange temporality and spatiality. While our relationships to Derrida and Foucault may have involved personal encounters of one sort or another, these exchanges, too, take place mostly in texts and are separated in time by years if not decades. These exchanges are asymmetrical; they may, from time to time, speak in their own words (those we select, mind), but 'Derrida' and 'Foucault' are who we, their students, make them out to be.[7]

I do not mean to malign any of their interpreters nor do I mean to court the old and tired charges of nihilism often attached to these two figures (as heralds of 'postmodernity' among other allegedly calamitous turns). Rather, as both Derrida and Foucault were well aware, these are the dynamics of reading and writing. The process of formation runs both ways; I am formed by what I read, what I read in turn (in)forms what I write. That I write about texts signed, sealed and delivered by eminences like Derrida or Foucault in no way guarantees that what I say will match what they (thought they) intended to say. (Death arguably exacerbates these dynamics, as an observation Derrida makes in *The Work of Mourning* suggests. There, he speaks of the impossible obligation of putting loss into language to honour the dead. We long to speak *with* the deceased, not *about* him or her. Yet the dissymmetry of the relationship of mourner to mourned – the deceased *is* now only as we remember them – means that what we say in the deceased's honour may miss its target. This inevitable ambiguity would certainly apply to Derrida's selection of a portion of 'Justice' as his tribute to Foucault – in spades, we might say, given its place in their exchange.)[8]

BETWEEN FOUCAULT AND DERRIDA IV: THE END OF MAN

Approaching what lies between Foucault and Derrida through the auto-bio-graphical has taken us through terrain perhaps more personal than political, more psychoanalytic than philosophical. I want to explore one last dimension of what lies between Foucault and Derrida that cashes out in a more philosophical and political vein the import of the auto-bio-graphical. I opened this essay with two epigraphs – one from Foucault, one from Derrida – that bespeak a motif in their work, the question of the end of man, that has been particularly generative for me. Significantly, this motif and these epigraphs appear early in both philosophers' *oeuvres* between the publication of *History of Madness* and the exchange that I've been tracking: in Foucault's *The Order of Things* (published in 1966) and in an essay of Derrida's entitled 'The Ends of Man' (published in 1972, but originally written in 1968). Though he says nothing explicitly about it in the essay itself, Derrida selected as an epigraph for 'Ends' the epigraph from *The Order of Things* that I cite above. Thus, these two texts fit within the long lineage of exchange I outlined earlier. Extending our inquiry into what lies between Derrida and Foucault via this motif and these texts will return us one last time to the question of the relationship of history, philosophy and psychoanalysis with particular attention to its relevance to our time and place.

As its readers know, *The Order of Things* traces the emergence of the modern *episteme* as an order of knowledge of words and things (as per its French title, *Les mots et les choses*, Words and Things). Life (*bios*) comes to replace nature as that which is to be known, an object (or, better, set of objects) characterised by finite depth rather than as before by infinite breadth. At the centre of this *episteme* is man, who has displaced God as the one who knows (things and the order of things, in so far as that's possible). To displace, though, is not to replace. For one thing, the scope of man's knowledge does not equal that previously imputed to God. For another, misknowing in the modern *episteme* is no longer accidental to but rather constitutive of knowing. Most important for our purposes is man's unique relationship to this new order. According to Foucault, 'Man, in the analytic of finitude, is a strange empirico-transcendental doublet';[9] at once the one who knows and, as a living being himself, an object of knowledge. This distinctive status makes man's attempt to know himself a very peculiar – and limited – affair; a matter simultaneously of the empirical and the transcendental, of knowing as the accumulation and analysis of data and of knowing *how* he knows, a project that ultimately exceeds his (finite) grasp.

Psychoanalysis occupies a place of particular significance in Foucault's account of the modern *episteme*. It is among those human sciences (along with history and what Foucault calls ethnology) positioned where the transcendental and the empirical meet. If the other human sciences (e.g., philology, economics) seize upon a particular sphere of human behaviour (e.g., speaking, exchanging), psychoanalysis lays claim to an account of what gives rise to them. And that account, centred as it is (as we've seen) in death and desire, is deeply redolent of finitude as both biological and epistemological. But finitude applies not only to individual instances of modern subjectivity, but to man himself *as* a structure of subjectivity. Notably, *The Order of Things* ends with Foucault envisioning man's end. Man was born in and by 'a change in the fundamental arrangements of knowledge', Foucault writes. When and if *those* arrangements 'crumble, as the ground of Classical thought did, at the end of the eighteenth century, then one can certainly wager that man would be erased like a face drawn in sand at the edge of the sea'.[10] While Foucault stops short of announcing – much less pronouncing – man's end as a *fait accompli*, he clearly anticipates and perhaps even welcomes it.

Per my second epigraph, if man is a peculiarly modern invention for Foucault, it would seem to be quite the opposite for Derrida. If according to Foucault, man's beginning lies in the shift from the classical to the modern *episteme*, Derrida locates it in the co-belonging 'since always' of man and Being. In 'The Ends of Man', man names the subject at the heart of metaphysical humanism; that is, the philosophical discourse that distinguishes human being from other forms of being based on their properties and their proper ends (*teloi*). Derrida's 'man' is co-extensive with the history of (western) philosophy, as the Aristotelian allusions in the previous sentence suggest. References to Heidegger, though, are more prominent in 'Ends'. What distinguishes man from other beings is a distinctive relationship to Being that constitutes his proper (if not precisely his property). This mapping seems, then, to anticipate the exchange in 'Cogito' and 'My Body' over the relationship between history and philosophy.

The two philosophers may differ on the historical *moment*, if you will, of man's beginning, but thinking of this claim *as* a matter of history in the banal sense (of a what-where-when) short-changes the philosophical import – for *our* time and place, especially – of this particular between. We misread these claims if we read them as only or primarily temporal; we need also to read them as philosophical claims about the conditions of possibility that gave rise to man. More to the point, though Derrida may claim an older and wider provenance for (his version of) man, he, too, sees man's spatial and temporal reach as limited and man's end (as limit if not death) as imminent. Significantly, for both philosophers, man's end lies in his beginning; a beginning that is, for both, marked by unknowing as forgetting and thus as loss. Modern philosophy begins in the forgetting of madness (Descartes via Foucault); philosophy *per se* begins with the forgetting of man's primordial relationship to Being (Heidegger via Derrida).

Neither Foucault nor Derrida is endorsing the position of the philosopher they credit with this development nor are they seeking to resurrect what has (purportedly) been lost. Foucault is not advocating that we replace asylums with Ships of Fools nor is Derrida following Heidegger's pursuit of the meaning of Being, in other words. Rather, what concerns both is the impact of this past on our present and future; the import of the traces of these pasts for our time and place and for what is to come. We can, I think, better grasp that import by bringing psychoanalysis – and the figure of Freud – back into the conversation. Might we consider Freud as a hinge or a door now not just into Foucault's *oeuvre* (as per Derrida), but into what lies between Derrida and Foucault, between man's origin and his end? Do both of them – or more significantly do we as their readers – owe a debt to Freud for rendering legible what lies between each philosopher's pursuit of the figure of the end of man? Might we read this between as constituted by yet another series of *fort/da* games: those played between Derrida and Foucault (and their readers), yes, but also one played between man and his end? Between man and what he knows – and cannot know – of his end and thus of himself? As noted above, unknowing is constitutive of both man's origin and man's end in a complex array of senses: as misknowing or forgetting, as disavowal and inaccessibility. Not only are man's past origin (and future end) to a large degree inaccessible to him, but, as the product of desires and needs that are hidden from him, man – the one who is supposed to know – cannot (fully) know himself.

I am not speaking here only of death drives and pleasure principles or of other dynamics internal to man, but also of external dynamics, of man's relationship to others and to his world. 'The Ends of Man' was originally delivered as a lecture for an international colloquium on philosophical anthropology held in the United States in 1968. On the one hand, the mere event of the colloquium – an international gathering of philosophers around the question of man – performs metaphysical humanism. The philosophers gathered there constitute a collective that simultaneously marks and elides boundaries such as those of nation, ethnicity and political persuasion; a performance that presumes the common ground, 'man', that is the colloquium's topic. Note, for example, the specific topic Derrida was asked to address: 'where is France with regard to man?' But Derrida also suspects that the colloquium as an event also bears silent witness to metaphysical humanism's – and man's – limits. Observing that such an event is quite literally unthinkable in many places in the world, he asks whether the 'anxious and busy multiplication of colloquia in the West' may indicate awareness of a 'mute, growing and menacing pressure, on the enclosure of Western collocution',[11] a pressure that such a gathering attempts to master by reassuring those gathered, at least, of man's universality.

Shortly after making that observation, Derrida identifies as 'belonging to the field and problematic of our colloquium'[12] several of the significant political events of that year – the assassination of Martin Luther King, Jr., the ongoing Vietnam peace talks, the Paris student uprisings – expressing his solidarity with the civil rights movement, peace movement and student movement connected with them. As I suggested when I first took up this essay of Derrida's, these events and movements might be productively read as symptoms of that pressure to which he alludes.[13] This pressure is symptomatic, Derrida goes on to say (a few sentences before the epigraph I cite above), of a 'trembling' in the presumed 'co-belonging and co-propriety of the name of man and the name of Being' that is 'played out in the violent relationship of the whole of the West to its other'.[14]

Nearly fifty years later, ours is a time and place where the trembling Derrida noted is, if anything, more acute (and perhaps less metaphorical). We confront conflicts and crises that are global and local, military and ecological, personal and political. These conflicts and crises are not unrelated to the events Derrida mentions; they are, moreover, integrally connected to the events whose photographs anchor *Signs and Wonders*. Thus, though I cannot make the case here, all of these events are symptomatic of the fractures and fissures in what bio-disciplinary power, *channelled through the fourfold of man and his others*, has wrought. We are, after all, man's heirs. We bear the traces of his legacy for good or ill; those we can know and name and those we cannot. Following both Foucault and Derrida in thinking through that legacy as best we can in all of its complexity is, I would argue, necessary if we are to *responsibly* live out our present and into our future.

NOTES

1. Ellen T. Armour, *Signs and Wonders: Theology After Modernity* (New York: Columbia University Press, 2016).
2. Michel Foucault, *History of Madness*, ed. Jean Khalfa, trans. Jonathan Murphy and Jean Khalfa (New York: Routledge, 2006), p. 47.
3. Sigmund Freud, *Beyond the Pleasure Principle*, ed. and trans. James Strachey (New York: W.W. Norton, 1961), p. 14.
4. Jacques Derrida, *The Postcard: From Socrates to Freud and Beyond* (Chicago: University of Chicago Press, 1987). For more on this, see my 'Beyond Belief?: Sexual Difference and Religion After Ontotheology' in John Caputo (ed.), *The Religious* (New York: Blackwell Press, 2002), pp. 212–6.
5. Jacques Derrida, '"To Do Justice to Freud": The History of Madness in the Age of Psychoanalysis', trans. Peggy Kamuf, in *Resistances of Psychoanalysis* (Stanford: Stanford University Press, 1996), p. 76.
6. Jacques Derrida, 'Signature Event Context', *Limited, Inc.* (Chicago: Northwestern University Press, 1988), pp. 1–24; Michel Foucault, 'What is an Author?', *Language, Counter-memory, Practice: Selected Essays and Interviews*, ed. and trans. Donald F. Bouchard (Ithaca, NY: Cornell University Press, 1977), pp. 113–38.
7. For very productive pursuits along this line, see, for example, Lynn Huffer, *Mad for Foucault: Rethinking the Foundations of Queer Theory* (New York: Columbia University Press, 2010), David M. Halperin, *Saint Foucault: Towards a Gay Hagiography* (New York: Oxford University Press, 1995), and Geoff Bennington and Jacques Derrida, *Jacques Derrida* (Chicago: University of Chicago Press, 1993).
8. Jacques Derrida, *The Work of Mourning*, ed. Pascale-Anne Brault and Michael Nass (Chicago: University of Chicago Press, 2001).
9. Michel Foucault, *The Order of Things: An Archaeology of the Human Sciences* (New York: Vintage Books, 1994), p. 318.
10. Ibid., p. 387.
11. Jacques Derrida, *Margins of Philosophy*, trans. Alan Bass (Chicago: University of Chicago Press, 1982), p. 113.
12. Ibid., p. 114.
13. See 'Derrida as *Supplément:* Deconstruction and Race on Philosophy's Terrain', the fifth chapter of my *Deconstruction, Feminist Theology and the Problem of Difference* (Chicago: University of Chicago Press, 1999).
14. Derrida, *Margins of Philosophy*, pp. 133, 134.

PART III

The Voice

CHAPTER 9

'Murmurs' and 'Calls': The Significance of Voice in the Political Reason of Foucault and Derrida

Fred Evans

Between Foucault and Derrida restarts a dialogue that Derrida heralded in his 1963 lecture on Foucault. In that lecture, Derrida cites the 'master's voice' – Foucault's – that he says already resounds within and precedes his own. He adds that to reclaim his proper voice he must now break the hold on him of his former professor's discourse.[1] Similarly, Foucault indicates in an address years later that he would have liked 'to lodge' himself 'in a nameless voice' that had 'long preceded' his, so that he would be freed from all 'beginnings' and institutional directives.[2] These references to voices and related terms, especially 'calls' and 'murmurs', continue throughout the works of Derrida and Foucault. We might think that they are only rhetorical flourishes. But I will follow Derrida and Foucault's allusions to voices across a number of their texts and show that they play a crucial role in their competing views of political reason. I will argue, moreover, that voice allows us to remedy some of the two philosophers' ideas that others have found unsettling. The most important of these are Derrida's claim that democracy suffers from 'autoimmunity' and Foucault's declaration that 'power-resistance' is the inescapable character of all societies.[3] In other words, we will find that focusing on their uses of voice and its derivatives is an efficacious way to reopen the dialogue between the two philosophers who have been waiting in the wings for their return encounter.

THE 'MURMURINGS' OF HISTORY

The dialogue between Derrida and Foucault begins with a disagreement over the relation between reason and madness.[4] In response to Foucault's *History of Madness*, Derrida identifies two 'projects' in the text of his former teacher. The first is an 'archaeology' of the 'silence' that occurred once the classical age (seventeenth- to eighteenth-century Europe) had confined and then transformed madness into the muted object of psychiatric science (WD, 34; cf. HM, 497, 516–17). Because this silence occurred at a particular time, it has the character of a decision of reason to protect itself from madness. But this event presupposes its occurrence within a logos preceding it, one that 'from within itself permitted dialogue between what were later called reason and madness' (WD, 38). If Foucault could not appeal to this primordial logos, his archaeology would leave him with only two alternatives: he would have to speak in the 'classical language' of 'the jailer' and thus betray madness to reason; or he would have to literally disappear in 'the wild and inaccessible silence of madness' and thereby lose all reason (WD, 37). Thus Foucault's only recourse was to inaugurate 'a second project' and appeal to 'the historic liberation of a logos' that would allow us to articulate 'the broken dialogue' between the 'two monologues' (WD, 37).

Derrida is right to highlight this second project. Foucault explicitly describes an original symmetrical relation between reason and madness in three related registers and suggests that 'murmurings' are central to each. The first register concerns 'the unity and the opposition of sense and senselessness' (HM, xxxiii). To hear the echo of that 'originary confrontation' we must 'strain our ears, and bend down towards the murmuring of the world'. The second register is similar to the first: an opposition between 'the *oeuvre* of the history of the world' and the 'absence of history'. This 'absence' and basic meaning of 'silence' is 'a great space of murmurings' and the 'pure origin' of the *oeuvre* of history. The *oeuvre*, in its turn, uses its syntax and consistent vocabulary to conquer the region's 'confusion'. But it is always 'indelibly accompanied' by the murmuring or absence which 'runs unaltered in its inevitable void the length of history'. Indeed, this absence is 'already there in the primitive decision' that produced the division between it and the *oeuvre*. It therefore exists 'before history' but also remains after this decision and will 'triumph in the last word uttered by history' (HM, xxxi–ii; see also 535–8). Foucault finds traces of this triumph in the works of Nietzsche, Van Gogh, Artaud, and others who express madness as a 'lyrical experience' rather than as the reductive results of 'reflective thought' (HM, 519, 169–70, 521).

The third and last register is more specific but no less expressive of the originating structure and the murmurings that gave birth to sense and history. This register is the reference to two voices, that of 'the man of reason' and 'the man of madness'.[5] Foucault says that we must stop supposing that the caesura between these two has meant a victory for the man of reason and the complete silence of madness. Only when we put aside this supposition will a 'domain' appear 'where men of madness and men of reason, departing from each other and not yet separate, can open, in a language more original, much rougher and much more matutinal than that of science, the dialogue of their rupture, which proves, in a fleeting fashion, that they are still on speaking terms' (HM, xxvii). In other words, this language will help us put aside momentarily the 'horizontal reason' of the classical age and modern psychiatry and bring to the surface the 'constant verticality' of the 'Reason-Unreason relation' that runs 'the length of Western culture', from the ancient Greek idea of hubris, through the art of Hieronymus Bosch and 'long after Nietzsche and Artaud' (HM, xxix). It would be a language, a liberated logos, remaining 'sufficiently open for the decisive words through which the truth of madness and of reason are constituted to find their place without being betrayed' (HM, xxxv). In short, it would be the language, at once lyrical and rigorous, of Foucault's *History of Madness*.

These comments establish that in Foucault's early work murmurings, if not 'speaking subjects' (HM, xxxi), have an originary role in the emergence of history and the dialogue between madness and reason. They also imply more broadly what is clearer in Foucault's later philosophy: that there are many voices, many versions of reason, and not just the one that a particular historical period might privilege. In contrast, Derrida accepts neither Foucault's pluralistic view of reason nor the symmetrical dialogue between madness and reason. He claims that the language for articulating these claims – Foucault's liberated logos – can be nothing more than the same 'adventure of Western reason' that Foucault wishes to escape; nothing more than the 'tradition of meaning' that 'alone can give meaning and rationality in general to Foucault's discourse and to any discourse on the war between reason and unreason' (WD, 35, 42; see also 55–6, 57, 308 n.4).

Derrida's and Foucault's different views of reason – pluralised versus continuous – are clarified further in their famous debate about the role of madness in Descartes' *Meditations*. Derrida argues that madness is vanquished as an opponent of reason in the totalising scope of Descartes' rational arguments (WD, 55–6). In contrast, Foucault claims that Descartes and the classical period arbitrarily and perhaps fearfully, rather than argumentatively, exclude madness as a rival of Cartesian rationality (HM, 45–7, 550–74). Moreover, Foucault claims in a later article that Derrida's insistence upon the continuity of a single tradition of reason overlooks the 'events' or discursive practices that constitute Descartes' meditation and fracture it into different types of reason. In other words, the *Meditations* or any other verbal tract is a constellation of contesting voices, for example, the Descartes who speaks sometimes as a subject committed to doubting all things, and then as the one wishing to hold on to himself as reasonable, and again as the one provoked by the fear of being mad or being declared so, and finally as the cultural voice that rejects the mad (HM, 573, 564–7).

Foucault's rebuff of Derrida, however, is complicated because both thinkers value difference and heterogeneity. Thus Derrida indicates that the continuity of reason in the *Meditations* or elsewhere is nonetheless always 'an economy, a structure of deferral whose irreducible originality must be respected', a 'regulated relationship between that which exceeds and the exceeded totality: the *différance* of the absolute excess' (WD, 62). In other words, Derrida views reason as a continuous tradition that nonetheless exceeds itself internally and thereby safeguards difference. But Foucault finds this way of valorising difference inferior to his own emphasis on the plurality of reason. He therefore concludes his article by castigating Derrida's 'oversight' of the plurivocity of Descartes' text and the existence of many kinds of rationality. Indeed, he derisively declares that Derrida provides us with only a 'historically well-determined little pedagogy' that 'inversely gives to the voice of the masters that unlimited sovereignty that allows it indefinitely to re-say the text' and teach 'the student that there is nothing outside the text' – that we only find the 'origin' or 'the meaning of being' in the 'reduction of the discursive practices to textual traces' and the 'elision of events that are produced there' (HM, 573).

Evaluating this conflict between Derrida and Foucault will require that we look more closely at how they develop their views of reason in later work and at the role that voice takes on in that process. We can begin with Derrida.

THE 'CALL' OF HISTORY

Throughout his work, Derrida indicates that important ideas function as 'calls'. He says, for example, that 'a certain appeal to or call by [*appel de*]' his famous method of 'deconstruction' is 'necessary' for it 'to get off the ground'.[6] This idea of a call is even more pronounced when he speaks of the event of all events, the '*khora*'. He says that this idea from Greek antiquity 'comes before everything' and designates the 'place' of 'the call for a thinking of the event *to come*, of the democracy *to come*, of the reason *to come*'. He also states that we can 'invoke a certain *reason to come*, as *democracy to come*', and thus speak of 'democratic reason'. Moreover, Derrida sees democracy to come as 'the political' itself and its 'khora'.[7] It is therefore this version of political reason and its self-exceeding totality that he thinks Foucault cannot escape.

The idea of the call or an anonymous voice is a necessary element in Derrida's political philosophy. It allows him to combine a political injunction with his temporal notion of 'to come'. He says that much of the world now experiences the increasingly 'globalatinizing' idea of democracy and claims that the centuries old legacy of this idea is an 'injunction' that calls upon us 'hermeneutically' to 'elucidate its meaning' and 'call for its advent'.[8] Derrida adds that this normative injunction is 'real' and 'sensible': it asserts a force upon those who share its legacy, never letting us 'put it off until later', seizing us '*here* and *now*'.[9] But this call also involves a temporal structure that implies that democracy can only ever be 'to come'.

Derrida refers to this temporal structure as *différance* or 'spacing'. More specifically, he thinks that any present moment includes the 'past' and the 'future' as an 'absence' without which it would lose its duration and disappear into nothing. This differing from itself as both a presence and an absence means that the spacing of the present moment is at once the 'becoming-space of time' and the 'becoming-time of space'. Because the temporal interior of the present and thus of our experience of things necessarily opens onto an 'outside', that is, onto its past and future, spacing is the becoming-*space* of time. It is the becoming-*time* of space because it also 'defers' the future of the present moment and its contents. Therefore, this moment and the identity of anything that takes place within it always remain still to come, always deferred and hence 'indecidable'. This indecidability implies that *khora*, reason, democracy and any of the other calls or voices Derrida treats 'can only be but a trace' of themselves as they disappear into the past and open onto their indeterminate future, always deferring and differing from themselves, forever 'an unforeseeable coming of the other'.[10]

Because democracy to come has the structure of spacing, it is an 'unconditional' injunction. This means that it 'opens' or is 'vulnerable' to whatever or whoever '*comes* and comes to affect it'.[11] It is therefore always beyond any conditions that could ever render it foreseeable; its 'to come' character would always interrupt any possible determination of its meaning. More specifically, it necessarily remains outside the realm of 'the theoretical, the descriptive, the constative, and the performative',[12] always 'indifferent to any content', always transcending or heterogeneous to any possible democracy,[13] 'possible only as im-possible'.[14]

Despite their 'absolutely heterogeneous' relation to each other, Derrida claims that unconditional democracy and its conditional counterparts are 'indissociably' related to each another. On the one hand, possible democracies require the unconditional idea of democracy to come for their 'guidance' and 'inspiration', indeed for their very possibility as democratic: it is their unconditional condition.[15] On the other, this 'quasi-transcendental' injunction must engage in 'conditions of all kinds' in order to 'arrive' and be more than utopian thought or 'nothing at all'. Only between the benign oracle of unconditional democracy to come and the earthly voices of possible democracies can 'decisions and responsibilities' be taken.[16]

But if unconditional democracy is going to guide possible democracies, it must at least have enough content that it can be linked to them in thought or practice. Perhaps realising this necessity, Derrida proclaims that '[i]t is on the basis of freedom that we will have conceived of the concept of democracy', and proceeds to qualify this freedom in several ways.[17] He identifies it as 'a freedom of play, an opening of indetermination and indecidability *in the very concept* of democracy', and holds that this distinguishes the 'constitutional paradigm' of democracy from all other political rationalities. Most importantly, he further specifies this freedom as the 'right [in principle] to criticize everything publicly, including the idea of democracy'.[18] Derrida adds three more qualifications to this freedom. The first is its quasi-transcendental status: unconditional freedom makes possible the conditional sort of freedom that involves the 'I can' or individual initiative of 'liberty and license'.[19] This freedom also absolutely renounces 'sovereignty' and its inherent 'abuse of power',[20] its subordination of free 'decision' and 'responsibility' to the '*determinative* knowledge' of a norm or law.[21] Derrida also sees an 'incalculable' form of equality as 'an integral' and 'unconditional' part of '[pure] freedom'.[22] This equality is also linked to unconditional hospitality: Derrida thinks we have an absolute obligation to expose ourselves to 'the coming of the others, beyond rights and law', especially those who are absolutely unlike us.[23]

This mediating freedom, then, permits Derrida to link the unconditional injunction of democracy to come with conditional democracies: the commitment to critique, especially self-critique, is an identifiable aspect of each. Because of this linkage, Derrida says that the indecidability of the idea of democracy is not due to the interminable 'deferral' of the becoming-time of spacing but to something much stronger – 'autoimmunity'.[24] More specifically, unconditional freedom and equality imply that the invitation to participate in a democracy must be extended to even those who would argue against democracy and would vote it out of existence. Immunising democracy against this self-destruction would require restricting it to those who absolutely uphold it. But Derrida thinks such a restriction would contradict democracy's demand for universal inclusivity and equality. It would therefore immunise democracy against itself, that is, make it undergo a fatal and latent autoimmunity.[25] Derrida cites the Islamists in Algeria and fascist and Nazi regimes in Europe as illustrations of his claim that the 'general form' of autoimmunity has to do 'with . . . the freedom at play in the concept of democracy'. It permits 'the worst enemies' of democracy to 'put an end to democratic freedom in the name of democracy' by achieving a 'numerical majority' in a popular election. The intrinsic autoimmunity of democracy, derived from its joint demand for unconditional freedom and equality, therefore ensures that democracy can never make itself present and will always be lacking a 'proper meaning', will always be possible only as impossible.[26]

Despite its pessimistic appearance, Derrida thinks that autoimmunity carries a positive implication for democracy. The indecidability it implies means that no country can view its democracy as the true one and then use that as a reason for imposing its model on others or for curtailing needed changes at home.[27] Indeed, Derrida proposes that we adopt 'reasonableness' instead of 'calculable rationality' as our form of political reason. This type of reason would take into account unconditionality, the always 'to come' temporality of pure democracy, and thereby seek the sort of 'maxims of transaction' for possible democracies that would ward off totalitarian temptations.[28]

Derrida's desire to interrupt the sclerosis of democracy is laudatory. But is the vehicle of this interruption – autoimmunity – really intrinsic to democracy? We can agree with Derrida that freedom as unlimited critique is a primary meaning of democracy. But contrary to what he thinks, this claim implies that for any electoral process to qualify as democratic it must preserve an 'open space' for always further critical commentary. If a 'numerical majority' votes out democracy and eliminates dialogic practice, then we cannot legitimately say it is acting democratically. The majority would merely be using a formal voting procedure and not one that meets the Derridean requirement of operating 'in the name of democracy'. The triumph of the majority would be due to the external factor of the polity's susceptibility to demagogy, fear, or some other foible and not to a factor intrinsic to democracy itself. Even if the idea of an 'open space' is itself subject to Derrida's structure of spacing, questioning the former's meaning would require that it always remain open for a rejoinder to any of the proposed interpretations of it: the open space mandate would always reassert itself. Democracy, then, is not immune to an overthrow from fascist or other non-democratic regimes through a procedural vote; but it is not autoimmune, not destructible in its own name.

This argument also implies that the injunction of democracy to come is not unconditional in at least one sense: with some qualification that will be introduced later, only those committed to the open space or unlimited dialogue and critique count as legitimate participants – as equal members – in a democratic polity; said otherwise, democracy to come is not indifferent to content. We may say that the open or dialogic space is now the unconditional injunction as well as the quasi-transcendental basis of possible democracies. But if so, then the injunction cannot be a univocal call that trumps the many contesting voices that compose the dialogic space of a democratic society; it must instead be a plurality of injunctions, the manifold of voices that constitute the open, dialogic space of society and that are enunciated by the subjects who find themselves articulating these different voices, that is, answering their calls. In other words, the call is not the one issued by the continuous, if self-deferring, voice of the all-encompassing tradition of reason that Derrida spoke of in his comments on *History of Madness* and elaborated in his later work; rather, it is more like the pluralistic murmurings that Foucault favours, the interminable interplay or contestation among the voices that constitute (and sometimes betray) the open dialogic space of political reason.

But to see what the pluralistic murmuring and hence the open space of democracy and political reason might really mean, we must return to Foucault for help and, as we will see, once more to Derrida and some of his further remarks about the voices animating us.

FOUCAULT'S PARRHESIASTIC VOICES

After *History of Madness*, Foucault may seem to replace murmurings and voices with the formal *epistemes* and 'discursive formations' of his archaeological period. But this conjecture is mistaken. Foucault's references to voices occur throughout his archaeological period. In *The Order of Things* he speaks of 'something like a will [*un vouloir*] or a force' that 'constitutes' the 'modern experience' and that indicates the demise of the classical age by 'giving voice [*se énonçant*] to . . . the order that lay dormant within things'.[29] He also signals that each of the three *epistemes* of western culture – resemblance in the Renaissance, representation during the classical epoch, and finitude in the modern period – involves the 'murmurs' of an underlying reality: in the Renaissance, things are filled with 'the murmur of words' that indicate what they resemble;[30] in the classical age, it is the 'murmuring resemblance of things' that now 'furnishes the infinite raw material' for the 'divisions and distributions' filling taxonomic representations of reality;[31] and in the modern age, 'the whole of modern thought is imbued with the necessity of thinking the unthought [and] . . . of straining to catch its endless murmur', of hearing the 'murmur' of 'the people' in the '*energeia*' of their language and 'the murmuring of death' beneath life now seen as the evolution that endlessly devours its creations.[32] Beyond these *epistemes*, Foucault declares that there are 'inexhaustible values' in language that will allow us to 'speak within it in that endless murmur in which literature is born' and in which the 'Man' of modernity will 'perish'.[33]

Foucault continues to refer to murmurings in *The Archaeology of Knowledge*. He says there that a statement could not be spoken of 'if a voice had not articulated it'.[34] He also makes clear that this voice is not a Hegelian one, not 'a great, anonymous voice that must, of necessity, speak through the discourses of everyone'.[35] Indeed, in the places where he depreciates the notion of voice it is always and only when a voice is depicted as transhistorical, totalising, or hidden beneath and secretly animating the ones we are hearing.[36] As we will see more clearly, the voices that count for him are always ones existing, like madness and reason, in agonistic or dialogic relations.

Foucault's references to anonymous murmurings and voices are especially numerous and significant in 'Language to Infinity', 'The Thought of the Outside', 'A Preface to Transgression',[37] *This is Not a Pipe*[38] and other writings during this time.

I have systematically discussed these references elsewhere and hence will not repeat that effort here.[39] In their place, we can note Deleuze's enthusiastic remark that Foucault sees 'the speaking subject located within a deep anonymous murmur' and that 'what comes first' is 'a ONE SPEAKS, an anonymous murmur in which positions are laid out for possible subjects'.[40] Moreover, Deleuze takes Foucault's notion of 'thought of the outside' to designate the murmurings and voices that resist the dominant power in society – the topic of Foucault's later power-resistance period.[41]

Foucault's references to murmurings and voices during his archaeological period are not gratuitous rhetoric. The 'statements' that are the core elements of Foucault's archaeological efforts cannot float in an ether of disembodied discursive formations. Nor do their emergence and interaction with each other occur *ex nihilo*. They require murmurings and voices as their anchors and for their status as forces lest they be no more than the 'textual traces' Foucault derides in his attack on Derrida's 'little pedagogy'. This attack continues as Foucault inaugurates the genealogical method of a new period in his thinking. This method has both a critical and an affirmative side. The critical side joins Derrida in rejecting the Enlightenment's notion of 'humanism' and valorising its practice of 'critique'.[42] But Foucault favours his genealogical form of critique over Derrida's idea of deconstructive autoimmunity and a single tradition of reason. Rather than attempting to deduce 'what it is impossible for us to do and to know' from supposed universal structures of our existence, Foucault critically examines historically specific power formations.[43] These examinations free us from the constraining 'individualizations' and 'totalizations' sanctioned by the state[44] and thereby give 'new impetus . . . to the undefined work of freedom',[45] create 'new forms of subjectivity',[46] and make room for 'the claims of bodies, pleasures, and knowledges, in their multiplicity and possibility of resistance'.[47]

In a related article, Foucault indicates that part of genealogy is to re-establish 'the hazardous play of dominations' where freedom and creation occur. He describes the location of this interplay among contesting 'dominations' or voices as a 'non-place' that 'divides them' and 'through which they exchange their threatening gestures and speeches'. In other words, the interplay among these voices simultaneously separates and holds them together, forming the social body they inhabit. Foucault adds that new discourses 'emerge' from this interplay, ensuring that history will not be driven by a 'voiceless obstinacy toward a millennial ending'.[48] We can think of Foucault's development of this idea of a non-place and its vocal forces as the affirmative side of his genealogical critiques, as that in the name of which these critiques are offered, and as his pluralistic substitute for Derrida's continuous but self-deferring ideas of *khora* – the place of all places – and political reason.

We can see Foucault's development of 'non-place' as happening in two phases. The first concerns his notion of 'power-resistance' and the second his ideas of 'care of the self' and *parrhesia*. In the first phase, there is little use of voice-derived terms, and subjects are almost reduced to the mere effects of power. But these terms reappear when Foucault attempts to allow more room for subject-like forces that play a role in their own destiny. In a late paper, 'The Subject and Power', Foucault indicates that 'power-resistance' is the basic structure of all societies: he declares that 'a society without power relations can only be an abstraction' and adds that the analysis of the 'agonism' between 'the intransitivity of freedom' and these relations is 'the political task that is inherent in all social existence'. He also states that the real theme of his research is the subject and not power – more specifically, how 'human beings are made subjects' in our culture.[49]

In *The History of Sexuality* (1978) Foucault provides a theoretical characterisation of power-resistance and a preliminary answer to his subject question. He designates modern society as 'biopower' and says that it or any other form of power is 'both nonintentional and nonsubjective': it operates strategically in society but is not the product of the individuals and institutions that it shapes from below and that serve as the vehicles of its objectives.[50] Indeed, Foucault thinks the direction of the 'complex strategic situation' of modern society is the 'complete administration' of its inhabitants and their distribution 'in the domain of value and utility'.[51] He adds that power and resisting forces are symbiotically related: power requires resistance to it in order to persist as power, and resistance is impossible without a force attempting to limit freedom.[52]

In 'The Subject and Power', Foucault attempts to clarify his concepts of freedom and subject. He argues that power-resistance requires subjects to be free in the sense of possessing a 'field of possibilities' in which several ways of conduct are always possible. Power relations thus refer to how the actions of subjects or institutions modify other subjects' fields of possibility. The desire of these targeted subjects to preserve or increase their possibilities means that power is always a relation of 'mutual incitation' between those possessing it and those resisting it.[53] Without freedom, power turns into domination and the silencing of other voices. Power-resistance then is the status of all societies except when it is transformed into absolute domination, if that is ever really possible.[54]

Foucault brings us back to voice and a fuller concept of subjectivity when he says that 'anti-authority struggles' today 'revolve around one question: Who are we?'[55] He re-emphasises that answering this question can release us from our subjection to biopower, including the 'identity' to which it ties us through our 'conscience or self-knowledge', that is, to a particular voice and its accompanying discourse. Only by accomplishing this release can we create new forms of subjectivity.[56] In what many call his ethical period, Foucault attempts to characterise further the idea of a subjectivity that will make this goal possible. He therefore introduces his notions of 'care of the self' and *parrhesia*.

The first of these ideas – care of the self – replaces the self as a 'substance' with an active relationship to oneself. On this view, we 'constitute ourselves in an active fashion through practices of the self'. Nonetheless, these practices are not invented by the individual; they are 'models' already 'proposed, suggested, or imposed' on us by our culture.[57] The practices, rules, or *ethos* constituted by these models amount to a 'quasi-subject' or 'voice' established inside us. This voice is the basis of our freedom and obligation to our particular discourse of truth; it guides us in our interactions with ourselves and others.[58]

Foucault stresses that the care of the self and hence the voices involved in it are linked to western culture's acceptance of 'the obligation of the truth'.[59] He has in mind not a single universal truth, even one only ever to come, but a variety of 'games of truth'. Each of these is 'a set of procedures that lead to a certain result, which on the basis of its principles and rules of procedure, may be considered valid or invalid, winning or losing'.[60] The obligation of the truth or of following these procedures is ultimately political as well as ethical: a game of truth may be linked to establishing strategies of domination, and another to resisting such strategies.[61] Indeed, Foucault refers to these procedures as 'strategic games between liberties' that take place in different power-resistance regimes or non-places. Because these contests for audibility are based on the freedom of the participants, and because the only alternative to them is domination, the aim of 'governmentality' and the care of self or of others is to allow these voices to remain audible 'with as little domination as possible'.[62]

In his last works, Foucault links the ancient Greek idea of *parrhesia* to care of the self and governmentality. He defines *parrhesia* as 'true discourse in the political realm', a 'political structure' that is related to 'the freedom for citizens to speak' in democracies and, with certain restrictions, in autocratic polities.[63] In particular, it upholds the ethico-political obligation to tell the truth. This obligation involves 'binding' oneself to one's statement and its content and making a 'free pact' to run the personal risks it entails in the agonistic contests of the political realm.[64] This pact, moreover, is not only the parrhesiast's commitment to communicate truth courageously; it is also the hearer's willingness 'to demonstrate his greatness of soul by accepting being told the truth'. The two together are 'at the heart of what we could call the parrhesiastic game'.[65] Care of the self, then, requires that one courageously speak and hear the truth as part of its primary aim of making a 'creative activity' of the relation we have to ourselves, of 'creating ourselves as a work of art'.[66]

This discussion of care of the self and *parrhesia* suggests a more explicit characterisation of the notion of voice and also presents three problems. With respect to voice, Foucault's references to 'cultural models', our 'obligation' to 'truth', and 'truth games' might allow us to say that each voice has three dimensions: the body that enunciates it, the discourse that it expresses and that confers a cultural identity or 'model' on the enunciating body, and the other voices to which it is always responding. These contesting, intertwined voices make up the 'non-place' or social body of society: the murmuring depths from which emerge the audible 'speaking subjects' of society.

But Foucault's more specific treatment of this non-place or dialogic body as involving care of the self and *parrhesia* raises the three problems I just mentioned. One is solvable within his view, the second possibly, but the third is not and returns us to the role of voices in his thought and also in Derrida's. The first problem concerns *parrhesia* and brings us back to the dilemma of democracy that we encountered in our critical reflections on Derrida's notion of autoimmunity. Foucault delineates four 'conditions' of democracy and points out how Plato, Aristotle, and other ancient thinkers took them to imply that equal rights to free speech for everyone, combined with the persuasive powers of certain citizens, could lead an unwary polity to mistake flattery, demagoguery, and other 'false truth-telling' for speech based on care. They would see themselves as adhering to the conditions of a 'good' democracy when in fact it was a 'bad' one.[67] In other words, equal freedom is necessary for democracy and, at the same time, the source of its undoing.

An extension of Foucault's reflection on Prince Cyrus of Persia indicates a way to escape this dilemma. Foucault says that the Emperor enjoyed a parrhesiastic pact with his counsellor because he 'did not' punish him and thus 'open[ed] up the space within which his counsellor's truth-telling [could] be formulated and appear'.[68] This suggests that democracy too can maintain the same sort of open space and parrhesiastic pact among its citizens as that characterising Cyrus's relation to his counsellor. The risks it might run would be extrinsic to it, the product of the foibles of some of its participating voices, rather than the autoimmunity Derrida proposed.

Foucault's presentation of care of the self raises our second problem. Foucault appears favourable to the idea that care of the self is ethical in itself and 'ontologically' and 'ethically' prior to care for others: we must first be able to care for ourselves before we can treat others properly.[69] But this claim makes care of others appear as only a derivative concern and care of the self as narcissistic. However, Foucault indicates one case in which care of others is primary: the Cynics hold that their care of the self directly means looking after others. The basis for this 'ethical universality' is an 'individual bond with all individuals'. For the Cynics, holding to this bond is 'true political activity, the true *politeuesthai*', the 'true sovereignty', and applies to the whole world.[70] More specifically, the Cynics think that caring for the humanity in others is at the same time to care for oneself. Foucault uses the word 'solidarity' to capture the Cynics' relation to humanity: 'thus it is his own solidarity with humankind which is questioned, which is the object of his care, concern, and supervision when he looks at how men act and spend their lives, and when he enquires into what they take care of'.[71] Foucault also thinks the Cynics represent a 'historical category' that runs throughout all of western history.[72] His lengthy treatment of this group suggests that he might have thought in his waning days that something like the Cynics' *parrhesia* and the care it upheld might provide a worthy way of life in our own time.

If Foucault did uphold a version of the Cynic's form of *parrhesia*, then the form of power-resistance or 'non-place' he valorises would be composed of parrhesiasts who practise care of the self as the way in which each relates to his or her self and to the other participants. This interaction would involve courageous speaking and hearing one another as well as listening to the 'quasi-subject' or ethical voice inculcated in oneself. This implies that Foucault's notion of the 'work of freedom' would not be entirely 'undefined': it would involve *parrhesia*, a truth telling and hearing that can also serve as a 'counter-memory' when power-resistance threatens to become domination.

But now we encounter the third problem: what is the basis for the solidarity valorised by the Cynics, for their declared ethical commitment to others? As it stands, it seems no more than a declared desire. Our criticism of autoimmunity (if it was successful) rules out the universal hospitality contained in Derrida's unconditional democracy as a possible basis for this desire. Nor can we find this ground in Foucault's notions of power-resistance, care of self, and *parrhesia* by themselves. Stated more generally, Derrida's and Foucault's shared emphasis on creativity and heterogeneity would amount to domination by the new and different if it could not also affirm solidarity at the same time. Similarly, a solidarity that homogenised society – a 'homo-hegemonization'[73] – would be equally abhorrent in an age that sees diversity as a value as well as a fact. We have overcome Derrida's autoimmunity and Foucault's dilemma of democracy, but not the dilemma of diversity: without solidarity a unified society is not possible, but with it neither is heterogeneity.

We must return to Derrida and some of his direct comments about voices for a possible response to this dilemma.

DERRIDA'S HYBRID VOICES

Like Foucault, Derrida continues mentioning voices throughout his work. We have already seen that he refers to the *khora*, deconstruction and his key political idea 'democracy to come' as 'calls', as disembodied voices that bid us reply. We can now add that he sometimes considers himself to be an interplay of many voices, ones that constitute him and speak through him. He says that for himself 'a monologism, univocity, a single voice . . . is impossible, and plurivocity is a non-fictional necessity'. He adds that in writing a text he often has 'to change voices . . . to make several persons speak . . . and that the essential thing comes from another voice in some manner, from another voice in [him] . . . which is the same and not the same'.[74] In another text, he reveals that he was inspired to start writing by 'the adolescent dream of keeping a trace of all the voices which were traversing me', and that 'this is still my most naïve desire'.[75] Part of this 'tracing' includes an allusion to his roots in French Algeria as an 'over-colonized European hybrid'.[76] Moreover, Derrida often structures his arguments as a dialogue between two or more voices.[77] In discussing Husserl, Derrida argues that a pure voice is intrinsically open to its other.[78] We can take 'other' to include different voices, so that each voice is a dialogic hybrid of the rest. Similarly, Derrida depicts Europe as shot through with 'other headings' or non-European voices,[79] a Europe that 'consists precisely in not closing itself off in its identity and . . . assign[s itself] identity from alterity'.[80]

As noted earlier, each of these voices is always already responding to the rest. The vocal interplay among them simultaneously holds them together and keeps them separate, forming a dialogic body. But Derrida's remark that each 'heading' or voice 'assign[s itself] identity from alterity' suggests a stronger form of this interrelationship: that each voice is part of the identity and, at the same time, the other of the rest – that each is what it is through its difference from the rest. Because of this 'identity from alterity', the affirmation of one's own voice would be immediately the valorisation of the others and hence of our unity composed of and by difference. It would therefore also be the simultaneous affirmation of solidarity and heterogeneity, of an identity shared with those who are at the same time our other. It would, that is, provide the basis for resolving the dilemma of diversity that plagued the unity Foucault stressed in the Cynic's love of humanity.

Concretely, this affirmation of the voices resounding within our own implies hearing them in a manner that is not merely recording their words. It signifies instead the willingness to court changes in one's own discourse on the basis of what others say. In short, it is the *parrhesia* of which Foucault spoke. This *parrhesia* would be hospitality to all ears and therefore opposed to the 'homo-hegemonization' that both Derrida and Foucault reject and to any other material (especially economic) or spiritual barriers to equal audibility and to the freedom to be other than we are. The affirmation of this dialogic society, of this mutual hearing and speaking, also ensures its indecidability but without appeal to the injunction of a continuous 'tradition of reason', even if it is one that exceeds itself and is indifferent to content. Indecidability still would be assured because the interplay among these heterogeneous voices would continually produce new ones. Because each voice is established by its difference from the rest, these new creations would immediately be a change in all the rest. The dialogic body would therefore continually change and its meaning would always be open to new significations. The becoming-space of time would be the differences between the voices, each the outside of the other that it also inhabits; and the becoming-time of space would be the continual interplay among them and the metamorphosis of society it occasions. This 'spacing', then, would bequeath to the dialogic body its intrinsic status as always to come.

On this view, the dialogic body of society is unconditional in at least one of Derrida's senses of that word: such a body is intrinsically productive of and open to any new vocalisation of its meaning and incarnations of its being. In its injunction or rather celebration of parrhesiastic speaking and hearing, this dialogic social body valorises hearing all voices. But it also affirms that only certain voices can legitimately make government policy for society at any given time. These policy-making voices would be those whose proposals include an affirmation of the open space and parrhesiastic bond of society. Democracy would therefore commit itself to keeping that space and bond permanent. Thus the polity must be hospitable even to continual debate with the voices it provisionally deems hostile to dialogic exchange and thus illegitimate as possible policy makers. This openness allows us to correct the misunderstandings we might have of anti-democratic voices or of our own position. It also creates the possibility for enunciators of white supremacy, patriarchy and other anti-dialogic views to adopt a different discourse. Once again, the major commitment based on the unconditional dialogic hybridity of all voices is that we affirm the open space and parrhesiastic bond as the condition of the acceptability of public policy. This condition supports Derrida's exhortation for all of us 'to hear each other [*nous devons nous entendre*]' in '[each others'] languages'[81] and Foucault's valorisation of *parrhesia*. It therefore suggests a formulation of political reason – parrhesiastic speaking and hearing – that echoes the voices of both Derrida and Foucault within the framework of an immanent dialogic body.[82]

NOTES

1. Jacques Derrida, 'Cogito and the History of Madness', in *Writing and Difference*, trans. Alan Bass (Chicago: University of Chicago Press, 1978), pp. 31–2. Hereafter cited in the text as WD.
2. Michel Foucault, 'The Discourse on Language', in *The Archaeology of Knowledge*, trans. A. M. Sheridan Smith (New York: Pantheon Books, 1971), p. 215.

3. Jacques Derrida, *Rogues: Two Essays on Reason*, trans. Pascale-Anne Brault and Michael Naas (Stanford: Stanford University Press, 2005), pp. 33–4, 90; Michel Foucault, *The History of Sexuality, Vol. I: An Introduction*, trans. Robert Hurley (New York: Vintage/Random House, 1978), pp. 95–6, 157; Foucault, 'The Subject and Power', in *Power: Essential Works of Michel Foucault, Volume 3*, trans. Robert Hurley et al., ed. James D. Faubion (New York: The New Press, 2000), p. 343.
4. Or, more broadly, 'unreason'; on the relation between 'unreason' and 'madness' see Ian Hacking's 'Foreword' to Michel Foucault, *History of Madness*, ed. Jean Khalfa, trans. Jonathan Murphy and Jean Khalfa (London: Routledge, 2006), pp. ix–xii. Hereafter cited in the text as HM.
5. Foucault uses the term 'voice' throughout *History of Madness* when he is speaking of madness and reason as cultural forces. For occurrences not already cited above, see 'voice of madness', 44, 107, 330, 393, 511, 'voice of wisdom', 175, 'voice of man's desire', 372, 387, 'voices of the world', 387, 438, 'voice of a truth', 438, and 'voice of the masters', 673; for other uses of 'murmuring', xxxi, xxxiii, 529; for 'dialogue' between madness and reason, xxxviii, 165, 168, 171, 497.
6. Jacques Derrida, 'The Spatial Arts: An Interview with Jacques Derrida', trans. Laurie Volpe, in Peter Brunette and David Wills (eds), *Deconstruction and the Visual Arts: Art, Media, Architecture* (Cambridge: Cambridge University Press, 1994), p. 27.
7. Derrida, *Rogues*, pp. xiv, xv, xii–xiv, 29, 82.
8. Ibid., pp. 9, 28–9, 18; Jacques Derrida, *The Other Heading: Reflections on Today's Europe*, trans. Pascale-Anne Brault and Michael B. Nass (Bloomington: Indiana University Press, 1992), pp. 77–8.
9. Derrida, *Rogues*, p. 84.
10. Ibid., pp. 35–6, 37–9, 84, 144; see also Jacques Derrida, *Speech and Phenomena*, trans. David B. Allison (Evanston, IL: Northwestern University Press, 1972), pp. 85–6.
11. Derrida, *Rogues*, p. xiv.
12. Ibid., pp. 84, 144.
13. Jacques Derrida, *Specters of Marx*, trans. Peggy Kamuf (New York: Routledge, 1994), pp. 74, 91–2.
14. Derrida, *Rogues*, p. 144; see also pp. 83–4.
15. Jacques Derrida and Anne Dufourmantelle, *Of Hospitality*, trans. Rachel Bowlby (Stanford: Stanford University Press, 2000), p. 79–80; Jacques Derrida, *The Politics of Friendship*, trans. Georges Collins (London: Verso, 2005), pp. 104, 106, 134, 142.
16. Jacques Derrida, *On Cosmopolitanism and Forgiveness*, trans. Mark Dooley and Michael Hughes (London: Routledge, 2001), pp. 44–5; Jacques Derrida, 'Autoimmunity: Real and Symbolic Suicides – A Dialogue with Jacques Derrida', trans. Pascale-Anne Brault and Michael Naas, in Giovanna Borradori (ed.), *Philosophy in a Time of Terror* (Chicago: Chicago University Press, 2003), p. 130; Derrida, *Rogues*, pp. 91–2.
17. Derrida, *Rogues*, p. 22.
18. Ibid., pp. 24–5, 87; see also pp. 48, 72, 90 and 'Autoimmunity: Real and Symbolic Suicides', p. 121.
19. Derrida, *Rogues*, p. 25.
20. Ibid., pp. xiv, 102.
21. Ibid., pp. 85–5, 158.
22. Ibid., pp. 48–9, 53–4.
23. Ibid., pp. 60, 86, 149.
24. Ibid., p. 86; see also p. 35.
25. Ibid., pp. 40–1, 63, 86–7, 101–2; 'Autoimmunity: Real and Symbolic Suicides', pp. 128–9.
26. Derrida, *Rogues*, pp. 33–4; see also pp. 30–1.
27. Ibid., pp. 86, 96, 105.

28. Ibid., pp. 150–1, 158–9.
29. Michel Foucault, *The Order of Things: An Archaeology of the Human Sciences* (New York: Random House, 1970), p. 209; *Les mots et les choses* (Paris: Gallimard, 1966), p. 222.
30. Foucault, *The Order of Things*, p. 27; see also p. 41.
31. Ibid., p. 58; see also pp. 69, 70, 119, 155, 207.
32. Ibid., pp. 327, 291, 279.
33. Ibid., pp. 103, 386.
34. Foucault, *The Archaeology of Knowledge*, p. 100.
35. Ibid., p. 122.
36. Ibid., pp. 6–7, 25, 27–8, 68, 117, 122.
37. Michel Foucault, *Aesthetics, Method, and Epistemology: Essential Works of Foucault, Volume 2*, ed. James Faubion (New York: The New Press, 1998), pp. 90–1, 94–5, 100–1; 148, 152, 153–4; 73, 74–5.
38. Michel Foucault, *This is Not a Pipe*, trans. James Harkness (Berkeley: University of California Press, 1982), pp. 34, 37, 47–9.
39. See Fred Evans, 'Foucault and the "Being of Language"', in *The Cambridge Foucault Lexicon*, ed. Leonard Lawlor and John Nale (Cambridge: Cambridge University Press, 2014), pp. 236–42.
40. Gilles Deleuze, *Foucault*, trans. Seán Hand (Minneapolis: University of Minnesota Press, 1988), pp. 7, 55.
41. Ibid., pp. 89–90.
42. Michel Foucault, 'What is Enlightenment?', in *Ethics: Essential Works of Michel Foucault, Volume 1*, trans. Robert Hurley et al., ed. Paul Rabinow (New York: The New Press, 1997, p. 314; Derrida, *Rogues*, p. 142.
43. Foucault, 'What is Enlightenment?', pp. 315–16.
44. Foucault, 'The Subject and Power', p. 336.
45. Foucault, 'What is Enlightenment?', p. 316.
46. Foucault, 'The Subject and Power', p. 336.
47. Foucault, *The History of Sexuality, Vol. I*, p. 157.
48. Foucault, 'Nietzsche, Genealogy, History', in *Aesthetics, Method, and Epistemology*, pp. 377, 380.
49. Foucault, 'The Subject and Power', pp. 343, 326–7.
50. Foucault, *The History of Sexuality, Vol. I*, pp. 94–5.
51. Ibid., pp. 93, 139–41, 144–5.
52. Ibid., pp. 95–6.
53. Foucault, 'The Subject and Power', pp. 340–2; 'The Ethics of the Concern for the Self as a Practice of Freedom', in *Ethics*, p. 292.
54. Foucault, 'The Subject and Power', pp. 346–8; 'The Ethics of the Concern for the Self as a Practice of Freedom', p. 292.
55. Foucault, 'The Subject and Power', p. 331.
56. Ibid., pp. 331, 336.
57. Foucault, 'The Ethics of the Concern for the Self', p. 291.
58. Ibid., pp. 285–6.
59. Ibid., p. 295.
60. Ibid., p. 297.
61. Ibid., p. 295.
62. Ibid. p. 298. Foucault refers to the different modes of truth-telling as 'voices', for example, in the contrast he makes between parrhesiastic discourse and the 'prophetic' way of telling the truth. See Michel Foucault, *The Courage of Truth: The Government of Self and Others*, vol. 2, ed. Frédéric Gros, trans. Graham Burchell (New York: Palgrave Macmillan, 2011), p. 16, also p. 77; and Foucault, *The Government of Self and Others*, ed. Frédéric Gros, trans. Graham

Burchell (New York: Palgrave Macmillan, 2010), pp. 104–5, 125–7, 135, 211–13, 233, 269 for various other uses of 'voice' in relation to truth telling.

63. Foucault, *The Government of Self and Others*, pp. 6, 71, 301.
64. Ibid., pp. 65–6, 156.
65. Foucault, *The Courage of Truth*, pp. 12–13.
66. Foucault, 'On the Genealogy of Ethics', in *Ethics*, p. 262.
67. Foucault, *The Government of Self and Others*, pp. 173–4, 182–4; *The Courage of Truth*, pp. 44–5.
68. Foucault, *The Government of Self and Others*, pp. 202–3.
69. Foucault, 'The Ethics of the Concern for the Self', p. 287.
70. Foucault, *The Courage of Truth*, pp. 302–3.
71. Ibid., p. 312.
72. Ibid., p. 174.
73. Jacques Derrida, *Negotiations: Interventions and Interviews, 1971–2001*, ed. and trans. Elizabeth Rottenberg (Stanford: Stanford University Press, 2002), p. 373.
74. Hélène Cixous, 'Jacques Derrida: Co-Responding Voix You', trans. Peggy Kamuf, in Pheng Cheah and Suzanne Guerlac (eds), *Derrida and the Time of the Political* (Durham, NC: Duke University Press, 2009), p. 50.
75. Jacques Derrida, 'This Strange Institution Called Literature', in *Acts of Literature*, ed. D. Attridge (London: Routledge, 1992), p. 35.
76. Derrida, *The Other Heading*, p. 7.
77. Derrida, *Rogues*, pp. 82–4.
78. Derrida, *Speech and Phenomena*, p. 86.
79. Derrida, *The Other Heading*, pp. 10, 15, 77–8.
80. Ibid., pp. 29–30.
81. Derrida, *The Other Heading*, pp. 60–1.
82. My thanks to Jim Bahoh for superlative research help on this article.

CHAPTER 10

'Let Others Be Ends in Themselves': The Convergence Between Foucault's *Parrhesia* and Derrida's *Teleiopoesis*

Leonard Lawlor[1]

Early in their careers, both Foucault and Derrida recognise the originality of the idea of the performative.[2] In his 1969 *The Archaeology of Knowledge*, Foucault turns to the 'speech act' as 'one last possibility, and the most probable of all, of defining the statement [*l'énoncé*]'.[3] After describing the performative, Foucault concludes that a 'bi-univocal relation' between the statement and the performative cannot exist.[4] There is one primary reason, according to Foucault, why the performative cannot define the statement. Even if one says that an illocutionary act is complete, one has to admit that the act is complete only if several statements have already been made, prior to the act. The illocutionary act is made possible by the juxtaposition of statements. Foucault concludes that the statement is 'indispensable'; it is that 'on the basis of which' we can determine speech acts. A statement then is a prior or even an a priori 'verbal performance'.[5] The statement is a 'place of emergence', an 'irruption'; the statement is an event.[6] In his 1971 'Nietzsche, Genealogy, History', Foucault will define an event as 'the irruption of forces'.[7] Nevertheless, despite the irruption of forces, a statement, Foucault tells us, is in principle 'remanent', that is, repeatable.[8]

Similarly, in 1971, Derrida, in 'Signature Event Context', turns to the 'problematic of the performative' because he thinks that speech act theory has transformed the concept of communication.[9] He stresses, however, that the 'infelicities' that Austin encounters with the performative arise from what Derrida calls 'a common root'. These linguistic 'impurities', 'parasites', or 'abnormalities', for instance, non-serious speech and citations, are rooted in the linguistic codes. As Derrida claims, no performative statement (*un énoncé performatif*) would succeed if it 'did not repeat a coded . . . statement'. In other words, Derrida is claiming that a performative statement is able to function only if the statement conforms to a code whose forms are 'repeatable' or 'iterable'. Therefore, iterability is necessarily prior to all utterances or statements, a necessary or structural possibility of all speech acts, whether serious or non-serious, of all success and all failure in communicating, in short, for any event. Because of the priority of iterability, all linguistic utterances are in reality 'marks'.[10] Nevertheless, while formally prior to events, iterability, for Derrida, is also and necessarily 'emergence', 'a force of rupture'.[11] And finally, like Foucault in 1971, Derrida mentions Nietzsche as the philosopher who initiates the thought of force.[12]

For Derrida, the force of iterability requires us to rethink 'the eventhood of an event'.[13] For Foucault, the force of the statement requires us to 'restore discourse's event character'.[14] Despite the similarity, if not identity, between Derrida and Foucault in regard to the task of rethinking and restoring the event, the very wording of the task discloses a difference. The 'event character' (*caractère d'événement*), for Foucault, leads to discourse's existence or reality. In contrast, for Derrida, 'the eventhood of an event' (*l'événementalité d'un événement*) leads to language's essence or ideality. In *The Archaeology of Knowledge*, Foucault defines the statement, which must be coded in order to be 'remanent', as 'repeatable materiality'.[15] For Derrida, because he develops the idea of iterability from the materiality of language (writing), we can say that a coded statement is 'material repeatability'.[16] In other words, for Foucault, it is the *material* of the repeatable that produces emergence, while, for Derrida, it is the *repeatability* of the material that produces emergence. In still other words, for Foucault, it is the verbal performance or act (of speaking) that makes something emerge, while, for Derrida, it is the mark or form (of speaking) that makes something emerge. These precise differences derive from Foucault interrogating the *act* itself that makes an event happen, while Derrida interrogates the *form* itself that makes an event happen. The most basic question that both Foucault and Derrida seem to be asking is: how, in what manner or way, does an event take place?[17] What sort of act *and* what sort of form produces a change in us, in our thinking and behaving, in our way of living? As the subtitle of this chapter states, the answer lies in *parrhesia* and *teleiopoesis*. It is the question of the *act* that leads Foucault, in his final courses at the Collège de France, to the investigation of the ancient practice of 'speaking freely' (*parrhesia*). In these investigations, Foucault constructs what he calls an 'ethics of speech'. It is the question of the *form* that leads Derrida, in the courses from which he writes *Politics of Friendship*, to the investigation of 'speaking distantly' (*teleiopoesis*).[18] In these investigations, Derrida constructs a kind of formalism, which we can call a 'logic of speech'.

In this chapter, I plan to examine the practice of speaking in both Foucault and Derrida.[19] Without ignoring the complexity of each one's thought, I have placed emphasis on the 'ethics of speech' in Foucault and the 'logic of speech' in Derrida. The accentuation will allow us to see the divergence between them in regard to speech acts. But it will also allow us to see their convergence. The hinge between Foucault's *parrhesia* and Derrida's *teleiopoesis* is, as the title of the chapter suggests, Kant's categorical imperative.[20] In fact, the hinge is the categorical imperative in this form: one should never treat the person in oneself or in others as a mere means to an end, but always as an end in itself. I know that my placing of Kant's moral theory in the background of the thought of Foucault and Derrida is controversial.[21] What happened to Foucault's idea of self-formation? What happened to Derrida's idea of justice? Although I will not argue this point here, it seems to me that the treatment of others in a non-economic or non-useful way is at the heart of their thinking. In any case, even if I am wrong about the ends in itself form of the categorical imperative playing a crucial role in their thinking, I am really interested in the philosophical resources found in Foucault and Derrida. Instead of a correct interpretation, I am more interested in a creative appropriation of Foucault's and Derrida's thinking – in order to develop a solution to the problem of how to speak out against violence. Even if it is impossible to completely eradicate violence, speaking-freely (*parrhesia*) and speaking-distantly (*teleiopoesis*) aim at letting others be free. The force of language in these ways of speaking strives to effectuate the intensification of the freedom: 'let others be ends in themselves!'

CLARIFICATION OF THE CONCEPT OF FORCE

There is no question that force plays an essential role in both Foucault's and Derrida's conceptions of language. The concept of force that we find in Foucault and Derrida seems to have three components. First, the starting point from which we can approach the concept of force is linguistic codes (or codes in general). As we shall see below, the codes are not what is most fundamental: they are based in something like a consensus. The point we need to make here, however, is that for any statement or utterance to function effectively, either well or badly, for it *to have force*, the utterance must conform, at least loosely, to the forms of phonemes and graphemes, to the sounds and shapes of the words and meanings that are given in a particular linguistic system. If I want to change your mind, confess my love for you, or provoke you to anger, I *must* produce shapes or sounds that you, the hearer, are able, at the least, to recognise. This 'must' expresses a 'necessary condition', something 'indispensable' to speech. The possibility of re-cognition by means of a minimal conformity to the codes is the only way for me, the speaker, to have an effect (any effect) on you, the hearer. Without minimal conformity to the codes, the speaker would produce nothing but noise, and the hearer would recognise nothing. The force of murmuring and stammering, and even the force of a ritornello, relies on the recognition of them as such.[22] Thus, the formal character of a linguistic system *exerts force* over any and all speakers. Second, while the repeatable forms exercise force over speakers, speakers exercise force over the forms through the use or 'performance' of them. Even though I have no force over others, through speech, without the force of the codes, I still have force over the forms. I can transform the forms through thought, imagination, or memory, through archaeology or deconstruction. In fact, I am able to intensify and exaggerate the forms.[23] The exercise of force over the forms is the freedom of speech. There is one more aspect to this concept of force: either the effects can be intended, known in advance and predictable, or the effects can be unintended, unknown and unpredictable. The utterance, which projects the form (transformed or not), is subject to the force of chance. The utterance might reach its destination or it might *not*. Even more than not reaching its destination, the uttered form might go further and beyond its destination, having indefinite effects over an indefinite space and for an indefinite time. To summarise, the three components of the concept of force are: (1) the force of the codes (or the forms); (2) the force of the speaker (the act of intensification and exaggeration); and (3) the force of chance. It is this last component that makes speaking risky and dangerous.

We can see these three components in both Foucault's and Derrida's thinking. First, both recognise the essential necessity of the repeatable nature of codes, even though both criticise the idea of codes.[24] Indeed, both want to move discourse, as we have seen, to a level prior to codes. In *The Archaeology of Knowledge*, Foucault speaks of this formal level in terms of historical a priori. At that time (1969), these prior structures or *epistemes* are inseparable from institutions. Later, Foucault will speak of power-relations instead of institutions.[25] In contrast, Derrida in his early writings speaks of networks of traces. Later, he will speak of spectrality. Neither will ever speak of origins. Second, with *parrhesia* and *teleiopoesis*, both Foucault and Derrida are aiming their sights on the freedom of speech, the decision to stand up and speak out. And, third, both are taking aim at the effects of free speech, which necessarily have the chance of successful effects or the risk of unsuccessful effects. However, Foucault eventually takes aim at the actual subject who speaks: 'the culture of self'.[26] Derrida takes aim at the form of speech projected by the speaker: 'the "perhaps"'.[27] Through these differences, we can see already the divergence between an 'ethics of speech' and a 'logic of speech'.

'ETHICS OF SPEECH': SPEAKING FREELY (*PARRHESIA*) IN FOUCAULT'S FINAL LECTURE COURSES AT THE COLLÈGE DE FRANCE

Taking up themes found in his earliest writings like *History of Madness*, in particular, the theme of freedom,[28] Foucault's late studies of ancient and medieval thought move from the care of the self, that is, from the conversion of the self into being a subject of truth, to spiritual exercises, to the need for spiritual guidance, and therefore to the need for someone who can guide. After locating it within ancient Greek democratic practices, *parrhesia* appears in the context of the late Greek and early Roman idea of a spiritual director.[29] In order for the practices of the self to 'save' someone, someone else – the spiritual director – is 'indispensable'.[30] Besides calling the spiritual director by the traditional names of 'master', 'sage', 'philosopher' or 'priest', Foucault calls him 'an effective agency for producing effects [*un opérateur*] within the individual's reform and formation as a subject'.[31] The word *opérateur* suggests that the spiritual director is someone who makes something function. In *parrhesia*, the spiritual director 'operates' speech (the *logos*). *Parrhesia* is a 'verbal activity' or a 'speech activity', a 'doing'.[32] It is wisdom or philosophy considered in 'its allocutionary force',[33] that is, in its effects on the listener. *Parrhesia* is always an address to an other, on whom it produces effects. And in so far as it produces effects on an other, *parrhesia*, like the statement in *The Archaeology of Knowledge*, is an event. Left unanswered in *The Archaeology*, the question of how statements come into existence is answered by *parrhesia*.

In the final courses, Foucault distinguishes *parrhesia* from the performative, just as he had distinguished the statement from the performative in *The Archaeology*. In the course, *The Government of Self and Others*, Foucault outlines three characteristics, through which he isolates *parrhesia* from the performative.[34] First, a performative utterance, as is well known, requires an institutionalised or coded context or a well-defined situation. Because of the institutionalised, defined or coded context, the effect of the performative utterance is known in advance. Therefore, the performative utterance takes place in a world that guarantees that the saying effectuates the content of the utterance. In contrast, *parrhesia* opens the situation to effects that are not known. While the performative is 'a completely determined event as a function of the general code and institutional field in which the utterance is made', *parrhesia* is an 'irruptive event'. *Parrhesia* does not produce a coded effect; it produces 'an unspecified risk', the worst of which is the death of the speaker. *Parrhesia* is dangerous. This danger, Foucault says, is 'the crux of *parrhesia*'.[35] Second, in performative utterances, the subject's status is indispensable for the performative utterance to have its effects. The person who performs a wedding must have the authority to do so. He (or she) must be a priest, minister or judge. However, the performative utterance does not require something like a 'personal relation between the person who utters and the statement'. In contrast, *parrhesia* formulates the truth at 'two levels'. The first level is the statement of the truth itself, the content. The second level is that of the parrhesiastic act itself. Here one authentically thinks that what is said is genuinely true. The parrhesiastic statement is the affirmation of the affirmation. With *parrhesia*, there is a 'pact of the speaking subject with himself'. The subject 'binds' himself to the statement he has made and to the act of making it: this is the truth and I am the person saying it. This intensification, or even 'exaggeration', as Derrida would say, of the statement of truth, Foucault says, is 'essential to the parrhesiastic act'.[36] Third, while the performative utterance assumes that the person speaking has the status required for the intended effect, it does *not* require the person speaking to exercise his (or her) own freedom as an individual speaker. According to Foucault, *parrhesia* is 'the exact opposite'. What makes the parrhesiastic act different from the performative utterance is that, despite the status that the subject might have, the individual who speaks in *parrhesia* asserts 'his own freedom'.[37] The exercise of one's own freedom is why we find 'courage in the heart of *parrhesia*'. It is why the Romans translated *parrhesia* as *libertas*: speaking freely.[38] Thus with these three characteristics we have 'the crux', 'the essence' and 'the heart of *parrhesia*': the danger of speaking the truth; the intense binding of oneself to the stated truth; and the assertion of one's own freedom, in a word, courage. These three characteristics define, for Foucault, 'the ethics of speech'.[39]

The ethics of speech distinguishes *parrhesia* not only from performative utterances, but also, and equally importantly, from flattery and rhetoric.[40] According to Foucault, and this is well known, flattery and rhetoric are connected. The basis of rhetoric, as a technique of persuasion, is flattery, while the instrument of flattery is rhetoric, especially its 'tricks' (*ruses*).[41] Flattery is the moral adversary of *parrhesia*, while rhetoric is its technical adversary. More strongly, flattery is the enemy and *parrhesia* must get rid of it, because flattery is false discourse. Of course, in contrast, *parrhesia*'s 'ethics' consists in telling the truth. For Foucault, what is most important, as in Kant, is telling the truth. More specifically, while we just saw that flattery is connected with rhetoric, flattery is also coupled with anger. The anger and consequent abuse of power by a superior causes the inferior to engage in flattery (for instance, a tyrant over his subjects or a master over his slaves). In the general schema of flattery, we have a ruler who cannot control his temper.[42] The tyrant has not been able to form himself so as to have self-control and independence. Lacking self-control, the ruler 'exceeds the real function of his power over others'.[43] Complementary to and opposite from the superior's angry exercise of power, the inferior has only one instrument to use in order to manipulate the superior's power: speech. Here is where the flatterer uses the art of rhetoric.[44] The inferior 'praises'; he tells the tyrant what he wants to hear. And by addressing the superior in this way, the flatterer 'boosts' and 'reinforces' the superior's excessive power. However, being 'mendacious', 'lying' and 'duplicitous', the discourse blinds the superior. In fact, because of his insufficient relation to himself, the flattered ruler finds himself dependent on the flatterer and his discourse. In his dependency, the ruler's self-relation is mediated by the other. And as mediated by the other (the flatterer), the ruler finds himself subject to the flatterer's wickedness. Thus, the 'dialectic' of flatterer and flattered reverses the relation of inferior and superior.[45] The flatterer's discourse allows him to make use of the superior's power, leaving the flattered ruler 'impotent'.[46] In short, the flatterer gets what he wants.

Parrhesia, therefore, is anti-flattery. Unlike flattery, *parrhesia* speaks to an other in such a way so that the other 'will be able to form an autonomous, independent, full and satisfying relation to himself'.[47] Because the parrhesiastic speech is true, the addressee is able to internalise and subjectivise this true discourse, allowing the other to do without the speaker. In effect, in *parrhesia*, there is no dialectic. After the internalisation and subjectivation of the truth, the other does not become the same as the one who spoke freely to him. The other addressed is able to become free of the speaker, move away, and become distant. *Parrhesia* is also anti-rhetoric. In contrast to the rhetorical flourishes, images and ruses used to persuade the addressee, *parrhesia* tells the truth nakedly and without adornment. Several times, Foucault reminds us that the literal meaning of '*parrhesia*' is 'telling all'.[48] Moreover, unlike rhetoric, which is an art for which the subject-matter determines the 'how' of speaking, *parrhesia* is defined by the prudence and skill for saying truth at this very moment (the *kairos*).[49] Finally, in contrast to rhetoric whose aim is the advantage of the speaker, *parrhesia* aims to establish the other's autonomy. *Parrhesia* 'acts on others, but always to the greater advantage' of the other.[50]

Nevertheless, *parrhesia*'s relation to rhetoric is more complicated than its relation to flattery. While Foucault claims that *parrhesia* is not an art and therefore not rhetoric, he also claims that *parrhesia* has certain practices and even tactics.[51] The tactics of *parrhesia* explain why the ancients compare *parrhesia* to navigation and medicine.[52] In other words, in order to obtain the intended effect of speaking freely, it may be 'necessary' to make use of rhetoric. It may be necessary to take up rhetoric 'obliquely, and use it only if need be'.[53] When needed (the *kairos*), *parrhesia* might use rhetoric, including its images and ruses. The tactical use of rhetorical devises means that, when Foucault reminds us of *parrhesia*'s literal meaning as 'telling all', he is not implying that 'telling all' is *parrhesia*'s primary meaning. In fact, Foucault locates the literal sense of telling all only within Christian confessional practices. In regard to *parrhesia* in the ancients (Plutarch, for example), Foucault speaks of there being a 'pejorative sense' to *parrhesia*, a 'bad' *parrhesia*, which consists in being a 'chatterbox'.[54] When needed, *parrhesia*, in order to be 'good', does not tell all. While Foucault speaks of 'the automatism of the work of the *logos*', he also notes that true discourse's automatic effects on the hearer do not always occur. There are always those who hear the discourse, but who do not listen.[55] It might then be necessary to speak in a way that is 'rough, violent, and abrupt'. It might be necessary 'to tell the truth as quickly, loudly, and clearly as possible'.[56] Therefore, *parrhesia* is 'a particular way of telling the truth',[57] a way that, Foucault states, even includes the aphoristic form.[58] With this particular way of telling the truth, we see that, for Foucault, *parrhesia* is not always completely naked. As Derrida would say, the truth is not always and in fact cannot be wholly revealed.

Parrhesia also includes the form of 'irony'.[59] Of course, Socratic irony (and critique), for Foucault, is the model of *parrhesia*.[60] Yet, he says that the 'matrix scene of *parrhesia* [*scène matricielle*]' is the drama between Plato and Dionysus.[61] In fact, 'the birth of *parrhesia*' really occurs from this maternal scene, when (according to Plutarch) Dionysus asks Plato why he came to Sicily. Plato responds with the statement: 'I came to Sicily in search of a good man.' Through this statement, Plato 'lets it be understood' (*laissant entendre*) that Dionysus is not a good man. In other words, somewhere 'below' (*sous*) what the statement gives explicitly to be 'heard' (*entendu*), like a 'subtext' (*sous-entendu*), is the truth about Dionysus. The effects of this statement with its implicit or indirect truth are well known. Dionysus's reaction is violent, angry power exercised against Plato.[62] Dionysus becomes Plato's enemy.

Therefore, the parrhesiastic statement or utterance might fail (with the effect of animosity) – or it might succeed. When it succeeds, Foucault tells us, *parrhesia* increases the benevolence of the hearers towards one another. In short, when it succeeds, *parrhesia* increases friendship.[63] *Parrhesia* is the 'opening of the heart'.[64] Importantly, Foucault says that 'The exercise of *parrhesia* must be dictated by generosity. Generosity towards the other is at the very heart of the moral obligation of *parrhesia*.'[65] It is only by *giving* the truth to the other in a particular way, through this linguistic act of generosity, that one may increase the other's freedom. Through its tactics, *parrhesia* aims to 'intensify' freedom; it is 'the highest exercise of freedom'.[66]

'LOGIC OF SPEECH': SPEAKING DISTANTLY (TELEIOPOESIS) IN DERRIDA'S *POLITICS OF FRIENDSHIP*

Just as Foucault's lectures on *parrhesia* extend his earliest reflections on freedom, Derrida's concept of *teleiopoesis* extends his earliest reflections on language.[67] We have already spoken of the fundamental role of Derrida's iterability. In *Politics of Friendship* and in other later works,[68] iterability becomes the call (or the address or the declaration).[69] A call calls someone to presence (the one called is the intentional pole of my utterance); and yet, the call calls someone to presence because the one called is not present (the intentional pole of my utterance has not yet been reached). The one called is at once present and absent; he (or she) comes near without coming near. The structure of the call, therefore, consists in an unstable balance of presence and absence. The unstable balance of the call is the 'crux' of *teleiopoesis*. *Teleiopoesis*, for Derrida, 'makes' (*poesis*) speech so that it hits its goal immediately, thereby bringing the goal nearby (*telos*), and so that speech opens a distance, thereby delaying the hitting of the goal (*tele*).

We can see the unstable balance of presence and absence in Aristotle's statement, reported by Diogenes Laertius: 'Oh my friends, there is no friend'.[70] Derrida's analysis focuses on the opening omega (in Diogenes' Greek) of Aristotle's alleged statement. The opening omega (ω) could be interpreted as either a vocative interjection ('*Oh* friends') or the dative of a pronoun ('he *for whom* there are friends').[71] The ambiguity of the opening omega has led to two different ways of rendering Diogenes' Greek: either as 'Oh my friends, there are no friends' or 'he for whom there are [a multitude] of friends has no friend'. According to Derrida, the ambiguity of the opening omega refers to the difference between the performative and the constative. *Either* we have a call that does something (the call out to absence) *or* we have an assertion that reports something (the call into presence). The contradiction between the performative and the constative internal to the opening omega shows us the structure of every teleiopoetic statement, and also what is implicit in *every utterance*, whether it be constative or performative. We have a 'logic of language' functioning here, which the 'oh my friends, there is no friend' makes explicit. This one statement makes the structure of all utterances explicit.

The teleiopoetic logic works in this way. *Explicitly*, as we just saw, the 'oh my friends, there is no friend' is at once a performative and a constative: at once, it is a call *to* friends *and* a report *about* the lack of friends. Yet, *implicit to every assertion or report* is the fact that it must be addressed to someone. Implicitly, every assertion, even one about the lack of friends, *calls out to friends*, who are not present, not yet reached, and still to come. The call implicit to every utterance implies necessarily what is stated explicitly in Aristotle's statement: 'there is *no* friend'. Here is the *negation* essential to all teleiopoetic statements. Similarly, *implicit to every call or performative* is the fact that it must report. Implicitly, every call, even one addressed to an enemy, reports *that there are friends*. The negation (the call to someone not present) implicit to every assertion is always coupled necessarily to a position or affirmation, made explicit in Aristotle's statement: 'Oh my *friends*'. Therefore, due to the negation, the teleiopoetic logic, for Derrida, is *not* synthetic.[72] Nevertheless, if the negation separates to the point of a contradiction, then the teleiopoetic logic is also *not analytic*. It also essentially affirms or asserts. In other words, the teleiopoetic logic is neither an analytic logic that separates into opposites nor a synthetic (or dialectical) logic that unifies the opposites into a synthesis. The teleiopoetic logic is neither a logic of non-contradiction nor a logic of contradiction overcome. This dis-unity of negation and affirmation is the 'essence' of *teleiopoesis*.

Derrida uses the image of the chiasm (the 'crux') to define this unstable balance between the 'enveloped constative assertion' in every performative and the 'silent interjection' in every assertion.[73] Where the chiasm crosses, there is a presupposition about consensus. The consensus is even more fundamental than the linguistic codes we discussed at the beginning. For language to function at all (well or badly), there must have been a consensus established about the codes (constative), and yet for language to function, again at all, there must be a consensus to be called forth (performative). In other words, for me to say anything to you, you must minimally understand the meaning of the words I utter. Silently, it must assert that a consensus has already been established about the meanings and forms of my words for there to be the beginning of understanding. And yet, for me to say anything to you, I must minimally call to you about whether you understand what I'm saying. Silently, I call to you to fulfil the consensus about the meanings and forms of my words. An agreement must have already been struck and yet, at the same time, an agreement is still to be struck. The force of *teleiopoesis* to bring forth a possible friendship is based in a prior friendship. Derrida expresses the chiasm of friendship within the teleiopoetic statement with the phrase 'real possibility'.[74] It's *real*: the event of friendship has already happened; and it remains *possible*: the event of friendship is still to come. Like *parrhesia* in Foucault, *teleiopoesis* in Derrida answers the question of how an event takes place.

With teleiopoetic logic we have been speaking of a general structure that underlies all linguistic utterances: every utterance is at least implicitly, at once and necessarily, undecidably, constative and performative. However, the teleiopoetic statement as such (and as differentiated from every kind of utterance) is defined by the undecidability being made explicit enough for the statement to be recognised as paradoxical or aporetical.[75] In fact, and this requirement cannot be underestimated in Derrida: the undecidability must be intensified and exaggerated. It must even be shouted out in the loudest voice possible. The requirement of exaggerated explicitness is the very 'heart' of *teleiopoesis*. Through its exaggerated paradox, *teleiopoesis* brings about not just the experience of friendship, but also what lies beyond friendship: love. Love is precisely the exaggeration of the structure of the call.

The unstability of love lies in the fact that there is no love without the declaration of love *to* the other and that 'speech [*of* the other] ruins friendship'.[76] In other words, love means that, on the one hand, that if I want you to be my friend, I must tell you that 'I love you'. With this explicit declaration, we have the call into absence and into distance – the distance of *teleiopoesis* explains why we are calling it 'speaking distantly' – we have the call to establish a consensus. Not yet are you my friend and lover. Therefore you might be my enemy. This distance and enmity is what lies in the 'subtext' (*sous-entendu*) of the explicit call to love. What grows out of this concealed distance and enmity is violence. When I declare my love to you, when I call you 'my love', I make you *of* me: *my* love, the same as me. I try to bring you as close to me as possible so that you are my possession. We do not need to appeal to the countless stories of jealousy in order to recognise that love is usually possession. We also know from common experience the outcome of this kind of love: when I attempt to possess you, you pull back from me and rupture the intimacy. Love ends.

The excessive friendship that is love usually exaggerates the constative side of the call. It simply asserts, 'you are *mine*'. Love usually simplifies the complication of love into possession. In love, at the same time, I am your friend and your enemy.

The truth of love is that love wants to establish a bond of intimacy, which means that it wants to possess the beloved; and then, when possession becomes excessive, it breaks the bond and produces enmity. But, this enmity is usually not said out loud. In love, I always say 'I love you', while silently I think 'I hate you'. We can see already that there are possibilities, real possibilities in love. The possibility of saving the other from possession, and letting the other be free, appears when one reverses what is said out loud and what is said silently, what is implicit and what is explicit, what is posited and what is presupposed.[77] Derrida finds this reversal in Nietzsche. Through his reading of Nietzsche in *Politics of Friendship*, and in particular, through his reading of Nietzsche's reversal of the Aristotle statement into 'oh my enemies, there are no enemies', Derrida shows us how, through what form, to truly love the other.[78] This form is *teleiopoesis* itself, its crux, essence and heart.

Instead of declaring one's love explicitly, out loud, or with a loud voice, one declares one's hatred explicitly, out loud, and with a loud voice. The statement of enmity is true because, as we saw, love is implicitly violent. The statement is a veridiction, but it is formed in such a way that truth-telling of enmity is still love. Implicitly, *silently*, *to oneself*, *secretly*, one says to oneself that one loves the ones called 'enemies'. It is as if one is saying out loud, 'Stay away, I am your enemy'; but, silently, one is saying 'I need you, be close to me! I love you, my enemies'. Therefore, out of love, this statement – 'oh my enemies, there is no enemy' – in its explicit call to enmity, pushes those called farther out than the distance required by the essential structure of the call. In other words, this enmity is an extreme form of Kantian respect. By pretending to be or giving oneself off as the enemy, through a 'ruse', one explicitly repels the others away from oneself; you distance the beloved from yourself – even as you implicitly call the beloved in love. Consequently, the beloved is too distant for fusion and identification; she is too distant to be *of me*. She can no longer be a possession that can be used. Most importantly, she is too distant for one's loving actions to be deadly and violent. This distancing 'operates' an excessive act of love. With an 'open heart', the exaggeration of friendship into explicit enmity drives the beloved away in order to save her (him, or it).

To make this point as clear as possible: when you speak this statement of enmity, you implicitly love the ones called. Even as you call them 'enemies', you love them and want them to be near. But this love is still, up to this point, the desire for possession. The desire for possession explains why your speaking is always malicious and wicked, even evil.[79] You want to speak of them as your beloved; you want to assert that the other is a possession or a good.[80] Here however, the implicit love goes further. The teleiopoetic statement renounces love out loud (negation) without renouncing it silently (affirmation). Renouncing the love out loud, the secret love is more than the desire for possession, more than avarice, more than lust, more than self-love.[81] This love loves the others too much to do the evil one wants to do. This love is hyperbolic, but it is excessive in its desire to free the ones called from possession.[82] Therefore, the explicit declaration of enmity ('oh, my enemies') seems to be more loving than love. The teleiopoetic statement gives to the other the gift of freedom without any desire for reciprocation. Its generosity aims to never use the other as a means to an end. As Derrida says, 'The dream of an *unusable* friendship survives, a friendship beyond friendship.'[83] Although the wisdom is never to reveal the hyperbolic love as such, as such the hyperbolic love of dispossession is 'the highest exercise of freedom'; it intensifies the freedom of the other.

'LET OTHERS BE ENDS IN THEMSELVES'

If there is a difference between Foucault's *parrhesia* and Derrida's *teleiopoesis*, the difference lies between ethics and logic. It is probable that this difference is at the root of the terminological difference between 'repeatable materiality' and 'material repeatability'. It is even probable that the difference between ethics and logic is at the root of the original dispute between Foucault and Derrida. While Foucault, in *The Archaeology of Knowledge*, describes the form of the statement, and while Derrida, in 'Force of Law', describes an ethics of deconstruction, it seems to me that we can claim that Foucault's entire corpus, from *History of Madness* to *The Courage of Truth*, is directed towards an ethics, while Derrida's entire corpus, from *Writing and Difference* to *The Animal That Therefore I Am*, is directed towards a logic. For Foucault, it seems that what one says in speaking, the truth-content, is more important, while, for Derrida, how one speaks, the truth-form, is more important. Of course, in all of these statements, the name 'Derrida' could replace the name 'Foucault', and vice versa. They converge because the act of *parrhesia* exaggerates the bond of truth, while the act of *teleiopoesis* intensifies the friendship for others.

Thus from this divergence, we are able to move to a convergence. Of course, the title of this essay alludes to Kant's moral theory. As I said in the introduction, I know that placing Kant's moral theory in the background of both Foucault's and Derrida's reflections on ethics is controversial. Nevertheless, it seems to me that speaking-freely, either in Foucault or Derrida, strives to obey what we could call 'the highest practical vocation' for humans: never to treat the person in oneself or in others merely as a means, but always as an end in itself. As Derrida says (and I just quoted this comment), 'The dream of an *unusable* friendship survives, a friendship beyond friendship.'[84] An unusable friendship aims never to use the other within an economy that increases my power; it only ever strives to increase the freedom of the other. Then we have Foucault saying (and I also quoted this comment above): '*Generosity towards the other* is at the very heart of the moral obligation of *parrhesia*.'[85] It is precisely the moral imperative of generosity that distinguishes speaking-freely from flattery; once again, speaking freely only ever strives to increase the freedom of the other. What is most clear in both *parrhesia* and *teleiopoesis* is that these ways of speaking aim never to make the hearer of the speaking be dependent on the speaker. This truth-telling aims always for the advantage of the other.

I have just used verbs like 'to aim' and 'to strive'. I used these words of incompleteness because the intensification of the freedom of others encounters a problem that is perhaps irresolvable. The problem can be expressed in this question: how are we able, through action taken in the broadest sense to include speaking, to make others be independent? As we saw, starting from the idea of allocutionary force, both *parrhesia* and *teleiopoesis* have effects on the hearer. However, like all speaking this effect is violent. When I speak *to* the other, I always speak *of* the other because

I presuppose as an assertion that he or she is my friend, a member of my community, in consensus with me, and thus the same as me. More precisely, speaking is always violent because I capture the singularity of the other (its interior life) under a general concept. In this case, I capture alterity itself. Thus the problem has to be expressed in this question: how is it possible to speak to the other without doing violence to the other, or at least to reduce the violence done to its lowest level?

With this question we move from ethics to logic. The logic of both *parrhesia* and *teleiopoesis* is a specific way of formalising speech. With this formalisation, we are far from Kantian logic. The fundamental form for speaking-distantly is that the phrase includes *undecidably* both a negation and an affirmation. Then one exaggerates the undecidability itself. One exaggerates and makes explicit the absence, distance, negation and enmity concealed in every utterance. One exaggerates and says out loud the negation and the enmity in order to open as wide a distance and as dark an absence as possible. But the phrase negates proximity and presence, not out of hatred. There is no hatred here because the affirmation of friendship into love is also exaggerated. Silently, your love for your apostle is so excessive that you want the apostle to be so independent that she is able to survive without you. You say to yourself, 'I love you more than you can imagine.'

We saw the crystallisation of this logic in the omega of Aristotle's reputed statement and in Nietzsche's reversal of the statement. There are other examples, and these too are exemplary 'atypical expressions'.[86] We saw in Foucault: 'I came in search of an honest man (and you are not he).' And Derrida provides other forms of the teleiopoetic statement. From Nietzsche he takes: 'If you only knew, how soon, how very soon, something is coming.'[87] This sentence starts with non-knowledge and ends with the hearer knowing that something is coming. But the phrase does not complete the conditional clause, leaving the hearer free to respond to the knowledge. Another example from Derrida, one that is well known, is 'tout autre est tout autre'. This sentence asserts that every other is every other (redundancy), but also that every other is wholly other, meaning that every other is singular (wholly other) and therefore not like any other.

In each case, the phrase exaggerates the unstable balance of the call. The consensus has been established; I affirm that you are my friend. And, the consensus is still to be established; you are not yet my friend. The negation of friendship is exaggerated to the point of enmity. The force of the speaking then has the effect of pushing the hearer away, distancing him or her, and therefore of letting the hearer be free. It lets be the other 'so that' the other may take care of itself.[88] And thus, the exaggeration of the negation simultaneously exaggerates the affirmation of friendship. This exaggeration is true love. This exaggerated form of linguistic force shows us how we might be able to intensify the freedom of others. As Foucault and Derrida knew, the speaking of an utterance formed in this way is dangerous. Speaking-out requires courage. It requires courage because speaking-out, we hope, always produces an event: 'let others be ends in themselves!'

NOTES

1. I have written two companion texts to this essay: '"A Bird as Rare upon the Earth as a Black Swan": The Dream of an Unusable Friendship in Derrida's *Politics of Friendship*', forthcoming in Leonard Lawlor, *From Violence to Speaking Out* (Edinburgh University Press); and 'Speaking out for Others: Philosophical Activity in Deleuze and Foucault (and Heidegger)', co-authored with Andrea Janae Sholtz, forthcoming in Daniel W. Smith, Thomas Nail and Nicolae Morar (eds), *Between Deleuze and Foucault* (Edinburgh University Press). I am also writing another companion essay called 'Three Ways of Speaking', which will summarise this research project into modes of philosophical speech.
2. J. L. Austin, *How to do Things with Words* (Cambridge, MA: Harvard University Press, 1962). Paul Ricoeur's *Interpretation Theory* (Fort Worth: The Texas Christian University Press, 1976) provides a useful summary of Austin's idea of the speech act (see pp. 14–15). Speech acts refer to what happens by means of speech. The classical examples are well known: 'I now pronounce you man and wife'.
3. Michel Foucault, *L'archéologie du savoir* (Paris: NRF Gallimard, 1969), p. 110; *The Archaeology of Knowledge and the Discourse on Language*, trans. A. M. Sheridan Smith (New York: Pantheon, 1972), p. 82. Further references will cite page numbers for the French editions, followed by page numbers for the English translations in parentheses. On the statement, see Richard A. Lynch, 'Statement' in Leonard Lawlor and John Nale (eds), *The Cambridge Foucault Lexicon* (New York: Cambridge University Press, 2014), pp. 482–5.
4. Foucault, *L'archéologie du savoir*, p. 111 (83).
5. For an excellent study of *The Archaeology of Knowledge*, see David Webb, *Foucault's Archaeology: Science and Transformation* (Edinburgh: Edinburgh University Press, 2013).
6. Foucault, *L'archéologie du savoir*, p. 159 (121).
7. Michel Foucault, *Dits et écrits, I, 1954–1975* (Paris: Quarto Gallimard, 2001), p. 1012; *Aesthetics, Method, and Epistemology: Essential Works of Foucault, Volume 2*, ed. James D. Faubion (New York: The New Press, 1998), p. 376.
8. Foucault, *L'archéologie du savoir*, p. 163 (124).
9. Jacques Derrida, *Marges de la philosophie* (Paris: Minuit, 1972), p. 383; *Margins of Philosophy*, trans. Alan Bass (Chicago: University of Chicago Press, 1982), p. 322.
10. Ibid., p. 388 (326).
11. Ibid., p. 377 (317).
12. Ibid., p. 383 (322). In *Force de loi*, Derrida says, 'What we have to think is the exercise of force in language itself, in language's most intimate essence, as in the movement by which it would disarm itself absolutely from itself'. Jacques Derrida, *Force de loi* (Paris: Galilée, 1994), pp. 26–7, my translation. This sentence does not appear in the English translation. It is probably a later addition Derrida made for the French publication.
13. Derrida, *Marges de la philosophie*, p. 388 (326).
14. Michel Foucault, *L'ordre du discours* (Paris: NRF Gallimard, 1971), p. 53; *The Archaeology of Knowledge and the Discourse on Language*, p. 229.
15. Foucault, *L'archéologie du savoir*, p. 138 (105).
16. Jacques Derrida, *Positions* (Paris: Les Éditions de Minuit, 1972), pp. 69–70, 87; *Positions*, trans. Alan Bass (Chicago: The University of Chicago Press, 1981), pp. 50–1.
17. The question of the event (the *Ereignis*) was already Heidegger's question. It is still the question that animates much contemporary philosophy.
18. Samir Haddad's *Derrida and the Inheritance of Democracy* (Bloomington: Indiana University Press, 2013) is one of the few that has an illuminating chapter on *Politics of Friendship* (see pp. 100–18). Michael Naas also has a helpful essay in his *Taking on the Tradition: Jacques Derrida and the Legacies of Deconstruction* (Stanford: Stanford University Press, 2003), pp. 136–53.

19. Claire Griffin, philosophy doctoral student at Penn State University, provided essential research on Foucault's relation to the ancients. Daniel J. Smith, also a Penn State philosophy doctoral student, provided essential research on Derrida's *Politics of Friendship*. My sincere thanks to both Claire and Danny for their hard work and assistance.
20. It is important that, in *The Order of Things*, Foucault places Kant between ancient ethics, in particular Stoicism and Epicureanism, and modern ethics. The movement Foucault charts in the section of chapter nine called 'The "Cogito" and the Unthought', places Kant in the middle as the 'hinge' between the two. The Stoics and the Epicureans based ethical action on natural laws; Kant moved the law to the interiority of the subject; and apparently 'modern thought' moves the law to the unthought (like the unconscious). Michel Foucault, *Les mots et les choses* (Paris: Tel Gallimard, 1966), p. 339 n.1; *The Order of Things* (New York: Random House, 1970), p. 328 n.2.
21. It is worth noting that Foucault completes his discussion of the genealogy of ethics with Kant (*Dits et écrits II, 1976–1988* (Paris: Quarto Gallimard, 2001), p. 1230; *Ethics, Subjectivity, and Truth*, ed. Paul Rabinow (New York: The New Press, 1997), pp. 279–80). It is also worth noting that despite the immense influence of Levinas on Derrida, Derrida resorts to the feeling of respect in 'Violence and Metaphysics' (*L'écriture et la différence* (Paris: Points Minuit, 1967), p. 142; *Writing and Difference*, trans. Alan Bass (Chicago: University of Chicago Press, 1978), p. 96). In Marc Djaballah's excellent study of the relation between Foucault and Kant, Kant's moral philosophy appears only once (*Kant, Foucault, and the Forms of Experience* (London: Routledge, 2008), p. 36). See also Djaballah's 'Kant' in Lawlor and Nale, *The Cambridge Foucault Lexicon*, pp. 641–51.
22. Deleuze and Guattari have spoken of 'stammering' (*bégaiment*) as the beginnings of what they call 'minor language'. And for them a minor language, which is not a dialect, is based in a 'tensor' (a word or phrase repeated with varying intensities) or a ritornello. See Gilles Deleuze and Félix Guattari, *Mille Plateaux* (Paris: Minuit, 1980), p. 138; *A Thousand Plateaus*, trans. Brian Massumi (Minneapolis: University of Minnesota Press 1987), p. 109; for the ritornello (refrain) see ibid., pp. 366–77 (298–306).
23. Deleuze and Guattari state that a minor language is formed by two tendencies: 'an impoverishment, a shedding of syntactical and lexical forms; but simultaneously a strange proliferation of shifting effects, a taste for overload and paraphrase' (ibid., p. 131 [104]); see also Gilles Deleuze and Félix Guattari, *Kafka: Pour une littérature mineure* (Paris: Minuit, 1975), pp. 34–5; *Kafka: Toward a Minor Literature* (Minneapolis: University of Minnesota Press, 1986), p. 19. These acts of proliferation and impoverishment should be added to the acts of intensification and exaggeration that transform the codes of a language. All of these acts insert 'variation' into the 'constants' of a language system. In Deleuze and Guattari, variation is power and power – the 'perhaps' in Derrida – is freedom.
24. Foucault, *L'archéologie du savoir*, p. 39 (27); Derrida, *Marges de la philosophie*, p. 390 (329). Deleuze also recognises the necessity of codes and also criticises the idea of codes through the performative, which leads them to a 'pragmatics of language'. See Gilles Deleuze, *Différence et répétition* (Paris: Presses Universitaires de France, 1968), p. 160; *Difference and Repetition*, trans. Paul Patton (New York: Columbia University Press, 1994), p. 143. Also Deleuze and Guattari, *Mille Plateaux*, p. 98 (77). It seems to me that both *parrhesia* and *teleiopoesis* could be called a 'pragmatics of language'.
25. Michel Foucault, *Le pouvoir psychiatrique. Cours au Collège de France, 1973–1974* (Paris: Seuil Gallimard, 2003), p. 16; *Psychiatric Power: Lectures at the Collége de France 1973–1974*, trans. Graham Burchell (London: Palgrave Macmillan, 2006), pp. 14–15.
26. Michel Foucault, *Le gouvernement de soi et des autres. Cours au Collège de France, 1982–1983* (Paris: Seuil Gallimard, 2008), p. 43; *The Government of Self and Others: Lectures at the Collège de France 1982–1983*, trans. Graham Burchell (New York: Palgrave Macmillan, 2010), p. 43.

27. Jacques Derrida, *Politiques de l'amitiés* (Paris: Galilée, 1994), p. 86; *Politics of Friendship*, trans. George Collins (London: Verso, 1997), p. 67.
28. See the discussion of libertinage in Michel Foucault, *Histoire de la folie* (Paris: Tel Gallimard, 1972), pp. 134–9; *History of Madness*, ed. Jean Khalfa, trans. Jonathan Murphy and Jean Khalfa (London: Routledge, 2006), pp. 96–101.
29. Michel Foucault, *L'Hermeneutique du sujet. Cours au Collège de France, 1981–1982* (Paris: Seuil Gallimard, 2001), p. 132; *The Hermeneutics of the Subject: Lectures at the Collège de France, 1981–1982*, trans. Graham Burchell (New York: Palgrave Macmillan, 2005), p. 137.
30. Ibid., p. 123 (127).
31. Ibid., p. 125 (130).
32. Michel Foucault, *Fearless Speech*, ed. Joseph Pearson (Los Angeles: Semiotext(e), 2001), p. 13.
33. Foucault, *Le gouvernement de soi et des autres*, p. 322 (350).
34. Ibid., pp. 59–64 (61–6). This discussion takes place in the lecture of 12 January 1983, Second Hour.
35. Ibid., p. 56 (56).
36. Foucault had anticipated this intensification of the truth in *Lectures on the Will to Know*, when he speaks of sophism. Late in the course, he describes the intensification of truth as 'truthful truth' (*la vérité veritable*). See Michel Foucault, *Leçons sur la volonté de savoir. Cours au Collège de France, 1970–1971* (Paris: Seuil Gallimard, 2011), pp. 61 and 210; *Lectures on the Will to Know: Lectures at the Collège de France, 1970–1971* (New York: Palgrave Macmillan, 2014), pp. 62 and 219.
37. Foucault, *Le gouvernement de soi et des autres*, p. 63 (66).
38. Ibid., p. 46 (46).
39. Foucault, *L'Hermeneutique du sujet*, p. 132 (137). See Edward McGushin, *Foucault's* Askésis*: An Introduction to the Philosophical Life* (Evanston, IL: Northwestern University Press, 2007), especially Part 1, for an extensive treatment of *parrhesia*. See also Frédéric Gros and Carlos Lévy, *Foucault et la philosophie antique* (Paris: Kimé, 2003) for several essays that examine Foucault's relation to Stoicism.
40. The three characteristics also distinguish *parrhesia* from strategies of demonstration and teaching (Foucault, *Le gouvernement de soi et des autres*, pp. 52–5 [52–5]).
41. Foucault, *L'Hermeneutique du sujet*, p. 357 (373).
42. Ibid., p. 358 (374).
43. Ibid., p. 361 (377).
44. Ibid., pp. 365–9 (383–6). Foucault presents a shorter version of the definition of rhetoric (in relation to *parrhesia*) in *Le gouvernement de soi et des autres*, p. 53 (53).
45. Foucault, *L'Hermeneutique du sujet*, pp. 359–60 (376).
46. Ibid., pp. 359–62 (375–8).
47. Ibid., p. 362 (379).
48. Ibid., p. 356 (372); Foucault, *Fearless Speech*, p. 12.
49. Foucault, *L'Hermeneutique du sujet*, p. 367 (384).
50. Ibid., p. 368 (385).
51. Ibid., p. 369 (385)
52. Ibid., p. 372 (388).
53. Ibid., p. 369 (386).
54. Foucault, *Fearless Speech*, p. 13; *L'Hermeneutique du sujet*, p. 325 (342).
55. *L'Hermeneutique du sujet*, p. 321 (337).
56. Foucault, *Le gouvernement de soi et des autres*, p. 55 (55).
57. Ibid., p. 52 (52).
58. Ibid., p. 55 (56).
59. Despite the fact that the lectures *The Government of Self and Others (I)* and *The Courage of*

Truth (*The Government of Self and Others II*) occur in consecutive years, Foucault seems to change his mind about the relation of *parrhesia* and irony, or implicitly he is distinguishing a bad irony from a good irony. See *Le gouvernement de soi et des autres*, p. 54 (54), and *Le courage de la vérité. Le gouvernement de soi et des autres II. Cours au Collège de France, 1984* (Paris: Seuil Gallimard, 2009), p. 215; *The Courage of Truth: The Government of Self and Others II. Lectures at the Collège de France 1983–1984*, trans. Graham Burchell (New York: Palgrave Macmillan, 2011), p. 233.

60. Foucault, *Le courage de la vérité*, p. 215 (233).
61. Foucault, *Le gouvernement de soi et des autres*, pp. 50, 63 (50, 65).
62. Ibid., p. 65 (67).
63. Foucault, *L'Hermeneutique du sujet*, p. 372 (389).
64. Ibid., p. 132 (137).
65. Ibid., p. 369 (385).
66. Foucault, *Le gouvernement de soi et des autres*, p. 64 (67).
67. Although hardly noticed, in the 1967 *Voice and Phenomenon*, Derrida had spoken of *parrhesia*: '[intuitive knowledge] does not oppress what we could call the freedom of language, *the speaking-freely [franc-parler]* of a discourse, even if it is false and contradictory. One is able to speak without knowing'. Jacques Derrida, *La Voix et le phénomène* (Paris: Presses Universitaires de France, 1967), p. 100; *Voice and Phenomenon*, trans. Leonard Lawlor (Evanston, IL: Northwestern University Press, 2011), p. 76; my emphasis.
68. Derrida, *Force de loi*, p. 36; 'Force of Law: The "Mystical Foundation of Authority"', in *Deconstruction and the Possibility of Justice* (London: Routledge, 1992), p. 15.
69. Derrida, *Politiques de l'amitiés*, pp. 243–4 (215–16). Derrida's idea of the call seems to be based in what Heidegger says about the call in *On the Way to Language*. See Martin Heidegger, 'Die Sprache', in *Gesamtausgabe, Band 12, Unterwegs zur Sprache* (Frankfurt am Main: Klostermann, 1976), p. 18. The essay has been translated into English by Albert Hofstader as 'Language', in Martin Heidegger, *Poetry, Language, Thought* (New York: Harper Collins, 2001), p. 196.
70. Derrida's almost endless repetition of Aristotle's alleged statement is what is best known about *Politics of Friendship*.
71. Derrida, *Politiques de l'amitiés*, pp. 235–6 (209).
72. In *Politics of Friendship*, Derrida frequently mentions Plato's dialogue on friendship, the *Lysis*, a name that literally means 'to unbind', as in the word 'ana-*lysis*' (ibid., p. 176 [153]).
73. Ibid., pp. 241–2 (213–14).
74. Ibid., p. 154 (131).
75. I have developed this relation of sufficiency, necessity and hyperbolisation in Leonard Lawlor, *This is not Sufficient* (New York: Columbia University Press, 2007).
76. Derrida, *Politiques de l'amitiés*, pp. 26, 72 (9, 54).
77. Ibid.
78. The quotation is from Nietzsche in *Human, all too Human* (Book I, §376, called 'Of friends'): 'Perhaps to each of us there will come the more joyful hour when we exclaim: "Friends, there are no friends!" thus said the dying sage; "Foes, there are no foes!" say I, the living fool.' Derrida, *Politiques de l'amitiés*, p. 78 (59).
79. Ibid., p. 79 (60).
80. Ibid., p. 37 (17).
81. Ibid., pp. 198, 240 (174, 213).
82. Ibid., p. 79 (60).
83. Ibid., p. 245 (217), my emphasis. In addition to 'unusable friendship', Derrida speaks of 'love in friendship' (*aimer d'amitié*), which is the title of *Politics of Friendship*, chapter two, and the more well known 'lovence' (*aimance*) (ibid., p. 54 [35]).
84. Ibid., p. 245 (217), my emphasis.

85. Foucault, *L'Hermeneutique du sujet*, p. 369 (385), my emphasis.
86. See Deleuze and Guattari, *Mille Plateaux*, p. 126 (99).
87. Derrida, *Politiques de l'amitiés*, p. 49 (31). The actual sentence comes from Nietzsche's *Beyond Good and Evil*: 'Alas! If only you knew how soon, how very soon, things will be – different' (ibid).
88. In *What is Philosophy?*, Deleuze and Guattari transform 'speaking for' (*parler pour*) into 'speaking so that' (*parler pour que*). Gilles Deleuze and Félix Guattari, *Qu'est-ce que la philosophie?* (Paris: Minuit, 1991), p. 105; *What is Philosophy?*, trans. Hugh Tomlinson and Graham Burchell (London: Verso, 1994), p. 109. One speaks for the Indians (as they say) so that the Indians become otherwise (or care for themselves).

PART IV

The Placeless Place

CHAPTER 11

The Aporia and the Problem

Paul Rekret

> What is the answer to the question? The problem. How is the problem resolved? By displacing the question.
>
> (Michel Foucault)[1]

> There, in sum, in this place of aporia, there is no longer any problem.
>
> (Jacques Derrida)[2]

In defence of accusations of a relativism inherent to so-called 'post-structuralist' thought, Stephen White has proposed conceiving recent continental theory in terms of Gianno Vattimo's notion of 'weak ontology'.[3] This entails affirming the 'essential contestability' of concepts and theoretical frameworks while nonetheless accepting that ontological and theoretical 'generalisations' are an irreducible element of all theorising.[4] In other words, White argues that while what Jean-François Lyotard famously called 'grand narratives' – totalising accounts of the world – are jettisoned, the articulation of a 'grander narrative', no matter how implicit, is irreducible.

Conceived as a heuristic device, White's account of theory as 'grander narratives' is not dissimilar to the by now well-known neologism of 'correlationism' proffered by Quentin Meillassoux in *After Finitude* in reference to the move, ubiquitous in post-Kantian philosophy, whereby 'what is' always correlates to 'what is thought'.[5] Meillassoux's argument implies in part that social constructions function as a priori 'media of givenness' and so convey an idealism wherein nothing can be said to exist apart from its relation to thought. Even if we might admit that thinkers such as Friedrich Nietzsche, Jacques Derrida or Michel Foucault theorise some 'extra-correlational' medium to undermine the self-sufficiency of the subject by dispersing it to the media of will to power, *différance* or power relations, they nonetheless, Meillassoux argues, posit some socially constructed 'structural invariant' as conditional of thought. Accordingly, theirs is merely a 'sickened' or 'misfired' correlationism which nonetheless, confines thought to a medium which 'always already dominates us'.[6]

The logic described by both White and Meillassoux, albeit in different inflections, whereby the assertion of the finitude of thought seeks to undermine the self-sufficiency or totalising pretensions of a 'grander narrative', is a useful heuristic device. This is succinctly exemplified in certain themes central to Nietzsche's work. In putting to theoretical investigation his well-known meta-question regarding the 'value of values', Nietzsche leads thought to reflect upon its own point of departure since, if behind every truth there lies a will, if as he asserts, '[t]his world is will to power and nothing besides!',[7] logic dictates that the claim must be reflexively folded back upon itself. All knowledge, including Nietzsche's own account of the world as will to power, must be situated in terms of its finite and situated origin and thus must by definition be partial since it is the product of a particular will. 'Perspectival seeing', Nietzsche says, 'is the only kind of knowing.'[8] Once truth is located in a differential play of forces, as it is by Nietzsche, a new question emerges for theory: that of the relation between a generalised ontological vision and the finitude that the perspectival epistemological position of the latter implies. While the claim is frequently made that the circularity in Nietzsche's work between epistemological perspectivism and the ontology of will to power brings him to espouse a contradictory self-referentiality,[9] his advocates argue that it amounts to an ethical 'recoil' whereby his account resists 'authoritatively re-establishing itself' and that, moreover, the grounds upon which Nietzsche's genealogy ought to be evaluated are pragmatically tied its ability to depict the conditions and beliefs of other perspectives.[10] White pushes his own argument in parallel directions to Nietzsche's defenders in his analysis of recent Anglo-American political theory, while Meillassoux famously mobilises the logical dead-ends of the correlate as the setting off point for his own attempt to develop a post-Kantian realist epistemology.

This rather lengthy introductory digression by way of Nietzsche, White and Meillassoux serves to preface the questions of the analysis that follows of the debate between Derrida and Foucault: how should we conceive polemics wherein two such 'grander narratives' come into dialogue with one another? How are we to navigate competing claims to situate a finite thought within a medium and what can the nature of this competition or polemic reveal to us about these theories? The wager animating these questions and the analysis that follows is that while assertions of finitude may undermine the self-sufficiency of Derrida's and Foucault's 'grander narratives', in looking to the debate between them it becomes apparent that the self-sufficiency of the account in turn undermines the affirmation of finitude. I will seek to support this claim first, by locating the effects of this sufficiency in the well-known 'cogito debate' between Derrida and Foucault. I will then seek to demonstrate that the terms of the debate are inherent to the theoretical strategies adopted by both thinkers and which I thematise here with the concepts of 'problem' and 'aporia' indicated by my title. Finally, I will seek to demonstrate the way in which their incommensurability permeates their later works, exemplified in their engagements with ethics in particular.

FINITUDE, VIOLENCE AND MADNESS

The themes of the relationship between epistemological finitude, the ontological account of the media of givenness, and the irreducibility of epistemic violence are central to both Derrida's and Foucault's *oeuvres* and are especially apparent in their own engagements with Nietzsche.[11] First, as the progenitor of a vision of an ontological play of differences, Nietzsche assumes a singular position in both Derrida's and Foucault's works not only for having thus placed the unity of the signifier and signified in question, but for celebrating rather than mourning the consequent loss of the permanence of truth that this implies.[12] Secondly, the absence of a transcendental signified implies for both Derrida and Foucault that thought is always situated and finite in a medium. Nowhere is this more apparent than in Derrida's often quoted claim that '[t]here is nothing outside the text', which Foucault, almost as notoriously, echoes: 'there is no point where you are free from power relations'.[13] No reference to the real transcends the differential play of the media in which thought is situated. Third, both Derrida and Foucault retain the Nietzschean claim that truth is inseparable from power or violence. Exemplary in this regard is Derrida's analysis in *Of Grammatology*, described as a 'genealogy of morals', of Lévi-Strauss's *Tristes Tropiques*.[14] Lévi-Strauss's confessional account of the cultural violence involved in anthropological fieldwork is shown to betray its own Rousseauist nostalgia which disavows and so masters 'originary violence'. Only a 'presumed difference between knowledge and power', Derrida says, allows Lévi-Strauss to maintain the metaphysical myth of an originally nonviolent tribal society which the anthropologist then corrupts.[15] Similarly, the enduring theme of Foucault's work has been the rupture or disjunction, originating with Plato but still dominant in the modern age, between knowledge and power.[16] For the pre-Socratics true discourse was differentiated from mere rhetoric or flattery by its capacity to inspire, to contest and to command, and thus Foucault, himself employing a favourite concept of Derrida's, locates Plato as having enacted the 'logocentric' ground of philosophy operative today.[17] Yet despite these parallels, or more accurately, arising out of them, is a fundamental incommensurability between Derrida and Foucault.

In order to locate this incommensurability, I shall begin by looking to the most explicit and well-known polemical moment between Derrida and Foucault, the infamous 'Cogito debate', first, by briefly summarising what I take to be Derrida's central claims in his essay, 'Cogito and the History of Madness', before doing the same for Foucault's reply in 'My Body, This Paper, This Fire'. This will permit me to demonstrate what I take to be the central terms of the debate: that of two competing claims to have located the medium in which reason is differentiated from madness, where each contends that the interlocutor, having failed to correctly identify this medium, commits an epistemic violence against madness.

Derrida's target in 'Cogito and the History of Madness' is the indexical status Foucault accords to Descartes' *Meditations* of an epochal shift in attitudes to madness in seventeenth-century Europe. Derrida's critique involves more than a mere claim regarding textual or historical interpretation.[18] It involves rather, the claim that Foucault does not correctly recognise what Derrida elsewhere calls 'the prior medium in which differentiation in general is produced'.[19] That is to say, Foucault is said to posit an illegitimate transcendent or Archimedean point of departure for his discourse in so far as he 'violently' disavows what Derrida argues is the medium and thus the condition of both Descartes' and his own discourse.

Derrida seeks to demonstrate this disavowal by interrogating Foucault's claim that the significance of the Cartesian exercise of doubt lies in the way errors of the senses, illusions and dreams form obstacles to overcoming subjective doubt while Descartes accords to madness a categorically different status in so far as it is disqualified a priori from the activity of doubting, and so is opposed to a reasonable investigation of truth. 'I who think, cannot be mad', as Foucault puts it.[20] Contra Foucault, Derrida argues that this exclusion of madness is merely a minor moment in Descartes' argument. He contrasts it with the invocation in the *Meditations* of an evil genius who represents the possibility of total error and delusion, as the truly radical instance of doubt whereby even rational inferences may be false. This is a form of doubt so radical, Derrida says, that only a Godly guarantee of rational truths invoked by Descartes could free us from its power.[21] For Descartes, Derrida argues, 'the Cogito is valid even if I am mad'.[22]

Derrida's argument hinges upon a broader claim regarding thought's situatedness in an anterior medium and the question of how this medium is to be negotiated. For Derrida, this medium is located in the formal conditions of any differentiation of reason from madness. The Cogito's inseparability from the hyperbolic doubt of the evil genius is, he argues, the 'zero point . . . which no longer belongs to a determined reason or determined unreason' and so is a zone of indeterminacy which can only be 'violently' transcended.[23] The condition for a differentiation of reason from madness would thus be the violent reduction of madness through the invocation of a Godly guarantee of truth.

Accordingly, against Foucault's account of the exclusion of madness from reason, Derrida posits the anteriority of the formal conceptual aporia of what is in principle the inseparability of madness and reason such that their separation is only ever 'violently' accomplished in practice.[24] That is, Derrida's central claim is that in failing to situate the condition for both the Cartesian exclusion and his own discourse through his disavowal of the hyperbolic excess of doubt with a determinate discursive location, Foucault disavows what Derrida claims are the conditions of his account: the unmasterable excess whereby reason and madness, meaning and nonmeaning, are *de jure* inseparable. For that reason, Foucault's disavowal of the latter posits his enterprise in the position of an 'evasive transcendence' in so far as the differentiation is reduced to a particular event.[25]

If I am correct in asserting that Derrida's argument amounts to the claim that Foucault fails to situate his thought then it should also become evident that Foucault's reply in 'My Body, This Paper, This Fire' analogously mirrors Derrida's. This time however, it is Derrida who is said to disavow the anterior medium conditioning his analysis and, thus, to repeat the Cartesian exclusion by ascribing a transcendent position for his discourse. Foucault reiterates here what he had already asserted in *History of Madness*: that the condition for the Cartesian exercise of doubt comes prior to the exclusion of madness from the activity of doubting, since the exercise must first acquire the status of a rational discourse capable of formal veridiction. The exercise of doubt is conditioned first of all, Foucault claims, by the separation of a subject qualified to make axiomatic statements and the disqualification of a 'mad' subject who, through his objectification in seventeenth-century juridical and medical discourse as *demens*, is not. Anterior to the engagement with the hyperbolic doubt brought on by the evil genius, upon which Derrida's reading centres, is the qualification of the subject of doubt. In so far as the madman's act does not qualify as that of a rational subject, he is not qualified to speak the truth since 'the exercise of meditation has excluded the risk of being mad'.[26] Derrida disavows the exclusion of madness by asserting the philosophically mastered madness of an evil genius which puts in question only the object but not the subject of knowledge.

This argument is underlined by a broader one: Derrida's erroneous interpretation arises from his failure to have correctly located what Derrida had called the 'medium of differentiation'. It is Derrida this time who is said to have repeated the Cartesian exclusion in so far as he interprets the text from a position which has already violently excluded or mastered madness in advance. In revoking 'philosophical status' from the exclusion of the mad subject in the *Meditations*, Derrida's interpretation is thus said to 'efface differences within the text' in the name of a philosophical discourse which, in order to preserve its own sovereignty, must disavow its own conditions.[27] For Foucault, Derrida's interpretation of the text is constituted through an a-historical idealism which 'avoid[s] placing discursive practices in the field of transformations where they are carried out' and, thus, it is Derrida and not Foucault who makes the metaphysical move of occupying a position totally transcending its conditions in so far as the text is subsumed to a pre-determinate philosophical discourse.[28] In 'calling into question . . . the totality of beingness', as Foucault puts it, Derrida reads all discourses through a single determinate horizon that is thus reductive of the singular and specific status of madness in Descartes.[29]

Conceived in these terms, the debate reflects the tripartite Nietzschean schema outlined above. Given that thought is always finite, it is inevitably violent, yet the necessary avowal of that violence hinges upon indexing the medium from which it emerges. The claim being pursued here is that both Derrida and Foucault ultimately ground their polemics upon the notion that their interlocutor has failed to accurately affirm the conditions of both Descartes' and his own discourse. For both thinkers this failure thus amounts to the interlocutor's violent reduction and mastery of the object of thought through the illegitimate claim to have adopted a perspective which transcends its medium. Derrida's and Foucault's arguments both hinge upon the question of how the relation between finite thought and its generalised medium is to be conceived.

A CASE OF MISTAKEN NON-IDENTITY

It is not surprising that the secondary literature on the Cogito debate has not reckoned with the incommensurability between Derrida and Foucault, since commentators have generally been invested in defending the 'grander narrative' conceived by either Derrida[30] or Foucault[31] or in seeking a rapprochement on the grounds that

Derrida and Foucault simply pursue different terrains of thought.[32] A more profound challenge to my own thesis appears through Giorgio Agamben's influential argument that Derrida and Foucault ought to be situated as two divergent post-Heideggerian trajectories defined by ontologies of immanence (Foucault) and transcendence (Derrida).[33] While a valuable heuristic, Agamben's dichotomy omits the extent to which Derrida and Foucault are engaged in parallel enterprises. Insistence upon a 'formal structure of transcendence' as definitive of Derrida's work overlooks the deconstructive claim that transcendental grounds are irreducible from, or contaminated by, the empirical realm from which they are delimited.[34] Derrida and Foucault are both engaged in the articulation of a medium anterior to or 'outside' thought to which subjectivity is dispersed, thus to restrict the debate to the decision over an ontology of immanence or transcendence too quickly disregards their parallel yet incommensurable recastings of epistemology, ontology and the irreducible violence this relationship involves.[35] There is a basic shared conceptual architecture to Derrida's and Foucault's work which forms the terrain for their polemic.

If we might delimit a structure of transcendence underlying Derrida's work, it is in so far as, while Foucault views the discursive and non-discursive media of knowledge in their positivity as transformable regularities through the metaphor of 'battle' or 'struggle',[36] Derrida insists on the irreducibility of an aporetic logic or 'passage' through the transcendental which, while inescapably contaminated by the empirical, is conditional for meaning.[37] While Foucault attempts to disengage from questions of the limits of man in the name of the positivity, exteriority or outside of his knowledge – a level of reality not reducible to a subject – the Derridean response is the one he makes in 'Cogito and the History of Madness': to transcend the transcendental merely reinstates it at a different level of abstraction.

Yet this divergence between Derrida and Foucault involves first of all a shared refusal to posit some transcendent or Archimedean position for their work from which the medium of thought would be appropriated as a totality. For both thinkers, to think is to commence from some determinate time and place such that there is no access to the medium of differentiation in itself. If this is indeed the case, then we should expect that the terms of the debate exceed that of the dispute over the Cogito and define Derrida's and Foucault's *oeuvres* as a whole, since they involve questions broader than that of how particular texts or thinkers are to be interpreted. The very nature of questioning itself would be at stake, as I seek to show in the following section.

QUESTIONS OF THE OUTSIDE

Any claim to delimit and define the nature of Derrida's and Foucault's equally extensive and far-reaching *oeuvres* risks a crude reductionism. Rather than seeking merely to provide such an account, I seek here to outline the strategies of theoretical investigation employed by both thinkers, thematised as 'problematisation' and 'aporia', and characteristic of each of their *oeuvres*. This will provide us with the means for drawing out the terms of the 'Cogito debate', as I have defined them, more broadly. This analysis, I claim, must begin with the question of the 'outside' – that is, of the interrogation of the inappropriable exteriority of thought.

From his earlier works of the 1960s on, Foucault consistently seeks to effect a shift away from the formal line of questioning by which philosophy has proceeded (who are we? what ought we to do?) to the conditions of those questions themselves in the exteriority or 'outside' of discourse, time, space and bodies conceived as anonymous media of ordering. Most explicitly thematised in the series of early essays on literature and art, Gilles Deleuze and Pierre Macherey both extend the notion of a 'thought of the outside' whereby all forms of subjective interiority are conceived as an 'operation of the outside', to the general thematic of Foucault's work as a whole.[38] This insight is confirmed by Foucault who himself refers to his whole *oeuvre* in terms of a 'thought of the outside' in an important late methodological reflection.[39] In Foucault's earlier 'archaeological' works this is articulated in terms of a thought that seeks to think the rules and logics within which it takes place in order to produce a 'pure experience of order and its modes of being'.[40] With the genealogical trajectory announced in the early 1970s, the principles ordering discourse are theorised more explicitly than in earlier texts in terms of conceptions of 'force', 'battle' or 'contest'.[41] That is, no longer primarily seeking to formalise the 'rules of formation of concepts', Foucault's genealogical works attend to what he describes as the 'objectives, the strategies that govern [discourse], and the program of political action [discourse] proposes'.[42] Knowledge is dispersed to the exteriority or outside of an 'economy' of power relations which produce and sustain it and which knowledge tends to disavow. Thus, for instance, in *Discipline and Punish* Foucault seeks to demonstrate that nineteenth-century prison or factory reforms do not arise from a new humanist morality but from a concern with social order effected not through the visual theatre of violent punishment, but by a more efficient and effective protracted disciplining of the body.[43] Similarly, Foucault's late works on ethics are grounded upon the claim that the study of moral codes 'only shows the poverty and monotony of interdictions' to the exclusion of the ascetic practices by which humans transform themselves into moral subjects.[44] Consequently, Foucault contrasts his own study of dietary, sexual, physical and textual practices through which pleasures are exercised and restrained to a 'hermeneutics of desire' which seeks only formal criteria for ethical truth by which desire would then be regulated.

By the 1980s this theorisation of the exteriority or 'outside' of thought is formalised by Foucault through the concept of 'problematisation', defined as 'the conditions in which human beings problematise what they are, what they do, and the world in which they live'.[45] The concept of problematisation reflects the broader thematic defining Foucault's *oeuvre* as a whole in so far as it displaces historical analysis of established objects by examination of mechanisms by which phenomena emerge as objects of thought. In Foucault words, an analysis of the 'development of the given into a question' seeking 'to rediscover at the root of . . . diverse solutions the general form of problematisation that has made them possible – even in their opposition'.[46]

Foucault's notorious revisionism should not subtract from the fact that the concept of problematisation accurately functions as a placeholder for the act of situating thought central to his work. Thus, the archaeological works can be understood as formalising the 'network which defines the conditions of possibility of a controversy or problem'.[47] By contrast, the genealogical works of the 1970s look to the strategies, institutions and practices which respond to the 'problem' of increasing social power without impeding economic production.[48] Finally, the works on ethics problematise the practices by which individuals constitute themselves as ethical subjects.[49] All of these trajectories of Foucault's career reflect his refusal to presume some prior ground to be presented, since problematisations of objects of thought are themselves constitutive of being in so far as they are the different ways 'through which being offers itself to be, necessarily, thought'.[50] Being is not represented in nor precedes particular problems since, as Foucault argued throughout his career, anterior to any particular theoretical response to the world lie merely anonymous regularities among the media in which thought is situated.

If for Foucault the move of reducing thought's medium to some ground which it can appropriate can be disturbed by seeking to identify the conditions of particular questions in anonymous fields of discourses and practices, the Derridean rejoinder lies with the claim that any delimitation of a given problem involves a prior disavowal of the conditions which make it possible. In other words, we can presume that any Derridean interpretation of Foucault's concept of problematisation would claim that the latter amounts to what in 'Cogito and the History of Madness' he calls Foucault's 'structuralist totalitarianism', since it appears that Foucault seeks to delimit that which 'cannot be objectified'.[51] As we have already seen, Derrida's work proceeds by establishing an aporetic and un-objectifiable relation between terms, such that thought is situated upon a liminal position neither totally inside nor outside of a determinate structure but rather at the point of the production of differentiation itself. This aporetic logic has the effect of making the absolute delimitation of a concept from its other (the differentiation of reason from madness for instance), or a determinate inside from its outside, impossible. This in turn entails that for Derrida the condition of the constitution of any object, including any 'problematisation', would be the 'decision' to violently delimit what in principle cannot be so delimited.[52] In effect, Derrida posits a medium anterior to the delimitation of any questions, including Foucault's, and which he sees the latter as violently reducing. 'The question', Derrida says, in an important early text, 'is already enclosed' since it involves some delimitation of phenomena; accordingly, it is the aim of Derrida's own work to pose the 'question about the possibility of the question' in seeking to think the conditions of that delimitation.[53]

Derrida's attempt to affirm the conceptual impasse or aporia evident through his account of 'the question' as a finite objectification, delimitation or determination of an anterior medium has functioned as a defining theme of his work for his defenders and his detractors alike.[54] This is evident not only in the important early essay 'Violence and Metaphysics', referenced above, but throughout a number of later works. In *Of Spirit*, Derrida affirms our being 'thrown' into '[l]anguage always before any question' and in that text goes on to call for an affirmation of the finitude which 'overflows the question itself'.[55] In *Politics of Friendship* he refers to an affirmation 'more originary than the question and which, without saying yes to anything possible, can only affirm the possibility of the future by opening itself to determinability'.[56] But it is in 'To Do Justice to Freud', written almost ten years after

Foucault's death that, while having gone unremarked by commentators, Derrida posits an expansive engagement, encompassing their whole *oeuvres*, between his and Foucault's theoretical strategies of displacing the question in attending to its medium. In this later engagement with Foucault's work, much as he does in 'Cogito and the History of Madness', Derrida once again identifies an illegitimately empiricist and thus violent reduction by Foucault of his object. But here the move is related to Foucault's *oeuvre* as a whole, and to my central line of questioning, since Derrida addresses the concept of problematisation itself.[57] At stake is thus the fundamental mode by which both thinkers have sought to conceive a thought which seeks to affirm the medium in which it is situated.

In 'To Do Justice to Freud' Derrida ostensibly targets the objectification and mastery of another figure central to Foucault's works besides Descartes: Freud. Foucault's epistemically violent gesture, Derrida argues, is 'to situate Freud in a historical place that is stabilisable, identifiable, and open to a univocal understanding'.[58] Given that Freud sees the death drive as a hyperbolic force operating in the ego it by definition cannot be mastered nor confined to any epoch, discursive formation or given problematisation. Foucault's objectification of psychoanalysis within a discursive regime or an apparatus of power-knowledge is premised upon taking what in 'Cogito and the History of Madness' Derrida calls an 'evasive transcendence' to the hyperbolic excess of the death drive.[59] Freud thus acts as a 'supplement' in Foucault's text, he is only included in history in so far as his concepts are violently reduced and objectified, yet excluded in so far as his work is the disavowed condition of Foucault's own approach. Freud's status is thus aporetic in so far as he can only lie at the indeterminable 'border' of Foucault's history since Foucault's objectification of madness is founded upon psychoanalytic concepts he must first disavow.[60]

Much as in 'Cogito and the History of Madness', Derrida claims that Foucault has failed to ask 'the question of the question' in so far as he disavows the medium of his analysis conditional as it is upon the figure of Freud. Yet in 'To Do Justice to Freud' Derrida extends this argument to encompass Foucault's *oeuvre* as a whole. A 'problem' he argues, can only appear through the promise of the presence of knowledge of a given field, yet since the presence of an object is always already aporetically divided and deferred, any problem is only constituted in the violent and reductive disavowal of its own conditions:

> The self-identity of its age, or of any age, appears as divided, and thus, problematic, problematizable . . . as the age of madness or an age of psychoanalysis – as well as, in fact, all the historical or archeological categories that promise us the determinable stability of a configurable whole.[61]

Derrida repeats this claim in *Rogues*, claiming that Foucault's work is governed by a teleological 'infrastructure of technoscientific discovery'.[62] In other words, only by ascribing to himself a position transcendent to his medium can Foucault violently 'decide' the object of his analysis.

This critique of Foucault becomes clearer when informed by Derrida's etymological analysis of the word 'problem' in his book *Aporias*, wherein it is traced to its

Greek origins as a reference to 'projection' or 'protection'. The ancient meaning of the term, he suggests, echoes the constitution of a problem as the ordering or delimitation of a domain or field. That is, the constitution of problems in disciplinary, ontological or territorial terms, Derrida says, refers to the constitution of a border, identity or, in short, a closure.[63] By contrast, he situates his own work as an experience of interminable aporia wherein 'we are exposed absolutely without protection, without problem'. The claim here is for the anteriority of the aporetic structure of language: the setting up of a problem or limit, Derrida argues, is always already threatened; it is always already marked by the 'experience of nonpassage' of the aporia which denotes the impossibility of any total or non-negotiable border. The aporia is that milieu where 'it would no longer be possible to constitute a problem, a project, or a projection'.[64] Viewed in this light, Foucault's conception of problematisation fails to affirm its finitude since it disavows the violent closures which are conditional of its enterprise, or of any theoretical enterprise for that matter. In his most explicit claim to attend to a medium anterior to and conditional of Foucault's *oeuvre*, Derrida says that, in contrast to Foucault, he conducts 'the problematization of problematization'.[65]

Let me at this point reaffirm my thesis: given their shared axiomatic situating of thought, Derrida and Foucault efface the possibility of any resolution to their polemic. The very claim to situate thought within a more expansive medium over which the debate ultimately results precludes the possibility of any resolution of the polemic. As Derrida puts it in *Of Grammatology*, it is 'impossible to justify a point of departure absolutely', and thus, he goes on, deconstruction always proceeds from some particular locus, it always begins 'in a text where we already believe ourselves to be'.[66] For Derrida, to affirm the finitude of one's categories is to sustain what he calls a 'radically empiricist' point of departure, one which seeks neither to transcend and master its medium nor a purely empiricist position which maintains the telos of complete knowledge, but which rather proceeds through a 'minimal' consensus in the interpretation of given phenomena or texts.[67] But the decisions involved in any point of departure are by definition always open to critique. Accordingly, the criticisms of Derrida by David Wood and Peter Dews, albeit in different inflections, are perceptive in this regard. Both argue that inherent to the first step of Derridean deconstruction is a sustenance of metaphysics or logocentrism by which Derrida first constructs his medium as the singular unity of western metaphysics.[68] Such an argument mirrors Foucault's own attack in 'My Body, This Paper, This Fire' upon what he says is Derrida's privileging of the sovereignty of philosophy in his interpretation of Descartes. Derrida must first conceptualise the medium within which he can then situate his conception of finitude in Descartes' text. Yet Foucault too, as we will see below, makes an analogous 'strategic' affirmation about the truth status of his work.

Both thinkers affirm the finitude of all concepts and the consequent violence which all concepts do to their objects. Yet, the implications they draw from this notion of finitude are radically different and perhaps irreconcilable. Derrida persists with the 'quasi-transcendental' question of the impossibility of the concept in order to disturb all attempts to appropriate the medium of thought. Foucault, on the other hand, concludes that if a transcendent truth does not exist, if all interpretation is an 'infinite task' which violently 'upset[s], shatter[s] with the blow of a hammer', then thought must affirm itself as an event of power.[69] As Foucault puts it, 'knowledge is always a certain strategic relation in which man is placed . . . that's why it would be completely contradictory to imagine a knowledge that was not by nature partial, oblique, and perspectival . . . Knowledge simplifies, passes over differences, lumps things together, without any justification in regard to truth.'[70] The impossibility of transcendence signals for Foucault the affirmation of thought itself as performative of the economy of power and not in terms of the Derridean notion of the aporia inherent to any conception of truth, since such an aporia is tied a mode of veridiction linked to formal criteria independent of its expression.

Accordingly, Foucault says his work 'does need to be true in terms of academic, historically verifiable truth'.[71] It must accord with certain functions and demands of the particular institutions in which it functions. However, his work should be judged, he argues, not in terms of its capacity to prove demonstrable truths, but in terms of its 'effectiveness', in so far as its 'fictions become true' and thus 'arrive at an establishment of truth but also experience something that permits a change'.[72] Like Derrida, Foucault thus affirms the necessary reductions which any theoretical analysis will entail. Yet for Foucault, if all knowledge is 'error' and 'fiction', then questioning need not proceed by traversal of the aporetic nature of any formal justification or truth. Conversely, as Derrida argues in 'Cogito and the History of Madness' and 'To Do Justice to Freud', Foucault can only proceed by disavowal and, thus, attempted transcendence of the aporias conditional of his exercise.

Unless we are to posit some Archimedean point from which the debate could be adjudicated and thus renounce the finitude which underlies both their *oeuvres*, then the polemic cannot be resolved. This state of irresolution and incommensurability is a direct result of the claim to finitude which, in positing the self-sufficiency of its own medium, nonetheless knows exactly where its limits lie. The 'grander narratives' posited by Derrida and Foucault are not only exclusive but totalising in a way that they must disavow in order to continue to function. This thus leaves them caught in a game of one- upmanship where the polemic hinges upon competing claims to the anteriority of their 'grander narrative' over that of the other.

ALTERITY AND INCOMMENSURABILITY

In this final section I seek to substantiate my argument in briefly suggesting that any attempt to construct a dialogue between Derrida and Foucault only functions to confirm my thesis. Given the influence their competing conceptions of alterity or 'otherness' had on debates over ethics and politics in the 1990s and early 2000s, and because it is in terms of ethical questions that a dialogue has most often been sought between them, these discussions form a propinquitous terrain upon which to end.[73]

As is well known, Derrida's engagement with the concept of alterity takes place primarily through his career-spanning engagement with the works of Emmanuel Levinas.[74] Levinas's work centres upon the attempt to displace the Cogito as the ground of all social and ethical relation and, thus, to inscribe the totalising force of identity (what he calls the 'Same') with a notion of inappropriable infinity which undermines consciousness's mastery of its object.[75] In turn, Derrida's critique of Levinas, premised as it is upon the latter's empiricism, reflects the claims to finitude he makes against Foucault. Levinas seeks, Derrida argues, a nonviolent relation to the other by transcending existence itself, and thus his ethical teleology disavows its finitude.[76] Given that 'the Same' is the 'only possible point of departure' for any relation to the other, the violence of this relation is irreducible and its disavowal would amount to a further violence.[77]

This insistence upon the avowal of the violence inherent to any relation to alterity by a finite thought is crucial to Derrida's *oeuvre*. This is perhaps best illustrated in a well-known text where Derrida describes as paradigmatic of any decision Abraham's willingness to suspend the law that 'though shall not kill' in order to sacrifice his son Isaac in response to the absolutely other's (God's) ethical demand. The undecidable or aporetic decision between responding to the demand of the absolutely other and that of the particular other reflects the violence conditional of every ethical response to alterity and, in fact, of every decision.[78] Even feeding one's cat, Derrida says, represents the sacrifice of all other cats in the world whom one does not feed.[79] Situated and finite decisions are by definition unjustifiable.

The thematic of messianicity and futurity, often referred to by the hyphenated refrain of 'to-come' which peppers Derrida's later works, are also inscribed by this same ethical logic of finitude. Take for example one of Derrida's earliest accounts of the logic of the concept of event as 'invention' in *Psyche: Inventions of the Other*. The status of an invention or event qua event is said to only be recognised by its re-insertion into an economy of conventions. In other words, the concept of event implies an inaugural instance which only acquires its status in a system in which it can be recognised but through which its singularity is lost.[80] The 'other' cannot be incorporated into any *de facto* relation since it always exceeds any finite or determinate horizon or objectification and, accordingly, the other is always 'to-come', since the event of the other marks both the impossibility of the closure of the horizon of its arrival and the impossibility of anything coming to presence on that horizon. This is of course an aporetic logic which Derrida draws out most famously in terms of democratic politics in *Rogues* and elsewhere.

Drawing on this approach Judith Butler and Gayatri Chakravorty Spivak, among others,[81] have been critical of Foucault for the lack of an engagement with the question of alterity in his work, while others have sought to defend Foucault by avowing the 'openness' or 'generosity' to the other in his work.[82] Yet as several perceptive interpreters have pointed out, questions about whether 'the subaltern can speak' or one can 'receive recognition from the other' are precisely the sort of questions which Foucault seeks to displace since they reduce the medium in which they're posed to an 'oppositional' logic.[83] As I have suggested, Foucault's genealogy of ethics displaces analyses of morality as quasi-juridical systems of rules and prescriptions with what is conceived as an anterior multiplicity of historical problematisations to which ethical practices respond. Philosophical analysis of the aporia of moral demands and codes would merely, as Foucault says, 'show the poverty and monotony of interdictions'.[84]

This fundamental distinction between juridical morality and ethical *askesis* is defined by Foucault in terms of two broad modes of conceiving the subject's relation to truth – a dichotomy between a knowledge of the self and a care of the self defined as two modes of 'ethical differentiation'.[85] Foucault argues that in Ancient Greece and Rome a transformative care of the self or subjective *askesis* had been a precondition for philosophical access to truth, while the role of knowledge was primarily limited to assisting in the formation of ethical being.[86] It is only with the rise of Christianity under Platonic influence that a gradual prioritisation of knowledge over care takes hold. Man begins to seek to interpret the forces giving birth to his thoughts and to differentiate experiences as originating either with God or with Satan.[87] This process reaches its zenith in the Cartesian *Meditations* since there the subject with the right to truth is identified through a correct method to the exclusion of conversion. Once formalised, the conditions of truth exclude questions of power, deliverance or conversion and are reduced to the assertion of the adequation of concept and object.[88] This practice of mining the interiority of the subject in an examination of his consciousness through a technique of confession eventually develops into a care of the self by the other in Foucault's accounts of discipline and governmentality, as some of his more perceptive interpreters have noted.[89]

To claim, as Spivak and Butler do, that Foucault lacks a theoretical articulation of a constitutive responsibility or desire for recognition by an other, or to claim as William Connolly has that such a responsibility is indeed present in Foucault's work, is to submit his ethics to the horizon of precisely the sorts of questions for which he criticises Derrida in 'My Body, This Paper, This Fire'. It is, in other words, to make a claim for the anteriority of irreducible and unconditional demands in their finite inscription and thus to begin from the premise of a subjectivity independent to an alterity or exteriority which acts as interlocutor, adversary, confessor or expert. Yet such an argument relies upon the submission of Foucault's work to the 'oppositional' difference of Same and Other while in fact it sets off from a different conception of ethical differentiation in so far as exteriority is located in the anonymity of the discourses, rules, practices and institutions by which an ethical subjectivity is formed.[90] Accordingly, in the Foucauldian dichotomy, a care of the self and a free relation to one's own ethical aims is distinguished from a care by the other and a subjection to truth, as characterised by the Christian apparatus of confession or the modern apparatus of discipline.

Conversely, even a sympathetic reading of Derrida's ethics in Foucauldian terms as a form of ethical *askesis*, as suggested by both McGushin and Calcagno, wherein subjective transformation is propelled by the experience of aporia, must first posit the ethical problematisation of subjective truth as conditional of the quasi-juridical and unconditional demand of alterity.[91] Yet this once again involves the move of claiming the priority of one 'grander narrative' over another. That is, conditional for the reading of deconstruction as a Foucauldian ethics is the delimitation, and thus violent appropriation, of the ethical relation to a particular set of practices, and thus of a reduction of the other to the Same and a doubly violent disavowal of that reduction.

As a final point, provided we maintain the theoretically uncompromising position I have taken, I think there are three primary conclusions to be drawn from the claims made above. First, and most narrowly, that the Cogito debate be understood as a polemic over the means and terms by which the medium of differentiation is to be thought, and that this in turn results in a series of incommensurable claims to the priority of one account over the other. Second, and more broadly, that these terms extend to Derrida's and Foucault's *oeuvres* as a whole. The means by which they seek to affirm the finitude of their categories entails the self-sufficiency and, accordingly, the exclusivity of their competing 'grander narratives'. Given that the basic conceptual architecture of their work remains stable throughout their *oeuvres*, the terms of the debate are thus not merely reducible to the Cogito debate, but are implicitly or explicitly present throughout all of their work. Finally, and most broadly, any thought which seeks to affirm its finitude through the articulation of a nonetheless generalised and self-sufficient medium thereby undermines that finitude. In other words, a theory which affirms its finitude but which can nonetheless locate the precise limits of that finitude is caught in an endlessly circular self-referentiality. A self-referentiality, moreover, most evident in polemic.

NOTES

1. Michel Foucault, *Aesthetics, Method, and Epistemology: Essential Works of Foucault Volume Two*, trans. Robert Hurley et al., ed. James Faubion (Harmondsworth: Allen Lane, 1998), p. 359.
2. Jacques Derrida, *Aporias: Dying – Awaiting (One Another At) the 'Limits of Truth'*, trans. Thomas Dutoit (Stanford: Stanford University Press, 1993), p. 12.
3. Stephen White, *The Strengths of Weak Ontology in Political Theory* (Princeton: Princeton University Press, 2000); Gianno Vattimo, *The End of Modernity: Nihilism and Hermeneutics in Post-Modern Culture*, trans. John R. Snyder (Cambridge: Polity Press, 1988).
4. White, *The Strengths of Weak Ontology in Political Theory*, p. 12.
5. Quentin Meillassoux, *After Finitude: An Essay On The Necessity Of Contingency*, trans. Ray Brassier (London: Continuum, 2008), p. 51.
6. Quentin Meillassoux, 'Interview with Quentin Meillassoux', in Graham Harman, *Quentin Meillassoux: Philosophy in the Making* (Edinburgh: Edinburgh University Press, 2011), p. 166; Meillassoux, 'There is Contingent Being Independent of Us, and This Contingent Being Has No Reason to Be a Subject of Nature', in Rick Dolphijn and Iris van der Tuin (eds), *New Materialism: Interviews and Cartographies* (Ann Arbor: Humanities Press, 2012).
7. Friedrich Nietzsche, *The Will to Power*, trans. Walter Kaufmann and R. J. Hollingdale (New York: Vintage, 1968), p. 550.
8. Ibid., p. 95.
9. Walter Kaufmann, *Nietzsche: Philosopher, Psychologist, Antichrist* (Princeton: Princeton University Press, 1950), p. 176; Jürgen Habermas, *The Philosophical Discourse of Modernity*, trans. Frederick Lawrence (Cambridge: Polity Press, 1990), p. 74; Arthur C. Danto, *Nietzsche as Philosopher* (London: Collier-Macmillan, 1965), p. 62.
10. Charles E. Scott, *The Question of Ethics: Nietzsche, Foucault, Heidegger* (Bloomington: Indiana University Press, 1990), p. 15; Maudemarie Clark, *Nietzsche on Truth and Philosophy* (Cambridge: Cambridge University Press, 1990), p. 141; David Owen, *Nietzsche's Genealogy of Morality* (London: Acumen, 2007), pp. 33, 46; John P. Richardson, *Nietzsche's System* (Albany: SUNY Press, 1996), pp. 279–80.
11. An equally legitimate starting point for this analysis would of course be Martin Heidegger's analysis of Dasein, who, finding itself 'thrown' into its existence, is the being who poses the question of Being. While Heidegger may have an equally important place in the intellectual

formation of Derrida and Foucault, such an analysis would equally demand an engagement with Derrida and Foucault's parallel defence of Nietzsche against Heidegger's interpretation and, accordingly, their Nietzschean transpositions of Heidegger. Lack of space precludes this discussion here.

12. Jacques Derrida, *Writing and Difference*, trans. Alan Bass (London: Routledge, 2001), pp. 354, 369; Michel Foucault, *Power: Essential Works of Foucault, Volume Three*, trans. Robert Hurley et al. (London: Penguin, 2002), pp. 14, 248; Foucault, *The Order of Things* (London: Routledge, 2002), p. 420. On this similarity between Derrida's and Foucault's Nietzsche interpretation see Alan D. Schrift, 'Foucault and Derrida on Nietzsche and the End(s) of Man', in David Farrell Krell and David Wood (eds), *Exceedingly Nietzsche: Aspects of Contemporary Nietzsche Interpretation* (London: Routledge, 1988).
13. Jacques Derrida, *Of Grammatology*, trans. Gayatri Chakravorty Spivak (London: Johns Hopkins University Press, 1997), p. 158; Michel Foucault, *Ethics: Subjectivity and Truth: Essential Works of Foucault, Volume One*, trans. Robert Hurley et al. (Harmondsworth: Allen Lane, 1997), p. 167.
14. Derrida, *Of Grammatology*, p. 140.
15. Ibid., pp. 112, 128.
16. Michel Foucault, 'The Order of Discourse', trans. Ian McLeod, in Robert Young (ed.), *Untying the Text: A Post-Structuralist Reader* (Boston: Routledge, 1981); *Aesthetics, Method, and Epistemology*; *Psychiatric Power: Lectures at the Collége de France 1973–1974*, trans. Graham Burchell (New York: Palgrave, 2006); *The Government of Self and Others: Lectures at the Collège de France 1982–1983*, trans. Graham Burchell (New York: Palgrave Macmillan, 2010); *The Courage of Truth: The Government of Self and Others II. Lectures at the Collège de France 1983–1984*, trans. Graham Burchell (New York: Palgrave Macmillan, 2011); *Lectures on the Will to Know*, trans. Graham Burchell (London: Palgrave Macmillan, 2013).
17. Foucault, *Power*, p. 12.
18. We put aside here Derrida's critique of Foucault's attempt to recover an undifferentiated 'original presence' of madness which modernity is said to violently reduce, since Foucault explicitly acceded to this argument. Foucault, *The Order of Things*, pp. 358–65; *The Archaeology of Knowledge*, trans. A. M. Sheridan Smith (London: Routledge, 2002), p. 16.
19. Jacques Derrida, *Dissemination*, trans. Barbara Johnson (London: Continuum, 2004), p. 125.
20. Michel Foucault, *Histoire de la folie à l'âge classique* (Paris: Gallimard, 1972), p. 57.
21. Derrida, *Writing and Difference*, p. 395 n.28.
22. Ibid., p. 67.
23. Ibid., pp. 68, 70, 395 n.28.
24. Ibid., p. 395 n.28
25. Ibid., p. 69.
26. Foucault, *Aesthetics, Method, and Epistemology*, p. 415.
27. Ibid., p. 412.
28. Ibid., p. 416.
29. Ibid., p. 412.
30. Geoffrey Bennington, *Interrupting Derrida* (London: Routledge, 2000); Arthur Bradley, 'Thinking the Outside: Foucault, Derrida and Negative Theology', *Textual Practice*, 16:1 (2002), pp. 57–74; David Carroll, 'The Subject of Archeology; or the Sovereignty of the Episteme', *Modern Language Notes*, 93 (1978), pp. 695–722; Marion Hobson, *Jacques Derrida: Opening Lines* (London: Routledge, 1998).
31. Edward Said, 'The Problem of Textuality: Two Exemplary Positions', *Critical Inquiry* (Summer 1978), pp. 673–714; Michael Sprinker, 'Textual Politics: Derrida and Foucault', *Boundary 2*, 8 (1980), pp. 75–89.
32. Roy Boyne, *Foucault and Derrida: The Other Side of Reason* (London: Unwin-Hyman, 1990); Alan Schrift, 'Foucault and Derrida on Nietzsche and the End(s) of Man', in Farrell and

Wood (eds), *Exceedingly Nietzsche*; Jean-Luc Nancy, 'Mad Derrida: Ipso Facto Cogitans Ac Demens', in Costas Douzinas (ed.), *Adieu Derrida* (London: Palgrave Macmillan, 2007).

33. Giorgio Agamben, 'Absolute Immanence', in *Potentialities*, trans. Daniel Heller-Roazen (Stanford: Stanford University Press, 1999).
34. The term 'formal structure of transcendence' is used by Daniel Smith, 'Deleuze and Derrida, Immanence and Transcendence: Two Directions in Recent French Thought', in Paul Patton and John Protevi (eds), *Between Deleuze and Derrida* (London: Continuum, 2003), pp. 46–66.
35. Leonard Lawlor has insisted that both Derrida and Foucault are thinkers of immanence in so far as both seek to think the priority of difference prior to some ground. See his *Thinking Through French Philosophy: The Being of the Question* (Bloomington: Indiana University Press, 2003) and *The Implications of Immanence: Towards a New Concept of Life* (New York: Fordham University Press, 2006).
36. Foucault, *The Archaeology of Knowledge*, p. 118.
37. On this point, see Lawlor, *Thinking Through French Philosophy* and *The Implications of Immanence*.
38. Gilles Deleuze, *Foucault*, trans. Seán Hand (London: Continuum, 2006); Pierre Macherey, *In A Materialist Way*, trans. Ted Stolze (London: Verso, 1998).
39. Michel Foucault, *Security, Territory, Population: Lectures at the Collège de France, 1977–1978*, trans. Graham Burchell (London: Palgrave Macmillan, 2007), pp. 116–20.
40. Foucault, *The Order of Things*, p. xxi.
41. Foucault, *The Archaeology of Knowledge*, p. 205; 'The Order of Discourse'; *Lectures on the Will to Know*.
42. Foucault, *Security, Territory, Population*, pp. 36, 118; *Power*, pp. 11–14.
43. Michel Foucault, *Discipline and Punish: The Birth of the Prison*, trans. Alan Sheridan (London: Allen Lane, 1977).
44. Michel Foucault, *The History of Sexuality, Vol. II: The Use of Pleasure*, trans. Robert Hurley (New York: Vintage, 1990), p. 250.
45. Ibid., p. 4.
46. Foucault, *Ethics*, p. 118; *Foucault Live: Collected Interviews, 1961–1984*, trans. Lysa Hochroth and John Johnston (New York: Semiotext(e), 1996), pp. 296, 421.
47. Foucault, *The Order of Things*, p. xxi.
48. Foucault, *Discipline and Punish*, pp. 208, 219–220.
49. Michel Foucault, *Politics, Philosophy, Culture: Interviews and Other Writings 1977–1984*, trans. Alan Sheridan et al., ed. Lawrence D. Kritzman (New York: Routledge, 1988), pp. 242–54.
50. Foucault, *The History of Sexuality Volume II*, p. 111; *Foucault Live*, p. 421.
51. Derrida, *Writing and Difference*, pp. 69, 70.
52. Ibid., p. 98.
53. Ibid., p. 90.
54. Simon Critchley, *The Ethics of Deconstruction: Derrida and Levinas* (Edinburgh: Edinburgh University Press, 1999); Bennington, *Interrupting Derrida*; David Farrell Krell, 'Spiriting Heidegger', in David Wood (ed.), *Of Derrida, Heidegger and Spirit* (Evanston, IL: Northwestern University Press, 1993), pp. 11–40.
55. Jacques Derrida, *Of Spirit: Heidegger and the Question*, trans. Geoffrey Bennington and Rachel Bowlby (Chicago: University of Chicago Press, 1989), p. 94.
56. Jacques Derrida, *Politics of Friendship*, trans. George Collins (London: Verso, 2005), p. 38.
57. Jacques Derrida, '"To Do Justice to Freud": The History of Madness in the Age of Psychoanalysis', *Critical Inquiry*, 20 (1994), p. 264.
58. Ibid., pp. 233–4.
59. Ibid., pp. 232–9.
60. Ibid., pp. 235, 242.
61. Ibid., p. 259.

62. Jacques Derrida, *Rogues: Two Essays on Reason*, trans. Pascale-Anne Brault and Michael Naas (Stanford: Stanford University Press, 2005), p. 128.
63. Derrida, *Aporias*, p. 40.
64. Ibid., p. 12.
65. Derrida, 'To Do Justice to Freud', p. 264.
66. Derrida, *Of Grammatology*, pp. 162–3.
67. Ibid., p. 162.
68. Peter Dews, *Logics of Disintegration: Post-Structuralist Thought and the Claims of Political Theory* (London: Verso, 1987); David Wood, *The Deconstruction of Time* (Atlantic Highlands: Humanities Press, 1989).
69. Foucault, *Aesthetics, Method, and Epistemology*, pp. 274–5.
70. Foucault, *Power*, p. 14.
71. Ibid., p. 243.
72. Michel Foucault, *Power/Knowledge: Selected Interviews and Other Writings* (London: Harvester, 1980), p. 93; *Aesthetics, Method, and Epistemology*, p. 244.
73. For a development of the Derrida-Foucault polemic upon a political terrain see Paul Rekret, 'Post-Metaphysical Political Thought: On Derrida and Foucault', *Telos*, 161 (2012), pp. 79–98.
74. Jacques Derrida, *Adieu: To Emmanuel Levinas*, trans. Pascale Anne-Brault and Michael Naas (Stanford: Stanford University Press, 1999); *Acts of Religion* (London: Routledge, 2002; *Psyche: Inventions of the Other*, trans. Catherine Porter (Stanford: Stanford University Press, 2007).
75. Emmanuel Levinas, *Totality and Infinity: An Essay on Exteriority*, trans. Alphonso Lingis (Dordrecht: Kluwer, 1991).
76. Derrida, *Writing and Difference*, pp. 142, 185.
77. Ibid., pp. 146, 158, 162, 191.
78. Jacques Derrida, *The Gift of Death*, trans. David Wills (Chicago: University of Chicago Press, 1995), p. 68.
79. Ibid., p. 66.
80. Derrida, *Psyche: Inventions of the Other*, p. 16.
81. Judith Butler, *Giving An Account of Oneself* (New York: Fordham University Press, 2005); Gayatri Chakravorty Spivak, 'Can the Subaltern Speak?', in Cary Nelson and Lawrence Grossberg (eds), *Marxism and the Interpretation of Culture* (Urbana: University of Illinois, 1988), pp. 271–313; Barry Smart, 'Foucault, Levinas, and the Subject of Responsibility', in Jeremy Moss (ed.), *The Later Foucault* (London: Sage, 1998), pp. 78–92; Johanna Oksala, *Foucault on Freedom* (Cambridge: Cambridge University Press, 2005).
82. William Connolly, 'Beyond Good and Evil: The Ethical Sensibility of Michel Foucault', *Political Theory*, 21:3 (1993), pp. 365–89.
83. Warren Montag, 'Can the Subaltern Speak and Other Transcendental Questions', *Cultural Logic*, 1:2 (1998); Nathan Widder, 'Foucault and Power Revisited', *European Journal of Political Theory*, 13:4 (2004), pp. 411–32; Widder, *Reflections on Time and Politics* (University Park: Pennsylvania State University Press, 2008).
84. Foucault, *The History of Sexuality Volume II*, p. 250.
85. Michel Foucault, *The Hermeneutics of the Subject: Lectures at the Collège de France 1981–1982*, trans. Graham Burchell (London: Picador, 2005), *The History of Sexuality Volume II*; *The Government of Self and Others*; *The Courage of Truth*.
86. Foucault, *The Hermeneutics of the Subject*.
87. Michel Foucault, *Fearless Speech* (New York: Semiotext(e), 2001), p. 109.
88. Foucault, *The Hermeneutics of the Subject*, p. 190.
89. Beatrice Han, 'The Analytic of Finitude and the History of Subjectivity', trans. Edward Pile, in Gary Gutting (ed.), *The Cambridge Companion to Foucault* (Cambridge: Cambridge

University Press, 2005), pp. 176–209; Edward McGushin, 'Foucault and the Problem of the Subject', *Philosophy and Social Criticism*, 31:5–6 (2005), pp. 623–48; Sergei Prozorov, *Foucault, Freedom and Sovereignty* (Aldershot: Ashgate, 2007); Sebastien Harrer, 'The Theme of Subjectivity in Foucault's Lecture Series L'Hermeneutique Du Sujet', *Foucault Studies*, 2 (2005), pp. 75–96.

90. Macherey, *In A Materialist Way*; Deleuze, *Foucault*.
91. McGushin, 'Foucault and the Problem of the Subject'; Antonio Calcagno, 'Foucault and Derrida: The Question of Empowering and Disempowering the Author', *Human Studies* 32:1 (2009).

CHAPTER 12

The Folded Unthought and the Irreducibly Unthinkable: Singularity, Multiplicity and Materiality, In and Between Foucault and Derrida

Arkady Plotnitsky

INTRODUCTION: IN-BETWEENS

The space between Foucault and Derrida or, as I prefer to see it, the 'in-between' of Foucault and Derrida, is inconceivable apart from Derrida's two overt engagements with Foucault's first book, *Folie et déraison: Histoire de la folie à l'âge classique*, published in French in 1961.[1] The first of these engagements, the 1963 'Cogito and the History of Madness', marked the beginning of, and helped to launch, Derrida's career;[2] and the second, '"To Do Justice to Freud": The History of Madness in the Age of Psychoanalysis', in 1991, marking the thirtieth anniversary of the book's publication, occurred at the apex of his career.[3] The in-between of Foucault and Derrida is defined no less by a thirty-year-long silence between these two engagements, with Freud added to the second, Freud between Foucault and Derrida, just as Descartes was added to the first. The silence was mostly on Derrida's part. Foucault died seven years before Derrida's 1991 lecture, in part compelling his long silence, according to Derrida.[4] This is not to say that Foucault's voice was not heard during the intervening years, even apart from overt engagements, comments, references and so forth. Thus, Foucault's reply to Derrida was added to the second edition of *History of Madness* in 1972. Indeed, has either Foucault or Derrida ever been, could either of them have ever been, silent about each other's work, beginning with *History of Madness*, in this 'infinite conversation' (*entretien infini*), as Blanchot would have it? Blanchot's book, under this title, is also not without its relations to the in-between of Foucault and Derrida, and to *History of Madness*, 'an almost unreasonable book'.[5] The unreasonable here means literally 'un-reasonable', beyond reason, or beyond reason and madness. The difficulty one faces is that *History of Madness* and the infinite conversation between Foucault and Derrida about it could neither be engaged sufficiently to do them justice within the limits such as those of this chapter, nor, conversely, could it ever be avoided in dealing with the in-between of Foucault and Derrida. This chapter, accordingly, will spend most of its time in other regions of this immense, abyssal in-between, and will return to *History of Madness* by way of an epilogue.

According to Gilles Deleuze, Foucault's 1966 *The Order of Things: An Archaeology of the Human Sciences* 'represents the most decisive step yet taken in the theory-practice of multiplicities'.[6] This formulation, qua *formulation*, would also apply to Derrida's *Dissemination* (1972) and to Derrida's work in general. Foucault's and Derrida's *concepts* of multiplicity are, however, not the same: their conceptual architectures are partially matching, but are ultimately different. They are, in the language of mathematics, homomorphic (they have a structure-preserving mapping between them) but not isomorphic (their overall structures are different). Deleuze refers to a particular type of 'multiplicity' (*multiplicité*), introduced by Bernhard Riemann (*Mannigfaltigkeit*) in mathematics. It might be more accurate to translate the term into English as 'manifoldness' or (the technical English term) 'manifold'. This translation would also preserve the French *pli*, fold, a key concept for Deleuze,[7] including in his reading of Foucault. The concept of the fold is also explored by Derrida in his reading of Mallarmé in *Dissemination*, and is germane to Derrida's concept of dissemination.[8] I shall, however, while speaking of manifolds when discussing Riemann, retain multiplicity as my main term, because it is a broader term which also applies to both discrete and continuous multiplicities (Riemann spoke of both as 'manifolds'). The type of multiplicity that Deleuze has in mind here is not only *topological* (spatial) but is also *topologically continuous*. As such, it is defined by spaces and trajectories, by the 'continuity of line', as Deleuze says. The concept of the 'singular' in Foucault (as in Deleuze) is, too, defined in terms of singular, unique trajectories, haecceities, rather than in terms of point-like events, discontinuities, interruptions and so forth, as it is in Derrida.

At stake in Derrida are, most essentially, multiplicities of discontinuous events that cannot be connected by continuous trajectories. This is also more customary than seeing singularities as lines or trajectories. Derrida, however, gives this concept a radical sense, in part by developing the ideas of such figures as Nietzsche, Heidegger, Bataille, Blanchot, Levinas and Lacan, the sense in particular defined the fact that continuous connections between singular events are precluded in principle. This brings Derrida's concept of the singular closer to quantum theory than to Riemann's topology and geometry of manifoldness or Einstein's relativity, grounded in Riemann's mathematics, theories that exhibit strong affinities with Foucault's thinking, or that of Deleuze. Derrida and the other thinkers just mentioned do, however, engage with these Riemannian and Einsteinian conceptualities as well, and make them part of the architecture of their concepts. It is a matter of a different balance and different relationships between these two types of conceptual architecture, of their in-between (a complex question in physics itself, which thus far has been unable to bring relativity and quantum theory together), rather than giving a unique significance to one or the other. The role of Einstein's relativity, especially the so-called general relativity, Einstein's non-Newtonian theory of gravity, is also crucial in view of the role of materiality, essential to Foucault, or Deleuze. Materiality is crucial to

Derrida as well, but is, again, conceived by him more on quantum-mechanical than relativistic lines.

The argument of this chapter proceeds via these connections to mathematics and physics. The nature of these connections merits a brief reflection here, via Niels Bohr. In commenting specifically on quantum theory, Bohr said:

> we are not dealing here with more or less vague analogies, but with an investigation of the conditions for the proper use of our conceptual means shared by different fields. Such considerations not only aim at making us familiar with the novel situation in physical science, but might . . . be helpful in clarifying the conditions logical relations which, in different contexts, are met with in wider fields.[9]

In other words, we deal with parallel – homomorphic, if not necessarily isomorphic – conceptual architectures, arising from such investigations, rigorously pursued.

As noted above in the case of their concepts of multiplicity, the conceptual architectures defining, respectively, Foucault's and Derrida's investigations are also homomorphic but not isomorphic. This is not only due to the different nature and balance of continuous and discontinuous multiplicities in each, a balance shifted towards continuous multiplicities in Foucault and discontinuous ones in Derrida. More significant are the differences in the nature of the *efficacities* (multiple in Foucault and Derrida alike) that are responsible for both types of *effects* in each theory; although, as will be seen, the nature and balance of both types of effects may depend on the nature of their efficacities. In Derrida, or in quantum physics, these efficacities, while giving rise to both types of effects, cannot be seen as either continuous or discontinuous, or indeed allow for any conception of them, including that of efficacity (which is a provisional and ultimately inapplicable term). They are literally unthinkable, ultimately unthinkable even as unthinkable. This view, thus, reaches beyond Kant's concept of *noumena* or things-in-themselves, because, while the latter are unknowable, they are in principle thinkable.[10] It also follows that these efficacities cannot be causal (because that would give them at least a partial conception). This combination of the unthinkable and non-causal makes these efficacities quantum-mechanical-like in character, and, as in quantum mechanics, makes the role of chance and recourse to probability unavoidable in dealing with the effects considered.

One does find a similar, homomorphic, conception in Foucault's later works. This conception is defined by Deleuze in terms of an interfold of 'an Outside, more distant than any exterior', and 'an Inside that is deeper than any interior', an interfold that reaches beyond this Outside and this Inside as well, to the unthought in thought.[11] I shall call this concept 'the folded unthought', in contrast with 'the irreducibly unthinkable' found in Derrida and quantum theory. (Materiality would be understood accordingly in each case.) The unthought in Foucault, as the term implies, may be and appears likely to be (a definitive claim would be difficult) in principle thinkable, and thus is closer to Kant. The unthinkable in Derrida and quantum theory cannot be thought in principle, not even as unthinkable (one can make a definitive claim here).

The *degree* of difference and homomorphic proximity (there are both) between Foucault's architecture of the multiple and the unthought and Derrida's architecture of the multiple and the unthinkable may well be the main philosophical question of the in-between of Foucault and Derrida. 'What is at stake here is enormous', no less than 'a general reinterpretation of everything', a radical reinterpretation of everything, from physics to justice (the ultimate concern of Foucault and Derrida alike), which may be closer, or allow for a deeper and more rigorous in-between, than one might think. Those two quotations come from Derrida.[12] The first refers to the in-between of Hegel and Derrida, and the second to the in-between of Plato and Mallarmé, or Hegel and Mallarmé, or Derrida and Mallarmé, which absorbs its poles and merges Derrida's philosophy and Mallarmé's literature. The in-between of Foucault and Derrida is the in-between of all the in-betweens here mentioned, beginning with that of quantum physics and relativity, and a few that were not mentioned and will not be addressed here, in particular that of Nietzsche and Heidegger, crucial to Derrida's encounter with *History of Madness*. The in-between of reason and madness was the first of these in-betweens, brought about by Foucault's 'almost unreasonable book', and it has never left the in-between of Foucault and Derrida, itself almost unreasonable, not least because it reaches the highest spheres of thought, which are always between reasons and madness. But then, what is not between them?

MATTER AND MULTIPLICITY IN FOUCAULT

It may be worthwhile to follow Deleuze's argument concerning the multiple in Foucault a bit further. Deleuze comments on Foucault's concept of the 'statement' as manifesting a shift (not a break), in *The Order of Things*,[13] from his preceding works, but at stake is the multiple in general. Deleuze says: 'this is our definition of a group of statements, or even a single statement: they are multiplicities. It was Riemann in the field of physics and mathematics who dreamed up the notion of "multiplicity" and different kinds of multiplicities.'[14] Riemann 'uprooted the multiple from its predicative state and made it into a noun, "multiplicity",' which signalled 'the end of dialectic and the beginning of topology and typology of multiplicities'.[15] Deleuze links Riemann and Foucault:

> The core of the notion is the constitution of a substantive in which 'multiple' ceases to be a predicative opposed to the One, or attributable to a subject identified as one. Multiplicity remains completely indifferent to the traditional problems of the multiple and the one, and above all to the problem of a subject who would think through this multiplicity, give it conditions, account for its origins, and so on. There is neither one nor multiple, which would at all events entail having recourse to a consciousness that would be regulated by the one and developed by the other. There are only rare multiplicities composed of particular elements, empty places for those who temporarily function as subjects, and cumulable, repeatable and self-preserving regularities. Multiplicity is neither axiomatic not typological, but topological. Foucault's

> [*The Order of Things*] represents the most decisive step yet taken in the theory-practice of multiplicities.[16]

This concept of multiplicity is as crucial as that of the statement, even more so, because the latter concept is only an instantiation of the former, albeit an important one. This concept also traces a trajectory across Foucault's thought, beginning with *History of Madness*. One needs, however, to establish the architecture of this concept as a philosophical concept; and, as with every philosophical concept, this architecture is, according to Deleuze and Guattari, multiple.[17] This is also true of mathematical or physical concepts, such as that of Riemann's manifoldness or Einstein's spacetime in relativity, from which the concept of multiplicity is derived by Deleuze, and perhaps by Foucault, although Riemann or Einstein are not their only sources. The history of the concept of the multiple in Foucault and Deleuze, and in Derrida, is itself multiple, Foucauldian.

The concept of a manifold was introduced by Riemann in his famous Habilitation lecture 'On the Hypotheses That Lie at the Foundations of Geometry' (*Ueber die Hypothesen, welche der Geometrie zu Grunde liegen*), presented in 1854, but first published in 1868, after Riemann's death in 1866.[18] The lecture was a revolution in our understanding of the nature of spatiality and geometry. A manifold may be either discrete or continuous, although in effect these are two different concepts in Riemann. In modern usage the term 'manifold' is usually reserved for continuous manifolds, which can be either a flat (Euclidean) or curved, positively or negatively. A continuous manifold was defined by Riemann on the model of two-dimensional surfaces, which, as was discovered by his teacher, Karl Friedrich Gauss, could be understood in terms of their intrinsic, immanent, geometry, rather than in relation to the ambient Euclidean space. This immanence is crucial to Riemann, who allows for higher dimensions, and then to Einstein, because it liberates geometry from Euclid and physics from Newton. The same type of immanence defines Foucault's multiplicity, which is also that of his 'physics', the microphysics of power, liberated from 'the traditional problems of the multiple and the one, and above all to the problem of a subject who would think through this multiplicity, give it conditions, account for its origins, and so on', as Deleuze says.[19] Each continuous manifold is a conglomerate of local, continuously connected spaces, and specifically of small neighbourhoods around each point. This concept of a manifold and, hence, of space, as 'glued' or 'quilted' out of these neighbourhoods, is Riemann's great invention, extendable to a still more general concept of topological space, in which such neighbourhoods need no longer be Euclidean. Indeed, every Riemannian manifold is underlayed by a topological space. In the case of properly Riemannian manifolds, each neighbourhood is infinitesimally flat, Euclidean or Cartesian, and can be treated accordingly, while the manifold as a whole is, in general, not, except in the case of a Euclidean homogeneous (flat) space itself. Consider a sphere as an example. Imagine small circles on the surface around each point and project each such circle onto the tangent plane to this point to a regular flat circle on this plane. If the first circle is very small, the difference between two circles becomes very small as well and can be neglected, allowing one to treat the first circle as Euclidean. A manifold can not only be negatively or positively curved, but (one of Riemann's major innovations) this curvature can also be variable, giving a manifold a greater heterogeneity. Riemann, again, extended this concept to any dimensions, even to infinite-dimensional manifolds. A discrete manifold has a (topological) dimension zero. It may, however, be conceived of as multiply extended spatially if it forms a lattice with intervals between points, which could be 'filled' to form a continuous space of the corresponding topological dimensions. Riemann allows for a possibility that the physical 'reality underlying space' might be 'a discrete manifold' at the microscopic scale.[20] Deleuze and Guattari see Riemannian manifolds or spaces as reflecting 'the most important features' of the 'smooth and nonmetric' manifoldness, as opposed to 'the metric manifoldness', and thus defining 'the *nomos* of smooth space'.[21] They describe Riemann spaces as follows:

> Riemann spaces are devoid of any kind of homogeneity. Each is characterised by the form of the expression that defines the square of the distance between two infinitely proximate points. . . . The result [as Elie Cartan said] is 'that two neighboring observers in a Riemann space can locate the points in their immediate neighborhood [*voisinage*], but they cannot locate their spaces in relation to each other without a new convention.' Each neighborhood is therefore like a small shred of Euclidean space, *but the linkage between one neighborhood and the next is not defined and can be effected in an infinite number of ways. The most general Riemann space thus presents itself as an amorphous collection of juxtaposed pieces that are not attached to one another.*' It is possible to define this multiplicity without any reference to a metrical system, in terms of the conditions of frequency, or rather *accumulation*, of a set of neighborhoods; these conditions are entirely different from those determining metric spaces and their breaks (even though a relation between the two kinds of space necessarily results). In short, if we follow Lautman's fine description, Riemannian space is pure patchwork. It has connections, or tactile relations. It has rhythmic values not found elsewhere, even though they can be translated into a metric space.[22]

While in accord with the technical mathematical terminology, the cartographical language and conceptuality is crucial to Deleuze and Guattari's, and of course to Foucault's, 'new cartographer'.[23] There is a cartographic genealogy to Riemann's concept. Gauss arrived at his key geometrical ideas, preparing those of Riemann, in part through his work in land surveying. Riemann was able to introduce for three or still higher dimensions what was only available previously for two-dimensional surfaces – a multidimensional cartography.

The architecture of Riemannian manifolds is, thus, defined by the multiplicity and connectivity of local spaces and, therefore, local mappings, and thus also movements, connecting these spaces and maps, as against being defined as a set of points. The concept, mathematical and philosophical (it is both), of Riemann space is defined as a conglomerate of *spaces* through the (contiguous) connectivity of such spaces. It is *composed* of spaces, rather than of points, akin to the way this happens in certain art works, for example, in Claude Monet's *Nympheas* murals in the Musée de l'Orangerie in Paris.[24] Multiplicities are composed, in the manner of paintings, but composed more of spaces than of points.

The difference between geometry and topology becomes important here, because it allows one to see multiplicities in terms of a composition that precedes geometry. While both geometry and topology are concerned with the mathematics of space, each is distinguished by its different provenance. Geometry (geo-*metry*) has to do with measurement, while topology disregards measurement or scale and only deals with the structure of space qua space and with the *essential* shapes of figures. Topological figures are continuous spaces. In so far as one deforms a given figure continuously (i.e., in so far as one does not separate points previously connected and, conversely, does not connect points previously separated) the resulting figure is considered the same, a topological equivalent. Thus all spheres, of whatever size and however deformed, are topologically equivalent, despite the fact that some of the resulting objects are no longer spheres geometrically speaking. They are, however, topologically distinct from tori, because spheres and tori cannot be converted into each other without disjoining their connected points or joining the disconnected ones: the holes in tori make this impossible. Topology, it is sometimes said, measures not distances, as geometry does, but the number of holes in a given space.

Technically, Riemann spaces are defined in mathematics as geometrical, but, as Deleuze and Guattari (rightly) suggest here, these spaces are better seen as *allowing* for a geometry, while being topological, 'smooth', spaces first: 'It has connections, or tactile relations. It has rhythmic values not found elsewhere, even though they can be translated into a metric space.' In mathematics, smooth is synonymous with differentiable, but in Deleuze and Guattari, the term refers to *continuous* topological multiplicities, allowing for uninhibited trajectories of movement, haecceities or lines of flight. A topological space is also a multiplicity of the (rhizomatically) interconnected haecceities. Each haecceity is a multiplicity, too, in so far as it changes from point to point, a change that, in a metric Riemann space, may become a change of curvature.

Riemann, thus, defines a space topologically and then, if necessary, geometrically, not as a constitution of points but as a space composed of other spaces, and thus, again, composed by continuities. (Discrete manifolds are, again, given a different concept by Riemann, and are composed of points.) Topology describes a space not so much by its points but by its so-called *open* subspaces, the concept that underlies Riemann's concept of a manifold but that allows for a more general mathematical definition of topological spaces, which need not be locally Euclidean. Consider, again, a sphere, and a small circle on it around each point; removing the boundary of each circle makes it an open neighbourhood (a closed neighbourhood would include a boundary). All such circles together cover and indeed, topologically, constitute the sphere, or any given surface, although there will be mathematical conditions that allow us to distinguish different surfaces (such as different spheres) or different types of surfaces (such as spheres vs. tori). This procedure can then be used to define the topology of curves or higher-dimensional spaces, flat or curved. It enabled Riemann to define manifolds of any dimensions, even infinite-dimensional ones, as collections of subspaces, and to do so in terms of their inner properties rather than in relation to an ambient Euclidean or Cartesian space, where such a manifold might be embedded. This is also a key feature of any Foucauldian multiplicity: it is defined immanently or in relation to other immanent multiplicities, rather than assumed to inherit its architecture from a preordained domain, analogous to Newton's absolute space in physics.

This approach allows for a more general definition of space as comprised by, composed of, other spaces. One would need some primitive space, but it need not be Euclidean, or a single, absolute space of any kind, in so far as such a space could be different once the situation changes and, moreover, may itself emerge from the relational architecture of spatiality, rather than be a starting point for the building of this architecture. A topological or geometrical space is, then, defined as a collection of open spaces, as subspaces or even exterior spaces (without assuming a single all-encompassing space, absolute space), by providing certain rules for the relationships between these spaces. Modern topology allows for such esoteric constructions as spaces consisting of a single point and yet having a relational architecture that defines them, rather than structure-less entities (classical points), or conversely, spaces without points, sometimes slyly referred to by mathematicians as 'pointless topology'. These constructions are far from 'pointless', however, in so far as each suggests that 'space', or something space-like in character, is a more primary concept than that of 'point'. Spaces can be without points but they cannot be without spaces: they are multiplicities, ultimately multiplicities of multiplicities, just as Foucault's statements are. Deleuze and Guattari see Foucauldian multiplicities in the same way: as assemblages of spaces, neighbourhoods and trajectories, lines of flight traversing through them.

Lautman's description of Riemann spaces, cited by Deleuze and Guattari, is inflected by Einstein's relativity, via the idea of 'observers in a Riemann's space', whose curvature is defined by matter. In Einstein's account of general relativity, his non-Newtonian theory of gravity, the topology and geometry of a given physical space are defined by the materiality of the bodies and energy fields in it, or indeed that give rise to it. For, as Leibniz (a major inspiration for both Einstein and Deleuze) already argued, there is no preexisting background space, Newton's absolute space, in which material bodies are then placed. As Einstein did (more rigorously) later on, Riemann argued that physics defines the nature of space, especially in the infinitely small, that is, in a microphysics, just as Foucault's microphysics of power defines the topology and geometry of multiplicities materially shaped by power. While space, Riemann argued, may be assumed to be a three-dimensional manifold (we no longer take this for granted either), what kind of manifold it is will be defined by physics. For Riemann and then Einstein, whether the physical space is Euclidean or non-Euclidean, or whether it has a positive or negative curvature, or whether this curvature is permanent or variable, is defined by material bodies and forces. 'The reality underlying space' may be different from our phenomenal experience of space (which is continuous) or, depending on scale, our understanding of the physical character of space.[25] Physics may also find that this reality is different on different scales.

Einstein's theory of general relativity gave a rigorous physical content to these insights by bringing together the physics of gravitation and Riemannian geometry. The spaces or spacetimes of general relativity are continuous and are three-dimensional or, in the case of spacetimes, four-dimensional. Also, as noted above, not only may the curvature of a *manifold* and hence of physical space, or, again, the physical reality underlying space, not be zero, it also need not be constant, which was a ground-breaking concept of Riemann's. It is in general not constant in a gravitational field, and establishing this in rigorous terms was the equally ground-breaking contribution of Einstein. We now know that Euclidean geometry and even the non-Euclidean geometry of constant curvature do not necessarily correspond to the physical reality underlying space, except that, at the very large scale of the Universe itself, it appears to be on average flat, as current observations suggest. In sum, one needs physics to establish the facts that would enable us to form and test hypotheses concerning physical space, or the reality underlying space.[26] By, roughly, 1900, the facts of experience no longer corresponded to the concepts of Newton's physics, and required relativity and then quantum mechanics. Matter defines a given space and its architecture immanently as a Riemannian manifold, whose topology and geometry have a Baroque variability to them.

The Baroque, Deleuze argues, frees its spacetimes from the imposition of the 'Cartesian' or 'Renaissance' architecture (mathematical, physical or cultural).[27] This imposition was presumed to enable a *rational* coordination of points or events in space or time, or spacetime, in terms of a Cartesian absolute grid imposed on all multiplicities. Ultimately, one would have a single global coordination of all events. The Renaissance concept of perspective, grounded in Euclidean geometry and grounding the corresponding view of the world, Descartes' analytic geometry (which algebraically codifies geometrical lines and figures), and Newton's absolute space and time are among the primary models of this philosophy and the ideologies based on it. By contrast, while Baroque spaces or (in their mathematical and physical incarnations) Riemannian and then Einsteinian spaces allow for local coordinations and grids, they do not in general allow for global coordinations.

It is this immanence and variability of the multiple, defined by materiality, that is at stake in Deleuze's analysis of multiplicity in Foucault. While Riemannian as concerns its manifold-multiple conceptual architecture, the picture is grounded in a material microphysics, that of material entities acting upon each other and, as a result, developing in time, enabling some of the 'bodies' involved to move along particular trajectories, which in smooth spaces become and shape the 'lines of flight'. Deleuze once remarked: 'I consider myself Bergsonian, in the sense that Bergson says that modern science has not found its metaphysics, the metaphysics it needs. It is this metaphysics that interests me.'[28] This metaphysics is Leibnizian, that of matter that defines the multiple and the manifold, although, like Riemann and Foucault (or Leibniz and Bergson), Deleuze appears to be more concerned with continuous, Baroque multiplicities, 'the pleats of matter' and 'the folds of the soul'.[29] It is also this metaphysics that Deleuze derives from or gives to Foucault's multiplicities, ultimately linking them to the concept of the folded unthought, which I shall discuss after considering Derrida. I close here, by giving voice to Foucault, with an elaboration that returns us to his concept of the statement, based in the Baroque, Riemannian, Einsteinian principles of variability, multiplicity and materiality:

> We are concerned not with a criterion of individualization for the statement, but rather with the principle of variation: it is sometimes more diverse than the structure of the sentence (and its identity is then finer, more fragile, more easily modifiable than that of a semantic or grammatical whole), sometimes more constant than that structure (and its identity is then broader, more stable, more susceptible to variations). Moreover, not only can this identity of the statement not be situated once and for all in relations to that of the sentence, but it is itself relative and oscillates according to the use that is made of the statement and the way in which it is handled.[30]

Individualisation, or individuation, is still important, of course. It must, however, be understood in relation to and as the theory-practice of variability, multiplicity and materiality, and its criteria defined accordingly: as those defining a haecceity. Although it can have punctual states or effects, a statement is a singularity as a continuous haecceity (which underlies and connects such punctual states) that changes on its trajectory across the manifold from which it emerges. It is a line of flight across a Riemannian-Einsteinian manifold and field of forces. Indeed, as he extends this elaboration, Foucault's language becomes more Riemannian and Einsteinian:

> Too repeatable to be entirely identifiable with the spatio-temporal coordinates of its birth (it is more than the place and date of its appearance), too bound up with what surrounds it to be as free as a pure form, . . . [the statement] is endowed with a certain modifiable heaviness, a weight relative to the field in which it is placed, a constancy that allows of various uses, a temporal permanence that does not have the inertia of a mere trace or mark . . . This repeatable materiality that characterises the enunciative function reveals the statement as a specific and paradoxical object, but also as one of those objects that men produce, manipulate, use, transform, exchange, combine, decompose and recompose, and possibly destroy. Instead of being something said once and for all – and lost in the past like the result of a battle, a geological catastrophe, or the death of a king – the statement, as it emerges in its materiality, appears with a status, enters various networks and various fields of use, is subjected to transferences or modifications, is integrated into operations and strategies in which its identity is maintained or effaced.[31]

This is the language of Einsteinian relativistic materiality, and more than only the language. At stake, to return to Bohr's phrase, is 'an investigation of the conditions for the proper use of our conceptual means shared by different fields', which creates a correspondence, a homomorphism, between Foucault's theory of statements and Einstein's general relativity. There is no isomorphism, for one thing, because Foucault's theory is not, is too rich to be, mathematical. On the other hand, Riemann's and Einstein's theories are also philosophical.

THE MULTIPLE AND THE UNTHINKABLE IN DERRIDA

I begin with Derrida's reading of Kafka's parable 'Before the Law', eventually included in *The Trial*,[32] in Derrida's essay under the same title, 'Before the Law [*Devant de Loi*]'.[33] Apart from the fact that Derrida's essay offer an instructive exposition of his key ideas, Kafka is arguably the best literary 'in-between' of Derrida and Foucault, or Derrida and Deleuze, especially in relation to Foucault's *Discipline and Punish*, and Deleuze and Guattari's *Kafka: Toward a Minor Literature*.[34] Derrida's reading explores the difficulties of applying spatial or topological concepts to the domain (*topique*) or a-domain (*atopique*) of the law in Kafka, and as a consequence to law in general. At the same time, such concepts are unavoidable in our thinking, including our thinking beyond them, or beyond anything, in dealing with the unthinkable.

Any attempt to configure or even to conceive of the determinable, or decidable, space of law is, Kafka shows and Derrida argues, bound to fail. While we are always in front of (before, *devant*) its doors (as in Kafka's parable), we cannot think of law as a space we can enter, or conversely in which we can exist. We are never inside and never outside the law, and the doors of the law only appear to separate the two. This is not contradictory: the (unthinkable) efficacy of the law, the *différance* of the law, has topological effects, and we are within these effects, but we cannot conceive of, and in this sense are outside, this efficacity, which, by the same token, cannot be causal. The unthinkable affects us through its *effects*. The efficacity of these effects is 'a radical alterity' that is beyond thought. As Derrida argues, via Freud, who is central for his readings of Kafka and Foucault as well:

> A certain alterity – to which Freud gives the metaphysical name of the unconscious – is definitively exempt from every process of presentation by means of which we would call upon it to show itself in person. In this context, and beneath this guise, the unconscious [refigured in the regime of *différance*] is not, as we know, a hidden, virtual, or potential self-presence. It differs from, and defers, itself, which doubtless means that it is woven of differences, and also that it sends out delegates, representatives, proxies; but without any chance that the giver of proxies might 'exist', might be present, be 'itself' somewhere, and with even less chance that it might become conscious. In this sense, contrary to the terms of an old debate full of metaphysical investments that it has always assumed, the 'unconscious' is no more a 'thing' than it is any other thing, is no more a thing than it is a virtual or masked consciousness. This radical alterity as concerns every possible mode of presence is marked by the irreducibility of the aftereffect, the delay. In order to describe traces, in order to read the traces of 'unconscious' traces (there are no 'conscious' traces), the language of presence and absence, the metaphysical discourse of phenomenology, is inadequate. (Although the phenomenologist is not the only one to speak this language.)[35]

Importantly, while always unthinkable, this alterity is each time different, different with each given effect or set of effects. This also compels Derrida to multiply, in principle interminably, the names (neither words nor concepts as he sees them) which reflect various aspects of these efficacities and effects – 'dissemination', 'trace', 'supplement', 'writing' and so forth. What Derrida calls 'dissemination', a structural, irreducible part of *différance*, conjoins and makes irreducible both types of multiplicities – those of efficacities and those of effects.

That which produces the effects of law ('power', Foucault would say, within his scheme) cannot be ascribed a spatial, or temporal, character any more than any other character. By the same token, this conception, a conception of the inconceivable, is not merely the product of a philosophical imagination. The unthinkable is inferred, as rigorously necessary, in view of the particular nature of the effects in question. This dynamics is material, but it in turn compels us to rethink, against all metaphysical materialism (which becomes as precluded as metaphysical idealism), materiality, as a radical alterity.[36] The situation is also transferred by Derrida to the structure and law of reading. A reading, such as Derrida's, or Kafka's writing in the first place, is subject to the same law, the same law of law, as law itself.

Différance, then, is an atopological efficacity of topological multiplicities, and of the multiple temporalities associated with or dissociated from them. As I said, this efficacity is itself multiple, is an uncontainable field of efficacities, none of which can ever be reached because they always differ and defer from themselves (the movements conjoined in *différance*), without an absolute origin. Hence, allegorically, in Kafka, the doors and guardians of the law only lead to other doors and other guardians, interminably:

> This differantial topology [*topique différantielle*] adjourns, guardian after guardian, within the polarity of high and low, far and near (*fort/da*), now and later. The same topology without its own place, the same atopology [*atopique*], the same madness defers the law as the nothing that forbids itself and the neuter that annuls oppositions.[37]

I shall return to madness, which would be difficult to think apart from Foucault, in the epilogue, merely noting for the moment that in Foucault and Derrida alike, the topology of reason and madness have parallel and interactive topological structures and atopological efficacities. They are interactive because there is always a law of reason and madness, and a law that attempts to define and demarcate them, either in an unconditional classical opposition (as in the classical age) or in their various mixtures, as Foucault, Deleuze and Derrida urge us to do. At the same time, as explained above, this atopology has topological or temporal effects. Like Kafka's K. in *The Trial* we can never cross the threshold of the law and have already, always already, crossed it, and hence can always be apprehended by the forces of law (in either sense).

More generally, *différance* produces, as its effects, the spatiality of space, the temporality of time, the spatiality of time, the temporality of space, and so forth.[38] Derrida's analysis of Plato's concepts of *khora* in *Timaeus* finds the same dynamics operative there as well, even if against Plato's own grain.[39] These efficacious *différantial* dynamics are homomorphic to those relativity, although the Derridean conceptual architecture is ultimately quantum-mechanical-like, rather than relativistic. As discussed earlier, in contrast to classical Newtonian physics, the spacetime of special and even more so of general relativity disallows a universal background with its (separate) absolute space and time, and thus also a uniquely privileged frame of reference in relation to which all physical events could be positioned. By contrast, in relativity, whatever happens, happens only in a local reference frame, is always relative to this frame (hence the name 'relativity'). The physics of bodies and forces becomes irreducibly local, which is why relativity needs Riemann's topology and geometry of manifolds as its mathematical expression. This makes the structure of relativistic spacetimes or events irreducibly decentred. The idea can be traced back to Galileo, as far as the relativity of space is concerned. Einstein's crucial contribution already in 1905 (before he considered gravity) was to add the relativity of temporality, correlative to the constancy of the speed of light in the vacuum, *c*, regardless of the motion of the source. This theory, which does not include gravity, is known as special relativity theory, as opposed to general relativity, which extends the same thinking to gravity. Indeed, space and time can no longer be unconditionally distinguished either, and can transform into each other, a situation eventually codified by the concept of spacetime, introduced by Herman Minkowski in 1908, and extended by Einstein to general relativity, which defines its spacetimes as Riemannian manifolds shaped by gravity.

In philosophical terms, then, the conceptual framework of relativity, especially general relativity, could be seen in terms of Derrida's sense of decentred play as not being controlled by a centre, interior or exterior, of a structure.[40] Derrida sometimes speaks, via Nietzsche, of 'the play *of* the world', as opposed to play *in* the world.[41] This shift, also found in Foucault's immanent concept of multiplicity, is crucial. The world is no longer given as a spacetime background in which the play of events takes place. Instead it is defined by the workings of the play of such effects as space and time, or spacetime, or even whatever appears to us as a world, while their ultimate efficacity remains inaccessible. At stake is the irreducible variability of the world, as opposed to the concept of the world as a background of events given once and for all, such as Newton's absolute space (with absolute time) in classical physics. Relativity is the play *of* the world, a play of material bodies and fields of forces that gives a rise to the world, and, through the technology of rods and clocks, to space and time themselves.

Derrida's concept of play, then, couples the world to *différance*, and thus the multiple (effects) to the unthinkable (efficacities). *Différance* produces, as effects, the spatiality of space and the temporality of time, and, under certain conditions, they, in the manner of relativity theory, give spatial aspects of time and temporal aspects of space.[42] It is, again, crucial that this production is material-technological. It is parallel to and philosophically grounds the fact, noted above, that in relativity space and time are effects of, *always local*, rods and clocks, rather than preexistents that are then measured by rods and clocks. The irreducibility of the technology of measurement in relativity and more radically in quantum physics becomes the *tekhne* of 'writing' in Derrida's sense, and thus makes relativity and, even more so, quantum mechanics sciences of *writing* in Derrida's sense. In quantum physics we only deal with traces *written* by the interactions between quantum objects and measuring instruments, without being able to describe or even conceive of quantum objects and their behaviour. These traces become written traces in Derrida's sense.

Derrida's argumentation concerning the multiple has, thus, affinities with both relativity and quantum physics, but because of the fundamental role of the unthinkable (*différance*), it is ultimately closer to quantum mechanics. It may not be possible to fully bring together these two dimensions of the multiple in Derrida. In physics, relativity and quantum theory have not been brought together thus far either, and indeed they are incompatible. I am quite content, however, to see Derrida's argumentation as heterogeneous (which does not mean inconsistent) in this respect. Its deepest and most fundamental affinities are, however, with quantum mechanics.

At stake in quantum mechanics is the behaviour of nature in the *very* small, but no longer the infinitely small, a concept ultimately inapplicable in quantum physics.[43] The smallness in question is measured by Planck's constant h, of a very small magnitude, which prevents physical continuity in quantum physics and defines all observable quantum phenomena, *manifest in measuring instruments*, as quantum in so far as we cannot disregard h in predicting them.[44] Unlike in classical physics, these observed phenomena are not the same as, indeed are irreducibly different from (hence my emphasis), quantum objects, which are unobservable and indescribable, and ultimately inconceivable. By the same token, one only deals with discrete phenomena, disconnected from each other. Observed effects of continuity merely manifest large multiplicities of discrete phenomena or events in close proximity to each other and not anything really continuous. Historically, this discreteness of quantum phenomena and, correlatively, the unavoidable recourse to probability in predicting them, came first. Quantum mechanics was developed as a response to this situation, just as Derrida's framework emerged in response to a certain, analogous, situation of language, meaning, thought, communication and so forth. Quantum mechanics only predict, in general probabilistically, the outcomes of quantum experiments, the *effects* of quantum objects upon measuring instruments, without describing quantum objects and their behaviour. Nobody has ever observed a moving electron or photon. We only observe traces of the impacts of quantum objects on measuring instruments. Indeed, the character of these effects is such that no description or even conception, however idealised, of quantum objects and their behaviour, and hence of the *efficacities* of these effects, appears to be possible.

This situation and the corresponding conceptuality are thus different from the Democritean and subsequent forms of physical atomism. Such theories conceive of the ultimate constitution of nature in terms of 'atoms' as conceivable and, at least ideally, describable entities. By contrast, quantum mechanics, at least in the present interpretation (there are alternative views), suspends any possible description or conception of the ultimate constitution of nature, for example, in terms of particles or waves, especially on the model of classical mechanics or classical wave theory. One can still speak of certain elementary entities, the so-called elementary particles, such as electrons or quarks, which cannot be decomposed into more elementary constituents and of which actual atoms (beginning with those of hydrogen), no longer seen as elementary, are composed. But these entities cannot be assigned any physical structure, discrete or continuous. As I said, the discreteness, defined by *h*, only enters at the level of what is observed, the effects in the measuring instruments involved and thus upon the world we experience.

These effects may be discrete, particle-like, or continuous, corresponding to discrete or continuous, wave-like, multiplicities. These two types of effects are mutually exclusive, or in Bohr's language complementary, so we need not worry about entities that are both continuous and discontinuous at once, which are in fact impossible to conceive. Moreover, as noted above, continuous or wave-like effects are, in actuality, sequences of traces of discrete and disconnected events, which occur too close to each other for their discreteness to be perceived. Rigorously speaking, we only deal with discrete – indeed singular, unique – effects or events and discrete multiplicities of such events, which is also true in the case of effects and multiplicities in Derrida. Effects of *différance*, individual or collective, are always ultimately unique, just as are quantum effects. Quantum objects, just like the efficacities defined by *différance*, are neither continuous nor discrete, nor anything else, and the concepts of object or quantum, or names such as *différance* (which is not a concept), are ultimately inapplicable to them.

Do the irreducibly unthinkable efficacities make the discreteness of effects inevitable? I would refrain from a definitive answer, in part for reasons (having to do with Foucault's continuous multiplicities) to be discussed in the next section. However, the absence of causality, which is an automatic consequence of the irreducibly unthinkable efficacities, at least strongly suggests the discreteness of their effects, for the following reasons. The classical concept of motion, which is continuous, is defined by the simultaneous assignment of both position and velocity or momentum to a moving body at each point, which also allows us to predict what happens, ideally exactly (i.e., neglecting small practical deviations). In other words, this behaviour is, jointly and correlatively, continuous and causal (what happens at any given point determines what happens at all future points) and our predictions are, ideally, deterministic, exact, at least in dealing with individual classical systems. Once the system under consideration is more complex, such as that of the weather, and we can no longer track its behaviour, we can no longer make exact predictions and must use statistical ones, but only for practical rather than fundamental reasons, as in quantum physics, where our predictions are always probabilistic even in dealing with individual quantum systems. Causality remains in place in relativity, special or general, as well.

By contrast, causality and even the classical (or any) concept of (continuous) motion are no longer sustainable in quantum physics in view of Heisenberg's uncertainty relations, which make the simultaneous assignment of position and momentum to a quantum object impossible at any point. As a result, it does not appear possible to develop the concepts through which we might describe or even conceive of quantum objects and their behaviour. What happens between the (discrete) events registered by measuring instruments is not known or, again, conceivable. The suspension of causality is an automatic consequence. In Erwin Schrödinger's words, 'if a classical [physical] state does not exist at any moment, it can hardly change causally'.[45] Hence, quantum predictions can only be probabilistic, even in dealing with individual quantum processes and events. Quantum mechanics is able to provide such predictions, strictly in accord with quantum experiments, without describing the behaviour of quantum objects in space and in time in the way classical physics or relativity do. Accordingly, we do not know why quantum mechanics works, and works so well. We are just lucky to have it. And in the absence of causality and continuity of motion, or, again, of any conception of quantum objects and behaviour, one could hardly expect continuous effects. There are no ascertainable or even conceivable connections between events to allow for continuity.

The homomorphic relationships between Derrida's conceptuality and that of quantum theory must now be apparent, including, it follows, by a reverse homomorphism, from the discussion of quantum mechanics just given, as concerns the discreteness of the effects or events considered. Both are conceptual architectures of the irreducibly multiple (effects) and the irreducibly unthinkable (efficacities). The 'effects' of the interactions between quantum objects and measuring technologies considered in quantum physics are effects, again always ultimately discrete, of quantum *différance*, as the efficacity or, again, efficacities (plural) without causality or in the first place without any conception of reality that we can give to these efficacities. By the same token, one is dealing with traces (without being able to trace their origins, which they cannot thus be assigned) as *writing* in Derrida's sense, the technology, *tekhne*, of Derrida's writings. Quantum multiples are effects of the quantum unthinkable, in the same sense as unthinkable *différance* is the efficacity, the multiple of efficacities (*différance* is dissemination!), without causality, of the irreducibly multiple effects, which are, in the absence of causality, always discrete multiplicities, simultaneous or sequential. The difference is that quantum mechanics has the mathematics to predict these effects. Like Foucault's Einsteinian-like field of the multiple, the Derridean quantum-like field is too rich to be mathematisable. But it is still defined by chance and probability, which is, again, inevitable in the absence of causality, in turn inevitable in the regime of the irreducibly unthinkable. Derrida speaks of

> the Nietzschean affirmation, that is the joyous affirmation of the play of the world and of the innocence of becoming, the affirmation of a world of signs without fault, without truth, and without origins which is offered to an active interpretation. *The affirmation then determines the noncenter otherwise than as a loss of the center* [but as multiple centres]. And it plays without security. . . . In absolute chance, [the Nietzschean] affirmation . . . surrenders itself to *genetic* indetermination, to the *seminal* adventure of trace.[46]

As in quantum mechanics, we can *only count* on a probability of what we expect to happen. But a probability is not nothing: we *can* count on it.

A MORE QUANTUM FOUCAULT?

Certain affinities with quantum theory may also be found or at least surmised in Foucault, although they appear to be hidden in most of his earlier works, and come into the foreground only in his later writings following *The History of Sexuality*. These affinities are, in my view, more tentative than in Derrida (hence 'surmise'), in part because of the dominant role of continuous multiplicities, or continuous effects, in Foucault, in contrast with the discontinuous effects in Derrida, which are more consistent with quantum mechanics, as explained above. Without invoking them as such, Deleuze's reading of Foucault poses the question of these affinities by considering the concept of, in my terms, 'the folded unthought' in Foucault.[47] Deleuze traces intimations of this concept to Foucault's earlier analysis of the life and death of 'infamous men' and sees it as emerging as such in *The Use of Pleasure*:

> few men more than Foucault died in a way commensurable with their conception of death. The force of life that belonged to Foucault was always thought through and lived out as a multiple death in the manner of Bichat. . . . What remains, then, except an anonymous life that shows up only where it clashes with power, argues with it, exchanges 'brief and strident words', and then fades back into the night, what Foucault called the 'the life of infamous men', whom he asked us to admire by virtue of 'their misfortune, rage or uncertain madness'? Strangely, implausibly, it is this infamy which he claimed for himself: 'My point of departure was those sorts of particles endowed with an energy that is all the greater for their being small and difficult to spot.' This culminated in *The Use of Pleasure*'s searing phrase: 'to get free of oneself'.[48]

One cannot perhaps avoid this eternal (but never the same) return of madness in Foucault. Most crucial here is the invocation of a quantum-theoretical concept of particle – 'particles endowed with an energy that is all the greater for their being small and difficult to spot' – particles in the high-energy regimes, governed by the so-called quantum field theory. The theory extends quantum mechanics and reflects an even greater quantum multiplicity than quantum mechanics does (indeed it is the ultimate theory of the quantum multiple), as well as the quantum unthinkable.[49] Ultimately these particles cannot be spotted at all: as I said, nobody has ever seen a moving electron or photon, but only the traces they leave in measuring instruments. But they have effects, including high-energy effects, which we observe in particle accelerators. The word 'infamous' might be read in its literal sense, as something that is beyond any 'fame'—beyond any knowledge and even thought itself. Thus, it is also, as in Nietzsche, 'beyond good and evil', and beyond reason and madness, law and lawlessness, and so forth. And, as is Nietzsche's 'beyond', this 'infamous' is the efficacy of effects thus designated, and various assemblages of and interactions between these effects. Similarly, in quantum theory, the term particle is provisional, for these particles are beyond any concept of particle we can form. Their interactions with measuring instruments and thus the world we experience can, however, have both types of effects, discrete and continuous, keeping in mind that in quantum physics all continuous effects are ultimately discrete multiplicities of proximate but disconnected effects. Continuous multiplicities mask the ultimately discontinuous character of effects or events, which discontinuity, while found in Derrida, does not appear to be found in Foucault. Foucault appears to think primarily in terms of continuous multiplicities, which, reversing the quantum-mechanical situation, would topologically underlie and connect, in however a hidden way, discontinuous multiplicities, in the same way as happens in Riemann's continuous manifolds. Deleuze reads Foucault in this way, which is, I think, correct and is also consistent with Deleuze's own thinking of the multiple. Could these continuous multiplicities still be effects of the unthinkable? Perhaps, although this is not what Foucault or Deleuze say, at least expressly. I shall return to the subject presently. For the moment, it is not surprising that Foucault's thinking leads Deleuze to his concept of, in my terms, the folded unthought, which is beyond any exterior and any interior, and yet is the efficacity of both, and their relationship. According to Deleuze:

> *The History of Sexuality* explicitly closes on a doubt. If at the end of it Foucault finds himself in an impasse, this is not because of his conception of power but rather because he found the impasse to be where power itself places us, in both our lives and our thoughts, as we run up against it in our smallest truths. This could be resolved only if the outside were caught up in a movement that would snatch it away from the void and pull it back from death. This would be like a new axis, different from the axes of both knowledge and power. . . . it is not an axis that annuls all others but one that was already working at the same time as the others, and prevented them from closing on the impasse. Perhaps this third axis was present from the beginning in Foucault (just as power was present from the beginning in knowledge). But it could emerge only by assuming a certain distance, and so being able to circle back on the other two. Foucault felt it necessary to carry out a general reshuffle in order to unravel the path which was so tangled up in the others that it remained hidden: it is this recentring which Foucault puts forward in the general introduction to *The Use of Pleasure*.
>
> But how was this new dimension present from the beginning? Up until now, we have encountered three dimensions: the relations which have been formed or formalized along certain strata (Knowledge); the relations between forces to be found at the level of the diagram (Power); and the relation with the outside, that absolute relation, as Blanchot says, which is also a non-relation (Thought). Does this mean that there is no inside? Foucault continually submits interiority to a radical critique. But is there *an inside that lies deeper than any internal world*, just as the outside is farther away than any external world? The outside is not a fixed limit but a moving matter animated by peristaltic movements, *folds and foldings* that together make up an inside: they are not something other than the outside, but precisely the inside *of* the outside. *The Order of Things* developed this theme: if thought comes from outside, and remains attached to the outside, how come the outside does not flood into

> the inside, as the element that thought does not and cannot think of? The unthought is therefore not external to thought lies at its very heart, as that impossibility of thinking which doubles or hollows out the outside.[50]

Deleuze develops this concept of the unthought within thought via Heidegger and Merleau-Ponty, whom Foucault follows and radicalises: 'An Outside more distant than any exterior, is "twisted", "folded", and "doubled" by an Inside that is deeper than any interior, and alone creates the possibility of the derived relations between the exterior and the exterior.'[51] One is dealing with what is beyond both the interior and the exterior, or even the inside and the outside, and yet is the efficacity of both, as 'the [folded] unthought beyond thought'.[52]

This conception has or suggests a proximity to Derrida and quantum mechanics. And yet it may also be seen as quite distant from them. The question is whether this 'beyond' is irreducibly unthinkable in the way quantum objects and processes are in quantum theory, or the radical alterity of *différance* is in Derrida, or whether, as the folded unthought, it could still be given a conception and in particular continuity. Indeed, this 'beyond' does appear to be seen as a topological, continuous (Baroque?) multifold, 'a "topological" . . . space which establishes contact between the Outside and the Inside', ultimately continuously folded to and unfolding the unthought.[53]

Chance enters the picture as well: 'Must this outside be called chance?' But this chance is connected to and even defined by dependency and continuity (a line), and hence implicitly causality: 'this is the outside: the line that continues to link up random events in a mixture of chance and dependency'.[54] What is the nature of this mixture? Neither Deleuze nor Foucault himself makes it entirely clear, and neither ever gives it a quantum-mechanical-like nature, unlike Derrida in his persistent invocations of chance.

These features of Foucault's thinking appear, thus, to be different from Derrida's conceptuality or that of quantum mechanics, where there no such lines or links, where the interplay of chance and necessity, when it occurs, takes a very different form, that of 'calculations without end', in which chance remains irreducible.[55] It could be argued that, in contrast to Foucault, or to Deleuze in *The Fold*, Derrida's analysis of the relationships between the outside and the inside in *Of Grammatology* and his analysis of the fold in Mallarmé in *Dissemination* show the outside and the inside, or folding, to be the effects of the irreducibly unthinkable, effects, moreover, ultimately composed of discrete singularities.[56] The concept of chance (*hazard*) in Mallarmé is inscribed, accordingly, more quantum mechanically as well. There is still the question whether the unthinkable efficacity, which, hence, can be neither continuous not discontinuous, can have strictly continuous effects, rather than only discrete ones, as in quantum mechanics or Derrida. For the reasons explained above, this seems doubtful, although perhaps not impossible, and the question is never posed by Foucault or Deleuze. In any event, against the folded unthought, as still possibly thinkable, it is never possible to ever think the irreducibly unthinkable.

It would be difficult to argue that the ultimate nature of things is necessarily defined by either of these two conceptual architectures. Hence, one need not accept either, and it is not my aim here to advocate one or the other. Each may be compelling in its own way. Einstein never accepted quantum mechanics, which he thought 'logically possible without contradiction', but 'contrary to [his] scientific instinct', and he debated the issue with Bohr throughout his life.[57] Einstein's thinking was closer to that of the folded unthought, and he saw the main goal of theoretical physics as being to think this as yet unthought, a project he himself continued to pursue, against quantum mechanics, all his life. Bohr was a thinker of the irreducibly unthinkable; for him the main role of theoretical physics was to find the mathematics to predict what happens in experiments, without describing or even conceiving the ultimate constitution of matter, which he saw as the irreducibly unthinkable.[58] This debate, thus initiated, continues with undiminished intensity in physics and philosophy alike, and is likely to do so interminably. The folded unthought and the irreducibly unthinkable offer a similar, or even philosophically the same, choice, if it is a choice. For, as Derrida observes, in this region, 'let us say provisionally a region of historicity' (a Foucauldian region?), 'the category of choice seems particularly trivial . . . we must fist try to conceive of a common ground, and the *différance* of this irreducible difference'.[59]

EPILOGUE: THE HISTORY OF REASON AND MADNESS IN THE BAROQUE AGE

A Baroque city, such as Venice, is a mad city. Following Foucault's analysis of madness in the classical age, the age of Cartesian reason, I give the phrase 'a mad city' a positive meaning. For one thing, Baroque architecture or the Baroque in general gives a certain 'madness' to urban spacetimes. Indeed, one could understand curvature as the madness of a straight line, the divine madness of its poetry, of which Plato spoke in *Ion*. A curve is a straight line gone astray, deflected, sometimes traumatically, by something within or outside it. Unless it is, on the contrary, the straight line that is a mad curve, and Cartesian coordination and reason are madness – not reason gone mad, but the madness of reason itself. Descartes perhaps already knew this, even if despite himself, as Derrida argues in his reading of Foucault, which may be more Foucauldian than it might appear even to Foucault or Derrida, who acknowledges its Foucauldian aspects.[60] It follows that madness and reason, even in mathematics, let alone in poetry, are not simply or unequivocally distinguishable so as to allow reason to isolate madness, just as Venice or its rulers wanted to isolate Torquato Tasso, or Paris or its guardians Antonin Artaud. Artaud, alongside Van Gogh and Nietzsche, is Foucault's principal example of madness judging reason, the latter defined, naïvely, by its self-proclaimed guardians placing it in the grid of the rational, defined equally naïvely by them. In the Baroque, Riemannian spacetimes and multiple boundaries between reason and madness are possible, too, and sometimes necessary. But, arising from the abyss of the folded unthought or, for Derrida, of the irreducibly unthinkable, the abyss that gives rise to reason and madness alike, these boundaries are never unconditional or established once and for all, or strictly boundaries, similarly to those of the law in Derrida's reading of Kafka. They are rather multiplicities as well – multiplicities between multiplicities, which give the multiple mixtures of reason and madness to reason and madness alike, as

Deleuze and Guattari argue in *Anti-Oedipus*, inspired by Foucault, and inspiring Foucault in his later work. Whether they arise from the folded unthought or from the irreducibly unthinkable, Baroque spaces combine reason and madness in the way Riemannian spaces in mathematics and Einsteinian spaces in physics combine coordinate grids or striations with the play of curvatures, or with topologies without any geometrical features or even without points.[61]

Shelley writes from the Baroque Milan, especially of its famous cathedral, after a visit to Como, which he describes in terms of a 'union of culture and the untamable profusion & loveliness of nature' which is 'here so close that the line where they are divided can hardly be discovered':

> Como is only 6 leagues from Milan, & its mountains are seen from the Cathedral. This Cathedral is a most astonishing work of art. It's built of white marble & cut into pinnacles of immense height & the utmost delicacy and workmanship, & loaded with sculpture. The effect of it, piercing the solid blue with those groups of dazzling spires relieved by the serene depth of this Italian heaven, or by moonlight when the stars seem gathered among those sculpture shapes is beyond anything I had imagined architecture is capable of producing. The interior tho[ugh] very sublime is of a more earthly character, & with its stained glass & massy granite columns overloaded with antique figures & the silver lamps that burn forever under the canopy of black cloth beside the brazen altar & and the marble fretwork of the dome, give it the aspect of some gorgeous sepulchre. There is one solitary spot among these aisles behind the altar where the light of the day is dim & yellow under the storied window which I have chosen to visit & to read Dante there.
>
> I have devoted the summer & indeed the next year to the composition of a tragedy on the subject of Tasso's madness, which I find upon inspection is, if properly treated, admirably dramatic & poetical.[62]

The phrase 'architecture is capable of *producing*' may be read in the literal sense, which is at work throughout Shelley's depiction of architecture in his poetry. Architecture produces a curved Baroque spacetime, just as matter, the architecture of matter, produces spacetime in Leibniz, Riemann and Einstein. The tragedy on the subject of Tasso's madness, a quintessentially Baroque subject, linked to the curved, mind-twisting spaces of the Baroque Venice, never materialised. The project mutated into *Julian and Maddalo*, a fortunate genetic mutation, perhaps. While keeping the same spacetime of the Baroque and the same city, Venice, the poem linked both poetry and madness to the 'agony' found in 'the text of every heart', as Shelley says in his Preface.[63] It is not possible to offer here a full reading of this extraordinary work. Nearly every line, by the very nature of the dynamic flow of its poetic curvature, inscribes the Baroque, both in Deleuze's broad sense and in terms of the Venetian Baroque. I shall only comment on the theme of madness in the poem from this perspective, and with Foucault's *History of Madness* in mind.

The poem is structured as a 'conversation' (the poem's subtitle) between its two main protagonists, Julian and Maddalo, and ostensibly suggests Shelley as a prototype for Julian and Byron for Maddalo, even giving their respective characters a few traits of each poet. The conversation is a confrontation between Julian's (roughly Enlightenment) views, explained in detail, and 'the darker side' taken by Maddalo, whose actual views are 'not exactly known'.[64] The case of the Maniac, the third main protagonist (whose name is not given), the case of madness, offers an occasion to settle the dispute. The reasons for the Maniac's illness are not exactly known and, as I shall explain, may ultimately not be important, although his disappointment in love appears to be the cause.

The debate remains unresolved, which is not surprising given the generally sceptical nature of Shelley's poetry. Instead, more profound questions are posed, giving the two protagonists and the poem's reader an opportunity to think more deeply about the case and the world. While Julian, the narrator, adopts an Enlightenment-like philosophy concerning human destiny (179–91), Maddalo argues from 'the darker side' (49) of this destiny. Julian initially attributes Maddalo's argument to 'pride', but ultimately sees it, rightly, as grounded in a complex understanding of the world, the complexity that the Maniac's case exemplifies (49). Maddalo does a few things that help the Maniac, perhaps not much, but as much as it may be possible to help, in so far as one can count on anything to work in this case. Julian, who initially thought that he could achieve more by a kind of proto-psychoanalytic treatment (Shelley knows his Freud!), appears to come to accept the limits of any possible help in this case, and leaves the situation in the hands of Maddalo and life itself (549–75). Julian realised that this might be a wiser course of action, even though, in the end, life showed little kindness to the Maniac – a story that the poem ultimately does not tell us: 'she [Maddalo's daughter] told me [Julian] how / All happened – but the cold world shall not know' (616–17). There emerges, however, a new space for relationship between the protagonists, a new space of friendship (the words 'friend' and 'friendship' appear throughout the poem, and dominate the closing part, after an encounter with the Maniac).

Shelley's strategy is to centre the poem on the long, disconnected monologue of the Maniac, or rather partly disconnected, between reason and madness, which is often the language of what reason sees as madness: 'The colours of his mind seem yet unworn; / For the wild language of his grief was high, / Such as in measure were called poetry' (540–2). One might say, with Foucault, that this is the voice of madness, which, however, also measures our reason, especially that part of reason (or a form of madness in its own right, a dangerous form of madness) which defines madness as that which is outside the *coordinates* (the Cartesian space) of reason. In responding to Julian's question: 'Alas, what drove him mad?', Maddalo replies:

> I cannot say;
> A Lady came with him from France, and when
> She left him and returned, he wandered then
> About yon lonely isles of desert sand
> Till he grew wild – he had no cash or land
> Remaining, – the police had brought him here –
> Some fancy took him and he would not bear

Removal; so I fitted up for him
Those rooms beside the sea, to please his whim,
And sent him busts and books and urns for flowers,
Which had adorned his life in happier hours,
And instruments of music – you may guess
A stranger could do little more or less
For one so gentle and unfortunate;
And those are his sweet strains which charm the weight
From madmen's chains, and make this Hell appear
A heaven of sacred silence, hushed to hear. (245–61)

The allusion to Milton's 'The mind is its own place, and in itself / Can make a heav'n of hell, hell of heav'n' (*Paradise Lost* I, 254–5) is extraordinary and remarkably to the point, which contributes to its powerful impact. The mind can equally make reason of madness, madness of reason. Heaven and Hell are both cities, and Venice may be both, just as was Dante's Florence. The police, part of the surveillance system of the city and of the maintenance of its coordinated order and social grid, bring the Maniac into his proper place of isolation, actually on an island and thus surrounded by the sea, the space beyond reasons, as Foucault tells us in *History of Madness*. The main point is that Maddalo creates a different spacetime, or as Leibniz would have it, a different *monadological* spacetime. This is the spacetime of the Baroque, now that of the Baroque interior, defined by the complex relationships between the pleats of matter and the fold of the souls, and of their curvatures.[65] In such a spacetime (Shelley knows his Foucault!), the relationships between reason and madness become redefined, preventing their unequivocal separation and thus a rigorous (in either sense) isolation of madness from reason, its exclusion from reason. There are no police, governmental or mental, that can do so without an abuse of power by the force that is supposed to protect us in reason and madness. The spacetime of the Maniac's room – or of Venice, to which it is metonymically related and which it, in part, metaphorically represents – is the allegory of these relationships.

This is a grand Foucauldian moment of the poem, which also allows us to bring together Foucault and Derrida, via Deleuze, as I have done throughout this chapter. The reason for the Maniac's madness is less important than his voice, as Maddalo suggests to Julian earlier, before Julian's Enlightenment ideas suffer a shipwreck in the Maniac's room, in the spacetime of the Baroque, beside the sea, a space without grid, upon which our navigation likes to impose (albeit for good reasons) coordinates. Madness, Foucault tells us, is an affair of the sea, but it is seen differently by classical reason and by the Baroque, whether old, such as that of Leibniz, or new, such as that of Riemann or Pierre Boulez, or Foucault.[66] Classical reason sees madness as an exile from reason. The Baroque sees it as interminably and indeterminably intermixed with reason in the Riemannian space, in the Einsteinian field of thought in its confrontation with chaos, as its greatest enemy and its greatest friend.[67]

As Foucault tells us in *History of Madness*, it is not only cases like those of Van

Gogh, Nietzsche or Artaud that cannot be measured by reason, if defined apart from madness, and that their 'madness' measures this 'reason' instead. The main point of appealing to these cases is, I would argue, in showing that every case of madness would, given space enough and time, reveal an equally great (it is never the same) complexity of the relationships between reason and madness, as thought-effects of that which is neither, even if still thought. These cases are *not essentially* different from most other cases of madness, which reason or, again, something that sees itself as reason, wants to isolate from itself, or from its world. This is why Foucault argues that each of these cases or any case of madness, or conversely reason, is both exemplary and yet unique in its mixture of reason and madness, which makes it difficult to separate them.

This is reason and madness in the age of Foucault and Derrida, perhaps no longer the age of psychoanalysis, but not entirely leaving it behind either (Shelley knows his Derrida!). Shelley gives no name to the Maniac and says in the Preface that 'of the Maniac I [the fictional author of the Preface] can give no information. He seems by his own account to have been disappointed in love.' Shelley suggests that 'the unconnected explanation of his agony will perhaps be a sufficient comment for the text of every heart'.[68] That his love story may be tragic, too tragic to be told and made known to 'the cold world', which is also the world of cold reason, as the poem's last line, again, tells us (617), only supports and amplifies Shelley's point. One need not be 'officially' declared 'mad' by reason to be oppressed by it or to prove it wrong when it tries to isolate madness from thought. In the Maniac's own words: '*Me* – who am as a nerve o'er which do creep / The else unfelt oppressions of this earth' (449–50, Shelley's emphasis). Yes, the Cogito is valid, even if it is mad, as Derrida says, against Foucault, and he might well be right that Descartes argued this case.[69] Foucault might have replied that, while this may be true, the point is that it should be especially valid because it can be mad, and in a certain, deep sense is always mad. Derrida, and perhaps even Descartes, could have agreed in turn. But then, could one still speak of the Cogito, rather than only of the history of madness and reason, many a madness and many a reason, incessantly passing into each other, a history of which the history of the Cogito is only an episode, long as it may be?

If there is reason, thinking reason, madness is its nervous system, and vice versa. And yet both are only effects – effects defined by their multiplicities, mixing reason and madness – of that which is beyond both, beyond anything, between Foucault's folded unthought and Derrida's irreducibly unthinkable. Indeed, this is also a neurological problem, as Deleuze and Guattari argue in their conclusion to *What is Philosophy?*, 'From Chaos to the Brain', even if without addressing the relationships between madness and reason, that is, without expressly addressing them.[70] The problem of the relationships between madness and reason cannot be avoided, especially by readers of Foucault, as Deleuze and Guattari are, in addressing the relationships between chaos and the brain, relationships that define thought. As the problem of the multiple distributed by and distributing between reason and madness, this problem may require a new way of thinking about the brain, which Deleuze and Guattari urge us to develop. Whether this multiple will reveal itself as arising from the folded unthought or from the irreducibly unthinkable (there are indications in both directions in neuroscience) remains a question, yet another question in the in-between of Foucault and Derrida.

NOTES

1. Michel Foucault, *History of Madness*, ed. Jean Khalfa, trans. Jonathan Murphy and Jean Khalfa (New York: Routledge, 2006).
2. Jacques Derrida, *Writing and Difference*, trans. Alan Bass (Chicago: University of Chicago Press, 1978), pp. 31–63.
3. Jacques Derrida, '"To Do Justice to Freud": The History of Madness in the Age of Psychoanalysis', in *Resistances of Psychoanalysis*, trans. Peggy Kamuf (Stanford: Stanford University Press, 1996), pp. 60–118.
4. Ibid., p. 71.
5. Maurice Blanchot, *The Infinite Conversation*, trans. Lydia Davis (Minneapolis: University of Minnesota Press, 1993), p. 196.
6. Gilles Deleuze, *Foucault*, trans. Seán Hand (Minneapolis: University of Minnesota Press, 1988), p. 14.
7. Gilles Deleuze, *The Fold: Leibniz and the Baroque*, trans. Tom Conley (Minneapolis: University of Minnesota Press, 1992).
8. Jacques Derrida, *Dissemination*, trans. Barbara Johnson (Chicago: University of Chicago Press, 1981), pp. 270–3.
9. Niels Bohr, *Philosophical Writings of Niels Bohr*, 3 vols (Woodbridge, CT: Ox Bow Press, 1987), vol. 2, p. 2; vol. 3, p. 7.
10. Immanuel Kant, *Critique of Pure Reason*, trans. Paul Guyer and A. W. Wood (Cambridge: Cambridge University Press, 1997), p. 115.
11. Deleuze, *Foucault*, pp. 110, 118.
12. Jacques Derrida, *Positions*, trans. Alan Bass (Chicago: University of Chicago Press, 1981), p. 41; *Dissemination*, p. 245.
13. Michel Foucault, *The Order of Things: An Archaeology of Human Sciences* (New York: Vintage, 1994).
14. Deleuze, *Foucault*, p. 13.
15. Gilles Deleuze and Félix Guattari, *A Thousand Plateaus*, trans. Brian Massumi (Minneapolis: University of Minnesota Press, 1987), pp. 482–3.
16. Deleuze, *Foucault*, pp. 13–14.
17. Gilles Deleuze and Félix Guattari, *What Is Philosophy?*, trans. Hugh Tomlinson and Graham Burchell (New York: Columbia University Press, 2003), p. 19.
18. Bernhard Riemann, 'On the Hypotheses That Lie at the Foundations of Geometry', in Peter Pesic (ed.), *Beyond Geometry: Classic Papers From Riemann to Einstein* (Mineola, NY: Dover, 2007), pp. 23–40.
19. Technically, the manifolds considered by Riemann were differential, which means that one can define calculus on them, but this point is secondary here.
20. Riemann, 'On the Hypotheses That Lie at the Foundations of Geometry', p. 33.
21. Deleuze and Guattari, *A Thousand Plateaus*, p. 485.
22. Ibid., translation modified. I bring Lautman's passage in accordance with Lautman's text, which cites Cartan, not mentioned by Deleuze and Guattari (Albert Lautman, *Mathematics, Ideas, and the Physical Real*, trans. Simon Duffy (London: Bloomsbury, 2011), p. 98).
23. Deleuze, *Foucault*, p. 23.
24. Arkady Plotnitsky, 'The Spacetimes of Nympheas: Matter and Multiplicity in Einstein, Monet, and Deleuze and Guattari', in Rosi Braidotti and Patricia Pisters (eds), *Revisiting Normativity with Deleuze* (London: Bloomsbury, 2012), pp. 37–50.
25. Riemann, 'On the Hypotheses That Lie at the Foundations of Geometry', p. 33.

26. Ibid.
27. Deleuze, *The Fold*, pp. 3, 32.
28. 'Interview with Gilles Deleuze', in Arnaud Villani, *La guêpe et l'orchidée: Essai sur Gilles Deleuze* (Paris: Belin, 1999), p. 130.
29. Deleuze, *The Fold*, pp. 3, 14.
30. Michel Foucault, *The Archaeology of Knowledge and the Discourse on Language*, trans. A. M. Sheridan Smith (New York: Pantheon, 1972), p. 104.
31. Ibid., pp. 104–5.
32. Franz Kafka, *The Trial* (Oxford: Oxford University Press, 2009).
33. Jacques Derrida, *Acts of Literature*, ed. Derek Attridge (New York: Routledge, 1992), pp. 181–220.
34. Michel Foucault, *Discipline and Punish: The Birth of Prison* (New York: Vintage, 1979); Gilles Deleuze and Félix Guattari, *Kafka: Toward a Minor Literature* (Minneapolis: University of Minnesota Press, 1986).
35. Jacques Derrida, *Margins of Philosophy*, trans. Alan Bass (Chicago: University of Chicago Press, 1982), pp. 20–1.
36. Derrida, *Positions*, p. 64.
37. Derrida, *Acts of Literature*, pp. 208–9.
38. Derrida, *Margins of Philosophy*, p. 8.
39. Jacques Derrida, 'Khora', in *On the Name*, ed. Thomas Dutoit (Stanford: Stanford University Press, 1995), pp. 89–130.
40. Derrida, *Writing and Difference*, pp. 292–3.
41. Jacques Derrida, *Of Grammatology*, trans. Gayatri Chakravorty Spivak (Baltimore, MD: Johns Hopkins University Press, 1998), p. 50; also *Writing and Difference*, p. 293.
42. Derrida, *Margins of Philosophy*, p. 8.
43. I have discussed the quantum-mechanical situation in detail in Arkady Plotnitsky, *Epistemology and Probability: Bohr, Heisenberg, Schrödinger, and the Nature of Quantum-Theoretical Thinking* (New York: Springer, 2009).
44. It is not the question of the actual size, because quantum objects may consist of a large number of elementary particles or even atoms.
45. Erwin Schrödinger, 'The Present Situation in Quantum Mechanics' (1935), in John A. Wheeler and Wojciech H. Zurek (eds), *Quantum Theory and Measurement* (Princeton: Princeton University Press, 1983), p. 154.
46. Derrida, *Writing and Difference*, p. 292.
47. Deleuze, *Foucault*, pp. 70–123.
48. Ibid., pp. 95–6.
49. Arkady Plotnitsky, 'Reality, Causality, and Probability, from Quantum Mechanics to Quantum Field Theory', in Theo M. Nieuwenhuisen et al. (eds), *Quantum Foundations and Open Quantum Systems* (Singapore: World Scientific, 2014), pp. 521–603.
50. Deleuze, *Foucault*, pp. 96–7.
51. Ibid., p. 110.
52. Ibid., p. 118.
53. E.g., ibid., pp. 110, 118, 120.
54. Ibid., p. 117.
55. Derrida, *Margins of Philosophy*, p. 7.
56. Derrida 1998, pp. 30–73; *Dissemination*, pp. 270–3.
57. Albert Einstein, 'Physics and Reality', *Journal of the Franklin Institute*, 221 (1996), p. 375.
58. I have considered Bohr's view and this debate in detail in Arkady Plotnitsky, *Niels Bohr and Complementarity: An Introduction* (New York: Springer, 2013).
59. Derrida, *Writing and Difference*, p. 293.
60. Ibid., p. 59.

61. Deleuze and Guattari, *A Thousand Plateaus*, pp. 482–92.
62. *The Letters of Percy Bysshe Shelley*, ed. Frederick L. Jones. 2 vols (Oxford: Clarendon, 1964), vol. 2, pp. 461–2.
63. Percy Bysshe Shelley, *Poetry and Prose*, ed. Donald H. Reiman and Sharon B. Powers (New York: W. W. Norton, 1977), p. 113. Line numbers for the poem will be given in parentheses in the text.
64. Ibid.
65. Deleuze, *The Fold*, pp. 2–5.
66. Ibid., p. 137; Deleuze, *Foucault*, p. 22; Deleuze and Guattari, *A Thousand Plateaus*, pp. 477–8.
67. Deleuze and Guattari, *What is Philosophy?*, pp. 208–10.
68. Shelley, *Poetry and Prose*, p. 113.
69. Derrida, *Writing and Difference*, p. 55.
70. Deleuze and Guattari, *What is Philosophy?*, pp. 208–18.

PART V

Crisis, Life and Death

CHAPTER 13

Living and Dying with Foucault and Derrida: The Question of Biopower

Jeffrey T. Nealon

Jacques Derrida's direct comments on Michel Foucault's concept of biopower are relatively few and somewhat mixed in his 20 March 2002 lecture (the penultimate session of the first year of *The Beast and the Sovereign* course). And I suppose it's a little bit unfair to wrest a full-fledged Derridean 'argument' concerning Foucault from them, in so far as these remarks are nested within what are (to my eyes) among the funniest pages in all of Derrida: his uncharacteristically severe smackdown of Giorgio Agamben's work on life, death and power. As Derrida says of Agamben's writings on biopower: 'I mention all these texts less because I understand them (I admit I often have to give up on that) than because they mark at least the currency of the problems and concerns that are ours here.'[1] When Derrida says he doesn't understand Agamben's work (or worse, that he's given up trying), and at least twice flat-out calls Agamben a purveyor of untruths,[2] while systematically dismantling the very basis of his thought (the zoe-bios distinction), it is I think fair to say that Derrida feels Agamben's project is suspect. (And there lingers in these pages a 'Limited Inc'-style sarcastically hostile tone that one seldom encounters in Derrida – a tone that's well worth thinking about in its own right.) In any case, Derrida remains clearly much more sympathetic to Foucault than to Agamben within this discussion of biopower. In addition to characterising Agamben's central claims about Foucault as 'literally false' (BS, 329), Derrida defends Foucault against Agamben's infamous claim that 'the Foucaultian thesis [on biopower] will . . . have to be corrected, or, at least completed' – which are not at all the same operations, 'correcting' and 'completing', as Derrida points out twice (BS, 315, 325). In the end, Derrida summarises Agamben's engagement with Foucauldian biopower like this: 'poor Foucault!', Derrida intones, 'He never had such a cruel admirer' (BS, 330).

Among his other pointed questions, Derrida accuses Agamben of wanting to be correct not once but twice when it comes to biopower – which is to say that

Agamben initially seems to concur with the Foucauldian thesis that biopower is a nineteenth-century invention (emerging at the threshold of modernity). But Agamben simultaneously wants to correct Foucault by suggesting that biopower is the structuring hidden secret of the west – that biopower has in fact been in effect since the very beginning. Derrida writes,

> In truth, Agamben . . . wants to be twice first, the first to see and announce, the first to remind: he wants both to be the first to announce an unprecedented and new thing [biopower], what he calls this 'decisive event of modernity', and also to be the first to recall that in fact it's always been like that, from time immemorial. He is telling us two things in one: it's just happening for the first time, you ain't seen nothing yet; but nor have you seen, I'm telling you for the first time, that it dates from the year zero. (BS, 330)

All this is very funny, and clearly Derrida has little patience for Agamben's reading strategy; but there is a real Derridean question to Foucault buried somewhere within this brinksmanship. Because if Derrida has to choose between Agamben's two 'firsts' for understanding Foucault's biopower – that it is a phenomenon born specifically in the nineteenth century, or that it is an originary western logic of political life itself – then he will clearly side with the latter characterisation. As Derrida insists more than once, 'biopolitics is an arch-ancient thing (even if today it has new means and new structures)', and he goes on to defend this claim as follows: 'I am not saying that there is no "new bio-power," I am suggesting that "bio-power" itself is not new. There are incredible novelties in bio-power, but bio-power or zoo-power are not new' (BS, 330). As he expands on his critique: 'What bothers me is not the idea that there should be a "new bio-power", but that what is "new" *is* bio-power; not the idea that there is something new within bio-power, which I believe, but that the idea of bio-power *is* something new' (BS, 329). In short, the Derridean scepticism surrounding biopower congeals around Foucault's historical claims that biopower is a novel form of life's imbrication with power, and that it emerged in Europe in the nineteenth century; whereas Derrida tends here to side with Agamben's more sweeping philosophical claim – that life and power will always already have been entangled (and likewise connected to the transversal question of sovereignty – to centralised decisions concerning who lives and who dies).

In this chapter, I'd like to explore this disagreement between Foucault and Derrida, and further to suggest that this dispute concerning the concept of biopower is symptomatic of their various philosophical and historical disagreements over the years. As a twist, however, I'll suggest that the *différend* between Foucault and Derrida may have less to do with a fairly recognisable dispute between philosophical historicism (the caricature of Foucault) and transcendentalism (Derrida), than it does with two different conceptions of life, and subsequently two very different ways of thinking about and responding to the immanence of death. Finally I'll suggest that this seemingly arcane philosophical distinction between Derrida and Foucault has particularly crucial stakes in our present era of climate change and impending ecological disaster – where, in less than a generation of thought and action, human death on a mass scale within a century or two has morphed from an abstract possibility into a nearly foregone historical conclusion.

FOUCAULT AND LIFE

If we begin by examining Foucault's specific claims to biopower's nineteenth-century emergence, to formulate a response to Derrida's sense that life and power will always already have been entangled, we almost immediately find another claim that one can imagine Derrida would have objected to *prima facie*. If one wants to begin reexamining the Foucauldian emergence of life as a central concern for power, one needs merely to cite these infamous lines from *The Order of Things*: 'if biology was unknown [in eighteenth-century Europe], there was a very simple reason for it: life itself did not exist. All that existed was living beings, which were viewed through a grid of knowledge constituted by natural history.'[3] Of course, this provocation – life did not exist until the nineteenth century, specifically until 1802 when Lamarck was the first to use the word 'biology' – functions as a bit of a dry run for Foucault's later, seemingly just as 'outrageous' idea that homosexuality was invented in 1870, or his declarations that the author, and indeed even 'man' itself, are products of recent invention.[4] This type of sentence-level provocation is one of Foucault's characteristic means for dramatising, in a very stark way, the crucial importance of social and historical emergence. Alongside the Foucauldian pleasure evident in the perversity performed by sentences like 'up to the end of the eighteenth century, in fact, life does not exist' (OT, 160), there's of course a consistent philosophical point being advanced: the historical emergence of a new way of handling topic X (here, 'life') gives rise to different problematics, different practices, and thereby different objects. A new form of practice literally remakes the (supposedly preexisting) object of the discourse: biology *creates*, rather than discovers, this object of study called life. This emphasis on discursive emergence constitutes Foucauldian Archaeology 101, and keeps us focused on the most basic terrain for all of Foucault's work: the question of how today is different from yesterday.

In schematic terms, Foucault's prey in *The Order of Things* is the epistemic shift from a classical regime of representation (natural history, where classification and nomination of visible 'living things' are the key practices) to a regime of modern knowledge – transcendentals like life, labour and language (where the 'object' of knowledge is no longer readily available to classification, but rather disappears into the shadowy half-light of discursive practice). In the birth of biology, the question of life unhinges itself from a practice of representation (the discourse is freed from what Foucault calls the 'pure tabulation of things' [OT, 131] in natural history's grids) and attaches itself instead to a mode of speculation about this murky thing called life – now understood not as a visible manifestation of similitude, but as a darkly hidden secret that connects living things. This movement from surface to depth signals the decline of natural history and the birth of biology, the emergence of the science of life. And in this movement across spheres, the modern human sciences and their era of transcendentals begin to replace the representational *episteme* – just as representation, in its turn, had replaced the early modern regime of fabulation or magic.

At the dawn of the nineteenth century, Foucault traces a mutation of the dominant epistemic procedures – from a representational discourse that maps external similitude and resemblance, to the emergence of a speculative discourse that takes as its object hidden internal processes. In short, we see emerge a discourse that 'opposed historical knowledge of the visible to philosophical knowledge of the invisible' (OT, 138): knowledge's privileged practices abandon the surface of objects in order to plumb their hidden depths instead. And first and foremost among those transcendental 'invisibles' was a little thing we like to call 'life': 'The naturalist is the man concerned with the structure of the visible world and its denomination according to characters. Not with life' (OT, 161), Foucault insists, because life is not representable. Life is in fact a kind of unplumbable depth, animating the organism from a hidden origin somewhere within. This birth of biology – which is to say, the emergence of 'life' itself as a bearing area for discursive power and a depth to be explored – constitutes the first birth of biopower, this one in Foucault's work of the mid 1960s.

In any case, if we return to Derrida's critique of Foucauldian biopower (Derrida insists that life was of course entangled with power for many centuries before the nineteenth – it's a foundational western concept or matrix, not a recent emergence), the Derridean concern begins to seem a bit off the Foucauldian mark. Clearly, Foucault doesn't believe that human life remained untouched by power before the nineteenth century any more than he believes that nothing was 'alive' until 1802, or that there were no homosexual acts performed before 1870. If nothing else, the opening pages of *Discipline and Punish*, the disquieting dismembering of the regicide Damiens, clearly demonstrate that Foucault wasn't blind to the imbrications of life, death and power before 1800. And one could probably split the difference in terms of Derrida's critique by suggesting that Foucault's historical argument concerns a decisive *intensification* of the relations among life and power in the nineteenth century, rather than an old-fashioned origin story.[5] In any case, one might say that they're decisively back on the same page when both Foucault and Derrida discuss and doggedly pursue contemporary innovations and further intensifications within power's relation to life – say, Derrida's work on the death penalty or the rogue state, or Foucault's work on neoliberalism or the medicalisation of society.

But of course one or several sticking points nevertheless remain here. As I've suggested, with a little further torque, you can pretty easily get Foucault's discourse to respond to Derrida's overarching concern: Foucault was never as naïve as to think that political power cared not one whit about life before 1800; biopower is the Foucauldian name for a decisive nineteenth-century intensification of political investment in the question of life, but it's surely not for Foucault the first time that power ever took notice of human life and death. So Foucault's discourse, it seems, has a ready response for Derrida's critique.

Conversely, though, I wonder if you can you get Derrida's discourse to respond to Foucault's proleptic historicist critique of Derrida? Because for Foucault, Derrida's overriding concern with biopower (it's an always-already, not a recent emergence) remains wholly symptomatic of Foucault's consistent and lifelong critique of Derrida, which we can summarise very economically from a little paragraph tucked into his 1969 essay, 'What is an Author': 'The conception of *écriture* sustains the privileges of the author through the safeguard of the a priori: the play of representations that formed a particular image of the author is extended within a gray neutrality. The disappearance of the author – since Mallarmé, an event of our time – is held in check by the transcendental.'[6] Foucault's critique focuses on Derrida's 'safeguard' deconstructive emphasis on the 'a priori' conditions of possibility for the emergence and functioning of a discourse – the 'gray neutrality' of the pre-originary and its ironic protection of a boundless depth for thinking to mime or mine. On that register, barely a page of Foucault's *Archaeology of Knowledge* goes by without some kind of stinging critique of any and all discourses of hidden depth or absent origin – a theoretical a priori of any kind, especially one of absence, gap, lack or trace. As Foucault clearly writes, what he seeks in concepts like the historical a priori is 'not a condition of possibility but a law of coexistence': the historical a priori and the statement constitute 'something more than a series of traces'.[7] The statements that comprise and transform the archive of the historical a priori are 'not defined by their truth – that is, not gauged by the presence of a secret content' (AK, 120). In other words, the domain of the historical a priori is characterised neither by the masked (historical) content of ideology, nor by a species of hidden originary (a priori) gap or lack that haunts all language usage. In either case, it's the 'hidden' nineteenth-century understanding of animating 'life' that constitutes Foucault's critical prey – the sense that all the important operations take place in some hidden, misty, unthematisable realm of life, which can be characterised equally by protean excess or its supposed opposite, tragic loss.

In his most pointed criticism of Derrida in the *Archaeology*, Foucault points out that the hazardous historical a priori of discourse 'can be purified in the problematic of trace, which, prior to all speech, is the opening of inscription, the gap of deferred time [*écart du temps différeré*]: it is always the historico-transcendental theme that is reinvested' (AK, 121). And just as deconstruction for Foucault entails a certain understanding of privileged subjectivity (the philosopher as the one who can uniquely hear the muffled call of the pre-originary), so too does the whole phenomenological legacy of Dasein, that 'subjectivity that always lags behind manifest history, and which finds, beneath events, another, more serious, more sober, more secret, more fundamental history, closer to the origin, more firmly linked to its ultimate horizon (and consequently more in control of all its determinations)' (AK, 121). In short, Foucault's archaeological apparatus insists that the historical archive of discontinuously constructed statements, and not the quasi-transcendental conditions of discourse's general possibility, governs the reception and impact of the statement: why certain statements are received as relevant and influential, and others – the vast majority of all statements – are not. The historical a priori does its work at the material level of discursive emergence – with positivities, things that are actually said – rather than ventriloquising the quasi-transcendental murmur that exists in the ether before things are said (the pre-originary realm that remains, on Foucault's reading, the privileged domain of deconstruction).

Which leads us to the upshot of Foucault's critique in 'What is an Author?', wherein he asks point blank: 'Is it not necessary to draw a line between those who believe that we can continue to situate our present discontinuities within the historical and transcendental situation of the nineteenth century, and those who are making a great effort to liberate themselves, once and for all, from this conceptual framework?'[8] Recall also in this vein his infamous charge in direct response to Derrida, where he calls deconstruction a 'historically well-determined little pedagogy'. In discussing this accusation, critics tend to pay attention to the 'petit pédagogie' aspect of Foucault's attack, but I think it's the other phrase ('historically well-determined') that contains Foucault's primary stinging claim: deconstruction is an anachronistic relic, the last gasp of a nineteenth-century transcendentalist mode of thinking, Hegel on steroids. Personal polemics aside, it seems to me that this is the difficult question that Foucault poses to Derrida: can you continue to locate the problems of the present always in reference to the horizon of nineteenth-century thought, or do you have to fashion a modality of thinking that moves beyond that (now long-gone) historicity?

While the question that Foucault poses to Derrida may initially seem a bit murky, I think it becomes clearer if we venture that Foucault pursues his overarching critique of Derrida less in terms of deconstruction's outdated 'metaphysics' than in terms of its portrait of 'life' as endless unthematisable desire (which for Foucault characterises the decisive intensification of biopower in the nineteenth century – this sense that life is a no longer a representable 'thing', but comprises a hidden secret animating living things from within). In short, and stated most polemically, Foucault argues that deconstruction mistakes a nineteenth-century European (essentially Hegelian) account of life and death for a transhistorical description of life 'itself'. And Derrida then deploys this historically quite specific conception of life as a bedrock definition of life itself, everywhere and since the year zero.

DERRIDA AND LIFE

To size up this Foucauldian counter-critique, we turn now to Derrida's work on the question of life. And this is a fortuitous turn, because at least since the publication of Martin Hagglund's *Radical Atheism: Derrida and the Time of Life*, Derrida has increasingly been seen as a philosopher of 'life itself'. This is obviously a big question, and one that would take us deep down the rabbit hole of Derrida's long engagement with Heidegger on the question of life, especially his work on Heidegger's parsing out of life among humans and animals. Recall Heidegger's infamous hierarchy of life-forms in his 1929–30 lecture course: the stone is *weltlos*, without world – stuck where it is; animals are *weltarm*, poor in world – more or less stuck where they are; whereas man has access to world, to possibility and transformation.[9] Derrida wants of course to question all kinds of moves within Heidegger's discourses on life – most consistently, he wonders about Heidegger's surety concerning humans' privileged access to these things called life and world, and likewise wonders whether there's ever any access to anything 'as such'.

Despite this thorough critique of Heidegger on the topic of animality, Derrida's late work continues to define life (and death) primarily through the conceptual horizon imported directly from Heidegger: that is, he continues to follow Heidegger in defining *life* through the thematic of *world*. For example, when it comes time to publish the French edition of his many memorial-funeral pieces (originally published in English as *The Work of Mourning*), Derrida re-names the collection *Each Time Unique, the End of the World* (*Chaque fois unique, la fin du monde*). In the introduction to *Chaque fois unique*, Derrida lays out what he calls the 'thesis' of the collection:

> The death of the other, not only but especially if one loves that other, does not announce an absence, a disappearance, the end of *this or that* life, that is to say, of the possibility of a world (always unique) to appear to a *given* living being. Death declares each time the end of the world in totality, the end of every possible world, and *each time the end of the world as unique totality, therefore irreplaceable and therefore infinite*. As if the *repetition* of the end of an infinite whole were once more possible: the end of the world *itself*, of the only world that exists, each time. Singularly. Irreversibly. For the other and in a strange way for the provisional survivor who endures this impossible experience. It is this that I would like to call 'the world'.[10]

As Derrida suggests, in a characteristically Levinasian challenge to Heidegger's sense of world as Dasein's relation to the abstract possibilities of Being, the Derridean world is opened by the radical singularity of the other(s), a finite world of future possibility that is each time unique. Understood as opening to the necessary finitude or alterity that marks 'our' lives, the world is haunted always by the end, by death, in so far as the finite temporality of mortality is what makes 'life' possible in the first place.

As Hagglund explains, it is the Derridean 'trace structure of time that is the condition for life in general. Whatever we do, we have always already said yes to the coming of the future, since without it nothing could happen.'[11] If life is defined by a singular being's relations to future possibilities (a being that is alive is inexorably open to the future and is likewise necessarily open to mortality), then death quite literally comprises the end of the world. At the end of a living thing's ability to endure through time, when it is no longer alive, that being does not escape time, but is left by death to live on (or not) through that very same trace structure (through, among other traces, the memories of the 'provisional survivor'). As Hagglund glosses this Derridean sense of 'world': 'The other is infinitely other – its alterity cannot be overcome or recuperated by anyone else – because the other is finite. . . . When someone dies it is not simply the end of someone who lives in the world; it is rather the end of the world as such, since each one is a singular and irretrievable origin of the world.'[12] Hagglund argues at great and convincing length that the Derridean world is a site where the only life is the life of finite beings open to the possibilities of the future (where there is no God or even the desirability thereof, hence the 'radical atheism' of Hagglund's title); and when one of those singular finite beings is no more, the unique 'world' that person had opened and inhabited ends as well.

Quite simply, if there is no other world, then death is each time the end of the whole world – the end of the infinite, of possibility. Derrida eloquently sums this up in his eulogy for Louis Althusser:

> What is coming to an end, what Louis is taking away with him, is not only something or other that we would have shared at some point or another, in one place or another, but the world itself, a certain origin of the world – his origin, no doubt, but also that of the world in which I lived, in which we lived a unique story. It is a world that is for us the whole world, the only world, and it sinks into an abyss from which no memory can save it – even if we keep the memory, and we will keep it.[13]

Which likewise explains Derrida's obsessive interest in the line from Paul Celan's 'Vast, Glowing Vault': 'The world is gone, I must carry you.'[14] After death, we 'live on' (or not) only as a series of traces in a series of other archives, other memories, other acts, other databases, other citations.

Importantly, Derrida's work on animality extends these concepts of life, death and world beyond the exclusively human realm (thereby posing his most serious question to Heidegger's analysis of death and world as exclusively the provenance of Dasein). For example, in the second year of the death penalty seminar (the session of 10 January 2001), Derrida insists that

> the death one makes or lets come . . . is not the end of this or that, this or that individual, the end of a who or a what in the world. Each time something dies [*ça meurt*], it's the end of the world. Not the end of a world, but of the world, of the whole of the world, of the infinite opening of the world. And this is the case for no matter what living being, from the tree to the protozoa, from the mosquito to the human, death is infinite, it is the end of the infinite. The finitude of the infinite [*Le fini de l'infini*].[15]

There is of course a lot that one could say about this astonishing Derridean opening of 'world' and (in)finitude beyond the human, but here I'd like to zero in on one very specific point: Derrida thematises world as a question of life and death, a unique relation wherein a 'living being' or a singular entity relates somehow to an 'infinite opening' (world as a drama wherein 'no matter what living being', human or otherwise, is dealing in some way with the 'finitude of the infinite').

However, given the definition of life that also gets configured here (as a singular entity's unique relation to the finitude of the world), it's not at all clear that many forms of what we routinely call 'life' – rhizomatic plants, for example – are technically among 'the living' in Derrida's scheme of things. (This despite Derrida's inclusion here of the tree, that most arborescent and individuated plant form.) As Rodolphe Gasché has written about Hagglund's work, it's becoming clearer that 'Derrida is essentially a philosopher of life, but of the only life there is – the life of finite beings'.[16] Here, I don't want particularly to put pressure on the Derridean sense that temporality is the decisive defining factor for 'finite beings' (the sense that living is essentially surviving – 'living on' in relation to an indefinite, but mortal, future). Rather I'd like to emphasise and put pressure on the Derridean requirement that life and world accrue only to singular, each time unique 'beings'. In short, if a kind of openness to the finite future within an individuated organism (a relation to world) is the ante to get in to the game of life, it seems clear that Foucault's concern about Derrida (he's mistaken a nineteenth-century, neo-Hegelian drama of life as desire for a transhistorical definition of life itself) is in fact spot on.

Hagglund is the commentator who has perhaps done the most extensive recent work on this question of life in Derrida. In a post-publication debate, Hagglund was asked about the ambiguity surrounding 'the question of the scope of "life"' in *Radical Atheism* – about the distinction between *différance* as a condition of (im)possibility for anything at all, and as the condition narrowly of living things and their logic of survival. He responds:

> My answer is that everything in time is surviving, but not everything is alive. . . . The isotope that has a rate of radioactive decay across several billion years is in fact surviving, since it remains and disintegrates over time, but it is indifferent to its survival, since it is not alive. The two midges [that Derrida recalls from a fossil dated 50 million years ago], on the other hand, have a project, need, and desire. Like any other living being, they cannot be indifferent to their own survival. This distinction is decisive for the definition of life in *Radical Atheism*. The reason I focus on life is because *only with the advent of life is there desire in the universe*. Survival is an unconditional condition for everything that is temporal, but only for a living being is the affirmation of survival unconditional, since only a living being cares about maintaining itself across an interval of time.[17]

Again, this all seems quite persuasive to me as a reading of Derrida: 'survival [living on] is the unconditional condition for everything' but not everything is 'a living being': isotopes or volcanoes exist in and change over time, but they are not 'alive' in so far as they have nothing analogous to interests or desires (which is to say, they have no world; to speak Lacan for a moment, one might say that they lack lack) – 'since only a living being cares about maintaining itself across an interval of time'.

But at the same time, this line of argumentation seems to double-down on the exigency of Foucault's critique of Derrida, and to deepen the Foucauldian suspicion concerning Derrida's refusal or inability to think historically about 'life'. Foucault would undoubtedly remain suspicious, in other words, of the stubborn Derridean sense that life is now, always was, and always will be primarily about a desiring relation to world – life everywhere entails a singular being that cares about maintaining itself across a desiring interval. However, you can't really think about the vegetable life of ecosystems, for example, on these terms – less because of the 'striving' requirement for life than because of the 'singular entity' requirement. And given the fact that out of the 100 trillion or so cells contained in a human body, only about 10 per cent are 'human' cells, it's not clear that we humans qualify as singular entities either.

In any case, here one could leave the specific orbit of Foucault and Derrida on the question of biopower to pivot to the growing consensus that, while Derrida's work on animality shows that his thought is not strictly speaking anthropomorphic, Derrida nevertheless remains a secretly human-subject-centred, or 'correlationist' thinker. The word 'correlationism' is coined by Quentin Meillassoux in *After Finitude* as an attempt to get back behind the Kantian Copernican revolution of subjectivity, and Meillassoux defines the term quite simply: 'Correlationism consists in disqualifying the claim that it is possible to consider the realms of subjectivity and objectivity independently of one another.'[18] For Meillassoux, and a series of other 'speculative realist' thinkers, it's the great 'outside' of the real that was lost with Kant, then further mystified by Hegel, bracketed by Husserl, and ignored as 'essentialist' or 'metaphysical' by virtually all continental existentialism and phenomenology. These modern and postmodern discourses remain (on Meillassoux's account) hopelessly filtered through (and thereby openly centred on) human subjectivity, precisely in so far as these philosophies all follow Kant in resolutely refusing to say anything at all about the real, or at least not without saying something at the same time about the perceiving subject. And it is precisely in this sense (accounting always for the each-time-unique human subject – for its language, idiom, finitude and history) that deconstruction has been painted as correlationist thinking par excellence. As Slavoj Žižek puts it, 'If there is a philosopher who effectively seems to be caught in the circle of what Meillassoux calls "failed correlationism", it is Derrida.'[19]

But I think that this critique fails to take into account Hagglund's argument that in Derrida not everything is alive – and even more importantly, that the conditions of possibility for life in Derrida (what he calls in various places *physis*, *différance*, the trace, etc.) are wholly indifferent to consciousness, much less to human life and death. I think one can grant to Meillassoux that 'life' is inexorably a correlationist discourse. However hard it is to define, the living is in practice most often differentiated from the nonliving precisely by the presence of a feedback loop of some kind; or at least virtually all definitions of life contain some defining sense of desire and response to immediate surroundings (to a thing's 'world'): feeding, growing, reproducing, 'stayin' alive'. I think it's easy to grant that life as we know it is correlationist (necessarily relational or supplemental in terms of the thing that's alive), without having to accept that reality is simply equitable with any subjective experience of it (human or otherwise). Arguing that life remains inexorably defined by relationality does not necessarily commit you to agreeing that, in Jacob von Uexkull's great correlationist phrase, '*All reality is subjective experience*.'[20] Life as we know it is certainly tied up with a singular entity's striving to persist in time; but it's certainly not the case (in Derrida, at least) that there is no reality at all without this particular sense of life. There exist myriad things that are not alive in Derrida, but that hardly means that nonliving things aren't real. In fact, it's not the human subject but the indifferent, violent emergence and passing away of *physis* or *différance* that is perhaps the privileged name for the real in Derrida:[21] *physis* is real, but not alive; nor is *différance*. But in the end, there's no 'correlating' with the real, in so far as these radically neutral principles of emergence are hardly beholden for their existence to human or animal life. Quite the opposite, as we have seen: *physis* or the trace or whatever name you'd choose for the Derridean real will necessarily pre-date (is in Meillassoux's terminology an 'ancestor' to) this or that being, species, or form of life.

Say what you will about Derrida's obsessive focus on various conditions of (im) possibility for human thought and action, but in the end there's no 'correlating' with the grey neutrality of Derridean concepts like *différance*. Which makes Derrida's view of life less vitalist or realist than, as Henry Staten suggests, 'naturalist' – materialist with a twist. As Staten writes, 'the strong naturalist view, from which Derrida does not deviate, holds that matter organised in the right way brings forth life, but denies that life is somehow hidden in matter and just waiting to manifest itself. . . . Life is a possibility of materiality, but as a vastly improbable possibility, by far the exception rather than the rule.'[22] While this seems quite convincing to me as a reading of Derrida, I would however point out that it does decisively reinscribe the very murky *je ne sais quoi* – the grey transcendental horizon – that Foucault diagnoses as the discursive move that birthed biopolitical 'life' as we know it in the nineteenth century. Life in Derrida remains defined as a singular finite entity's relation to abstract and largely empty possibility – to being and to a realm of world. Thereby, life remains an unfathomably rare thing, a nearly mystical occurrence, a 'vastly improbable possibility'.

Similarly, to circle back to the Agamben between Derrida and Foucault with which we began, for Derrida death remains the ultimate in tragic pathos (the loss of everything, of the whole world – which is again to say death remains understood wholly within the orbit of that tarrying with the negative that was birthed in Hegel and so decisively intensified in the nineteenth century). Whereas for Foucauldian biopower, death is less a tragic drama of unredeemable loss than it is a question of medico-political administration – in his famous formulation of biopower, it's a matter of managing populations by making some groups live and letting others die (in contrast to the anachronistic sovereign power of making die or letting live). And this *différend* concerning the primary sense of life and death is no longer merely an academic spat, as a whole 'baby boom' generation of folks born after the Second World War stares down this question of being made to live or left to die.

Meantime, in so far as we are beginning to see real signs of climate change leading to global mass extinction as a terrifying backdrop to these more prosaic questions of long-term disability and nursing-home care, it would seem there are substantial costs to continuing to see death in this individual, tragic, sovereign register – pivoting primarily on particular beings and their life or death. One might in addition wonder concerning Derrida, is there an 'each time unique, the end of the species'? Or does thinking life and death primarily through the individual organism largely preclude or at least de-emphasise that kind of aggregate, species-level or 'post-human' thinking?[23] At the dawn of the twenty-first century, staring down for the first time what looks like the inevitability (rather than the abstract possibility) of human extinction, maybe we are or soon will be experiencing a shift in our understanding and practices of life, a morphing every bit as radical as the one that Foucault suggests birthed life as we know it in the nineteenth century.

Perhaps it seems overly breathless to say that life itself is or soon will be undergoing a mutation, but it's probably worth remembering that the dominant human-sciences understanding of life has already changed radically at least twice in the past 100 years (from the vitalism of the late nineteenth century, to the sense of life as information with the discovery of DNA, to the micro-biological understanding of life and/as genetic manipulation in the present).[24] Likewise, I think we could agree that global climate disaster impacts conceptions of human life in a very different way than did the Cold War possibility of nuclear war leading to mass extinction. The apocalypse of so-called 'mutually assured destruction', as Derrida himself pointed out several times, tended to preserve the tragic, hidden pathos of unthematisable death visited upon us at a moment's notice.[25] But global climate change will likely prove to be a different kind of life and death situation, with less sudden tragedy and more slow erosion of human habitat and massive displacement of populations (about a quarter of the globe's population presently lives in areas projected to be under water by the end of this century). Which is to suggest that the question of human life and death in the twenty-first century will likely prove to be an even more intensely and thoroughly administrative quandary. And looking forward from the neoliberal consensus that seems to have formed in these early decades of the century, one has to wonder how humankind can respond to this large-scale administrative challenge in the era of the privatising, small-government triumph that both Derrida and Foucault diagnosed towards the end of their lives. Contemporary neoliberal nation-states are set up to protect and serve the very privatising pathos of nineteenth-century subjectivity; capitalism's dialectical drama is fuelled by individual desires (by consumption), and any 'we' remains based on a prior thought of the striving 'I', in Hegel's famous formulation. So any kind of large-scale inter-governmental thinking about the future (which is specifically to say, high global taxes on assets and fossil fuels coupled with massive, coordinated global nation-states' spending on huge protection projects) remains economic heresy in the present; and it likewise augurs electoral suicide in the future for any politicians either bold or stupid enough to propose such governmental (rather than privatising) solutions going forward. To paraphrase an observation of Fredric Jameson's, right now we're far better equipped to imagine extinction – the end of the world – than to imagine a viable alternative to global neoliberal capitalism.[26]

In the end, and given this portrait of the present and future, we may want to follow Foucault in thinking that death, like life, really *isn't* what it used to be; and that continuing to think about these species-level biopolitical questions on a nineteenth-century scaffolding may be less a philosophical or academic disagreement than it is quite literally a matter of life and death.[27]

NOTES

1. Jacques Derrida, *The Beast and the Sovereign, Vol. 1*, trans. Geoffrey Bennington (Chicago: University of Chicago Press, 2011), p. 317. Hereafter cited in the text as BS.
2. Derrida first suggests misrepresentation in Agamben's reading of Heidegger, and then in relation to Foucault (BS, 324, 329).

3. Michel Foucault, *The Order of Things: An Archaeology of the Human Sciences* (New York: Pantheon, 1970), pp. 127–8. Hereafter cited in the text as OT.
4. Re 1870 and homosexuality, see Foucault's 19 March 1975 lecture in *Abnormal: Lectures at the College de France, 1974–75*, trans. Graham Burchell (New York: Picador, 2004), p. 310, and *History of Sexuality, Vol. 1*, trans. Robert Hurley (New York: Vintage, 1980), p. 43; on the author, see Foucault's 'What is an Author?' in *Language, Counter-Memory, Practice*, ed. D. F. Bouchard (New York: Cornell, 1977), pp. 113–38.
5. On the concept of 'intensification' in Foucault, see my *Foucault Beyond Foucault* (Stanford: Stanford University Press, 2008). On the specific question of origin in and around Foucault, see his thoughts about Nietzsche's three senses of origin in 'Nietzsche, Genealogy, History', *Aesthetics, Method, Epistemology: Essential Works of Michel Foucault, Volume 2*, ed. James Faubion (New York: The New Press, 1998). Clearly, Foucault does not see the nineteenth century in Europe as the *Ursprung* of biopower, but as a point of decisive intensification, a 'descent' or re-working of human life's relations to power.
6. Foucault, 'What is an Author?', p. 120.
7. Michel Foucault, *The Archaeology of Knowledge*, trans. A. M. Sheridan Smith (New York: Pantheon, 1972), p. 107. Hereafter cited in the text as AK.
8. Foucault, 'What is an Author?', p. 120.
9. Specifically, Heidegger writes about life and world: 'the main points of our approach are encapsulated in three theses: [1.] The stone is worldless; [2.] The animal is poor in world; [3.] Man is world-forming.' Martin Heidegger, *The Fundamental Concepts of Metaphysics: World, Finitude, Solitude*, trans. William McNeil and Nicholas Walker (Bloomington: Indiana University Press, 2001), p. 184. If world is 'the accessibility of beings', then one might initially translate: stone has no access to things or beings; the animal has some constricted access to things or beings; and man, one might say in a Heideggerian turn of phrase, has access to the question of access itself – to what he will call elsewhere the 'worlding of the world'.
10. Jacques Derrida, *Chaque fois unique, la fin du monde*, ed. Pascale-Anne Brault and Michael Naas (Paris: Galilée, 2003), p. 9.
11. Martin Hagglund, *Radical Atheism: Derrida and the Time of Life* (Stanford: Stanford University Press, 2008), p. 96.
12. Ibid., p. 111.
13. Jacques Derrida, *The Work of Mourning*, ed. and trans. Pascale-Anne Brault and Michael Naas (Chicago: University of Chicago Press, 2001), p. 115, sentence rearranged. See also Derrida's thoughts in his letter to Max Loreau's widow: 'I lack the strength to speak publicly and to recall each time another end of the world, the same end, another, and each time is nothing less than an origin of the world, each time the sole world, the unique world, which, in its end, appears to us as it was at the origin – sole and unique – and shows us what it owes to the origin, that is to say, what will have been, beyond every future anterior' (ibid., p. 95). See also Derrida's recollection for his friend Jean-Marie Benoist: 'death takes from us not only some particular life within the world, some moment that belongs to us, but each time, without limit, someone through whom the world, and first of all our own world, will have opened up in a both finite and infinite – mortally infinite – way' (ibid., p. 107).
14. See Derrida's *Sovereignties in Question: The Poetics of Paul Celan*, trans. Thomas Dutoit (New York: Fordham University Press, 2005), especially pp. 141 ff., as well as numerous places throughout *The Beast and the Sovereign* lectures.
15. Jacques Derrida, *Séminaire: Peine de mort, II (2000–2001)*, ed. Geoffrey Bennington, Marc Crépon and Thomas Dutoit (Paris: Galilée, 2014), pp. 118–19. My thanks to Michael Naas, from the Derrida Translation Project, for offering me this citation from the not-yet-published English translation of the second year of Derrida's death penalty seminar. Naas cites it in his *The End of the World and Other Teachable Moments: Jacques Derrida's Final Seminar* (New York: Fordham University Press, 2014), ch. 2 n.14.

16. This quotation is from Gasché's endorsment of Hagglund's *Radical Atheism*, on the back cover.
17. Martin Hagglund, 'The Challenge of Radical Atheism: A Response', *New Centennial Review*, 9:1 (2009), pp. 245–6.
18. Quentin Meillassoux, *After Finitude*, trans. Ray Brassier (London: Bloomsbury, 2010), p. 5.
19. Slavoj Žižek, *Less Than Nothing* (London: Verso, 2012), p. 642.
20. Jacob von Uexkull, *Theoretical Biology* (San Diego: Harcourt Brace, 1926), p. xv.
21. For an attempt to reconcile Derrida's thought with 'speculative realism', see Michael Marder, *The Event of the Thing: Derrida's Post-Deconstructive Realism* (Toronto: University of Toronto Press, 2011).
22. Henry Staten, 'Derrida, Dennett, and the Ethico-Political Project of Naturalism', *Derrida Today*, 1:1 (2008), p. 40.
23. For some thoughts on Derrida and climate change, see the essays collected in Tom Cohen, *Telemorphosis: Theory in the Era of Climate Change* (Ann Arbor: Open Humanities Press, 2012). For the sharpest contemporary thinking about extinction, see Claire Colebrook, *Death of the Post-Human: Essays on Extinction* (Ann Arbor: Open Humanities Press, 2013).
24. On the latest in genetic manipulation and life (which is to say, the ability to manipulate genes to create life rather than merely to 'read' the life-information contained in DNA), see Ross Thyer and Jared Ellefson, 'Synthetic Biology: New Letters for Life's Alphabet', *Nature*, 509 (15 May 2014), pp. 291–2, and Denis A. Malyshev et al., 'A Semi-synthetic Organism with an Expanded Genetic Alphabet', *Nature*, 509 (15 May 2014), pp. 385–8.
25. See Derrida's essays on apocalypse, 'Of an Apocalyptic Tone Recently Adopted in Philosophy', *Oxford Literary Review*, 6:2 (1984) and 'No Apocalypse, Not Now', *Diacritics*, 14:2 (1984).
26. See Fredric Jameson, 'Future City', *New Left Review*, 21 (2003), p. 76.
27. This chapter is excerpted in part from my *Plant Theory: Biopower and Vegetable Life* (Stanford, CA: Stanford University Press, 2015).

CHAPTER 14

Philosophy on Trial: The Crisis of Deciding Between Foucault and Derrida

Peter Gratton

> On the basis of this juridical form of *krinein* [to judge, to decide, as in a *krisis*, which has its root in this word], a singular type of true discourse appears which is linked to the *dikaion* [the just], to the *nomos*, to the order of the world and the organization of the city. It is still *very far* from what is true discourse *for us*, but, through multiple transformations, *ours derives from it*. We belong to this dynasty of *krinein*.
>
> (Michel Foucault)[1]

> The instant of the *krinein* or *krisis* (decision, choice, judgment, discernment) . . . is one of the essential 'themes' or 'objects' of deconstruction.
>
> (Jacques Derrida)[2]

How are we to judge, to decide, to put in order the suits and countersuits between Foucault and Derrida generations after their mutual accusations were first levelled? Prosecutors and defenders have long been arrayed on all sides, even as, until this volume, the charges in this ongoing litigation – what Lyotard would have called their *différend*, their 'phrases in dispute' – were often little understood. Part of this has to do with academic politics: defenders of Derrida and Foucault were facing larger forces within and beyond the academy convicting both of crimes against reason, sentencing each to be ill-read as relativists or postmodernists. Part of this, too, has to do with the nature of their own testimony: Derrida's 'Cogito and the History of Madness' takes up an important text by Foucault, *History of Madness*, but a relatively early one, and Foucault's own replies in the early 1970s were both delayed and sharply polemical, to the point that readers could often suppose that there was more going on – something that history had not yet revealed in the personalities or psychologies between them – than competing testimonies over the proper reading of Descartes or the ostracism of madness in early modernity (or *as* modernity). After all, in the various trials over the fate of reason and history and hence what has been willed to us from post-Hegelian thought, should not both have been witnesses for each other against their often aligned prosecutors speaking in the name, if not always on the actual side, of reason, Enlightenment, and so on? Should they not have stepped forward together into open court to critique and question, *à la* Socrates, a series of plaintiffs who knew little of their work but perpetuated talk about protecting the children from their impieties in university classrooms and elsewhere? They were both, too quickly in philosophy, facing a summary judgment without evidence or explanation beyond the rumours of a French thought gone mad.

Both, of course, saw in Nietzsche a fundamental change in the west, a glimmer of the last daylight of a thinking beyond metaphysics, not least given his arguments concerning a long Greek thinking still with us. As Derrida puts it in *Of Grammatology*, Nietzsche 'has written that writing – and first of all his own – *is not originarily* subordinate to the *logos* and truth'.[3] Or per Foucault, just several years later in his first lectures at the Collège de France, 'Nietzsche was the first to release the desire to know from the sovereignty of knowledge (*connaissance*) itself: to re-establish the distance and exteriority that Aristotle cancelled, a cancellation that had been maintained *by all philosophy*.'[4] Each was interested in the limits of the performativity of language, of the declarations of knowledge, which philosophy disavows in order to get underway. For philosophy to be sovereign over truth means that it must have no inherent stake in the mundane games of power or any geographic, temporal situatedness out of which it arrived. Both followed Nietzsche in attempting to cut or rethread crucial strands in this tradition by pointing towards a certain thinking of *krisis* and *krinein* that marks the event or arrival of what we call philosophy: the model of philosophy as disinterested and without its own desire, as something standing beyond any political impetus and interests, which they both argued was aligned with the production from ancient Greece forward of a sovereign judging of and over the law. This for them was productive of the dominant juridical model in the west – denying the motives and motifs of the law of force behind that which has the force of law. There is no thinking of one without the other: the model of metaphysics is a certain political *nemein* or ordering, which then becomes the *theoria* that ought to lead all praxis.[5]

Key texts here for Foucault would be 'Nietzsche, Genealogy, and History', as well as his 1970–1 *Lectures on the Will to Know*, where in the first four seminars, Foucault moves in astounding order to demonstrate an isonomy between an incipient metaphysics and what he will later simply dub 'sovereign' or 'juridical power', while specifically looking at a genealogy of the meaning of the sign and a whole series of discourses around *krinein* – whose dynasty, he says, we still live under. Foucault argues that there is a fundamental division, itself a *krisis*, though he doesn't name it as such, that occurs when truth is moved away from the law courts and the arguments of sophists, since it is said to be irreconcilable with power.[6] The judge, those 'kings of justice',[7] are characteristic or even paradigmatic of a power/knowledge performed through the juridical, though of course, as the opening quotation above from the *Lectures* shows, Foucault will develop in the 1970s both how the west continues and discontinues this thinking of power – 'It is still *very far*', he writes, ' from what is true discourse *for us*, but, through multiple transformations, *ours derives from it*.' The footnote for this sentence in the *Lectures*, by the editors, notes:

> How not [to] recall here Heidegger's comment on Nietzsche: 'the primordial Greek conception of beings congeals into something well known and taken for granted in the course of Western history to date . . . We need not follow in detail this two-world doctrine and its historical transformations, which coincide with the main stages of Western metaphysics.'[8]

Everything will come down to or be decided between Derrida and Foucault concerning the just measure, the proper or right place to make the cut in the distance between that which is 'very far' but nevertheless is so close as to be familial, to be a given legacy that despite all our revolutions and transformations, despite all our denials about a given parentage, is still *ours*. In any event, this will bring Foucault, as is well known, to his thinking of discipline and other forms of power heterogeneous to the law and its long legacies going back to the Greek thinking of *krinein*. Here another decisive cut away from Derrida can be made, given the long focus in Derrida's explicit political discussions on sovereignty up to his last lectures in *The Beast and the Sovereign* (2001–3), even as both endeavoured to think the relation between propositional truth and the dominant western thinking of the law. Combining the thinking of these two, we arrive after many steps at the formal style of philosophy up to and perhaps including this chapter: the writer will present to you the facts of the case – textual evidence and other clues and traces left behind – all to adjudicate and decide, for example, between Foucault and Derrida, while suggesting that the facts could only have led to this coming formal conclusion, a summation and summing up of all the differences at issue, which one suspects led to the picking of the evidence in the first place. There is never a disinterested or third party on the scene to adjudicate between and among a given opposition, even as philosophy in its dominant modes is written in the third person.[9]

Let's for the instant, though, give in to this madness, that is, the sovereign presumption to decide between Derrida and Foucault – recalling that Kierkegaard's dictum that the 'instant of decision is madness' opens Derrida's 'Cogito and the History of Madness' and thus begins the litigation at issue.[10] The decision marks the perpetual *krisis* or originary *krinein* of philosophy: to occlude the decision, the instant of madness that can have no rational ground, by which it begins, and that it repeats. For both Foucault and Derrida, this problem of the sovereign *krinein* has been with us since Greece. By this point in this book, you are aware of the dossier of the case, but standing like a sovereign judge let me reframe the supposed facts of the case before rendering a decision or verdict between Foucault and Derrida. Is this not what I owe to you? To do justice, to paraphrase the title of Derrida's last extensive treatment of Foucault, to Derrida *and* Foucault? To render an account, to give my reasoning, to share it out while marking its irreducible instant of decision, all while providing a history of the present in which I arrived at that decision, a 'history of the present' that collates and combines under an *eidos* heterogeneous ensembles of events and touching contingencies, for example those events and texts under the names Derrida and Foucault? Is this not what any history as such wants – we are coming to the crux of the *krisis* between Derrida and Foucault – namely to present a course of reasoning, a rationale, to what has been decided about a given history or series of events, even as that decision itself is irreducible to that history: we narrate for want of something more, while each narration – history is economics; history is the unfolding of reason; history is great men and their patriarchy, and so on, no matter how complicated the historical apparatus or *dispositif* – is produced through and occludes this decision, as if the decision were rendered from on high, or, which is the same thing, as if this history could only lead to *this* decision. History is presented, even or especially in the case of the history of these two figures, as if – and this is the fiction of every sovereign moment[11] – the decision or *krisis* (to include this or that evidence, or even to think of such and such *as* evidence in the first place) had not happened, as if it arrived robotically and was causally determined by that history as presented by its very march of reason. As if the judge were rendering a disinterested and undecided result, a *fait accompli* always already accomplished before the historian or philosopher got underway. The result could not have been otherwise. Which is why any decision would have to be mad – following from no ground, historical cause or reason, and is thus exterior, extrinsic and exceptional to historical reason, and to any possible history. And which is why one should doubt any attempt to write a history or genealogy of the *krinein*, of the decision, of the event in its mad arrival.

As such, this dossier will be necessarily reductive, as all histories, even a 'history of the present', would have to be. As we will come to it – but you would rightly by now say it's already been decided – we will have to note that there are perhaps greater or lesser reductions or *epoché*, and this is precisely what is at issue between Derrida and Foucault, even as any comparison between them begins by trading on some common sense between and among us as to what these proper names mean. Given all of this, let's finally look at the bill of particulars.

'I would say there has been for several years a Heideggerian habit', Foucault argued in an oft-quoted 1975 interview, whereby 'all philosophy that takes up a history of thought or of a branch of knowledge at least ought to begin in ancient Greece and actually never go beyond it.'[12] This is, he notes, what is 'taken up in France by Derrida', producing a 'kind of history in the form of a metaphysical crystallization', through which everything is eventually found to be not just a footnote to Plato, as the old philosophical cliché goes, but directly emanating from that philosophy, such that no distance, no measure of transformation from the Platonic moment can be countenanced. In this view, Derrida would be arguing that we have never escaped Platonism, and his 'troubling' 'Hellenic archaism' avoids speaking to the ways in which 'one or two [of the most recent] centuries seem to yield a number of phenomena that are tied to our social structures, our economy, our way of thinking'.[13] For his part Derrida thought Foucault too often ignored something like the long term, since his 'typical gesture consists in hardening into an opposition a more complicated play of differences that stretches a more extended time'.[14] This allowed him to 'set up as ruptures and binary oppositions a range of complex differences', such as the move from an era of visibility of punishments (e.g., capital punishments and various tortures in juridical power) to its invisibility (e.g., disciplinary power). Thus we have the long and the short of their debate. But beyond this, which is documented well in this volume over the Cartesian Cogito and the history of madness, the crux of their dispute focused on the limits and legacies of Platonism and its continued applicability to what happens today – and hence how to think for what tomorrow.

In his 'Reply to Derrida', published in the Japanese journal *Paideia* in 1972, Foucault is clearer about the stakes at play than in his 'My Body, This Paper, This Fire', published in the 1972 edition of *Histoire de la folie*, not least since that paper's focus on Descartes acts against Foucault's avowed attempt to show that philosophy, far from the central locus of history, is subject to discourses it can never master. Foucault writes:

> What I have tried to show (but it was probably not clear to my own eyes when I was writing the *History of Madness*) is that philosophy is neither historically nor logically a foundation of knowledge; but that there are conditions and rules for the formation of knowledge to which philosophical discourse is subject, in any given period, in the same manner as any other form of discourse with rational pretention.[15]

Foucault picks out three postulates to which he believes Derrida assents. Given the legacies of deconstruction and the futures of genealogy, but also given that many have not kicked the Heideggerian habit, the questions Foucault raises are as relevant as ever.

1. First, Foucault argues that Derrida believes all knowledge *as such* has a fundamental relation to philosophy, that is, every diagnosis of a social dilemma leads back to some fundamental problem in metaphysics – one can think of much of Heidegger's post-1930s career: the rise of Nazism (and his part in it), the *Gestell* of technicity, and so on, all lead back, in one way or another, through Descartes' representationalism and further back to some lost origin from before Plato to which we can never return – or perhaps only if a god can save us. If there is a first precedent to be set in deciding between Derrida and Foucault, or a precedent left for us to think from this judgment, it remains here, since a whole slew of thinkers can be brought into the brig to stand charge for a certain archaic Hellenism, for example, not just Heidegger's rather rancid allegiance of Greek and German thinking, but also the early Nietzsche of *The Birth of Tragedy*, or Arendt's valorisation of an early Greek thinking of *archē* as 'leading' and not 'ruling' prior to Platonic philosophy, as well as Agamben's declaration that the west has not 'succeeded in constructing the link between *zōē* and *bios*' (a distinction he believes is grounded in Aristotle's writings) because it 'carr[ies] out the metaphysical task' that causes a 'fracture' that gives us modernity's biopolitics.[16] Such a Hellenism renders the west in a quite Christian fashion, as an unredeemable fall from a pre-philosophical grace, and we are only ever living out the wages of this fall.

2. Foucault argues, using the example of 'Cogito and the History of Madness',

that Derrida's suggestion is that if one can be shown to be wrong in a rendering of a philosopher, then this 'error . . . will have shown the law that unconsciously rules everything that [Foucault] could say about police regulations in the seventeenth century, unemployment in the classical era',[17] and so on. Without the truth of philosophy, one is 'naïve' (a term Derrida does pepper around in 'Cogito') and one is judged to have committed a 'mortal sin', as Foucault puts it, that condemns the whole of the work.[18]

3. Following from this, Foucault writes:

> [F]or Derrida, there is no sense in discussing the analysis that I propose of this series of events [that is, the events that would mark the separation of reason and madness, as well as the geographical incarceration of those deemed mad, as outlined in *History of Madness*] . . . in his view [it is naïve] in wanting to write history on the basis of the derisory events that are the confinement of a few tens of thousands of people, or the setting up of an extra-judiciary State police; it would have been sufficient, more than amply so, to rehearse once again the repetition of philosophy by Descartes, who himself repeated the Platonic excess. For Derrida, what happened in the seventeenth century could only be a 'sample' (i.e., the repetition of the identical) or a 'model' (i.e. the inexhaustible excess of origin). *He does not know the category of the singular event.*[19]

Here is the fundament of the charge, that Derrida's Platonist reading of history is ultimately homogeneous and ever reducible to an idea, even if one would have to ask if there is such as thing as a 'category' of the 'event', as if it could be given over to an *episteme* or a genealogy, although to begin to ask that question is to start to fall to the critique, that is, the *krisis* and *krinein* Foucault makes above.

Can one *think* otherwise? The *aporia* faced by any given history is that it must, as Foucault puts it in *History of Madness*, though it is a point continuous with all of his later writings – though by the end of this sentence, you will see we need to suspend any such thinking of 'continuity' – must at once begin with a working definition of such things as madness, power and even history while also denying that 'facts in their positivity', as he puts it, fit some 'immutable identity' awaiting the investigator.[20] This is the aporetic spiralling of the hermeneutic circle, where one must enter a given investigation with a pre-understanding of a given x in order to get underway. But as Derrida will ask, can one have this precomprehension concerning madness – or even alterity and death, as we will see? Can one reduce sovereignty to a law? And then what about the decision, the *krinein* of a *krisis*?

There is little doubt that from 1963 until his last mentions of Foucault in lectures forty years later, collected in *The Beast and the Sovereign*, Derrida read all of Foucault's work as continuous with the *History of Madness*, a point that, long after the 'Reply to Derrida', will have made Foucault right about a mortal sin, an inescapable guilt that damned him to a hell of a misreading by Derrida, who refused, as he had done for so many other figures, to read Foucault *otherwise*. Not only did Foucault move between the different strategies of archaeology and genealogy, but he repeatedly re-read and re-treated the same texts and sets of discourses in varied ways from Ancient Greece onwards. Nevertheless, Derrida's long-held view is that by offering to think the 'birth' of modernity, or periodising history into different *epistemes*, he risked reifying under an idea each side of what Foucault called the 'threshold' he was studying.[21] That is, he read history, according to Derrida, with an eye to reducing its multiplicity to an *eidos*. Instead of differing and deferring historical thinking, temporalising the very concept, Foucault spatialised history into strata that at the same time forced the event into a linear path. In order to describe a supposed event – the great internment of modernity, the expulsion of madness from reason, the birth of the clinic, the breakthrough from an *episteme* of representation to the empirico-transcendental doublet, or the 'birth of biopolitics', to cite only a few examples – means inscribing that event within a linearity of before and after and thus reducing temporalisation to the linearity of the line. Moreover, Derrida's long hypothesis is that marking any such event not only reifies it – and thus takes it out of its eventness – but occludes or disavows the *decision* that meant placing the event here and not there, etc., since one says the event happens in the 'positivity of things', and not in the writing of the event.

In his first year of *The Beast and Sovereign* lectures, Derrida returns to Foucault, by way of a longer critique of Agamben, both of whom should lead us 'to reconsider, precisely, a way of thinking history, of doing history, of articulating a logic and a rhetoric onto a thinking of the history or the event'.[22] The stakes here are decisive, and should provoke a crisis in anyone who thinks we can borrow on common sense notions of history and so forth. Derrida writes:

> To call into question . . . the concern to periodize [in Foucault but also Agamben] . . . is not to reduce the eventness or singularity of the event: on the contrary. Rather I'm tempted to think that this singularity of the event is all the more irreducible and confusing, as it should be, if we give up that linear history that remains, in spite of all the protests [Foucault and Agamben] would no doubt raise against this image, the common temptation of both . . . ([e.g.] the modernity that comes after the classical age, the *epistemés* that follow on from each other and render each obsolete . . .) . . . To give up the idea of a decisive and founding event is anything but to ignore the eventness that marks and signs, in my view, what happens, precisely *without any foundation or decision coming along to make it certain*.[23]

Where a Foucauldian history of the present looks to a given institution or *dispositif* to denaturalise it by demonstrating the place and time of its birth (even if that birth is not a punctual point but an occurrence over a long period) Derrida looks to show a certain relation to a metaphysics of presence and ontotheology. With Foucault, we could argue for thinking an excess of events irreducible to the legacies of metaphysics, however reread and deconstructed. The post-Heideggerian habit of rendering all in terms of metaphysics is not just reductive but chokes history to death. Everything then gets read not just in terms of an historical *a priori* (the emphasis on the latter, not the former), but in the Platonic manner of an anamnesis of a forgotten origin to which one's death could only mark a return. No doubt Derrida's texts are replete with references to events well beyond the scope of what is happening within the supposed texts of philosophy (how could it be otherwise?), but for Foucault these must bracketed as inessential to philosophy's own march, no matter what Derrida says about questioning philosophy's limits and deconstructing its founding concepts. But does not the obverse – the pretence not to be doing philosophy – risk offering a blind empiricism of the 'positivity of things'? Are there not *aporias* to the genealogical method that Foucault must paper over in order to get underway? Witnessing the 'positivity of things' disavows an *a priori* decision (even if Foucault always implicates himself in his own discourses' stakes in power/knowledge) by which certain strands of the legacies of the west are rethreaded while others are not. But more importantly – and this becomes the problem, I believe, of all thinking that offers an immanence of power relations – all must be knowable, in principle, to the genealogical gaze, that is, there is no *other* or unconscious to the archive. If the method is to show, with each passing concept or institution, its genealogy and heritage, then one brings the event always back within a totality all-too-determined and knowable. This is what is at stake in Derrida's 'Cogito and the History of Madness', where he asks if a history of *madness* is possible since to write such a history means, to use a Levinasian formulation, to reduce its alterity to a measure of the Same. And *mutatis mutandis*, so too with any *event* or even the Other as such (if there can be an Other 'as such'). As Derrida puts it in 'Cogito', but it is in principle a problem for the event and for anything *exceptional* to discourses, 'Everything transpires as if Foucault *knew* what "madness" means.'[24] To move along in the history of this debate and thus to be simplistic, one could see a Foucauldian looking to the widespread use of the 'event' in Continental circles to ask after its genealogy, that is, the historical a priori that is the condition of possibility for its thinking. And yet it is precisely such an alterity or exceptionality that it cannot think, since these are heterogeneous to the order of knowing, even as power/*knowledge*.

At one level, Derrida's critique of Foucault operates by asking after the metaphysical unthought that he nevertheless repeats. That is, what ontotheological trope does Foucault claim to resist – by taking his distance from philosophy – but despite himself reinscribes throughout his own work? We all think of this as a central *modus* of Derrida's works. A certain Derridean dictum would stipulate that one can't use a set of terms (history, subject, reason, fraternity, and so on) without bringing along a long philosophical heritage. And if the claim is to be doing 'nonphilosophy', then one already knows what counts for philosophy and its limits.

But following along from the hypothesis that genealogy must render all to a certain knowability and thus a structure with no outside, we should clarify another oft-used *modus operandi* of deconstruction. Derrida argues that philosophers often testify to a given concept while using a common sense notion that they then reify at a 'higher' theoretical level. This he clearly believes is at issue in Foucault's *History of Madness*, that he exports onto history a *known*, commonsensical notion of madness, even as he talks about it as reason's other. But one finds this often in Derrida's texts. Let's pull an important moment from Derrida's late set of lectures on the death penalty, which circle around a certain thinking of the decision and thus the dynasty of *krinein*:

> My hypothesis today is that all the alleged pre-comprehensions of the meaning of the word 'death' [he goes onto discuss the supposed 'refinements' of Heidegger] must rely, even as they deny it, on so-called common sense, on the alleged objective and familiar knowledge, judged to be indubitable, of what separates a state of death from a state of life, that is, of the supposed objectifiable instant that separates living from dying.[25]

Can one do a genealogy or archaeology of death? Is there a death *itself*, however historical, that is not 'beyond power', to cite Derrida's 1986 memorial lecture to Foucault, which is to say the same thing, 'beyond knowledge'? Does the archaeologist or genealogist ever touch *on* death? And where to begin if not from a pre-comprehension of what we know we mean when we say death, and, again, so too for a genealogy of alterity, of madness, of the event, of history, and indeed, of freedom, of sovereignty and the decision.

THE DECISION

By this point, you await the decision, the *krinein*, the judgment that divides and comes down to the moment of the instant, even if as a decision it accedes to no given rule or forseeability. Let me begin by saying that the decision *between* Foucault and Derrida, or which amounts to the same, *between* what we think we mean by 'genealogy' and 'deconstruction', cannot be on the order of an either/or, nor a both/and, such as those who find in them just differing projects taking on different types of discourses or 'regions of application'.[26] For there is no deconstruction as such, nor genealogies, without reducing them to a certain formula or formalism and thus removing the questions of historicity at the heart of these works. Which is to say, we cannot remove their thinking from the specific genealogies and events of deconstruction arriving in their texts, that is, the political interventions that mark their writings. There is, nevertheless, a world of difference between a thinking of immanence and the quasi-transcendental. The latter no doubt risks mystification: there is always an excess and thus one could simply privilege that excess over the known and the knowable, and hence surround oneself on all sides by what we could only know to be unknowable: death, freedom, the other, madness, and so on. It risks a never-ending trial – we fear it will never come to a decision – of our most closely held concepts, those that we think we know when we speak and whose genealogy we could write. It could simply privilege – and I would argue all of these oppositions are in principle aligned – *krinein* over *krisis*, transcendence over immanence, alterity over the same, the event over continuity, madness over reason, contingency over necessity, and so on, even if the thinking of each requires a thinking of the other, and therefore a genealogy of their uses even as we are attuned to a thinking beyond these oppositions.

To come down to a decision here would be precisely to rewrite and redetermine where each discusses the decision, the *krinein* and *krisis* of interminable critique. In Foucault's 1970–1 lecture course, and as his work on power/knowledge developed in the 1970s, the sovereign *krinein* will always be related to the 'central and unambiguous role' of *nomos* and the law,[27] and the decision is thus calculated in terms of the law, as if the sovereign moment were not that which exempted itself from the law, and as if the decision's utter relatability to the law meant one could render a law of its use.[28] The *krisis* would be that at once one should and justly write the history of the decision, of its conceptuality, of its determinations from within a system whose dating would be decisive. One would need to adjudicate, as Foucault and Derrida do in different places and different ways, the manner in which the decision comes to dominate what we think we understand by a 'western' 'tradition', that is, as a free act made on the basis of a previous knowledge, like the making of the judgment after passing through the evidence of a case. This informs the phantasm of the sovereign decision, one that is said to follow from the law and the evidence of the particular, an instant of God-like omniscience that orders the political and is an original presence giving it its meaning. Derrida writes:

> Even if it multiplies discourses to the point of an endless repetition of the theory of the law [and Foucault's work in such places *as Society Must Be Defended* was to follow many of these discourses, up to the present, in terms of biopower and nationalism] or of every political rhetoric, sovereignty itself (if there is one and if it is pure) always keeps quiet in the very ipseity of the moment proper to it, a moment that is but the stigmatic point of an indivisible instant. . . . This indivisibility excludes it in principle from being shared, from time and from language. From time, from the temporalization that it infinitely contracts, and thus, paradoxically, from history. [In contracts with language because as] soon as I speak to the other, I submit to the law of giving reason(s).[29]

Hence to 'confer sense or meaning on sovereignty . . . is already to compromise its deciding exceptionality, to subject it to rules, to a code of law'.[30] But the point is not to lend a faith and credence to the sovereign supposition, but to mark its heterogeneity of giving reasons for itself, of having a relation to the law, and thus its autoimmunity as soon as it sets out to give itself a history, a timing and a place. This is not to say sovereignty does not have some effectivity but to point to a form of interrogation, a way of putting it on trial even as one recognises that to put it on trial is to borrow from a set of languages and legacies we can't help but speak even as we contest it. As Foucault well understood, our given heritages provide our only manner for thinking otherwise, for example, in the banal sense of providing different ways of reading our heritage and by providing counterexamples to the present, and inasmuch as we think the limits of that heritage, we mark the limit where the future, as such, awaits. That is, over the horizon of thought, as the thinking of the ungroundable threshold of that horizon, one can begin to see, even if it's unforeseeable, another thinking of the decision, one that calls into question the 'dynasty of *krinein*' that has been decidedly sovereign over a long thinking of it. If the 'instant of decision is madness', it remains 'irreducible to presence or presentation', and cannot be stabilised under a given concept, even one historically well determined:[31] 'Between knowledge and decision, a leap is required, even if it is necessary to know as much and as well as possible before deciding.'[32] The condition of the decision is not the past as knowable and presented,[33] but is the incalculable event in the face of an alterity arriving in the moment of responsibility, which is not an alibi for *not* deciding based upon all of the above, or of not having on hand, as it were, genealogies of what has been willed to us in terms of our legacies, but of deciding for a certain thinking of the decision, of deciding otherwise, and hence never letting this case be closed, even if such a decision appears mad and unreasonable. Here, a whole thinking, identified by Foucault, that links knowledge and the *krinein*, know-how and the decision, power and knowledge, begins to tremble.[34]

NOTES

1. Michel Foucault, *Lectures on the Will to Know*, trans. Graham Burchell (London: Picador, 2014), p. 96, my emphases.
2. Jacques Derrida, 'Letter to a Japanese Friend', in *Psyche: Inventions of the Other, Volume II*, trans. Peggy Kamuf (Stanford: Stanford University Press, 2008), p. 4.
3. Jacques Derrida, *Of Grammatology*, trans. Gayatri Chakravorty Spivak (Baltimore: Johns Hopkins University Press, 1997), p. 19, my emphasis.
4. Foucault, *Lectures on the Will to Know*, p. 5, my emphasis. As many readers of them will witness, a key text for both is Nietzsche's *Genealogy of Morals*, and one could circle around and compare discussions of Nietzsche, pulling him from the vice of Heidegger's late 1930s reading, in such texts as Foucault's 'Nietzsche, Genealogy, and History', and Derrida's *Of Grammatology*, among numerous other places. What is cruel or violent about the above text is that it must make the cut somewhere in this trial of Foucault and Derrida, must stop somewhere the witnessing – thus is the trial, the *krisis* of finitude, as all writing has to be cut somewhere – and hence doesn't take up, for example, the theme of cruelty that runs through *Discipline and Punish* and 'Nietzsche, Genealogy, and History', as well as from Derrida's readings of Bataille to his later *Death Penalty* seminars – all engaging the second essay of the *Genealogy* and the cruelty of the law, of crime and punishment, in a manner that should continually throw all of our jurisprudential truisms into *krisis* – now as much as ever given the vagaries of prison-industrial complexes marking our geographies that are nothing but carceral.
5. Hannah Arendt offers perhaps a quicker rendition than is on offer in either Foucault or Derrida, though one, I think, continuous with both: for her Plato modelled not just the *polis* but his metaphysics on the ruler-ruled relation of the Greek household. Interestingly for what follows, she aligns a thinking of the 'decision' in politics with *poiēsis* or making, over and against political action, which for her is non-sovereign. See Hannah Arendt, *The Human Condition* (Chicago: University of Chicago Press, 1998), p. 222.
6. For an excellent overview of the lectures, see Michael C. Behrent, 'The Genealogy of Genealogy: Foucault's 1970–1971 Course on The Will to Know', *Foucault Studies*, 13 (2012), pp. 157–78.
7. Foucault, *Lectures on the Will to Know*, p. 96.
8. Ibid., p. 99 n.31.
9. Derrida writes, '[T]he order of *knowledge* is never a stranger to that of *power*, and that of *power* [*pouvoir*] to that of seeing [*voir*], willing [*vouloir*] and having [*avoir*]. It is not original but it is not false, no doubt, to recall that the scene of knowledge, and especially of knowledge in the

form of the objectivity of the ob-ject . . . supposes that one disposes, that one poses before oneself, and that one has taken over the object of knowledge.' Jacques Derrida, *The Beast and the Sovereign, Vol. 1*, trans. G. Bennington (Chicago: University of Chicago Press, 2009), p. 279.

10. Jacques Derrida, 'Cogito and the History of Madness', in *Writing and Difference*, trans. Alan Bass (Chicago: University of Chicago Press, 1978), p. 31.
11. See Michael Naas, 'Comme si, comma ça: Following Derrida on the Phantasms of the Self, the State, and a Sovereign God', in *Derrida from Now On* (New York: Fordham University Press, 2009), pp. 187–212.
12. Michel Foucault, *Dits et écrits, II* (Paris: Gallimard, 2001), p. 521.
13. Ibid.
14. Jacques Derrida, *For What Tomorrow . . .*, trans. Jeff Fort (Stanford: Stanford University Press, 2004), p. 12.
15. Michel Foucault, 'Reply to Derrida', in *History of Madness*, ed. Jean Khalfa, trans. Jonathan Murphy and Jean Khalfa (London: Routledge, 2006), pp. 575–91, 580.
16. I cite and discuss this further in *The State of Sovereignty: Lessons from the Political Fictions of Modernity* (New York: SUNY Press, 2012), p. 174. For more on Arendt's affirmation of a 'pre-philosophical Greek remedy for [human] frailty', see ibid., pp. 79–88.
17. Foucault, 'Reply to Derrida', p. 580.
18. It's hard not to read here Foucault's impatience with a long philosophical practice of engaging texts *only* through claims made about philosophy, or what is believed to be so, a narcissism that is perhaps philosophy's standard gaze upon all other disciplines and knowledge – to see it as but a poor rendering of itself.
19. Ibid., p. 581.
20. See the editor's note where he discusses Foucault's many uses of 'positivity' in the text to mean 'having its basis in fact' (Foucault, *History of Madness*, p. 597 n.83).
21. Michel Foucault, *The Order of Things* (London: Vintage Books, 1994), p. xxiv.
22. Derrida, *The Beast and the Sovereign, Vol. 1*, p. 332.
23. Ibid., p. 333.
24. Derrida, *Writing and Difference*, p. 41.
25. Jacques Derrida, *The Death Penalty, Vol. 1* (Chicago: University of Chicago Press, 2014), p. 238.
26. Alan Schrift, 'Genealogy and/as Deconstruction: Nietzsche, Derrida, and Foucault on Philosophy as Critique', in H. Silverman and D. Weldon (eds), *Postmodernism and Continental Philosophy* (New York: SUNY Press, 1988), pp. 193–213, 194.
27. Foucault, *Lectures on the Will to Know*, p. 96.
28. For a larger discussion of Foucault's conflation of sovereignty and the law, see my *State of Sovereignty*, pp. 122–4; see also *Lectures on Will to Know*, pp. 96–7.
29. Jacques Derrida, *Rogues: Two Essays on Reason*, trans. Pascale-Anne Brault and Michael Naas (Stanford: Stanford University Press, 2003), pp. 100–1.
30. Ibid., p. 101.
31. See Jacques Derrida, *The Gift of Death*, trans. David Wills (Chicago: University of Chicago Press, 1995), p. 65.
32. Derrida, *For What Tomorrow . . .*, p. 53.
33. This is what I think Derrida means when he writes, in 'Cogito and the History of Madness': 'The attempt to write the history of the decision, division, differences runs the risk of construing the division as an event or a structure subsequent to the unity of an original presence, thereby confirming metaphysics in its fundamental operation' (*Writing and Difference*, p. 40).
34. Derrida, *Rogues*, p. 84.

Notes on Contributors

Amy Allen is Liberal Arts Research Professor of Philosophy and Women's, Gender and Sexuality Studies at The Pennsylvania State University. She is the author of *The Power of Feminist Theory: Domination, Resistance, Solidarity* (1999), *The Politics of Our Selves: Power, Autonomy, and Gender in Contemporary Critical Theory* (2008) and *The End of Progress: Decolonizing the Normative Foundations of Critical Theory* (2016).

Ellen T. Armour is the E. Rhodes and Leona B. Carpenter Associate Professor of Theology at Vanderbilt Divinity School. Her research interests are in feminist theology, theories of sex, race, gender, disability and embodiment, and contemporary continental philosophy. She is the author of *Deconstruction, Feminist Theology, and the Problem of Difference: Subverting the Race/Gender Divide* (1999) and co-editor of *Bodily Citations: Judith Butler and Religion* (2006). Her current book project, tentatively entitled *Signs and Wonders: Theology After Modernity*, will diagnose and craft a theological response to the shifts in our understanding of 'man' and 'his' others (sexed/raced, animal and divine) as modernity declines.

Yubraj Aryal is a Postdoctoral Researcher at the University of Montreal and Visiting Scholar at New York University. He edits *Journal of Philosophy: A Cross-Disciplinary Inquiry*, and has interviewed scholars such as Richard Rorty, Brian Massumi, Lauren Berlant and Marjorie Perloff.

Jean-Marie Beyssade is Professor of Philosophy at University of Paris IV. He is the author of *La Philosophie Première de Descartes* (1979); 'Création des vérités éternelles et doute métaphysique', *Studia Cartesiana* (1981); and many essays on Descartes, Spinoza, Rousseau and other moderm philosophers. He is the translator of *L'Entretien avec Burman* (1981).

Vernon W. Cisney is a visiting Assistant Professor of Philosophy at Gettysburg College. He is the author of *Derrida's* Voice and Phenomenon: *An Edinburgh Philosophical Guide* (2014); as well as *Derrida and Deleuze: Difference and the Power of the Negative* (2016). He is also the co-editor (with Nicolae Morar) of *Biopower: Foucault and Beyond* (2016) and (with Jonathan Beever) *The Way of Nature and the Way of Grace: Philosophical Footholds on Terrence Malick's Tree of Life* (2016).

Jacques Derrida (1930–2004) is most closely associated with the term 'deconstruction', following upon Heidegger's notion of *Destruktion*. He, like many members of his 'generation', wrote broadly in areas concerning metaphysics, ethics, politics, literature and art. His first publication blitz came in 1967, with the publication of *Voice and Phenomenon*, *Of Grammatology* and *Writing and Difference*. These three works remain to this day some of Derrida's most famous books. Later in his life his thinking took what some call a 'turn' (though this is a complicated description) towards religion, politics and ethics. Some of the more noteworthy publications to come out of this later period are *Acts of Religion*, *Spectres of Marx* and *Politics of Friendship*. Throughout his lifetime, he was involved in many activist organizations, such as GREPH (Groupe de Recherches sur l'Enseignement Philosophique), dedicated to protecting the teaching of philosophy in French education against austerity measures being taken. He held many academic positions throughout his life, at Yale, the Sorbonne, University of California Irvine, Johns Hopkins and SUNY Stony Brook. Derrida was diagnosed with pancreatic cancer in 2002, and died 9 October 2004.

Fred Evans is Professor of Philosophy and Coordinator for the Center of Interpretive and Qualitative Research at Duquesne University. He is the author of *Psychology and Nihilism: A Genealogical Critique of the Computational Model of Mind* (1993), *The Multivoiced Body: Society and Communication in the Age of Diversity* (2009; 2011) and co-editor (with Leonard Lawlor) of *Chiasms: Merleau-Ponty's Notion of Flesh* (2000). Evans has published numerous articles and book chapters on continental thinkers in relation to issues concerning psychology, politics and technology. He is currently completing a new book, provisionally entitled *Citizenship and Public Art: An Essay in Political Aesthetics*, and beginning another one on cosmopolitanism. He also worked for five years at the Lao National Orthopedic Center and other positions in Laos, under the auspices of International Voluntary Services, and taught philosophy for a year at La Universidad del Rosario in Bogotá, Colombia.

Michel Foucault (1926–84) held the chair in the History of Systems of Thought at the Collège de France from 1969 until his death. He was heavily involved in political activist movements throughout his life, advocating on behalf of students, workers, prisoners, homosexuals and others. His vast body of research operates at the intersections of systems of knowledge, power and ethics. He is the author of *History of Madness* (1961), *The Birth of the Clinic* (1963), *The Order of Things* (1966), *The Archaeology of Knowledge* (1969), *Discipline and Punish* (1975), and *The History of Sexuality*, 3 volumes: *Introduction* (1976), *The Use of Pleasure* (1984), and *The*

Care of the Self (1984). Foucault died on 25 June 1984 from complications arising due to AIDS.

Peter Gratton is Associate Professor of Philosophy at the Memorial University of Newfoundland. He has published numerous articles in political, continental and intercultural philosophy and is the author of *The State of Sovereignty: Lessons from the Political Fictions of Modernity* (2012) and *Speculative Realism: Problems and Prospects* (2014). Peter has also edited three books: *Traversing the Imaginary* (2007), co-edited with John Mannousakis, *Jean-Luc Nancy and Plural Thinking: Expositions of World, Politics, Art, and Sense* (2012), co-edited with Marie-Eve Morin, and *The Meillassoux Dictionary*, co-edited with Paul Ennis (2014). He is editor, along with Sean McGrath, of the Edinburgh book series *New Perspectives in Ontology*.

Leonard Lawlor is Edwin Erle Sparks Professor of Philosophy at Penn State University. He is the author of six books: *This is not Sufficient: An Essay on Animality in Derrida* (2007), *The Implications of Immanence: Towards a New Concept of Life* (2006), *Derrida and Husserl: The Basic Problem of Phenomenology* (2002), *Thinking Through French Philosophy: The Being of the Question* (2003), *The Challenge of Bergsonism: Phenomenology, Ontology, Ethics* (2003), and *Imagination and Chance: The Difference Between the Thought of Ricoeur and Derrida* (1992). He is one of the co-editors of *Chiasmi International: Trilingual Studies Concerning the Thought of Merleau-Ponty*. He has translated Merleau-Ponty and Hyppolite into English. He has written dozens of articles on Derrida, Foucault, Deleuze, Bergson, Merleau-Ponty, Ricoeur and Gadamer. He is writing two books: *Never Will There be Enough Written: An Essay on the Problem of the Worst in Deleuze and Guattari* (for Columbia University Press) and *Early Twentieth-Century Continental Philosophy: Towards the Outside* (for Indiana University Press).

Edward McGushin is Associate Professor of Philosophy at Stonehill College in Easton, Massachusetts. He is author of *Foucault's Askesis: An Introduction to the Philosophical Life* (2007) as well as numerous journal articles and book chapters on continental philosophy. His research and teaching interests include the philosophy of film and media, the problem of violence and the possibility of non-violent disobedience, and the idea of philosophy as a way of life.

Nicolae Morar is Assistant Professor in Philosophy and Environmental Studies and an Associate Member with the Institute of Ecology and Evolution at University of Oregon. He specialises in bioethics, philosophy of biology and ecology, and recent continental philosophy. Morar is the co-editor of *Perspectives in Bioethics, Science, and Public Policy* (2013) and of a *Foucault Studies* special Issue on Foucault and Deleuze (2014). Forthcoming publications include *Between Foucault and Deleuze*, co-edited with Thomas Nail and Dan Smith (2016) and Pierre Klossowski, *Living Currency*, translated with Vernon Cisney and Daniel W. Smith (2016). Morar is currently completing a monograph titled *Biology, BioEthics, and BioPolitics: How To Think Differently About Human Nature*.

Jeff Nealon is Edwin Erle Sparks Professor of English and Philosophy at Penn State University. His research interests include literary and cultural theory, contemporary American literature and culture, and most recently he is working on a book about the inter-connections of American cultural and economic production since the 1980s. He is the author of five books, including *Alterity Politics: Ethics and Performative Subjectivity* (1998), *The Theory Toolbox: Critical Concepts for the New Humanities* (2003), *Foucault Beyond Foucault: Power and Its Intensifications Since 1984* (2007) and *Plant Theory: Biopower and Vegetable Life* (2015).

Christopher Penfield is a recent PhD in Philosophy from Purdue University, where he completed his dissertation, *Foucault, Kant, Deleuze, and the Problem of Political Agency*. He is the author of 'Toward a Theory of Transversal Politics' in *Foucault Studies* (2014), articles on Foucault in *The Cambridge Foucault Lexicon* (2014) and Springer's *Encyclopedia of Global Justice* (2011), a book review on Deleuze and theology in *Notre Dame Philosophical Reviews* (2014), and a forthcoming article for Tate Modern Research on a painting by Larry Rivers and the concept of artistic tautology in twentieth-century visual art.

Arkady Plotnitsky is Professor of English and Theory and Cultural Studies, and Director of the Theory and Cultural Studies Program, at Purdue University. His specialisations include critical and cultural theory, British and European romanticism, continental philosophy, modernism and postmodernism, relations among literature, philosophy and science. He is the author of several books, including *Reconfigurations: Critical Theory and General Economy* (1993), *In the Shadow of Hegel* (1993), *Complementarity: Anti-Epistemology After Bohr and Derrida* (1994); *The Knowable and the Unknowable: Modern Science, Nonclassical Thought, and the 'Two Cultures'* (2002), *Reading Bohr: Physics and Philosophy* (2006), *Epistemology and Probability: Bohr, Heisenberg, Schrödinger, and the Nature of Quantum-Theoretical Thinking* (2009), and co-editor (with B. H. Smith) of *Mathematics, Science, and Postclassical Theory* (1997) and (with T. Rajan) *Idealism Without Absolutes: Philosophy and Romantic Culture* (2004).

Paul Rekret is Assistant Professor of Political Science at Richmond American University, London. He has published on twentieth and twenty-first century conceptions of political ontology. His current research engages with the politics of contemporary theories of materialism.

Alan D. Schrift is the F. Wendell Miller Professor of Philosophy at Grinnell College and the author of *Nietzsche and the Question of Interpretation: Between Hermeneutics and Deconstruction* (1990), *Nietzsche's French Legacy: A Genealogy of Poststructuralism* (1995) and *Twentieth-Century French Philosophy: Key Themes and Thinkers* (2005).

Index

EU Authorised Representative:
Easy Access System Europe Mustamäe tee 50, 10621 Tallinn, Estonia
gpsr.requests@easproject.com

Printed and bound by CPI Group (UK) Ltd, Croydon, CR0 4YY
10/03/2026
02068803-0006